THE BEATLES IN CO

Since their first performances in 1960, the Beatles' cultural influence grew in unparalleled ways. From Liverpool to Beatlemania, and from Dance Halls to Abbey Road Studios and the digital age, the band's impact exploded during their heyday, and has endured in the decades following their disbandment. Beatles' fashion and celebrity culture, politics, psychedelia and the Summer of Love, all highlight different aspects of the band's complex relationship with the world around them. With a wide range of short, snapshot chapters, *The Beatles in Context* brings together key themes in which to better explore the Beatles' lives and work and understand their cultural legacy, focusing on the people and places central to the Beatles' careers, the visual media that contributed to their enduring success, and the culture and politics of their time.

KENNETH WOMACK is Dean of the Wayne D. McMurray School of Humanities and Social Sciences at Monmouth University, where he also serves as Professor of English. He is the author or editor of numerous books, including *Long and Winding Roads* (2007), *Cambridge Companion to the Beatles* (2009), and *The Beatles Encyclopedia* (2014). More recently, he is the author of a two-volume biography of Beatles producer George Martin, including *Maximum Volume: The Life of Beatles Producer George Martin (The Early Years, 1926–1966)* and *Sound Pictures: The Life of Beatles Producer George Martin (The Later Years, 1966–2016)*.

Understanding and appreciation of musical works is greatly enhanced by knowledge of the context within which their composers lived and worked. Each of these volumes focuses on an individual composer, offering lively, accessible and concise essays by leading scholars on the many contexts – professional, political, intellectual, social and cultural – that have a bearing on his or her work. Biographical and musical influences, performance and publishing history and the creative afterlife of each composer's work are also addressed, providing readers with a multi-faceted view of how the composers' output and careers were shaped by the world around them.

Titles forthcoming in the series

Beethoven in Context edited by Glenn Stanley and John D. Wilson
Liszt in Context edited by Joanne Cormac
Richard Strauss in Context edited by Morten Kristiansen and Joseph E. Jones
Stravinsky in Context edited by Graham Griffiths

THE BEATLES IN CONTEXT

EDITED BY

KENNETH WOMACK

Monmouth University, New Jersey

CAMBRIDGE
UNIVERSITY PRESS

University Printing House, Cambridge CB2 8BS, United Kingdom

One Liberty Plaza, 20th Floor, New York, NY 10006, USA

477 Williamstown Road, Port Melbourne, VIC 3207, Australia

314–321, 3rd Floor, Plot 3, Splendor Forum, Jasola District Centre, New Delhi - 110025, India

103 Penang Road, #05-06/07, Visioncrest Commercial, Singapore 238467

Cambridge University Press is part of the University of Cambridge.

It furthers the University's mission by disseminating knowledge in the pursuit of
education, learning and research at the highest international levels of excellence.

www.cambridge.org
Information on this title: www.cambridge.org/9781108409520
DOI: 10.1017/9781108296939

First published 2020
First paperback edition 2021

A catalogue record for this publication is available from the British Library

Library of Congress Cataloging in Publication data
NAMES: Womack, Kenneth, editor.
TITLE: The Beatles in context / edited by Kenneth Womack.
DESCRIPTION: [1.] | New York : Cambridge University Press, 2019. | Series: Composers in context
| Includes bibliographical references and index.
IDENTIFIERS: LCCN 2019030340 (print) | LCCN 2019030341 (ebook) | ISBN 9781108419116
(hardback) | ISBN 9781108296939 (epub)
SUBJECTS: LCSH: Beatles. | Beatles – Influence. | Popular music – 1961–1970 –History and criticism.
CLASSIFICATION: LCC ML421.B4 B415 2019 (print) | LCC ML421.B4 (ebook) | DDC
782.42166092/2–dc23
LC record available at https://lccn.loc.gov/2019030340
LC ebook record available at https://lccn.loc.gov/2019030341

ISBN 978-1-108-41911-6 Hardback
ISBN 978-1-108-40952-0 Paperback

Contents

Contents   vii

Illustrations

Contributors

MITCHELL AXELROD, *Fab 4 Free 4 All* Podcast

DAVID BEDFORD, *Liddypool* Podcast

ALLISON J. BORON, EDITOR, *Rebeat* Magazine

KENNETH L. CAMPBELL, Monmouth University

KATHRYN B. COX, Lake Forest College

MELISSA DAVIS, Liverpool Hope University

JACQUELINE EDMONDSON, Penn State University

WALTER EVERETT, University of Michigan

MICHAEL R. FRONTANI, Independent Scholar

CHUCK GUNDERSON, Independent Scholar

STEVE HAMELMAN, Coastal Carolina University

KATIE KAPURCH, Texas State University

JUDE SOUTHERLAND KESSLER, *The John Lennon Series*

JASON KRUPPA, *Producing the Beatles* Podcast

SPENCER LEIGH, BBC Radio Merseyside

STEVE MATTEO, Music Journalist

DAVID MELBYE, University of Tyumen, Russian Federation

KIT O'TOOLE, Independent Scholar

WALTER J. PODRAZIK, University of Illinois

JOE RAPOLLA, Monmouth University

ANTHONY ROBUSTELLI, *The Beatles Multi-Track Meltdown* Podcast

ROBERT RODRIGUEZ, *Something About the Beatles* Podcast

JEFFREY ROESSNER, Mercyhurst University

STUART ROSENBERG, Monmouth University

BRIAN SOUTHALL, Former EMI Press Director

AL SUSSMAN, *Beatlefan* Magazine

DAVID VENTURO, The College of New Jersey

KENNETH WOMACK, Monmouth University

JERRY ZOLTEN, Penn State University

Preface

The Beatles in Context offers an expansive introduction to the band, arguably the most critically and commercially successful musical fusion of all time. *The Beatles in Context* affords readers a wide-ranging analysis of the cultural contexts that led to the group's emergence and enduring global influence, while also providing students, general readers, and advanced scholars alike with a key point of departure for understanding the Beatles' vaunted place in twentieth- and twenty-first-century culture.

The Beatles in Context provides readers with an array of insightful scholarly essays. In so doing, it affords its audience vital information regarding the historical-, performance-, and reception-related aspects of the Beatles' achievement, especially in regard to the group's corporate successes as pop music's foremost composers and musicians. To this end, *The Beatles in Context* is arranged across six thematic sections: "Beatle People and Beatle Places"; "The Beatles in Performance"; "The Beatles on TV, Film, and the Internet"; "The Beatles' Sound"; "The Beatles as Sociocultural and Political Touchstones"; and "The Beatles' Critical Reception and Cultural Legacy."

The first section, "Beatle People and Beatle Places," examines the biographical and social contexts of the bandmates' origins, while the second section, "The Beatles in Performance," addresses the group's development as live performers from their early days in Liverpool and Hamburg through the world tours of their heyday. The third section, "The Beatles on TV, Film, and the Internet," explores the ways in which the evolving contexts of television, movies, and the World Wide Web have shaped the group's reception into the cultural main across successive generations. The fourth section, "The Beatles' Sound," provides a deeper understanding of the compositional and cultural contexts that influenced their emergence into the pantheon of twentieth-century popular music. The fifth section, "The Beatles as Sociocultural and Political Touchstones," investigates the band's abiding influence as social, fashion, political, and industry icons. Finally, "The Beatles' Critical Reception and Cultural Legacy" addresses the group's enduring impact upon global culture, particularly in terms of their artistic and musicological influence; their publishing and business forays; their place in the formation of heritage tourism in England and the USA; and their continuing and highly successful efforts to market their output to successive generations of fans.

KENNETH WOMACK

Acknowledgments

Special thanks are due to the many friends and colleagues who helped to bring this volume to fruition. The editor is particularly grateful for the supportive and highly professional staff at Cambridge University Press, especially Kate Brett and Eilidh Burrett. I am thankful for my amazing team at Monmouth University, including Lynne Clay, Judy Ramos, Nancy Mezey, Laura Moriarty, Joe Rapolla, and Michael Thomas. Special thanks are due, as always, to Nicole Michael for providing top-drawer publicity, and to Jeanine Womack, who makes all things possible

Chronology

NOTE: All release dates refer to official entries in the Beatles' UK catalog.

1926 January 3: George Martin born in London

1934 September 19: Brian Epstein born in Liverpool

1940 July 7: Ringo Starr [Richard Starkey] born in Liverpool

  October 9: John Winston Lennon born in Liverpool

1942 June 18: James Paul McCartney born in Liverpool

1943 February 25: George Harrison born in Liverpool

1957 July 6: McCartney meets Lennon after a Quarry Men performance at the Woolton Parish Church Garden Fête in Liverpool

  December: Harrison joins Lennon and McCartney as a member of the Quarry Men

1958 July 12: The Quarry Men record "That'll Be the Day" and "In Spite of All the Danger" at P.F. Phillips Professional Tape and Disk Record Service in Liverpool

1959 August 29: the Quarry Men begin an extensive engagement at Mona Best's Casbah Club in Liverpool

  October: The Quarry Men change their name to Johnny and the Moondogs

1960 January: Stu Sutcliffe's painting in a local competition is purchased by John Moores for £65. Stu purchases a Höfner bass at Lennon's behest.

  May: Allan Williams becomes the manager of The Beatals, who change their name, shortly thereafter, to Long John and the Silver Beatles

  May 20–28: As the Silver Beatles, the band embarks upon a nine-day Scottish tour in support of Johnny Gentle

  August 12: Drummer Pete Best joins the band, who change their name to the Beatles in advance of their upcoming Hamburg engagement

  August 17–November 29: the Beatles perform on the Reeperbahn in Hamburg, first at the Indra Club and later at the Kaiserkeller

1961 **February 9:** The Beatles perform at Liverpool's Cavern Club, eventually becoming the establishment's regular lunchtime act

April 1–July 1: The Beatles perform on the Reeperbahn in Hamburg's Top Ten Club; during this period, McCartney replaces Sutcliffe as the band's regular bassist

June: The Beatles record several songs as the Beat Brothers, the backing band for musician Tony Sheridan

November 9: NEMS record-store owner Brian Epstein watches the Beatles perform at the Cavern Club

December 10: Brian Epstein officially becomes the Beatles' manager

1962 **January 1:** The Beatles audition, unsuccessfully, for Decca Records in London

January 5: "My Bonnie"/"The Saints" by Tony Sheridan and the Beatles released by Polydor

April 10: Sutcliffe dies of a brain hemorrhage in Hamburg

April 13–May 31: The Beatles perform at Hamburg's Star-Club

June 6: The Beatles' first session at EMI Studios under the supervision of producer George Martin, who is impressed with their potential, with the exception of Best's drumming ability

August 16: Best is told he is being replaced by Ringo Starr in the Beatles

August 18: Starr performs as the Beatles' drummer for the first time

August 23: Lennon marries Cynthia Powell

September 11: The Beatles record "Love Me Do," "Please Please Me," and "P.S. I Love You" at EMI Studios

October 5: "Love Me Do"/"P.S. I Love You" single released by Parlophone; the single reaches no. 17 on the British charts

October 17: The Beatles' first television appearance on Granada's *People and Places*

November 1–14: The Beatles return for a brief engagement at Hamburg's Star-Club

November 26: The Beatles record "Please Please Me" at EMI Studios

December 18–31: The Beatles' final engagement at Hamburg's Star-Club

1963 **January 3–6:** Winter Scottish Tour

January 10–February 1: Winter UK Tour

January 11: "Please Please Me"/"Ask Me Why" single released by Parlophone. "Please Please Me" reaches the top position on the British charts.

January 19: The Beatles appear before a nationally televised audience on *Thank Your Lucky Stars*

February 2–March 3: Helen Shapiro Tour

February 11: The Beatles record the *Please Please Me* album in a - single day's session at EMI Studios

March 9–31: Tommy Roe/Chris Montez Tour

March 22: *Please Please Me* album released by Parlophone

April 2–May 17: Spring UK Tour

April 11: "From Me to You"/"Thank You Girl" single released by Parlophone

May 18–June 9: Roy Orbison/Beatles Tour

June 10–September 15: Summer UK Tour

August 23: "She Loves You"/"I'll Get You" single released by Parlophone

October 5–7: The Beatles' Mini-Tour of Scotland

October 13: The Beatles perform before a national television audience of some 15 million viewers on the popular British variety show *Val Parnell's Sunday Night at the London Palladium*. Beatlemania is born.

October 11–19: The Beatles' Autumn UK Tour

October 25–29: The Beatles' Tour of Sweden

November 1–December 13: The Beatles' Autumn Tour of Britain

November 22: *With the Beatles* album released by Parlophone

November 29: "I Want to Hold Your Hand"/"This Boy" single released by Parlophone

December 24–January 11: The Beatles' 1963 Christmas Show at the Astoria Cinema, London

1964 January 16–February 4: The Beatles' extended engagement at Paris' Olympia Theatre

February 7: The Beatles arrive at New York City's John F. Kennedy Airport, where they are greeted by thousands of ecstatic fans

February 9: The Beatles perform on the *Ed Sullivan Show* in New York City to a nationally televised audience of some 74 million viewers

February 11: The Beatles perform their first US concert at Washington, DC's Coliseum

February 12: The Beatles perform at New York City's Carnegie Hall

March–April: Principal photography for *A Hard Day's Night* feature film

March 20: "Can't Buy Me Love"/"You Can't Do That" single released by Parlophone

June 4–30: The Beatles' World Tour

July 6: *A Hard Day's Night* premieres at the London Pavilion

July 10: "A Hard Day's Night"/"Things We Said Today" single released by Parlophone

July 10: *A Hard Day's Night* album released by Parlophone

August 19–September 20: The Beatles' First American Tour

October 9–November 10: The Beatles' Autumn Tour of Britain

November 4: The Beatles' Royal Variety Command Performance at the Prince of Wales Theatre

November 27: "I Feel Fine"/"She's a Woman" single released by Parlophone

December 4: *Beatles for Sale* album released by Parlophone

December 24–January 16: The Beatles' 1964 Christmas Show at the Odeon Cinema, London

1965 February 11: Starr marries Maureen Cox

February–May: Principal photography for the *Help!* feature film

April 9: "Ticket to Ride"/"Yes It Is" single released by Parlophone

June 20–July 3: The Beatles' European Tour

July 23: "Help!"/"I'm Down" single released by Parlophone

July 29: *Help!* premieres at the London Pavilion

August 6: *Help!* album released by Parlophone

August 15–31: The Beatles' American Tour

August 15: The Beatles perform at Shea Stadium in New York City before an audience of 55,600 fans

August 27: The Beatles meet Elvis Presley in Los Angeles

October–November: Recording sessions for *Rubber Soul*

October 26: The Beatles receive their MBEs from Queen Elizabeth II

December 3: "We Can Work It Out"/"Day Tripper" single released by Parlophone

December 3: *Rubber Soul* album released by Parlophone

December 3–12: The Beatles' British Tour

1966 January 21: Harrison marries Pattie Boyd

April–June: Recording sessions for *Revolver*

June 10: "Paperback Writer"/"Rain" single released by Parlophone

June 24–July 4: The Beatles' Tour of Germany and Japan

July 29: American magazine *Datebook* republishes Lennon's March 1966 interview in which he proclaims that the Beatles are "more popular than Jesus"

August 12–29: The Beatles' Final American Tour

August 5: "Eleanor Rigby"/"Yellow Submarine" single released by Parlophone

August 5: *Revolver* album released by Parlophone

August 29: The Beatles play at San Francisco's Candlestick Park for their final concert before a paying audience

November 9: Lennon meets Yoko Ono at London's Indica Gallery

November–April: Recording sessions for *Sgt. Pepper's Lonely Hearts Club Band*

1967 **February 17:** "Strawberry Fields Forever"/"Penny Lane" single released by Parlophone

June 1: *Sgt. Pepper's Lonely Hearts Club Band* album released by Parlophone

June 25: The Beatles perform "All You Need Is Love" on the *Our World* international telecast

July 7: "All You Need Is Love"/"Baby, You're a Rich Man" single released by Parlophone

August 24: The Beatles meet the Maharishi Mahesh Yogi at the London Hilton

August 27: Brian Epstein is found dead in London from an accidental drug overdose

September–October: Principal photography and recording sessions for the *Magical Mystery Tour* project

November 24: "Hello Goodbye"/"I Am the Walrus" single released by Parlophone

December 8: *Magical Mystery Tour* EP released by Parlophone

December 26: *Magical Mystery Tour* film televised on the BBC

1968 **February–April:** The Beatles visit the Maharishi's compound at Rishikesh

March 15: "Lady Madonna"/"The Inner Light" single released by Parlophone

May 14: Lennon and McCartney announce the formation of Apple Corps at a New York City press conference

May–October: Recording sessions for *The Beatles (The White Album)*

July 17: *Yellow Submarine* cartoon feature premieres at the London Pavilion

August 30: "Hey Jude"/"Revolution" single released by Apple

November 22: *The Beatles (The White Album)* released by Apple

1969 **January 2:** Principal photography for the *Get Back* project commences at Twickenham Studios

January 17: *Yellow Submarine* album released by Apple

January 30: The Beatles' Rooftop Concert at Apple Studios on Savile Row

March 12: McCartney marries Linda Eastman

March 20: Lennon marries Yoko Ono

March 21: Allen Klein appointed as business manager for Apple Corps

April–August: Recording sessions for *Abbey Road*

April 11: "Get Back"/"Don't Let Me Down" single released by Apple

May 30: "The Ballad of John and Yoko"/"Old Brown Shoe" single released by Apple

August 22: The Beatles gather at Lennon and Ono's Tittenhurst Park estate for their final photo session

September 26: *Abbey Road* album released by Apple

October 31: "Something"/"Come Together" single released by Apple

1970 **March 6:** "Let It Be"/"You Know My Name (Look Up the Number)" single released by Apple

April 9: McCartney announces the Beatles' break-up

May 8: *Let It Be* album released by Apple

1973 **April 19:** *The Beatles, 1962–1966* and *The Beatles, 1967–1970* are released by Apple

1976 **March 5:** "Yesterday"/"I Should Have Known Better" single released by Parlophone

1976 **June 11:** *Rock 'n' Roll Music* is released by Parlophone

1976 **June 25:** "Back in the USSR"/"Twist and Shout" single released by Parlophone

1977 **May 6:** *The Beatles at the Hollywood Bowl* is released by Parlophone

1977 **November 19:** *Love Songs* is released by Parlophone

1978 **September 30:** "Sgt. Pepper's Lonely Hearts Club Band/With a Little Help from My Friends"/"A Day in the Life" single released by Parlophone

1979 **October 12:** *Rarities* is released by Parlophone

1980 **December 8:** John Lennon is assassinated in New York City

1982 **March 22:** *Reel Music* is released by Parlophone

1982 **March 24:** "The Beatles' Movie Medley"/"I'm Happy Just to Dance with You" released by Parlophone

1982 **October 11:** *20 Greatest Hits* is released by Parlophone

1985 **July 13:** Paul McCartney performs "Let It Be" at the Live Aid benefit concert at London's Wembley Stadium

1985 **October 9:** Yoko Ono dedicates the Strawberry Fields memorial in New York City's Central Park

1988 The Beatles are inducted into the Rock and Roll Hall of Fame

1994 John Lennon is inducted into the Rock and Roll Hall of Fame

1994 **November 30:** *Live at the BBC* released by Apple

1995 **November:** The Beatles' televised *Anthology* documentary is broadcast in six parts on the UK's ITV and the US ABC TV networks

1995 **November 21:** *Anthology 1* released by Apple

1995 December 4: "Free as a Bird"/"Christmas Time (Is Here Again)" released by Apple

1996 George Martin is knighted by Queen Elizabeth II

1996 March 4: "Real Love"/"Baby's in Black (Live)" released by Apple

1996 March 18: *Anthology 2* released by Apple

1996 October 28: *Anthology 3* released by Apple

1997 Paul McCartney is knighted by Queen Elizabeth II

1998 April 17: Linda McCartney dies of cancer in Tucson, Arizona

1999 Paul McCartney is inducted into the Rock and Roll Hall of Fame

1999 September 13: *Yellow Submarine Songtrack* released by Apple

1999 George Martin is inducted into the Rock and Roll Hall of Fame

2000 November 13: *1* is released by Apple

2001 November 29: George Harrison dies of cancer in Los Angeles

2003 November 17: *Let It Be . . . Naked* released by Apple

2004 George Harrison is inducted into the Rock and Roll Hall of Fame

2006 June 30: Cirque du Soleil's *Love* premieres at the Mirage in Las Vegas

2006 November 20: *Love* released by Apple

2009 September 9: The Beatles' remastered recordings are released by Apple

2010 November 16: The Beatles release their catalog digitally on iTunes

2012 July 24: *Tomorrow Never Knows* is released by Apple on iTunes

2013 December 17: *The Beatles Bootleg Recordings, 1963* is released by Apple on iTunes

2014 January 21: *The US Albums* is released by Apple

2016 March 8: George Martin dies in Coleshill, Wiltshire

2016 September 15: *The Beatles: Eight Days a Week – The Touring Years*, directed by Ron Howard, premieres at the Odeon, Leicester Square, London

2017 December 15: *The Christmas Records* is released by Apple

2018 Ringo Starr is knighted by Queen Elizabeth II

PART I

Beatle People and Beatle Places

CHAPTER I

Britain at Mid-Century and the Rise of the Beatles

Jude Southerland Kessler

The 1950s: life in Britain, for the last decade, had been austere and unsmiling. And in the post-war world, little had changed. In England, government debts had the country on the verge of economic ruin.[1] Furthermore, London, Liverpool, Birmingham – and all of the seaport villages – lay in scalded ruin. Children skittered about, slapdash, on heaps of rubble, and the once pastoral countryside was littered with abandoned military bases and equipment, quietly disappearing in a riot of weeds.

Beatles expert and author Mark Lewisohn offers this vivid 1956 description of Liverpool as viewed by author J. Brophy in his period piece, *City of Departures*: "Once progressive and proud, the city is now dilapidated and dirty, shabby and down and out ... still [replete with] unrepaired bombsites, many transformed into eternal temporary car parks, red brick buildings now black with encrusted soot, ruined shops run amok with police-dodging barrow boys, people queuing for almost everything."[2] From top to toe, England was ravaged.

Well into the 1950s, meat, butter, coal, and tea (*of all things!*) were still being rationed.[3] The oft-repeated, sighed refrain of, "Before the war ... before the war ... " began every sentence.[4] And to make strident measures even worse, the standard rate of income taxation was nine shillings in the pound – more than *double* today's rate.[5] Money was tight; belts were tighter. Life was grim.

In 1950, although England supplied one-quarter of the world's trade in manufactures, and employment was at an all-time high, her people were

---

[1] Philip Norman, *Shout! The Beatles in Their Generation* (New York: MJF Books, 1981), 247.
[2] J. Brophy, *City of Departures*, 56, cited in Mark Lewisohn, *All These Years: Tune In* (London: Little Brown, 2013), 137.
[3] Roland Quinalt, "Britain 1950," *History Today*, 51, 4 (August 2001), 2.
[4] Richard Davenport-Hines, *An English Affair: Sex, Class, and Power in the Age of Profumo* (New York: HarperCollins, 2013, Kindle edition), 1156.
[5] Quinalt, "Britain 1950," 2.

not thriving. More than half lived in rented housing – dreary bedsits with limited privacy and meager heater bars for comfort.[6] And lethal levels of coal smog choked the cities; in 1952, over 4,000 people in London died from lung and heart disease.[7]

But life in urban Britain was "elegant" compared to the paltry standard of rural living. Farms lacked basic water sanitation, electricity, and telephones. Life in British countryside cottages hearkened starkly back to the previous century. Despite the Agriculture Act of 1947, which had boosted farm income by approving subsidies for those raising livestock or cereal grains, England's farmers dwelt in dire poverty.[8] The world "was waiting for the sunshine," but it was yet to be found.

Across the nation, however, the stern mantra of "Keep calm and carry on" squelched any tendency to complain. Indeed, as author Richard Davenport-Hines observed, though drabness was the order of the day, "pinch and scrape suggested respectability."[9] Those who suffered were ennobled as moral and honorable.

Davenport-Hines goes on to say, "in 1957 [England] – dominated by the memory of two world wars – was more drilled and regimented than at any time in history, and more strictly regulated."[10] Indeed, "conformity in clothes, deportment, and opinions was the sign of trustworthiness."[11] Audiences still, for example, stood respectfully for the National Anthem.[12] The British government dispensed consumption pricing; contraceptive devices were not given to the unmarried, and homosexuality was illegal.[13] Conventionality reigned supreme.

But merely one decade later, life altered dramatically and irrevocably. In ten brief years, England hurtled into reformation. Evolution was radical and vast.

Davenport-Hines's first youthful inclination that the world was swiftly changing occurred one late afternoon in the early 1960s when his father

---

[6] Quinalt, "Britain 1950," 3, and P. Willis-Pitts, *Liverpool: The Fifth Beatle* (Littleton, CO: Amozen Press, 2007), 109. Willis-Pitts describes his post-war home in Liverpool as "unheated save by a fire" with "six people living in a space big enough for two." He says, "The outside toilet (the only one) stank, and there were rats in the alley."

[7] Quinalt, "Britain 1950," 3.   [8] Quinalt, "Britain 1950," 4.

[9] Davenport-Hines, *An English Affair*, 2435.   [10] Davenport-Hines, *An English Affair*, 464.

[11] Davenport-Hines, *An English Affair*, 338.

[12] As late as 1964, Derek Taylor and Neil Aspinall would make good use of this custom, employing it after Beatles performances as an apt technique for getting the Beatles off stage and safely into escape cars.

[13] Davenport-Hines, *An English Affair*, 464.

sped along London's Park Lane, a bright four-lane boulevard that had once been a sleepy dual carriageway. Observing his father's utter delight with the revamped roadway, Davenport-Hines concluded, "My father loved the swift, new Park Lane as a reminder that England was finished with slow coaches."[14] The thoroughfare, Davenport-Hines concluded, was a brash symbol that the Old Guard had lost its iron grip.

Indeed, as actor Michael Caine declares in his documentary, *My Generation: Celebrate the 60s, The Decade That Changed the World*, "Britain in the 1950s was stable, conventional, predictable … and dull. But that's the way our parents liked it. My generation demanded new beginning."[15]

Cultural Change Initiates

No one is certain when the transformation began. Perhaps the shift started when England "abdicated its status as a Great Power," losing India (1947), Pakistan (1947), Burma (1948), and Ceylon (1948), and for the first time in history, the sun actually set on the British Empire.[16] Or perhaps the change had roots in the Irish (1940) and Scottish (1950) unrest – desperate, heartfelt efforts to separate from England. Without a doubt, the fierce and unquenchable spirit of independence served as a pivot point in what was to come.[17]

Perhaps the kaleidoscopic shift from the world of the 1940s was further enhanced by the great influx of multi-cultural peoples to England's tiny island. The Irish had long since arrived in Liverpool, during the late 1840s.[18] Mark Lewisohn tells us that "three hundred thousand sick and poor Irish landed in Liverpool in 1847 alone [during the Great Potato Famine] … such were the numbers of Irish pouring into Liverpool alone that records of arrival could not be kept."[19] As he shrewdly observes, "The Irish … brought Ireland to Liverpool."[20]

---

[14] Davenport-Hines, *An English Affair*, 464.
[15] David Batty, Ian La Frenais, Dick Clement, et al., *My Generation: Celebrate the 60s, The Decade That Changed the World*, film documentary, XIX Entertainment, London, 2017.
[16] Jonathan Gould, *Can't Buy Me Love: The Beatles, Britain, and America* (New York, Harmony Books, 2007), 15.
[17] This spirit of independence was, essentially, the "father" of George Harrison's bold retort to George Martin's critique of the Beatles' behavior: "Yeah well, I don't like your tie." See Kenneth Womack, *Maximum Volume: The Life of Beatles Producer George Martin, The Early Years* (Chicago: Chicago Review Press, 2017), 94.
[18] Lewisohn, *All These Years*, 16.   [19] Lewisohn, *All These Years*, 16–17.
[20] Lewisohn, *All These Years*, 17.

But in the post-war 1950s, many others appeared on the scene: Caribbean West Indians, Africans, Dutch, Indians, and Greeks.[21] Their rich language, dress, customs, attitudes, and music became inexorably woven into a lush, multi-textured garment that was the new Great Britain.

In Britain's larger cities, Chinese "take-aways," Indian restaurants offering exotic "kebabs," and splendidly diverse Caribbean steel bands gradually became as common as Sunday pot roast dinners. Ports of call, welcoming sailors from all over the world, introduced Britons to the sounds of America. The music of Buddy Holly, Little Richard, Jerry Lee Lewis, and Elvis Presley filtered into the once proper BBC Light Programme-dominated British world.[22] The sounds of sentimental Celtic folk tunes, sensual syncopation, and live jive filtered out over England's rooftops; the music of the isle became rich, various, and diverse.

The times, they were indeed a-changing. Women – who in pre-war days, had been expected to marry, keep house, and raise a family – had taken jobs during World War II, and in the aftermath, many were reluctant to surrender the social and economic advantages of such employment. Wearing full, long skirts, nylons, and bright red lipstick, these newly autonomous young women began to reject the notion of being a "selfless housewife."[23] British women clung to their vocations, cherishing "the feeling of independence ... an escape from what home [had] come to mean."[24] Female employees eagerly filed into the workplace, and on Saturday nights, single girls, in confidence-building groups, filled the local dance halls.[25]

These inspired young women were after more than just a vocation, however. They were seeking recognition: validation of their worth. Because parliament tried to prevent them from serving in the political arena, females desired representation even more fervently. As early as 1918, with the Representation of the People Act, females over age 30 (*about 40 percent* of Britain's female population)[26] won the right to vote. That same year, they were permitted to stand as candidates and be selected as Members of Parliament.[27] In fact, Constance Markievicz won a seat in the House of Commons in 1918, but as an active and vocal member of Sinn Fein, she did

[21] Willis-Pitts, *Liverpool: The Fifth Beatle*, 103.
[22] Gary Popper, David Appleton, Dave Bedford, et al., *Looking for Lennon*, film documentary, Evolutionary Films, London, 2017.
[23] Davenport-Hines, *An English Affair*, 2025, and Quinalt, "Britain 1950," 7.
[24] Davenport-Hines, *An English Affair*, 1999.   [25] Quinalt, "Britain 1950," 9.
[26] "Women in Parliament," *Art in Parliament*, www.parliament.uk/worksofart/collection-highlights/portraits/women-in-parliament.
[27] Note: they were allowed to be elected to a seat in the House of Commons.

not take her seat, and the opportunity to introduce women into parliament passed. In 1919, however, Nancy Astor was elected as a Conservative for the Plymouth-Sutton constituency – a seat she held until 1945.[28]

But such extremely scanty representation did not signify that women were accepted as a part of Britain's political life. Indeed, in 1957, Robert Shirley, 13th Earl Ferrers, stated quite candidly, "Frankly, I find women in politics *highly* distasteful ... a man's judgement is generally more logical and less tempestuous ... We like women; we admire them. Sometimes, we even grow fond of them, but we do not want them here!"[29] This prevailing attitude galvanized the suffrage movement in England, and by 1958 (via the Life Peerages Act), women finally secured the right to hold a seat in the House of Lords.[30]

But elsewhere, little had changed. Because married women were forbidden by law to negotiate a legal contract or secure a loan without their husband's signature, they reacted with, "It's *his* house! It's *his* children!"[31] Women sought something all their own; they sought expression, acknowledgment, and identification.

Young men were hungry for meaning as well. In a journey toward identity, some began sporting tight drainpipe jeans and long Edwardian-style jackets with velvet collars, hallmarks of the edgy Teddy Boy movement.[32] And others found skiffle – an exceptional blend of American folk tunes, jazz, and primitive rock 'n' roll. Thirty thousand bands sprung up across the country: bare-bones ensembles comprising washboards, jugs, kazoos, tea-chest bass, harmonicas, and if very fortunate, a rare guitar or a banjo.[33]

The groups popped up overnight, rehearsing in the myriad bomb shelters that dotted Britain's crumbled neighborhoods, and inspired by British skiffle star Lonnie Donegan,[34] they ginned out "Cumberland Gap"

---

[28] "Women in the House of Commons," *Parliament uk*, www.parliament.uk/about/living-heritage/transformingsociety/electionsvoting/womenvote/overview/womenincommons/, 'Women in Parliament', *Art in Parliament*, and "Lady Nancy Astor Biography," *Biography*, www.biographyonline.net/politicians/uk/lady-nancy-astor.html.

[29] Davenport-Hines, *An English Affair*, 1902–03.   [30] 'Women in Parliament', *Art in Parliament*.

[31] Davenport-Hines, *An English Affair*, 1903.

[32] Bill Harry, *The Ultimate Beatles Encyclopedia* (New York: Hyperion, 1992), 646. Both Stuart Sutcliffe and John Lennon dressed in the Ted style at Liverpool College of Art in 1958.

[33] Ken Womack, *The Beatles Encyclopedia*, Vol. 2 (Santa Barbara, CA: Greenwood Press, 2014), 842–43.

[34] Harry, *The Ultimate Beatles Encyclopedia*, 203. Harry notes that Donegan "virtually created the skiffle phenomenon in England" beginning with his 1956 hit, "Rock Island Line." Harry says that after this entry song, Donegan had "ten Top Ten chart entries [in Britain] within an eighteen-month period."

and "Jack of Diamonds" (enhanced with the "ole ackey-dackey," as Gerry Marsden explained in the documentary *The Compleat Beatles*)[35] at golf clubs, birthday parties, and wedding receptions.[36]

Banned in stylish establishments, skiffle – and gradually its successor, rock 'n' roll – became the rugged voice of Britain's male youth. Young men in the post-war world were happy to be alive and determined to be heard. Fortunately, the press (also eager for change) heard them. By the late 1950s, "youth" had become the watchword of once-conservative newspapers such as London's *Daily Mirror*.

In August 1956, *Daily Mirror* reporter Patrick Doncaster penned the chilling article "Do We Want This Shockin' Rockin'?" in which he asked fellow Britons: "Can it happen here – the trouble that goes with rock 'n' roll music in the United States?"[37] But merely a handful of months later, the *Mirror* tuned in to the wavelength of the young, proudly carrying the life story of Tommy Steele – England's first rock 'n' roll teen idol.[38]

Teenagers – who, one generation ago, had been conveniently "seen and not heard" – now were finding themselves in music, fashion, the press, and even on "the big screen." In September 1956, as the American musical film *Rock Around the Clock* (starring rock 'n' roll DJ Alan Freed, along with Bill Haley and the Comets)[39] swept riotously from one theater to another across the British isle, the early stirrings of England's vibrant Youth Movement[40] horrified their elders. Mark Lewisohn notes that at a Paddington (West London) showing of *Rock Around the Clock*, a 15-year-old boy "punched the cinema manager."[41] Up in Liverpool, duck ass-coifed, 16-year-old John Lennon, the founder and leader of the Quarry Men skiffle group, eagerly anticipated the film's arrival on Merseyside as the perfect opportunity to flex his youthful independence and raise "a bit o' ruckus." But the ingénue guitarist was sadly disappointed when the local audience in Liverpool's Woolton suburb sat mutely staring at the screen and munching on popcorn. "Nobody," he complained forever after, "was screaming or dancing in the aisles. I was all set to tear up the seats, too, but nobody joined in."[42]

---

[35] Patrick Montgomery and Stephen Bennett, *The Compleat Beatles* (Los Angeles: MGM/UA, 1982).
[36] Harry, *The Ultimate Beatles Encyclopedia*, 688. Harry tells us that Nigel Whalley, who served as the first manager of the Quarry Men, got the group their first gig as a skiffle band at the Lee Park Golf Club – where he worked – in 1957. Harry (p. 540) also states that the Quarry Men, playing skiffle tunes such as "Rock Island Line," "Railroad Bill," "Cumberland Gap," and "Freight Train," also performed at "various parties" prior to their first "real gig" at the 22 June Roseberry Street carnival.
[37] Lewisohn, *All These Years*, 281.   [38] Davenport-Hines, *An English Affair*, 3426.
[39] Ray Coleman, *Lennon* (New York: McGraw-Hill, 1984), 53.
[40] Willis-Pitts, *Liverpool: The Fifth Beatle*, 103.   [41] Lewisohn, *All These Years*, 281.
[42] Philip Norman, *John Lennon: The Life* (New York: HarperCollins, 2008), 78.

Lennon's bitter disillusionment aside, films such as *Blackboard Jungle*, *Rebel Without a Cause*, and *Rock Around the Clock* were all litmus tests – indicators of a new and fervent infatuation with youth that had only begun to populate. As respected journalist Ray Coleman noted, these films were much more than entertainment; they were "clarion calls to confrontation."[43] And in 1956, the world was beginning to listen to that sound.

But this cultural metamorphosis was not restricted to teens alone. The British family was changing as well. As two-wage-earner families became the norm and the government supported two-week paid holidays for workers,[44] family travel took hold as an annual tradition. British "holiday camps" (such as Butlins) increased in popularity,[45] requiring proprietors to provide inexpensive entertainment. And nothing was more affordable than the eager, rabid-to-be-rich-and-famous skiffle and rock 'n' roll bands that had mushroomed across the nation. Enthusiastic groups such as Liverpool's Rory Storm and the Hurricanes could be had for the asking – with the promise of free caravan board, meals, and a paltry weekly rate.[46] It was an experience camp owners and families could afford.

But when unable to travel, the rapidly progressing field of technology was most happy to supply a new and unique diversion to Mum, Pater, and the kids.

Technological Change Augments

In 1963, English literary critic and author Cyril Connolly wrote: "Television is the single greatest factor for change in people's lives and probably has done much to undermine English Puritanism."[47] Indeed, the pervasive "goggle box" – as it was referred to in Britain – was solely responsible for bringing lurid stories and photos straight into the family living room.[48] As author Richard Davenport-Hines observed, "Television abolished shame."[49]

---

[43] Coleman, *Lennon*, 54.

[44] Tim Lambert, "A Brief History of Holiday," *Local Holidays*, 2019, www.localhistories.org/holidays .html. Two-week paid holidays were given after the first year of employment. It must be noted that seaside resorts and holiday camps had first appeared in the early 1900s when one-week vacations were instituted in the UK. With the two-week increase during the 1950s, their numbers and popularity spread.

[45] Quinalt, "Britain 1950," 10.

[46] Harry, *The Ultimate Beatles Encyclopedia*, 560. The drummer for Rory Storm and the Hurricanes was Ringo Starr.

[47] Davenport-Hines, *An English Affair*, 3491.   [48] Davenport-Hines, *An English Affair*, 3491.

[49] Davenport-Hines, *An English Affair*, 3491.

In the early 1950s, radio and TV – under the auspices of the British Broadcasting Company (the BBC) – politely refrained from dealing with unsavory subjects. Programs were cultured and refined. But as television audiences grew from 764,000 in 1951 to over 4 million in 1955, entrepreneurial eyes turned longingly toward the industry.[50] With the passage of the Television Act of 1954, the BBC's monopoly over TV was shattered and the next year, a commercial station known as Independent Television (ITV) was created.

Whereas the BBC had always "spoken with a conservative voice," the newly created, commercial ITV was determined to make money.[51] And realizing that smart businesses would only purchase commercials during well-liked programs, ITV strove to give the people what they wanted. The popular program *Danger Man* (featuring Patrick McGoohan as secret agent, John Drake)[52] and the beloved soap-opera *Coronation Street* premiered on ITV in 1960. Artfully appealing to public interests, ITV swiftly changed the landscape of the British television.

Indeed, with a jealous eye on ITV's ratings, the BBC began to reach out for public approval as well. From November 1962 to December 1963, the BBC courageously aired the wry political satire short *That Was the Week That Was*.[53] Irreverently poking fun at "the men in power," *TW3* (as it was called) dared to laugh at those in the public eye.

This razor wit was also the biting humor of a rapidly rising band from Liverpool known across Britain in 1962–63, a group once known as the Quarry Men but now heralded as the Beatles. Their innovative music and sharp retorts were capturing the imaginations of young people and the press alike, and on November 4, 1963, the boys won the staid approval of the Royal Family when the group performed to resounding applause at the Royal Command Performance.[54]

Politics Serves as Catalyst

Yet, none of these social, cultural, or technological changes held quite the impact on a society that British post-war politics wielded. The rise of the "working class" (correctly translated as "the lower class" in 1950s and 1960s

---

[50] Davenport-Hines, *An English Affair*, 3471.   [51] Davenport-Hines, *An English Affair*, 3474.
[52] "Patrick McGoohan," *IMDb*, www.imdb.com/name/nm0001526/.
[53] Davenport-Hines, *An English Affair*, 3483.
[54] Norman, *John Lennon: The Life*, 330–31. Also known as "The Royal Variety Show."

England)[55] had no greater ally than Harold Wilson, who – through a series of convoluted events – rose from member of parliament to prime minister in 1964.

For thirteen years (prior to the 1964 election of Labour's Harold Wilson as prime minister) the Conservative Party had been firmly, unequivocally in power. And for thirteen years strict conformity had been the order of the day.

"It was an epoch," Richard Davenport-Hines states, "in which it was unthinkable for a Cabinet Member to appear in shirt sleeves."[56] When Harold Macmillan was chosen as prime minister in 1957 (succeeding his fellow Conservative, Sir Anthony Eden), he immediately put on the mantle of "proper behavior." He began attending cricket matches, minimizing any mention of his Scottish heritage, and watching his speech quite carefully. For, "when an Englishman opens his mouth," author P. Willis-Pitts tells us, "he is automatically categorized as to birth, education, and area of origin . . . neatly pigeonholed."[57]

As young men and women of the post-war world began to discover new roles in society, this attitude of rigid conformity weathered and aged. And nothing did more to deflate the philosophy than did the Profumo Affair. In the words of Richard Davenport-Hines, "The Profumo Affair was a death-knell to . . . hierarchal authority" as it lay bare "the widespread decadence beneath the glitter . . . of stiff-lipped society."[58]

In 1961, Prime Minister Macmillan's secretary of state for war, John ("Jack") Profumo, was caught having an illicit affair with 19-year-old "would-be" model Christine Keeler.[59] And to make matters worse, Keeler was also involved with several West Indians, a property racketeer, a London osteopath named Stephen Ward, and most importantly, with Yevgeny Ivanov, an assistant naval attaché at the Russian Embassy in London.[60] Whilst the British Secret Service could reluctantly overlook Keeler's connection with other suitors, they could not ignore Profumo's involvement with a young woman so intimately enmeshed with a suspected Russia agent.[61]

---

[55] Willis-Pitts, *Liverpool: The Fifth Beatle*, 280. Willis-Pitts states, "It should be remembered that the term 'working class' in 1960s England does not equate with the American term. A better translation would be . . . as 'lower class.'"

[56] Davenport-Hines, *An English Affair*, 567.   [57] Willis-Pitts, *Liverpool: The Fifth Beatle*, 102.

[58] Davenport-Hines, *An English Affair*, 4714.

[59] Philip Norman, *Shout! The Beatles in Their Generation* (New York: MJF Books, 1981), 185 and Robert Rodriguez, Anthony Edmunds, Michael Foley, Jeffrey Sanders, Bradley Shreve, et al. *The Sixties Chronicle* (Lincolnwood, IL: Legacy Publishing, 2004), 143.

[60] Rodriguez et al., *The Sixties Chronicle*, 143.

[61] Rodriguez et al., *The Sixties Chronicle*, 143. Rodriguez states, "Ivanov was undoubtedly a spy, and the triangle exposed a Cold War security weakness in the British government. "

However, from the very beginning the manhunt for Profumo's vast indiscretions was never truly "about Profumo." It was a thinly veiled attack on a Conservative member of parliament in an attempt to upset the apple cart: to dislodge Macmillan and his cronies and issue in a new age guided by the common man and the Labour Party. And the newspapers led the fray.

As early as 1955 – faced with competition from ITV's programming – British newspapers had begun to recruit new readers by publishing the sensational. *News of the World* writers, for example, had been directed by management to "produce sizzling stories with lots of pictures to vie with screen images."[62] And no story could have filled that bill better than the tale of Jack Profumo. It was a story made for the front page!

When confronted with evidence of the shabby indiscretion, Profumo acted predictably; he vehemently denied the affair to parliament. Claiming that "there was no impropriety whatsoever in my acquaintance with Miss Keeler," the secretary of state for war thought to have closed the case. But infuriated, the press reacted by seizing on the Profumo scandal not just to "thump the Conservative Party," but also to, in effect, "kill off a political class."[63]

Still, the British Secret Service was reluctant to act in haste. MI5 informed the *News of the World* managing director, Mark Chapman-Walker, that "they were sure there had been no security risk."[64]

The ill-positioned Conservative Party – eager to sweep the story under the rug – readily agreed with MI5. In fact, they declared that the affair was merely "a private matter between Profumo and Keeler."[65] But the Labour Party, insisted that the scandal was "a security issue,"[66] and MI5 was forced to dig deeper.

When, at last, the complete facts were uncovered by the British Secret Service and made public, the jig was up. Profumo confessed to having "misled" parliament and resigned.[67]

At once, London's *Sunday Mirror* exploded in a bevy of articles deploring the wiles of "ruling-class corruption." Their top correspondent, James Cameron, penned the vitriolic "Why the World is Mocking Britain" whilst the equally vocal Malcolm Muggeridge depicted "The Sure Slow Death of the Upper Class."[68] Indeed, in *Shout! The Beatles in Their Generation*,

---

[62] Davenport-Hines, *An English Affair*, 3083.   [63] Davenport-Hines, *An English Affair*, 3442.
[64] Davenport-Hines, *An English Affair*, 4246.   [65] Davenport-Hines, *An English Affair*, 4382.
[66] Davenport-Hines, *An English Affair*, 5832.
[67] Norman, *Shout! The Beatles in Their Generation*, 185, and Rodriguez et al., *The Sixties Chronicle*, 143.
[68] Davenport-Hines, *An English Affair*, 4924, 4907.

author Philip Norman tells us that Macmillan and the Conservative Party were "mortally wounded." Their long-standing empire collapsed under the "devastating bombardment" by Fleet Street, and as the Tory Party fell, Macmillan resigned in disgrace.[69]

Meanwhile, waiting in the wings to capitalize on such a defeat was a man of the people – Harold Wilson of the long-scorned North.

Wilson cut an interesting figure. He was a symbol of the rising working class that despised "the idle rich."[70] Wilson approved of the rumbling lorries and vans that began to fill the British roadways in the wake of new technological advances. He smiled on the usage of once-elegant family lodgings as new office buildings. He understood that, unfortunately, tiny family-owned shops had to be replaced by large, national chains.[71] In an era when innovation was aching to do its work, Wilson was a man who championed progress.

Wilson had been elected to parliament from the Huyton district of Liverpool, a region of England generally snubbed. In the late 1950s, says author P. Willis-Pitts in *Liverpool: The Fifth Beatle*, "a Liverpool accent was the sign that a person was: a) potentially violent, b) definitely of the lower order of animals, c) stupid and violent (and therefore, dangerous) and d) to be avoided or exploited, depending upon the relative proportions of 'c'."[72] Willis-Pitts goes on to say, "This is by no means an exaggeration!"[73]

But attitudes shifted dramatically when Harold Wilson became prime minister. As the son of a grocer and a son of the once-reviled Merseyside, Wilson was, as Philip Norman has suggested, "attuned to the mass mood."[74] Promising a "New Britain," Wilson vowed to issue in "a hundred days of dynamic action"[75] that would be "forged in the white heat of the technological revolution."[76] Wilson pushed for reforms that would provide free secondary education for all. He vowed to create a welfare state designed to bolster those living in dire circumstances.[77]

Wilson was also very aware of the early 1960s arts renaissance in Britain's North. In late 1961, Liverpool School of Art student Bill Harry created the popular music newspaper *Mersey Beat*,[78] and noted Liverpool poets Roger

---

[69] Rodriguez et al., *The Sixties Chronicle*, 143.   [70] Davenport-Hines, *An English Affair*, 1334.
[71] Davenport-Hines, *An English Affair*, 1075–76.   [72] Willis-Pitts, *Liverpool: The Fifth Beatle*, 102.
[73] Willis-Pitts, *Liverpool: The Fifth Beatle*, 102.
[74] Norman, *Shout! The Beatles in Their Generation*, 245.
[75] Norman, *Shout! The Beatles in Their Generation*, 245.
[76] Norman, *Shout! The Beatles in Their Generation*, 245.
[77] Willis-Pitts, *Liverpool: The Fifth Beatle*, 103.
[78] Harry, *The Ultimate Beatles Encyclopedia*, 461.

McGough[79] and Adrian Henri[80] were being recognized for their work. Wilson extended unflagging support for artists from the "hick" North,[81] validating their search for acceptance.

In 1964, when John Lennon's rapidly burgeoning band, the Beatles, were selected for the annual Variety Club Award as the "Show Business Personalities of 1963," Wilson requested that as parliamentary representative from the Liverpool area he be permitted to present the honor to the lads at the Dorchester Hotel luncheon. Posing in front of the television cameras and having his photo made with the brilliant young group who had rocked the London Palladium in October 1963, and won the hearts of America in February 1964, Wilson neatly connected himself with "the latest rage."[82] He also endeared himself to young voters in the North.

Then, in May 1965, Wilson met with the Queen and recommended the Beatles for the Member (of the Order of the) British Empire award (MBE).[83] It was a bold move; Wilson's nomination was an intrepid act that would rock the once-stable world of the Conservatives. Resenting the nomination of the four young Northern rock stars, twelve MBE holders instantly returned their awards in protest.[84] But most of England nodded happily and thought Wilson cutting-edge and worldly wise.

In ten short years, from 1955 to 1965, England had undergone a remarkable transformation. Technology, the press, the arrival of television, broad changes in the cultural landscape, and the leadership of Harold Wilson had, as author Richard Davenport-Hines pointed out, "redrawn Britain's social landscape."[85] It was an age in which anything could happen, in which an unpolished band of brothers from a Cavern in the rugged North could overtake the known world.

[79] "Roger McGough," *The Poetry Archive*, www.poetryarchive.org/poet/roger-mcgough.
[80] "Adrian Henri," *The Poetry Archive*, www.poetryarchive.org/poet/adrian-henri.
[81] Lewisohn, *All These Years*, 1391. John Lennon states, "When we came down [to London] we were treated like provincials by the Cockneys ... looked down upon as animals. We were *hicksville*."
[82] Mark Lewisohn, *The Complete Beatles Chronicle* (New York: Harmony Books, 1988), 152. Lewisohn points out that "the BBC made a 30-minute programme of the luncheon – The Variety Club of Great Britain Annuals for 1963 – [to be] screened from 10.30 to 11.00 pm on Friday 20 March [1964]." This was a fact *not lost* on the shrewd Wilson.
[83] Harry, *The Ultimate Beatles Encyclopedia*, 698, and Norman, *Shout! The Beatles in Their Generation*, 246. Norman states that by June 12, 1965 it was announced that the Queen had approved the nomination and the Beatles were to receive the award.
[84] Harry, *The Ultimate Beatles Encyclopedia*, 444.   [85] Davenport-Hines, *An English Affair*, 5488.

America Succumbs

But in order for the Beatles to succeed, really succeed, America had to be complicit – to fall in love with the Fab Four. And without realizing it, "the States" were primed.

At the 1960 Edinburgh International Film Festival, author Al Sussman tells us that a quirky four-man troupe of actors dubbed "Beyond the Fringe" caught the public eye.[86] The group – Alan Bennett, Dudley Moore, Peter Cook, and Jonathan Miller – performed satirical comedy of the highest order.[87] They were a festival sensation and were rapidly booked in London's West End.[88]

By October 1962, *Beyond the Fringe* had found its wry and whimsical way to the States, where the production proved just as appealing to Americans. By February 7, 1964, when the Beatles stepped off Pan Am Flight 101 at John F. Kennedy Airport, *Beyond the Fringe '64* was already "all the rage."

Similarly, in autumn 1963, another cheeky British production was running on the Great White Way: *The Establishment*, starring Graham Chapman and John Cleese – later of Monty Python fame. Indeed, the Liverpool tradition of "takin' the mickey out" of literally anyone was becoming fondly familiar to the American public.

However, a third Broadway offering entitled *The Girl Who Came to Supper* – with a musical score and lyrics by Noel Coward – was only receiving lukewarm reviews. But happily, the show lasted long enough to introduce America to the brash, lovable, and bawdy babe from the British Isles, Miss Tessie O'Shea.[89] Playing her banjo and belting out numbers such as "Don't Take Our Charlie for the Army," and "Saturday Night at the Rose and Crown," O'Shea completely stole the show.[90]

In 1963–64, Broadway was madly in love with the British

In literature, there was a high tide of Anglophilia as well. British spy-novel writer Ian Fleming was a *New York Times* best-selling author, many times

---

[86] Al Sussman, *Changin' Times: 101 Days That Shaped a Generation* (Chicago: Parading Press, 2013), 131.

[87] Sussman, *Changin' Times*, 131,   [88] Sussman, *Changin' Times*, 131.

[89] "Tessie O'Shea: Biography," *IMDb*, www.imdb.com/name/nm0642697/bio?ref_=nm_ov_bio_sm. Tessie O'Shea was born in Wales but spent much of her life performing and living in London. She was dubbed "Two Ton Tessie" for her considerable girth and her abundant storehouse of talent. When the Beatles appeared on *The Ed Sullivan Show* on February 9, 1964, Tessie O'Shea was a guest that evening as well.

[90] Reviews from people who attended the 1963 Broadway production of *The Girl Who Came to Supper* may be read here: www.amazon.com/Girl-Came-Supper-Original-Broadway/product-reviews/B0000027WE.

over. His suave, ice-veined hero – British MI6 secret agent James Bond (007) – was an overwhelming hit with both male and female readers. But when President John F. Kennedy admitted to being besotted with the books, sales of Fleming's works skyrocketed[91] and movie deals were made: 1962 saw the premiere of *Dr. No*, 1963 gave film houses *From Russia With Love*, and in 1964, movie marquees advertised *Goldfinger*.[92]

But Fleming was not the only British writer in the spy-novel business. David John Moore Cornwell, writing under the *nom de plume* John le Carré, called upon his experience as a former agent for the British Security Service and the British Secret Intelligence Service to pen espionage thrillers with a more "realistic" portrayal.[93] His 1963 award-winning work, *The Spy Who Came in From the Cold*, spent an eternity on the *New York Times* best-seller list.

In the bright, new world of television, the pattern was identical. British actors and themes were *en vogue*. In Britain, *The Avengers* had been in production on ITV since 1961.[94] But within a few short years, the British-conceived program was "transplanted" to America, taking up residence on ABC (a contractor with ITV).

By 1963, America was looking to British television for inspiration and a breath of fresh air. Copying the successful BBC political lampoon *That Was the Week That Was*, NBC created its own version of the program.[95] Running a test pilot in November 1963 and then releasing a legitimate *TW3* series in January 1964, the American edition was jam-packed with stars. But sadly, the American rendition of *TW3* failed to deliver the punch that had made it so popular across the pond, and by May 1965, the American *That Was the Week That Was* was no more.

In England, the 1950s had been labeled "the Golden Age of British films,"[96] and by the early 1960s these talented British actors and actresses were shining on the American "big screen." The results were not surprising.

Tom Jones, starring Northern British actor Albert Finney (with an accent not unlike the Beatles' own)[97] was without a doubt "the film sensation of 1963."[98] It dominated the 1963–64 awards ceremonies – garnering four Academy Awards. A riotously clever adaptation of Henry Fielding's adventurous (and amorous) novel *The History of Tom Jones, a Foundling*, Richardson's 1963 film depicted the fast and carefree love life of handsome,

[91] Sussman, *Changin' Times*, 147.
[92] "James Bond Movies in Order," *Movie Order*, https://moviesorder.com/james-bond-list/.
[93] Sussman, *Changin' Times*, 148.   [94] Sussman, *Changin' Times*, 47.
[95] Sussman, *Changin' Times*, 168–69.   [96] Quinalt, "Britain 1950," 11.
[97] Sussman, *Changin' Times*, 158.   [98] Sussman, *Changin' Times*, 158.

charming bastard Tom Jones – whose questionable parentage prevented him from marrying well, but stopped little else. *Tom Jones* led audiences laughing and gasping down a bawdy trail of affairs, fanning the flames of American fervor for anything British.

Everywhere one turned in 1963, Britain was conquering the arts – in films, literature, comedy, poetry, art, and theater. Everywhere, that is, except in music.

The 1963 Hit Parade was replete with American stars. The Beach Boys topped the charts with "Surfin' USA." The Chiffons charted for "He's So Fine," and Bobby Vinton scored with "Blue Velvet." Andy Williams had a hit with "Can't Get Used to Losing You," and the Angels belted out "My Boyfriend's Back." Martha and the Vandellas were having a "Heat Wave" while folkie Trini Lopez "Had a Hammer." The Essex told us it was "Easier Said than Done," while Dion sang his heart out to "Ruby Baby."[99] It was a US-dominated Top 40 chart, all the way. Only one British group, the Tornadoes, seized the prized No. 1 slot with their instrumental tribute to a US satellite, "Telstar."[100] There was one British hit – that and nothing more.

Yet over in Britain, John Lennon, Paul McCartney, George Harrison, and Ringo Starr were front-page news. The term "Beatlemania" had been coined, and screaming fans followed the boys almost as relentlessly as the press. But could this phenomenon translate to America? Even the Beatles were unsure. Their February 7, 1964 flight from London to New York City on Pan Am's *Defiance* was a hushed one. John Lennon was sure that his group would fail in America, just as Cliff Richard had done before them;[101] no British group had ever succeeded in the US music market.[102] The lads from Liverpool relied on the fact that "I Want to Hold Your Hand" had recently captured the top slot on the American charts,[103] and they prayed that this accomplishment would be enough to give them an edge.

The Culmination of It All

When the Beatles landed in America, no one told them that on Broadway, in Hollywood, and in the high-rise offices of New York publishers,

---

[99] The complete list of hits from 1963 may be found at https://en.wikipedia.org/wiki/Billboard_Year-End_Hot_100_singles_of_1963.

[100] Sussman, *Changin' Times*, 184.

[101] The Beatles, *The Beatles Anthology* (San Francisco: Chronicle Books, 2000), 116. John Lennon states, "We didn't think we had a chance. We didn't imagine it at all. Cliff [Richard] went to America and died."

[102] Lewisohn, *The Complete Beatles Chronicle*, 136.

[103] Rodriguez et al., *The Sixties Chronicle*, 172 and Lewisohn, *The Complete Beatles Chronicle*, 136.

Americans had fallen under the spell of Britain. No one informed John, Paul, George, or Ringo that in the wake of the Profumo disgrace and the emergence of the working class, their unpolished Scouse status and Northern wit would be a blessing, not a curse. No one whispered that Betty Friedan had recently written a best seller called *The Feminine Mystique* which freed women to seek fulfillment outside the tight confines of marriage and home.[104] No one suggested that the increased emphasis on youth[105] would work in their favor.

The Beatles came to the States unaware, bearing only their complex childhood and teen experiences: dramatic events that had molded them perfectly for sacrifice, hard work,[106] and a unique gift for writing extraordinary music. They came determined to do anything to succeed.[107] They came with a modicum of trepidation – but an abundance of talent.

Thus, on February 9, 1964, the Beatles stood on the stage in the Ed Sullivan Theater and played to the largest television audience in television history.[108] And *that* was just the beginning.

Had the events of the 1950s aligned in the four Scousers' favor? Hindsight tells us that these measures certainly helped, that they mattered. But nothing was more important, that historic evening in 1964, than the four boys themselves – their unique smiles, talents, and biographies. Without these things, that pivotal moment would surely have fallen fallow – and left the 1960s stark and silent.

---

[104] Rodriguez et al., *The Sixties Chronicle*, 161.   [105] Rodriguez et al., *The Sixties Chronicle*, 170.

[106] The Beatles, *The Beatles Anthology*, 137. George Harrison states, "In 1964, we seemed to fit a week into every day."

[107] The Beatles. *The Beatles Anthology*, 110, and 157. John Lennon states, "when we got nearly big, people started telling us, 'You're the biggest thing since ... ' I got fed up that we were the biggest thing 'since.' I wanted The Beatles to be just the biggest thing!" (p. 110). He also stated, "You have to be a bastard to make it ... and The Beatles were the biggest bastards on earth" (p. 157).

[108] Rodriguez et al., *The Sixties Chronicle*, 172. Rodriguez tells us, "More than 72 million Americans tuned in, setting a record for a live entertainment show."

CHAPTER 2

The Beatles in Liverpool

David Bedford

In many books about the Beatles, the authors retell some of the popular and well-known stories from the Beatles' childhoods. However, for me, there was always something missing; there was no Liverpool feel to the stories. In fact, many authors had their facts wrong too, and it is still happening today.

What was missing was obvious to me: to understand the Beatles, you have to understand Liverpool.[1] The Beatles could not have come from any other city. Professor John Belchem, one of Liverpool's foremost historians summed it up beautifully: "Liverpool is in the North of England, but not really of it. We are living in the people's republic of Merseyside."[2]

"In The Town Where I Was Born"

John Lennon said about Liverpool:

> We were a port, the second biggest port in England . . . where all the brass and the heavy people were. We were the ones that were looked down upon by the southerners as animals . . . and also a great amount of Irish descent and blacks and Chinamen and all sorts there. It was like San Francisco, you know. And it was a very poor city and tough, but people had a sense of humour because they're in so much pain, so they're always cracking these jokes. They're very witty and it's err, an Irish place, y'know, where the Irish came when they ran out of potatoes, and it's where the black people were left, or worked as slaves, or whatever, and created communities. It's cosmopolitan, and it's where sailors would come home with the blues records on the ships![3]

---

[1] This was the quote on the cover of my first book, *Liddypool: Birthplace of The Beatles* (Deerfield, IL: Dalton Watson, 2009).

[2] Interview with Professor John Belchem for the documentary *Looking for Lennon* (Get Back Films, 2018).

[3] Interview by Jann Wenner with John Lennon for *Rolling Stone Magazine*, January 21, 1971. John was talking about Liverpool, and how his ancestors came to Liverpool during the Irish potato famine of the 1840s.

Figure 2.1 Beatles still good for business in their home town. The recently unveiled
new statues of Paul McCartney, George Harrison, Ringo Starr, and John Lennon of
the Beatles stand outside the Liver Building at Liverpool Waterfront on February 11,
2016 in Liverpool, England. Photo by Christopher Furlong/Getty Images

What is so special about Liverpool? Settlements can be traced back to the
Iron Age, and the Romans were certainly familiar with this sparsely
inhabited village, but its first mention was in 1190 as "Lieurpul." It seems
most likely that the name refers to a pool of muddy water that flowed
inland from the river. That pool, later covered by docks and the shopping
area of its modern city center, flowed toward the bottom of Mathew Street,
home of the Cavern Club. The borough of "Livpul" was established in 1207
under a charter issued by King John.

As a small fishing village, Liverpool did not expand until the seventeenth
century. As the Romans, Vikings, and King John all discovered, Liverpool's
location was significant. With trade with Ireland becoming established, the
fishing and agricultural industries in the town expanded. In 1648, the first
transatlantic cargo was being sent to America. From that day, Liverpool has
looked more across the Atlantic than to London. Liverpool began trading
with the world, though with Africa and America in slaves.

Liverpool's first slave ship, the *Liverpool Merchant*, set sail for Africa to
begin a regular route that would see the slaves transported to the West

Indies and the southern states of America. It was this slave trade that built modern Liverpool. With the increase in transatlantic trade, Liverpool was firmly established as one of the world's most important ports. To reflect this status, after the American War of Independence, it was in Liverpool, and not London, where, in 1790, the USA opened their first Consulate in the world.

It was one of Liverpool's greatest citizens, William Roscoe, who led the campaign for the abolition of slavery in parliament. Liverpool was firmly established as the second city of the British Empire.

"It's Where the Irish Came When They Ran Out of Potatoes"

Although John Lennon oversimplified it, with the rapid growth in population came a housing and health crisis, especially after the potato famine in Ireland during the 1840s, which resulted in over 1 million people leaving their homes in Ireland, and seeking a new life in the new world, via Liverpool. Many ran out of money by the time they reached Liverpool, so the town had to find room for around 100,000 new inhabitants, which was an impossibility. By 1851, approximately 25 percent of the town was Irish. Among these new "Liverpolitans" were the McCartneys and the Lennons. With them came a new culture, especially through music, and their lilting Irish accent would eventually be absorbed into the new Liverpool accent that became famous around the world through the Beatles.

These families lived in one room of a house, sharing one outside toilet with those they were living with. There was no bathroom, and there would often be just one tap of running water in the street, used by many families. Mortality, especially infant mortality, was very high among the working class.

Norwegians Would

The term "Scouser," often applied to people from Liverpool, became popular in the nineteenth century, deriving from a food that the visiting Norwegian fishermen had brought to Liverpool, known as "lobscouse." Scouse, as it became known, was a mixture of cheap cuts of meat, with potatoes and vegetables; a nutritious meal for a family on a limited budget. If they could not afford the meat, then they made "blind scouse." The people who ate scouse became known as Scousers.

From 1851 there was also a migration into the town of people from Wales. They helped to construct Victorian Liverpool, with many of their houses, including the home that Ringo was born in, still standing today. Madryn Street where he was born as Richard Starkey is named, like those around it, after places in Wales. Among those families to come from Wales was the family of John's mother, the Stanleys.

"How Did You Find America? Turned Left at Greenland"[4]

Although slavery had been abolished in Britain, the links with America, especially the southern states, saw Liverpool become involved in the American Civil War. Now at the epicenter of Britain's trade in cotton, sugar, and tobacco, the war between the North and the South had resulted in a blockade of southern ports by the Union ships, which stopped the export of the cotton that Liverpool and Lancashire relied upon. With no navy to call upon, the Confederates looked to the port with whom they had the greatest ties: Liverpool. They dispatched Commander James Dunwoody Bulloch to Liverpool to build a navy to help them compete with the North. Through the firm of Fraser, Trenholm & Company, a Liverpool cotton broker, the Confederates managed to finance the construction of ships on the Mersey, both in Liverpool and across the river in Birkenhead at Lairds. This almost led to another war between Britain and the USA. After the war, Britain was fined $15,500,000 for the damage inflicted by the ships built here.

Liverpool's importance in Britain was recognized in 1880, when Queen Victoria granted Liverpool city status. By the end of the nineteenth century, the city of Liverpool had a population of over 700,000, which was a huge increase from only 100 years before.

"Across the Universe"

With its shipping links established throughout the world, Liverpool became the location of the first Chinese community in Europe, and the second oldest Jewish community in Britain. There were also the Afro-Caribbean communities, and those from Germany, Italy, Scandinavia, and many more, each bringing their own cultures, customs, and music to the city. Liverpool's links with America were re-established during the wars in

---

[4] John Lennon's famous answer has often been mistaken for a real interview, though it took place during the film *A Hard Day's Night* as a satirical comment on their actual interviews in America.

a more positive way that brought them closer than ever before. The American influence over Liverpool and its would-be musicians would help to define twentieth-century culture.

"War is Over, if You Want It"[5]

During World War II, Liverpool, as the headquarters for the battle of the Atlantic, suffered more damage than any other city in Britain outside of London. It was key to the supplies coming in from America that kept Britain going. When America joined the war, it was through Liverpool that the armaments, planes, and soldiers would arrive in the country. Of greatest importance was the airbase at Burtonwood, just outside of Liverpool. Taken over by the USAAF in 1942, it became the biggest operational airfield in the war. At its peak, there were over 20,000 US servicemen based there.

It was into this great and unique city that the Beatles were born. A city that was so heavily bombed that nearly 4,000 people lost their lives, and thousands of homes were destroyed. The worst of the bombing came in the May blitz of 1941, when nine consecutive nights of bombing reduced much of the city center to rubble. When Paul McCartney was a baby, his family lived close to the docks on the Wirral, but the incessant bombing made them quickly move to safety. Much of Liverpool would not be rebuilt for many decades, with the scars of damage still visible in parts of Liverpool today. However, despite the stories, there was no bombing raid on the night that John Lennon was born.

For the boys growing up in post-war Liverpool, they were obsessed with everything American. They wanted the superhero comics and the candy, and to see the cowboy films at the cinema. John, like many boys, played cowboys and Indians with his friends. Then, as they grew older, these same boys would become just as obsessed with American music.

"Roll Over Beethoven"

The best ways to listen to this new music was through the medium of radio, and from the visiting American servicemen resident at Burtonwood. The BBC had the monopoly over the nation's airwaves. You could listen to

---

[5] When John Lennon and Yoko Ono released "Happy Xmas (War Is Over)" in 1971, they put up advertising boards in twelve cities around the world stating: "War Is Over! If You Want It. Happy Christmas from John and Yoko."

some jazz and classical music, but it was years before they allowed rock 'n' roll on the BBC. There were the radio comedians, a number of whom, like Ted Ray, Rob Wilton, Tommy Handley, and Arthur Askey were from Liverpool, though you could not tell from their newly acquired BBC accents. What the BBC did provide was the most influential comedy series in Britain: *The Goon Show*. Schoolboys like John Lennon became obsessed, and influenced, by the "Goons." You only have to study the writings of Spike Milligan, the principal writer for *The Goon Show*, to see the effect it had on John. This was reflected in *The Daily Howl*, John's hilarious school newspaper that he wrote and handed round, and later his books: *In His Own Write*, and *A Spaniard in the Works*. When, in 1962, the Beatles first met George Martin, they knew who he was, because he had made records with both Peter Sellers and Spike Milligan. If you go back and watch the interviews that the Beatles did, especially in America, then the humor they brought can be traced back to the natural wit of Scousers, and the influence of the Goons. When asked what he thought of Beethoven, Ringo replied: "I love him. Especially his poems."[6]

"In Our Ears and in Our Eyes"

Listening to the new, exciting music coming out of America was achieved by tuning in to Radio Luxembourg and the Armed Forces Network, the latter broadcasting across Europe to the American forces still resident in the many countries they had helped to liberate. Radio Luxembourg was a small station broadcasting the latest hit records all the way into bedrooms across Britain from the tiny European principality. Boys would stay up into the night listening to the shows from both British and American disc jockeys. John Lennon's Uncle George wired a speaker from the main radio downstairs into John's bedroom to enable him to listen to Radio Luxembourg.

In 1956, jazz musician Lonnie Donegan introduced a new sound, derived from American bluegrass and folk music called "skiffle," and sparked a musical revolution in Britain. Between 1956 and 1958, thousands of schoolboys, like John, Paul, and George, realized that music did not have to be something that you simply listened to. Now you could buy a cheap guitar and form your own group. When "Rock Island Line" hit the charts, Donegan laid the foundations for the revolution that the Beatles would lead in the 1960s. Its roots were in the rent parties in America during

---

[6] One of many funny "Ringoisms," this famous quote was recorded during an interview with Murray the "K" at John F. Kennedy International Airport on February 7, 1964.

the 1920s, when poor families would host a musical performance on their homemade instruments to raise the money for the rent. All you needed were three or four chords, and a few simple songs.

"Mother"

Inspired by his friend Geoff Lee, John Lennon formed a skiffle group at school, with his friends Pete Shotton, Bill Smith, and Eric Griffiths. John and Eric purchased guitars, though they did not enjoy the guitar lessons, so they turned to John's mum, Julia. A talented banjo player and singer, she taught the two boys to tune four of their guitar strings to her banjo, and how to play with banjo chords. They were making music. She even encouraged them to rehearse in her house.

Pete Shotton played washboard, which he borrowed from his mother at home; Bill Smith became the inaugural tea-chest bass player: a homemade upright bass. Rod Davis joined on banjo, with drummer Colin Hanton adding percussion; the Quarry Men were a group. The group performed in clubs and halls in Liverpool, including the Cavern, the city's leading jazz club. As skiffle had come via a jazz group, it was acceptable. Rock 'n' roll, however, was not allowed, even though Lennon tried to introduce it, much to the annoyance of the Cavern's owner. Beat music would have to wait a few years.

"A-Wop-bop-a-loo-lop a-lop-bam-boo"

It was rock 'n' roll that captured Lennon's heart and soul early on. A school friend, Don Beattie, was an avid listener to the Armed Forces Network, and heard a new star singing his latest recording, which took his breath away. The following day, he went to seek out his friend John Lennon and told him about this new phenomenon, whose name was Elvis Presley. John's world would never be the same again.

Little Richard's music had been introduced to John via one of his school friends, Michael Hill, who had purchased the record on a school trip to Amsterdam. On hearing "Long Tall Sally," John was dumbfounded. "That was the music that brought me from the provinces of England to the world. That's what made me what I am."[7]

---

[7] John's comments from Michael Hill in his book *John Lennon: The Boy Who Became A Legend* (CreateSpace Independent Publishing Platform, 2013). Michael purchased the record in Amsterdam and took it to his home to play to John, who sat there without saying a word at first.

"Lived a Man Who Sailed to Sea"

One of the unique ways of getting American music and culture into Liverpool was via Liverpool seamen who served on the transatlantic ships, traveling between Liverpool and New York. Both John's father Alf and George's father Harry used to make this journey, including during the war. However, it was the post-war seamen, known as the "Cunard Yanks," who would leave their impression on the city and its music. They disembarked in New York, and bought cameras, made-to-measure suits, aftershave, and, most importantly for the musical evolution in Liverpool, they brought records home. Groups were now listening to R&B, country and western and rock 'n' roll, before the records were ever released in Britain. As groups challenged each other to find songs that no other groups were performing, any advantage was welcomed. It was from one of these "Cunard Yanks" that George Harrison purchased his first Gretsch guitar.

Another unique way that American music made it into the city was through American servicemen at Burtonwood, who still had a presence in the city. With America still under segregation, the servicemen were separated both on base and when they came to enjoy themselves in Liverpool. The white servicemen headed for the bars in the city center, like the Jacaranda and Blue Angel, both owned by Allan Williams, who became the Beatles first manager.

"Ob-la-di, Ob-la-da"

However, of more importance to the musical evolution of the Beatles was visiting the black clubs in the Liverpool 8 area, where the Afro-Caribbean community had been established. The black American servicemen brought their records from Burtonwood to the clubs, and played them on the record player. Hanging out in these clubs were John, Paul, and George. They heard American records, and learned as many as they could, even the B-sides. But they also listened to, and took lessons from, local black musicians, like Vinnie Ismael. They were absorbing all of this music and culture, which was unique to Liverpool. Is it any surprise that the Beatles refused to play to a segregated audience on their US tour? The phrase "Ob-la-di, Ob-la-da" came from a Nigerian musician friend of Paul McCartney called Jimmy Scott-Emuakpor.[8]

---

[8] The phrase was from Jimmy Scott-Emuakpor (McCartney's Nigerian acquaintance) who later tried to claim a writer's credit for the use of his catchphrase in the song. McCartney claimed that the phrase was "just an expression." Scott argued that not only was the phrase not a general expression, but also

The only opportunities these Liverpool lads had to see and hear American artists in the early days were when Buddy Holly appeared at the Philharmonic Hall in March 1958, and when Gene Vincent appeared at a concert at Liverpool Stadium. John saw Buddy Holly with his friend Nigel Walley.[9]

Liverpool had a music scene unlike any other in Britain. From these roots came not only the Mersey Sound, but also the biggest country music scene in Britain, when Liverpool became known as the "Nashville of the North" in the 1960s. The Quarry Men's first business card reflects their repertoire and influences: Country, Western, Skiffle, Rock 'n' Roll.

"There Are Places I'll Remember All My Life"

Liverpool produced the sound that conquered the world through its most famous sons: the Beatles. They took American music, re-worked it with their own Liverpool sound, and sold it back to America and the rest of the world. They kept their Liverpool accents, spoke their minds, used humor and all that Liverpool had imprinted on them and in them. They knew where they came from, which is why it was reflected in their songs, both with the Beatles and as solo artists.

As Paul wrote, paraphrasing his old school motto: "Not for ourselves but for the whole world were we born, and we were born in Liverpool."[10]

---

it was in fact exclusively used in the Scott-Emuakpor family. He later dropped the case when McCartney agreed to pay his legal expenses for an unrelated issue. From Steve Turner, *A Hard Day's Write: The Stories Behind Every Beatles Song* (London: Carlton Books, 2005).

[9] Although never mentioned by John Lennon, Nigel Walley, in an interview with David Bedford, recalled seeing Buddy Holly and the Crickets at Liverpool's Philharmonic Hall on March 20, 1958.

[10] This quote is from "Movement II – School" from *Liverpool Oratorio* by Paul McCartney. The Liverpool Institute school motto was: "Non Nobis Solum Sed Toti Mundo Nati," which translates as "Not for ourselves alone, but for the whole world were we born."

CHAPTER 3

The Beatles on the Reeperbahn

Spencer Leigh

I was born in Liverpool and have lived there all my life. In 1963/64, my friends and I had a sense of pride that the Beatles had come from our home streets and that they often spoke of the city in their interviews. We knew that they had been to Hamburg but we thought that their sound had been formed in the clubs and church halls around Merseyside, building their repertoire from the R&B singles that they heard in shops like Brian Epstein's NEMS.

Having interviewed the Merseybeat musicians extensively for my programs on BBC Radio Merseyside, I decided in 2002 to make a series about the Beatles in Hamburg. It was a revelation as I discovered that many of those who went to the beat clubs in St. Pauli thought that those long working hours had made the Beatles and also that the rough surroundings had added an edge to their work.

Similarly, I have met people from London who say that the capital city made the Beatles and many Americans think that the Beatles accounted for little before *The Ed Sullivan Show* in February 1964. Strong arguments can be put forward for Liverpool, Hamburg, London, and America but, as with everything else, it was the combination that made the Beatles. They were blotting paper, soaking up influences and surroundings, but they were always able to add their own spin so that the results were original.

This sounds simplistic but it is not. In the 1990s, Oasis had a series of hits which were said to be inspired by the Beatles. Yes and no. Where was their "Eleanor Rigby"? Where was their "Yesterday"? Their inspiration was a Beatles' B-side, "Rain," and they returned to it time and again. That Oasis were able to sustain a long career with a similar sound showed the dearth of originality in rock around that time. In the 1960s, it was very different: the Beatles had to compete with the Rolling Stones, the Kinks, the Who, the Beach Boys, the Byrds and the songwriters Jimmy Webb and Burt Bacharach. The Beatles absorbed what was happening around them and came up with stunning work.

Referring to Hamburg, John Lennon said, "We would never have developed as much if we'd stayed at home." We can never test the validity of that remark but it does suggest that John Lennon, and by implication the rest of the Beatles, regarded Hamburg as crucial to their development.[1]

There are various low-fi tapes of the Quarry Men, recorded in Liverpool between 1957 and 1960. There is nothing to suggest that they would be world leaders, but their version of "That'll Be The Day," privately recorded by Percy Phillips in 1958, is as competent as the professionally released British rock 'n' roll cover versions of the time and easily superior to Larry Page's version, released by EMI's Columbia label.

Despite a passion for rock 'n' roll, the Quarry Men was an ad hoc band, making little effort to find regular bookings. At the start of 1960, they did not even have a drummer and Allan Williams, the owner of the Jacaranda coffee bar, did not consider them good enough to be a supporting act for a concert with Gene Vincent, whose agent was Larry Parnes. Shortly after the show at Liverpool Stadium, Williams arranged auditions for Liverpool groups to back Parnes's vocalists and the Beatles (then Lennon, McCartney, Harrison, Stuart Sutcliffe and drummer Tommy Moore) accompanied Johnny Gentle on a short tour in Scotland. Moore disliked Lennon's mockery and did not play with them again.

The Merseyside beat groups were copying Cliff Richard and the Shadows. Few of them paid any attention to the Beatles and none considered them serious competition. Without a drummer, they, as the Silver Beatles, sometimes played at the Grosvenor Ballroom in Wallasey but even these performances fell away on July 30, 1960 as the dances were canceled due to hooliganism. The Beatles were a ramshackle, drummer-less band, sometimes playing in the cramped basement of Allan Williams's Jacaranda coffee bar in the city center. Williams had a friend, Lord Woodbine (Harold Phillips), who played there in a Caribbean steel band and he fronted various ventures for Williams, including Liverpool's first strip club.

Liverpool and Hamburg were of a similar size, populated with proud residents who regarded themselves as somehow separate from the rest of the country. Both cities were ports, but despite elegant stores and beautiful houses, Hamburg had its dockland area of St. Pauli. It catered to the leisure activities of sailors and its sex shops and shows contrasted sharply with Liverpool. Certainly, there was nothing like the Herbertstrasse, a street where the prostitutes were on display in the front windows.

---

[1] Ian Inglis, *The Beatles in Hamburg* (London: Reaktion, 2012), 8.

Not to mention, Reste Ecke (Remainder Corner) off the Herbertstrasse which offered bargain basement prostitution. (Sometimes I feel I may have researched a subject a little too thoroughly.) Williams and Woodbine visited Hamburg to see how its sleaze could be transferred to Liverpool. Williams heard some abysmal rock 'n' roll from a German band and told the owner Bruno Koschmider that the Beatles were far superior.

What happened next has never been satisfactorily explained, but then I rarely accept coincidence. It may be correct as I do not have an alternative explanation. Larry Parnes had offered a Blackpool season to Derry and the Seniors, but then changed his mind. The group blamed Williams, who took them to London so they could play at the best-known teenage haunt, the Two I's coffee-bar. It so happened, or so the story goes, that Koschmider had come to the city looking for the "Peadles" and had been referred to the Two I's. He met Williams and offered Derry and the Seniors a residency at the Kaiserkeller. The club was at Grosse Freiheit (Great Freedom) 36, a street off the Reeperbahn: named for religious tolerance, it now applied to sex and drugs.

The first UK band to play at the Kaiserkeller was a London band, the Jets, who brought along a maverick rock 'n' roll singer from Norwich, Tony Sheridan. Sheridan had the looks, the talent, and the potential to be a big star but he was too argumentative and had been sacked by Larry Parnes for not following orders. He soon tired of Koschmider's dictatorial ways and pathetic accommodation but Derry and the Seniors accepted this. Koschmider extended their residency and asked Williams for a second group to play at a smaller club, the Indra, at Grosse Freiheit 64. The strip-club was not doing well as it was well away from the Reeperbahn, and prospective customers would have been enticed into other clubs long before they reached the Indra. The Seniors were unimpressed when Williams sent the Beatles as they considered them incompetent. However, there was little choice as Williams had to find a group without the commitment of day jobs.

Lennon and Sutcliffe were at art college, McCartney had left school, and Harrison was half-heartedly studying to be an electrician. They leapt at the chance but the contract stipulated a drummer and they asked Pete Best, whose mother ran the Casbah coffee club. He had done well in his O-levels and was waiting to go to college: he had O-level German, a useful bonus.

"My mother took a phone call from Paul McCartney," Best remembers, "He said that they'd had an offer to go to Germany and needed a drummer.

George Harrison had seen me play and knew I had a drum kit. I went to Allan Williams' house and auditioned. Two days later, I was a Beatle."[2]

In August 1960 Williams drove the Beatles to Hamburg, a momentous, incident-packed adventure in its own right. Their accommodation, behind the cinema screen at the Bambi-Kino, was appalling, but the wages were reasonable (30 DM per Beatle per day, that is, roughly $6). They had to play four hours a day and six at weekends. If they flagged, Koschmider, a hard taskmaster, would shout, "Mach Schau! (Make show)."

The long hours gave the Beatles the chance to experiment with their repertoire, their sound, and their harmonies, but they knew what was wanted from Day One. Howie Casey recalls, "I went to see the Beatles on their opening night as they started and finished earlier than us. They kicked off and my jaw went to the floor. There was such a difference from what I had seen before, and we became buddies. They were jealous that we were playing in this huge club and they would come down and jam. We had some great nights."[3]

The Beatles started on August 17 and they were soon attracting a following. However, a resident complained to the police that the Beatles and their followers made too much noise and Koschmider was ordered to return to strippers. The Beatles made their final appearance on October 3. With no increase in wages, Koschmider wanted the Beatles to replace the Seniors at the Kaiserkeller and he secured another Liverpool band, Rory Storm and the Hurricanes (with Ringo Starr on drums), so that it could be continuous live music all night. Oddly, Storm was given top billing on the posters.

Johnny Guitar from the Hurricanes remembered a supreme example of *Mach Schau*: "The rickety stage was very dangerous, so we came to an arrangement with the Beatles that we'd wreck it. First, they'd go on and stamp their feet and then we'd go on and jump up and down. Koschmider would say, 'Very good, boys, you *mach* good *schau*.' Little did he realise that this was a deliberate effort to destroy the stage. The club was packed one Saturday night when Rory got on top of the piano for 'Whole Lotta Shakin' Goin' On' and the whole stage collapsed. The orange boxes supporting the planks couldn't take the strain. Koschmider went berserk and dismissed Rory for breach of contract."[4]

The Beatles befriended German youths who were influenced by the intellectual movement on the Left Bank in Paris. The students, known as

[2] Spencer Leigh, "Germany Calling!," www.spencerleigh.co.uk/2013/05/germany-calling/2/.
[3] Leigh, "Germany Calling!"   [4] Leigh, "Germany Calling!"

Exis (short for existentialists), included the photographer Astrid Kirchherr, the illustrator Klaus Voormann and another photographer, Jürgen Vollmer. Considering that the Beatles were unknown, Kirchherr produced some remarkable, black-and-white photographs. She took them to the fairground for tough, unsmiling photographs amongst the machinery. Lesser photographers would have captured them on the rides. She never captured them in performance, although Vollmer was to photograph them at the Top Ten.

Borrowing from the Exis, the Beatles wore black leather jackets with black polo-necks. You can still stand in a doorway in Jägerpassage where Vollmer photographed John Lennon in his leather jacket. "That look inspired me," said Vollmer, "John's cool, arrogant, above-it-all rocker look. He wasn't that way, but he projected that image." In October 1961, Vollmer gave them their mop-top haircuts.[5]

Although John Lennon often mocked or impersonated Adolf Hitler on stage, it was not a sign that John was taking a great risk. There was nothing heroic about it as the audiences agreed with him. Astrid Kirchherr comments, "We loved it. We had this big guilt we carried around because of what our parents did in the war, and meeting English people was very special for us. They thought we were the krauts with big legs and eating sauerkraut all the time. It was unusual for teenagers from different countries to meet then and they would joke, 'We won' and we got used to that."[6]

A horse circus venue, the Top Ten at Reeperbahn 136 had been converted into a music club. Owned by the Eckhorn family, its young manager, Peter Eckhorn, re-opened in July 1960 with beat music. In December 1960, they were featuring Tony Sheridan and the Jets as well as a Liverpool band, Gerry and the Pacemakers.

Going from Liverpool to Hamburg is easy enough today but not back then when money was tight. Fred Marsden was the drummer with Gerry and the Pacemakers: "We had to drive from Liverpool to Hamburg. We had our own van and I did most of the driving. We got to Hamburg about two in the afternoon and the manager of the Top Ten said that we were going to play at seven o'clock. We had gone 36 hours without sleeping, so Peter Eckhorn gave us Preludins to keep us awake."[7]

Groups often took drugs to help them through the night. Amphetamines were available from chemists and most musicians were swallowing Preludin with their beers. John Gustafson of the Big Three was delightfully frank:

---

[5] Leigh, "Germany Calling!"   [6] Leigh, "Germany Calling!"   [7] Leigh, "Germany Calling!"

"Memories of Hamburg? 'Drunken insanity' sums it up. You were reduced to a physical wreck after four days, but it was enjoyable to be a physical wreck. It was wonderful to be lying in the gutter in a whisky-sodden heap in rainwater. I'll never do it again."[8]

Although Sheridan had fallen out with Koschmider, he was perfectly suited to the area. He hated set lists and played exactly what he felt. While other bands strove to copy American originals, Sheridan, like a jazz musician, would improvise around them. He said, "If you play 'Blue Suede Shoes' 2,000 times, you've got to find ways to do it differently and this is when innovation happens – you put in sevenths and ninths and elevenths. That is what Hamburg can do for you, and I believe that the only way to be is spontaneous. All those guys who plan their shows are not being creative. Of course, I had bad nights, but there were nights when I turned myself on and turned everybody else on."[9]

The Beatles had never met anyone like Sheridan and thought he was fantastic. Sheridan was equally impressed with the Beatles' ability to follow him. Peter Eckhorn offered the Beatles a residency for early 1961. Seeing this as a betrayal, Koschmider accused McCartney and Best of starting a fire in their lodgings. They were deported along with George Harrison, who at 17 was under age. Lennon found his own way home but Sutcliffe chose to live with Kirchherr, now his girlfriend, and to study art in Hamburg. Back in Liverpool, they were downhearted but not for long as they asked the disc-jockey Bob Wooler to arrange some bookings.

On December 27, 1960, the Beatles were a supporting act on a beat show with Kingsize Taylor and the Dominoes at Litherland Town Hall, eight miles north of Liverpool. Instead of the regulation suit and tie, they wore black leather: Pete Best bashed the drum-kit with a manic ferocity; and they performed as though the songs meant everything to them. The audience was astounded and local promoters rushed to sign them.

Kingsize Taylor and the Dominoes were opening the show, and John Kennedy sang with them. "We'd normally do our first spot and then go to the pub for a few pints. We never got to the pub that night. We'd just reached the door when the Beatles started off and that was it. We stayed there and watched them. They were brilliant. There was something raw and animal about them."[10]

Tony Sanders played drums for Billy Kramer and the Coasters: "A friend of mine told me about this fabulous group at Litherland Town Hall. He said, 'They're all German. They wear cowboy boots and they

---

[8] Leigh, "Germany Calling!"   [9] Leigh, "Germany Calling!"   [10] Leigh, "Germany Calling!"

stomp on the stage.' A week later, we were coming off stage at Aintree Institute and saw these guys coming on next. Lennon wore a leather jacket and McCartney had a jacket that looked as though he'd been sleeping in it for months, but when they kicked off, it was unbelievable. They were smoking cigarettes on stage and that went right against convention. Instead of trying to look good, they didn't give a damn. We were all smoking the next time we went on stage, but it didn't go with our short haircuts and boy-next-door image."[11]

Ray McFall was the new owner of a jazz cellar in the city, the Cavern, and was soon offering them regular bookings, thereby transforming the venue into a beat club. McFall's lunchtime beat sessions worked splendidly. This meant that the Beatles could play three venues in a day, roughly playing an hour in each: this was a very different set-up from St. Pauli, which only had four beat clubs and never all four at one time.

The Beatles returned to Hamburg to play at the Top Ten from March 27 to July 2, 1961. They were to play five hours on weekdays and six at weekends and would receive 35 DM per Beatle per day. A successful Schlager singer, Tommy Kent, was recording for producer Bert Kaempfert in Hamburg and having the evening free, he went into St. Pauli and heard Tony Sheridan with the Beatles. He told Kaempfert that he ought to hear them and the following night Kaempfert went to the club and gave Sheridan a contract. Kaempfert wanted a familiar song and told them to re-arrange "My Bonnie." The single, released under the name of Tony Sheridan and the Beat Brothers, is often derided but it is intense and exciting and one of the best rock 'n' roll records made in Europe. It reached the German charts, making No. 32 in December 1961, a year before the Beatles' had their first UK hit with "Love Me Do."

When the Beatles returned to Liverpool, they gave a copy of "My Bonnie" to Bob Wooler, who played it during the changeover between groups. Raymond Jones and other teenagers were to order copies from NEMS's record department, run by Brian Epstein. This led to him seeing the Beatles in the Cavern one November lunchtime and becoming their manager. One of his first tasks was to negotiate with Manfred Weissleder.

Manfred Weissleder was a key player in St. Pauli, running sex shows and making explicit films. He had seen the success of the Kaiserkeller and the Top Ten and Horst Fascher, a bouncer who had been in prison and who loved the British groups, encouraged him to open his own beat club.

[11] Leigh, "Germany Calling!"

Weissleder converted a sex cinema at Grosse Freiheit 39, opposite the Kaiserkeller and next to a church, into the Star-Club.

The distinctive stage included a gold-plated piano and a backdrop of the New York skyline. The club could accommodate 2,000 patrons and the poster for the opening on April 13, 1962 declared "Die Zeit der Dorfmusik ist vorbei!" ("The time of village music is over"). As well as British bands, Weissleder, through an arrangement with Don Arden, enticed US rock 'n' roll stars like Little Richard and Gene Vincent to play the club.

Weissleder wanted several bands each evening and so the Beatles would only play two hours a night. The money was good: 500 DM for each Beatle per week. The musicians had Star-Club pins which protected them from gangsters as they walked around St. Pauli. If they were in trouble, Fascher and friends were to hand. The accommodation was better too, although a postcard home from John Lennon stated, "All 24 of us sleep in one room but we're English."[12]

Epstein arranged for the Beatles to fly to Hamburg for the opening of the Star-Club. They were met by Astrid Kirchherr who told them that Stuart Sutcliffe had died. Despite Lennon's melancholia, they still opened the Star-Club and played there until the end of May. They returned to the UK for a session with Parlophone Records, which ultimately led to the dismissal of Pete Best. Because of the long hours they played in Hamburg, the Beatles were on stage far more with Pete Best as their drummer than Ringo Starr – 1,500 hours as opposed to 600.

The Beatles returned to the Star-Club with Ringo Starr, who had played with Storm and Sheridan, for two weeks in November, this time with pay of 600 DM. At Epstein's request, Kirchherr took studio photographs for publicity purposes. Although the cover of their album, *With The Beatles* (1963) was not taken by Kirchherr, it referenced her work.

Enjoying a hit single with "Love Me Do," the Beatles reluctantly returned to the Star-Club over the Christmas period, the pay now 700 DM. The Beatles had Christmas dinner with the Dominoes at the Seaman's Mission in Hamburg. John Frankland from the Dominoes recalls, "The minister attached to the Mission said, 'Would anyone like to say grace?' and George in his wonderful deadpan way said, 'Yes, thank Christ for the soup.' The minister said, 'Any more of that and you're all out.' We ate steaks and we found out later that they were horse steaks. We'd eaten a horse for Christmas."[13] The final night on New Year's Eve was recorded by Kingsize Taylor leading to the unofficial double-album,

---

[12] Leigh, "Germany Calling!"   [13] Leigh, "Germany Calling!"

The Beatles Live At The Star-Club. It is unfortunate that the sound is so poor as otherwise it would be a valuable historic document.

The Beatles had played 279 nights in Hamburg, seventy-five of them at the Star-Club. They were invited to return in 1963 but as George Harrison told a friend, "We'd be bloody stupid to go back." That sums up the Beatles. Unlike many other acts, the Beatles always looked forward. The most concise summary of this insane area comes from Lewis Collins of the Mojos, later a star of *The Professionals* TV series. "My God, I went there a greenhorn and still a virgin at eighteen. I came back an old man having experienced just about everything in the book." No wonder John Lennon said, "I didn't grow up in Liverpool: I grew up in Hamburg."[14]

[14] Leigh, "Germany Calling!"

CHAPTER 4

Brian Epstein, Beatlemania's Architect

Kenneth Womack

Born in Liverpool to Harry and Malka "Queenie" Epstein on September 19, 1934, Brian Samuel Epstein had been educated at a succession of schools before settling upon Wrekin College in Shropshire. In 1950, Epstein entered the business world as a furniture salesman in his father Harry's prosperous department store on Walton Road. His time in the department store was cut short after he was conscripted into the National Service, for which he only served one year of his expected two-year term. At one point, he was charged with impersonating an officer after being saluted, incorrectly, by a sentry. As a result, he was confined to barracks and later discharged on "medical grounds."

After his unsuccessful stint in the National Service, Epstein returned to Liverpool, and Harry subsequently assigned his son to manage the record department. With his wide-ranging knowledge of classical music, Epstein transformed it into a profitable business in short order. Yet to his parents' great chagrin, he decided to leave Liverpool in order to pursue an actor's life at London's Royal Academy of Dramatic Art (RADA). After dropping out of the RADA in his third term, he returned to his hometown once again. His unrelenting father then opened Clarendon Furnishings, an upscale furniture store on the Wirral peninsula, and installed Brian as manager. In 1958, Harry decided to capitalize on the booming record business by opening up a NEMS (North End Music Stores) location at Great Charlotte Street under Brian's management. Although his early years had been distinguished by a general inability to fit in – he was homosexual, which was criminalized in Great Britain at the time – Epstein had proved highly adept at consolidating NEMS's success, and within a few years, he was in charge of the family's entire record operation.

Epstein's homosexuality forced him to lead a double life. Given his elite social status in Liverpool, he was often the target of blackmailers and consequently enjoyed few genuinely happy love affairs. As Philip Norman points out, Epstein was "attracted to what homosexuals call the

Figure 4.1 Record producer and Beatles manager Brian Epstein at a press conference after the Beatles return from the USA, September 2, 1965 . Photo by Daily Mirror/ Mirrorpix/Mirrorpix via Getty Images

rough trade – to the dockers and laborers of whom their kind go in greatest mortal terror. Those who sought the rough trade in Liverpool in 1957 paid a high price, even in that currency of damnation. Rebuffed or accepted, they still went in fear. If there were not a beating up, then there would probably, later on, be extortion and blackmail."[1]

---

[1] Philip Norman, *Shout!: The Beatles in Their Generation* (New York: Simon and Schuster, 1981), 132.

With the August 3, 1961 issue of *Mersey Beat*, Epstein had even begun authoring a regular column entitled "Record Releases by Brian Epstein of NEMS." By the early 1960s, Epstein operated two NEMS outlets in Liverpool, including stores on Great Charlotte Street and Whitechapel, the latter of which was less than 200 yards away from the Cavern Club. On October 28, 1961, a patron named Raymond Jones reportedly entered NEMS – the largest record outlet in Liverpool and throughout the North Country – and requested a copy of the Beatles' "My Bonnie" from the store's owner, 27-year-old Epstein. In his autobiography, *A Cellarful of Noise* (1964), Epstein claims to have been unfamiliar with the Beatles before Jones's visit on that fateful day: "The name 'Beatle' meant nothing to me though I vaguely recalled seeing it on a poster advertising a university dance at New Brighton Tower, and I remembered thinking it was an odd and purposeless spelling."[2] Given his association with *Mersey Beat* – and its regular cover stories about the band – it is doubtful that the Beatles had so thoroughly eluded his notice. In addition to the *Mersey Beat*'s lavish attention upon the band, the Beatles were featured on numerous posters throughout Epstein's record stores. As Bill Harry pointed out, "He would have had to have been blind – or ignorant – not to have noticed their name."[3] A number of music historians have gone so far as to suggest that Epstein manufactured Raymond Jones out of thin air.[4] Yet in Epstein's defense, Spencer Leigh recently located the elusive Raymond Jones, now retired and living in Spain. As Jones remarked, "No one will ever take away from me that it was me who spoke to Brian Epstein and then he went to the Cavern to see [the Beatles] for himself."[5]

In any event, on November 9, 1961, Epstein attended a lunchtime performance by the group at the Cavern in the company of his assistant manager at NEMS, Alistair Taylor. They descended into the cellar, where the club's DJ, Bob Wooler, announced that Epstein of NEMS was in attendance. Mesmerized by their performance, Epstein met with the Beatles backstage, where he was greeted by Harrison: "Hello there. What brings Mr. Epstein here?" As with so many others who encountered the group, Epstein enjoyed their charm and good humor. But more

[2] Brian Epstein, *A Cellarful of Noise: The Autobiography of the Man Who Made the Beatles* (New York: Pocket, 1998), 94, 95.
[3] Bob Spitz, *The Beatles: The Biography* (Boston: Little, Brown, 2005), 266.
[4] Mark Lewisohn, *The Complete Beatles Recording Sessions: The Official Abbey Road Studio Session Notes, 1962–1970* (New York: Harmony, 1988), 34.
[5] Spencer Leigh, "Nowhere Man?," in *The Beatles: Ten Years That Shook the World*, ed. Paul Trynka (London: Dorling Kindersley, 2004), 21.

importantly, he was impressed with the reaction that they garnered from the kids in the audience. "They gave a captivating and honest show and they had very considerable magnetism," he wrote in his autobiography. "I loved their ad-libs and I was fascinated by this, to me, new music with its pounding bass beat and its vast engulfing sound."[6] Even as he walked away from the Cavern that day, Epstein was already thinking about managing the band. After an initial meeting on December 3, 1961, with the group – sans McCartney, who was allegedly at home taking a bath – Epstein began to make inquiries about the Beatles. Not surprisingly, Allan Williams warned him about what he believed to be the band's lack of ethics. "I wouldn't touch 'em with a fucking barge pole," he told Epstein.[7] But Epstein was once and truly hooked, and at a meeting on December 10, the Beatles accepted Epstein as their manager. They signed a formal, five-year contract with him on January 24, 1962, at Pete Best's house. Epstein pointedly declined to sign the contract in order to allow his clients to withdraw from the agreement at any time. Over the next few months, he entreated the band to improve their demeanor on stage – no more swearing, no more eating between songs. For his part, he ensured that their regular fee at the Cavern Club was doubled, and he vowed, more importantly, to win them a record deal with a major label. While the Beatles were famously rejected by Decca Records after their January 1962 audition in London, Epstein doggedly pursued a record deal for the band, eventually winning a Parlophone Records contract for them and the opportunity to work with producer George Martin.

Over the next four years, Epstein emerged as a genuine rock 'n' roll impresario, working as the veritable architect of Beatlemania – both in England and abroad – by consolidating the band's fame through thousands of concert appearances, press conferences, and photo opportunities. He also shrewdly negotiated the Beatles' intermittent film appearances in the mid-1960s, allowing them to circulate their music and image among a variety of different demographics. While he suffered key missteps along the way – most notably, the disastrous Seltaeb negotiation that forfeited many of the band's key marketing rights, as well as the traumatic Far Eastern leg of their German and Japanese tour during the summer of 1966 – the Beatles' manager succeeded in exporting the Mersey Beat sound associated with a host of the group's Liverpool contemporaries. In so doing, Epstein was a central cog in the establishment of the British Invasion that swept across North American shores in the months and years after the Beatles'

[6] Epstein, *A Cellarful of Noise*, 98, 99.   [7] Spitz, *The Beatles: The Biography*, 274.

legendary February 9, 1964 appearance on *The Ed Sullivan Show*. In addition to negotiating such landmark Beatles moments as their appearances at Carnegie Hall, the Hollywood Bowl, and Shea Stadium, Epstein assisted the bandmates in traversing the minefield associated with "The Beatles Are Bigger Than Jesus Christ" controversy during the summer of 1966 that culminated in their final paying concert appearance at San Francisco's Candlestick Park on August 9 of that same year.

Yet for Epstein, the post-touring world made for a bitter, unfulfilling life. As the architect of Beatlemania, he had been on a high-octane entertainment carousel for nearly five years, and toiling in its shadow was too much for him to bear. In late September 1966, he had dinner at his posh Chapel Street home with Peter Brown, who had recently moved into the manager's house in order to look after him in his erratic state. Later that evening, Brown discovered that his roommate had fallen unconscious in his bedroom. Unable to rouse Epstein, Brown took him to a private hospital in Richmond, where the medical staff pumped his stomach and saved his life. While Epstein described the event as a "foolish accident," Brown knew better. The next morning, he found an empty bottle of Nembutal and the manager's would-be suicide note: "I can't deal with this anymore," Epstein had written "It's beyond me, and I just can't go on."[8] For some members of Epstein's inner circle, his words proved to be prophetic. On August 27, 1967, as the Beatles enjoyed their spiritual excursion to Wales in the company of Maharishi Mahesh Yogi, the world learned the news of Epstein's untimely death, at the relatively tender age of 32.

As it happens, during one of his last interviews, Epstein expressed his all-consuming fear of loneliness: "I hope I'll never be lonely, although, actually, one inflicts loneliness on oneself to a certain extent."[9] When the London nightlife failed to rouse his aching soul during that fateful final weekend, he drove home in his beloved Bentley, dying alone in his bedroom. "At that time," Alistair Taylor remembered, "Brian was taking all sorts of medication. He lived on pills – pills to wake him up, pills to send him to sleep, pills to keep him lively, pills to quieten him down, pills to cure his indigestion."[10] While the shadow of suicide lingered over Epstein's sudden death, his passing was officially ruled as an accidental overdose of barbiturates mixed with alcohol. As Harrison later recalled, "In those days

---

[8] Spitz, *The Beatles: The Biography*, 647.
[9] Keith Badman, *The Beatles off the Record: Outrageous Opinions and Unrehearsed Interviews* (London: Omnibus, 2001), 299.
[10] Alistair Taylor, *With the Beatles* (London: John Blake, 2003), 187.

everybody was topping themselves accidentally."[11] But nothing could have prepared the Beatles for life without Epstein. They loved him, to be sure, and they were thunderstruck with grief. But they also intuitively understood his role as the architect of Beatlemania and their attendant superstardom. The tragedy of his untimely death notwithstanding, he also existed – for better or worse – at the center of their financial vortex. He had been the keeper of their business affairs, and his sudden absence from their world had left a power vacuum in his place. And it was a void that they were in absolutely no way prepared to fill. "I knew that we were in trouble then," Lennon later remarked. "I didn't really have any misconceptions about our ability to do anything other than play music. And I was scared. I thought, 'We've fucking' had it.'"[12]

Epstein's death indeed had far-reaching ramifications, as the Beatles' business affairs began to spiral out of control during the development of Apple Corps, the fallout associated with Lennon and McCartney's unsuccessful 1969 effort to acquire Northern Songs, and the eventual receivership of their collective affairs under the guidance of American businessman Allen Klein. Although it is perhaps disingenuous to suggest that the band's autumn 1969 disbandment might have been delayed or even avoided with Epstein at the band's helm, it is worth noting that Epstein successfully guided the group's business affairs by employing the finest minds in the London financial establishment to guide their business empire. With his death, the Beatles no longer followed such a course, paving the way for other parties – such as Robert Stigwood and later Klein – to enter the fray, while also leaving the bandmates themselves to attempt to create their own business solutions through Apple Corps and similarly half-baked efforts.

In a 1997 BBC interview, McCartney remarked that "if anyone was the fifth Beatle, it was Brian." In a poignant song about Epstein, Lennon composed "You've Got to Hide Your Love Away" for the Beatles' *Help!* album in 1965. The composition is generally understood to be Lennon's coy allusion to Epstein's homosexuality – and the associated pain that comes from secreting the very truth and nature about oneself from the world. In "You've Got to Hide Your Love Away," Lennon does his best Bob Dylan impersonation and sings about loneliness and the bitter effects that it stamps upon its victims. Epstein was memorialized in the group's "Free as a Bird" video as part of *The Beatles Anthology* project in the mid-1990s. As the video nears its conclusion, Epstein can be seen donning

[11] Spitz, *The Beatles: The Biography*, 718.
[12] John Lennon, *Lennon Remembers*, interview by Jann Wenner (New York: Verso, 1970), 25.

a scarf. In 2012, it was announced that British actor Benedict Cumberbatch would play Epstein in the as-of-yet-untitled biographical film about the Beatles' manager to be directed by Paul McGuigan. Over the years, Epstein has appeared as a character in several movies about the Beatles. Brian Jameson played the role of Epstein in *Birth of the Beatles* (1979), while Jamie Glover played him in the 2000 television movie *In His Life: The John Lennon Story*. In the most notorious film about the Beatles' manager, Christopher Münch's *The Hours and Times* (1991) offers a fictive imagining of an intimate encounter between Lennon and the Beatles' manager during a 1963 Spanish vacation.

CHAPTER 5

"Love, Love, Love": Tracing the Contours of the Beatles' Inner Circle

Kenneth L. Campbell

In his 2008 best-selling book, *Outliers: The Story of Success*, Malcom Gladwell, using the Beatles as a case study, introduced his readers to the "10,000 hour rule," explaining the Beatles' musical success as a product of the long hours the group had to play during their apprenticeship in Hamburg in the early 1960s.[1] Unnoticed by Gladwell, Hamburg played a decidedly important role in the Beatles' story for another reason: they met Astrid Kirchherr, who became a member of the Beatles' inner circle in 1960. When she asked them if she could take their photographs, she had no idea that the pictures of them in iconic poses around Hamburg would become an important part of the visual record of the most famous rock band in history. Astrid contributed to the Beatles' sense of style and fashion, most famously their famous mop-top hairstyle, but Pauline Sutcliffe – whose brother Stuart played bass for the Beatles at the time and married Astrid before his early death – thought Astrid had influenced the Beatles' music as well.[2] Astrid was a revelation for the Beatles; at the age of 22, she possessed both an air of mystery and an aura of sophistication that made her as much a muse as a friend.

Throughout the Beatles' existence as a group, they owed a deep debt to a few select individuals. The Beatles themselves frequently acknowledged this, nowhere more clearly than in the opening verse of John Lennon's "In My Life":

> There are places I remember
> All my life though some have changed
> Some forever not for better
> Some have gone and some remain

---

[1] Malcolm Gladwell, *Outliers: The Story of Success* (New York: Little, Brown, 2008).
[2] Tim Riley, *Lennon: The Man, the Myth, the Music – the Definitive Life* (New York: Hyperion, 2011), 113.

> All these places have their moments
> With lovers and friends I still can recall
> Some are dead and some are living
> In my life I've loved them all.

This represents an incredibly mature perspective from the 25-year-old Lennon, one painfully acquired through the loss of his mother, Julia, his uncle and surrogate father, George Smith, and his close friend, Stuart Sutcliffe. Lennon's childhood friend Pete Shotton claimed John had told him the sixth line in the stanza referred specifically to him and Stu Sutcliffe.[3] However, the genius of the song resided in Lennon's ability to translate memories of specific people to a reflection on life in general and the important roles that others play in the lives of each of us. In John's case, the lyrics could have easily reflected an appreciation for any members of the Beatles' inner circle or the other members of the Beatles themselves.

The members of the Beatles' inner circle fall roughly into three categories, each of which I will briefly consider here in turn. Astrid Kirchherr pointed out that she could not have hoped for personal gain out of the Beatles' fame, since they were not famous when she met them.[4] Shotton, Freda Kelly, Neil Aspinall, and Mal Evans could have all made the same claim. The Beatles had forged their friendships with each of these individuals *before* the band became famous. The second group consisted primarily of Brian Epstein, Peter Brown, Derek Taylor, Alistair Taylor, and George Martin, each of whom played different but vital roles in their rise to stardom. They helped the group make the transition from a talented and energetic but raw performance group to pop and rock superstars. Describing his first encounter watching the Beatles alongside Epstein, Alistair Taylor said, "'They could barely play and they were deafening and so unprofessional – laughing with girls, smoking onstage, and sipping from Cokes during their act."[5] Third, the Beatles' girlfriends and wives – Cynthia Powell (Lennon), Dot Rhone, Jane Asher, Pattie Boyd (Harrison), Maureen Cox (Starkey), Linda Eastman, and Yoko Ono – played important roles in both the band's success and whatever degree of personal happiness and satisfaction they managed to achieve in the maelstrom of worldwide fame, controversy, and dizzying public obsession in the 1960s. Significantly, four of the most popular, desired, and famous young men in

---

[3] Pete Shotton and Nicholas Schaffner, *John Lennon: In My Life* (New York: Stein and Day, 1983), 67.
[4] Astrid Kirchherr and Max Scheler, *Yesterday: The Beatles Once Upon a Time* (New York: Vendome Press, 2007), 6.
[5] Bob Spitz, *The Beatles: The Biography* (Boston: Little, Brown, 2005), 266.

the world chose some form of a committed relationship for most of the time they were together as a group.

Freda Kelly, as president of the Beatles' fan club in Liverpool, made such a positive impression on the Beatles' manager, Brian Epstein, that he hired her to serve as his and the group's secretary. Her relationship with the Beatles soon became as much personal as it was professional. As she related in the 2013 documentary *Good Ol' Freda*, she worked for the Beatles not because she desired close proximity to fame, but because she was primarily a fan who liked and believed in the group well before their reputation spread outside of Liverpool. She gained their trust because she took both her job and her personal relationship with each of them very seriously, careful then and later never to divulge anything too personal about them.

Mal Evans and Neil Aspinall became the Beatles' roadies in the early days of the group's tours throughout Britain, but by all accounts, they were much more to the Beatles than that. The band met Mal, an electrician who worked for the post office, during his job moonlighting as a bouncer at the Cavern Club, where the band regularly performed. According to Cynthia,[6] John became particularly close to Mal, though all four of them developed a great fondness for the man they often referred to as the "gentle giant." Neil was a friend whom Paul and George had met at school, but went on to develop a close relationship with the others as well. Neil and Mal performed all manner of tasks for the Beatles that went well beyond the routine assignments normally performed by roadies. For example, in the pre-Internet age, Neil and Mal scoured libraries for the photographs used on the iconic album cover for *Sergeant Pepper's Lonely Hearts Club Band*.

Pete Shotton was John's childhood friend and a member of his original band, the Quarry Men. John had practically forced Pete to join that band, but he placed such a value on Pete's friendship that they remained close even after Pete informed John that he did not possess the requisite musical talent to remain in the band. In fact, Pete may have been responsible for the fact that the Beatles existed at all; when asked by John if they should invite Paul to join their band, Pete gave his approval, replying, "I think he's okay. I like him."[7] Temporarily displaced by Stuart and Cynthia in the early 1960s, Pete remained close enough to the Beatles that they asked him to oversee the Apple boutique they had opened in London in the mid-1960s.

When Brian Epstein, a polished and refined manager of a retail record division in a Liverpool department store, walked into the Cavern Club on

---

[6] Cynthia Lennon, *John* (New York: Crown Publishers, 2005), 6.
[7] David Pritchard and Alan Lysaght, *The Beatles: An Oral History* (New York: Hyperion, 1998) 13.

a Thursday afternoon in early November 1961, it marked a crossroads both for his life and for that of the group he had come to see. John developed a deeper relationship with Brian than any of the other Beatles, perhaps rooted in an underlying sadness they both felt as social outcasts, despite Brian's polished and John's tough façade. Peter Brown, who probably knew Brian better than anyone and dealt extensively with John, thought their "close bond . . . was largely as a result of them sharing and seeing in each other complicated personalities which were often unhappy and frequently frustrated."[8] John went so far as to accompany Brian alone on a Spanish holiday in April 1963, later telling Barry Miles that it was "not quite" a love affair.[9] However, Brian got along famously with the rest of the Beatles as well, who were all impressed with his upper-class manners and sophistication and put their utter faith in his ability to shepherd them to fame and fortune.

When the Beatles decided to stop touring in 1966, Brian suddenly became slightly less important since tour bookings had represented a large part of his portfolio in managing the group. Brian's long downward spiral into depression and drug addiction is well known, becoming worse once he no longer felt as needed by the Beatles, who had given meaning to his life. On 27 August 1967, Alistair Taylor and Dr. John Galway broke down the door of Brian's bedroom door to find him unresponsive, dead of either an accidental or deliberate drug overdose. Brian's death absolutely devastated the Beatles.

The only person possibly more distraught over Brian's death was Peter Brown. Peter Brown, Brian's closest friend was, along with Neil Aspinall and Derek Taylor, among the few who survived the firings of Apple personnel when Allen Klein took over as Beatles' manager in 1969. Chris O'Dell, an American who worked at Apple, wrote in her memoir that Peter Brown was "one of the only people at Apple with direct and immediate access to the Beatles and their wives or girlfriends, and the only person at Apple who knew exactly what they were doing at any particular moment of the day or night."[10] In addition to serving as Brian's social secretary, Peter Brown became a close confidante of the Beatles. John and Yoko actually moved in with him early in their relationship and he receives mention in "The Ballad of John and Yoko" for the assistance he provided John in locating Gibraltar as a spot where the couple could legally marry.

[8] Yoko Ono, ed., *Memories of John Lennon* (New York: Harper Collins, 2005), 13.
[9] Barry Miles, ed., *John Lennon in His Own Words* (New York: Quick Fox, 1981), 43.
[10] Chris O'Dell with Katherine Ketcham, *Miss O'Dell: My Hard Days and Long Nights with the Beatles, the Stones, Bob Dylan, Eric Clapton, and the Women they Loved* (New York: Touchstone, 2009), 22.

Alistair Taylor had accompanied Brian Epstein on his first epiphany-inducing visit to the Cavern Club. Although Klein fired Taylor as general manager of Apple when he took over as the Beatles' manager in 1969, Alistair had played a transformative role as a member of the Beatles' inner circle for a decade. He had been particularly close to Paul, but Peter Brown told Bob Spitz that "whenever any of the boys needed something done, Alistair always saw to it."[11] Derek Taylor, on the other hand, first met the Beatles in 1963, leaving a "comfortable career as a newspaperman" to become the Beatles' press manager and personal assistant to Brian Epstein.[12] He did so because, like Epstein and George Martin, he both liked them and saw the potential in them at a time when they had not yet made it big. He never regretted the move and quickly became another indispensable member of the group's inner circle, as evidenced by his survival of Klein's purge of Apple personnel.

The Beatles were still not the polished act they later became when they auditioned for George Martin, who also saw something special in them. After the release of "Love Me Do," he later wrote, "I was by now absolutely convinced that I had a hit group on my hands, though I knew that I hadn't got it with the first record, feeling the quality of the song wasn't really up to it."[13] Martin became perhaps the most important member of the Beatles' inner circle because of his professional guidance and contributions to the actual music for which they became so famous. Paul's recollection of the band's relationship with George Martin focused on his transition from an omnipotent producer whose decisions they dare not question to a co-producer who worked alongside the Beatles in the control room.[14] Kenneth Womack notes that *Revolver* represented as much the creative efforts of George Martin and Geoff Emerick, who began working with them as audio engineer on that record, as those of the Beatles themselves.[15]

The longest romantic relationship of any of the individual Beatles during their career as a group occurred between John and Cynthia. They started dating in the autumn of 1958, just months after John's mother had been killed after being struck by a car driven by an off-duty constable. Cynthia provided an important sense of stability for John, all the more so because of her willingness to endure years of verbal and emotional abuse

[11] Spitz, *The Beatles: The Biography*, 827.
[12] Derek Taylor, *It was Twenty Year Ago Today* (New York: Simon & Schuster, 1987), 14.
[13] George Martin with Jeremy Hornsby, *All You Need is Ears* (New York: St. Martin's Press, 1979), 127.
[14] The Beatles, *The Beatles Anthology* (San Francisco: Chronicle Books, 2000), 206.
[15] Kenneth Womack, *Long and Winding Roads: The Evolving Artistry of the Beatles* (New York: Bloomsbury, 2007), 131.

and neglect, and at least one instance of physical violence. Cynthia possessed the two qualities required by John in a long-term relationship – complete devotion and unconditional love. As their marriage gradually disintegrated in the 1960s, John still proved himself capable of showing great affection and love for Cynthia and his son Julian, sentiments he strongly expressed in one letter written while on tour in Los Angeles in August 1965.[16] Home life still exercised a strong pull on John at that time and could have been one factor in his desire to stop touring altogether the following year.

The role Cynthia played for John, Dot Rhone played for Paul during the band's early years. A steady presence in his life after Paul lost his mother to cancer, Dot placidly agreed to fade into the background when the group performed to preserve the illusion of his availability for the group's burgeoning number of female fans. When Paul became involved with Jane Asher, she and her cultured family introduced the young Beatle to the world of sophisticated London, facilitating his growing self-confidence and *savoir faire*. Unlike Dot, Jane provided access to the glamorous London club scene and an elite show business circle, as well as a congenial family home that gave Paul a place to retreat from the world with people he liked and respected. Furthermore, not only did his relationship with Jane provide the inspiration for such songs as "I'm Looking through You" and "We Can Work It Out," but Jane also introduced him to classical music. Without this influence, Paul would not have gotten the idea for the string arrangement on "Eleanor Rigby" or the trumpet solo on "Penny Lane," two songs which as much as any define the distinctive sound of the Beatles as a group in the mid-1960s.[17]

George and Ringo both married at the height of their fame, George to Pattie Boyd, a beautiful young actress whom he met during the filming of *A Hard Day's Night*, and Ringo to a Liverpool girl Maureen Cox. Following their January 1966 wedding, Pattie accompanied George first to Barbados for a honeymoon, then to India in September. There George took sitar lessons from the famous Indian musician Ravi Shankar, who shaped George's musical sensibilities and whose influence would manifest itself on a number of Harrison compositions recorded by the Beatles, such as "Love You To" and "Within You Without You." Pattie introduced George to transcendental meditation, which in turn led him and the

---

[16] Hunter Davies, ed., *The John Lennon Letters* (London: Weidenfeld & Nicolson, 2012), 89.
[17] Dominic Sandbrook, *White Heat: A History of Britain in the Swinging Sixties* (London: Little, Brown, 2006), 215.

Beatles to take an interest in the teachings of Maharishi Mahesh Yogi and a subsequent trip to India by all four Beatles and their partners in 1968. They undertook the trip for personal reasons, but it turned out to inspire an amazing outburst of musical creativity, including the writing of most of the songs that would appear on *The White Album*, recorded later that year. Maureen, only eighteen at the time of her marriage to Ringo, felt less secure and comfortable in the limelight than Pattie, but she provided Ringo with a son, Zak, and a happy home life at a critical time in his career.

Yoko Ono may have been somewhat disingenuous when she first met John in telling him she had never heard of him or the Beatles. However, what mattered to John was that he thought Yoko did not know his identity, piquing his interest more than the average avid Beatles fan who would have viewed John only through the lens of his fame and stardom. Yoko was an artist in her own right, gaining her enough respect in John's eyes that her attempts to solicit his help with her career before they became romantically involved did not offend him. Although John was still married to Cynthia when he met Yoko and it took some time for their relationship to develop, once they had consummated it the pair became inseparable. Six years older than John, Yoko may have represented a close approximation to the mother figure he had missed since Julia's death; "mother," in fact, later became one of his nicknames for her.

Yoko loomed larger within the Beatles' inner circle than any other woman did, but she also became the cause of the greatest amount of friction among them. She made the Beatles suddenly of less importance to John, who no longer cared as much about hanging out with the boys. Yet her emergence as the dominant influence in John's life had less impact on the break-up of the band than people often assume. George Harrison was least comfortable with Yoko's presence because, having already tired of playing third fiddle to Paul and John, he was not about to allow Yoko to eclipse his influence in the studio as well. Paul, however, came around relatively quickly, wishing his friend nothing but happiness in his new relationship. Significantly, Paul was the only Beatle besides John to perform on the recording of the "Ballad of John and Yoko."

Paul's relationship with Linda Eastman, like that of John and Yoko, took over a year to get off the ground after their first meeting, despite Linda's oft-related prophecy that she would marry a Beatle. In fact, Linda seemed much less determined to pursue Paul than Yoko had John, who, according to Cynthia, Yoko bombarded with constant phone calls, in addition to writing to John during the couple's stay at the Maharishi's retreat in India. Paul, attracted to Linda's vibrant yet easygoing personality and blend of brash self-confidence and 1960s mellowness, found in her the rare woman with whom he could relate as an equal. Jane possessed some of these same qualities and as an actress was not lacking in self-esteem, but, unlike Linda, a professional photographer concentrating on the rock scene, Jane had been unwilling to set aside her own career or subordinate it to that of her famous boyfriend.

The public's obsession with the Beatles insured that for much of their time together they would live what Cynthia Lennon called a "cocoon-like existence that was wonderfully entertaining but very restricting."[18] In *Many Years from Now*, Paul reminisced fondly to Barry Miles about a vacation he took with Jane, Ringo, and Maureen to Greece, where nobody knew who they were.[19] Pattie Boyd wrote that the Beatles "had few real friends apart from each other."[20] John once tellingly said, "We have met some new people since we've become famous, but we've never been able to stand them for more than two days."[21] As a result, those in the Beatles' inner circle had a pronounced significance for both their lives and their art. Fame is always a blessing and a curse, no less so for the Beatles. Their inner circle – those who loved them, helped them, and worked with and for them, not because they were famous but because they genuinely liked them – provided an additional blessing and did much to help mitigate the curse of fame.

[18] Cynthia Lennon, *A Twist of Lennon* (New York: Avon Books, 1978), 107.
[19] Barry Miles, *Paul McCartney: Many Years from Now* (New York: Henry Holt), 120.
[20] Pattie Boyd and Penny Junor, *Wonderful Tonight: George Harrison, Eric Clapton, and Me* (New York: Three Rivers Press, 2007), 89.
[21] Beatles, *Beatles Anthology*, 109.

PART II

The Beatles in Performance

CHAPTER 6

The Love There That's Sleeping: Guitars of the Early Beatles

Walter Everett

There would be many ways to establish the Beatles' musical accomplishments, as varied as they are numerous throughout multiple domains. One could single out their formal innovations; rhythmic and metric design; melodic, harmonic, and contrapuntal arrangements of pitch; electronic enhancements; or their vocal delivery of poetry. For this chapter, however, I would like to examine their instrumental work, and look past their accomplishments on piano and other keyboards, drums and other percussion, harmonicas and other "sweeteners" – whether employed by themselves or by session players – to focus on their primary vehicles for instrumental performance: their guitars. To do so, we will look at both the tonal qualities of the instruments they utilized and the performance techniques they employed to get their desired sounds in particular songs. In order to achieve some comprehensive level of detail in our limited space, we will restrict our examination to the Beatles' foundational early work through 1964, produced at a time when they learned their playing skills from a very wide variety of styles, but we will also note a few parallels to later work, as well as to other artists, when appropriate. Although the Beatles are more often celebrated for the incredible variety they would create in their later releases, the early recordings – dominated by guitar playing – repay close listening as to how, *even then*, a diverse array of sounds was always under exploration. Although evident upon scratching the surface, the results of this instinct are almost hidden, sleeping amidst a seeming uniformity of texture generally growing out of a seamless stage presentation.

As teenagers, John, Paul, and George each began with acoustic guitars of varying quality (at times amplified by makeshift pickups), but with "Raunchy," George was able to get impressive enough pre-bends from his Höfner President to pass his Quarry Men audition. The group's front line moved to inexpensive electric models (made by continental firms

Höfner, Rosetti, and Futurama) as they began semi-professional gigging in 1959–60. These instruments, plus Stu Sutcliffe's Höfner bass, all variously heard in the clumsy April 1960 home recordings, were necessarily amplified (through weak equipment, some permanently "borrowed" from rightful owners), in order both to be heard over noisy crowds at the Casbah and other clubs and to sound more like the reverb-laden playing of their first inspirations: Scotty Moore, Chuck Berry, Carl Perkins, Buddy Holly, and Hank Marvin. Electric guitars were a fairly unusual sight in England through the early 1960s: the Shadows and Johnny Kidd & the Pirates were the only Brits to make names playing them before the Beatles appeared, along with the contemporaneous Rolling Stones and then the Animals, the Who, the Kinks and others soon following close behind.

Just as their first Hamburg residency in the fall of 1960 brought the Beatles' musicianship into new repertoires (huge in both depth and breadth), higher entertainment value, and greater stamina, it also provided the need for better gear. That November, John purchased the Rickenbacker 325 with which his rhythm playing eventually made the Beatles famous. George very likely borrowed this instrument, and featured its wobbly vibrato arm, as he "sang" the slightly distorted lead part in "Cry for a Shadow." (The vibrato had been modeled in several Shadows forebears; watch, for instance, Hank Marvin whammy his way through the bridge in the mimed "Apache" video, beginning at 0:54.) For his part, John seems to have preferred short-arm electrics, principally this ¾-scale Rickenbacker and the Epiphone Casino acquired in late 1964 (whose neck is ¾" shorter than normal length). These lengths bring frets closer together, making it easier for John to boogie with alternating hammer-ons, and to reach the more demanding left-hand barre chord positions that he would later seek out in, say, his wide-ranging Casino part for "Because." On his Rick 325, John plays a boogie with power chords in the introduction and retransition of "I Want to Hold Your Hand" with a high degree of compression, providing an organ-like attack with a steady-state minimal decay. This guitar is also heavily compressed for both George's solo for "I Wanna Be Your Man" and John's part throughout "Don't Bother Me," both songs recorded with the same mixing-board input on the same day in September 1963. (George would overdub the solo for the latter song, but all other featured guitar lines are John's.) In "Don't Bother Me," the compressor limits the depth of the wide amplifier tremolo John elects when he foot-taps his Vibrolux pedal "on" for the song's shimmering refrains (0:17–0:21) and "off" for his intricate but thick-sounding rhythm part for verses. (John's performing yeoman service on George's composition – so the latter can concentrate on his singing – reverberates much later in Paul's endeavors to steal George's spotlight with sterling bass parts underneath "While My Guitar Gently Weeps," "Old Brown Shoe," and "Something.")

At the time of their first two Hamburg visits, Paul moved from third guitar to piano to a jerry-built bass, created by stringing his Rosetti guitar with pilfered low-range piano strings. In April 1961 when it became clear upon Stu's quitting the group that Paul was to permanently take over this role, beginning with the group's first professional studio recordings just a few weeks hence, he bought the Höfner "violin" bass, a model he has continued to play throughout his career. When its strings were amplified from the mellow neck pickup as opposed to the slightly brighter second pickup, the set-up for which Paul typically opted, this instrument provided a deep, rich tone. As is well known, Paul's bass playing was to mature dramatically following his August 1965 acquisition of the Rickenbacker 4001S; on *Rubber Soul*, McCartney would demonstrate all manner of sensitive melodic playing that often added a predominantly contrapuntal aspect to what had previously been a mostly primitive bedrock of harmony and rhythm. But Paul's early playing is notable in several ways.

In these years, Paul chiefly alternated between roots and fifths of chords (which technique provides the sonic foundation for "She Loves You" and "I Want to Hold Your Hand"), but he also began "walking" his bass right from the start, as with the short connecting scalar lines in "My Bonnie" and "The Saints" that would also be heard in the contrasting bridges of "Please Please Me," "A Taste of Honey," "Do You Want to Know a Secret," and "Anna (Go to Him)," and would later stretch to scales of sometimes more than an octave in the verses of "All My Loving," "Tell Me Why," and in the stop-time bass breaks of "I'll Cry Instead." Paul contributed a jazzy shuffle rhythm to a combination of triad arpeggiations and walking parts in the "Chains" bridge.

As busy as Paul's lines could sometimes be, roots typically fell on downbeats along with chord changes, keeping both harmony and meter clear at all times. The decorated triads of the "Honey Don't" chorus, derived from boogie-woogie (scale degrees 1–3–5–6–8–6–5–3–1, adding the upper neighbor to 5 in an otherwise purely triadic arpeggiation of roots, thirds, and fifths), prefigure the outstanding ostinato figure of "Day Tripper" (1–$\sharp$2–3–5–8, etc.), the guitar/bass doubling of which was also predicted in the covers "I Got a Woman," "Slow Down," and "Boys," and in "Hold Me Tight." To be recaptured in "Birthday," this bass/guitar doubling would become a hard-rock staple in bands like Cream ("Sunshine of Your Love") and Led Zeppelin ("Heartbreaker," "Black Dog"). For an unusual color, Paul would occasionally enlist double-stops, plucking two strings simultaneously. The unusual muddiness of this procedure mires the verses of "All I've Got to Do" in a brooding funk relieved in the single-line verse endings where connections are made through phone calls and whispering. This song was taped a day before "Don't Bother Me," wherein Paul recoups the morose and stubborn double-stops in the second refrain (0:34–0:38). A month later, in "I Want to Hold Your Hand," Paul gives the first seven bars of the bridge an introspective cast with double-stops, bursting loose with an aroused thrumming on a repeated fifth scale degree for passionate retransitions. Paul's simple duet with Ringo toward the end of "What You're Doing" sets the stage for a more complex one that will prepare the psychedelic coda of "Rain."

By August 1961, George would have his first American-made guitar, a Gretsch – a line most closely associated with rockabilly players like Duane Eddy and Eddie Cochran, and country and western artists such as Chet Atkins. The smooth-fingering Gretsch Duo Jet was a much easier instrument to play well than the unresponsive Futurama, so George was able to improve his technique mightily in 1961–63. Note, for instance, his frequent usage of parallel thirds (as in "Memphis" and "Bésame Mucho" in the January 1962 Decca audition) and sixths (as in his invented solo for "Falling in Love Again"). In the Decca audition, George recreates Carl Perkins's sentimental strummed tremolo on his Duo Jet for the intro and solo of "Sure to Fall." This instrument had strongly contrasting mid-range and treble pickups, allowing George to switch from the darker neck pickup, when accompanying vocals, to the brighter bridge pickup for solos, as seen and heard in the August 1962 "Some Other Guy" footage. In the March 1963 version of the double-stops in his "One After 909" solo, George manipulates the Duo Jet's Bigsby vibrato bar to emulate a train whistle, similarly to the way Chuck Berry got his blaring car-horn effect in "Maybelline." (At the same time, John chugs away with boogie hammer-ons via his Gibson acoustic-electric, like a slowed-down performance of Berry's rhythm part to "Sweet Little Sixteen." George had boogied with hammer-ons a month previously on his own Gibson in "Misery.")

Both John and George acquired these matching Gibson acoustic-electrics when the Beatles needed new guitars for their fall 1962 EMI sessions. John favored this guitar throughout his career with the group; it is the hollow body of his Gibson that amplifies the vibration from Paul's single bass note to feed back at the start of "I Feel Fine," and the instrument on which John strums through "A Day in the Life." One technique that George loved to employ on his Gibson was to play his lead lines in octave double-stops, a jazz sonority rarely heard in rock playing before Jimi Hendrix's recordings began to appear four years later. Nevertheless, George introduced such octaves on the Gibson in his "Please Please Me" tattoos, always doubled by John's harmonica, and again in solo parts for "There's a Place," "From Me to You," and "I'll Be On My Way." George's Gibson makes several stage appearances for "This Boy," which always concludes as it does on disc, with George's repeated octave and sixth double-stops. (Electric Gibsons such as Berry's 335 and Hubert Sumlin's Les Paul were quite popular among other professionals but not associated with the Beatles before Eric Clapton was to give George his first Les Paul in August 1968.)

George replaced his Duo Jet in May 1963 with the Atkins-designed Gretsch Country Gentleman that – when played through the treble-boost circuit on the Beatles' Vox amps – would allow for ever-brighter timbres, a goal that George would continue to pursue through the twelve-string Rickenbacker acquired in February 1964, and would culminate in the complex upper-frequency sounds of the sitars he began playing in 1965. On the Country Gent, George took advantage of an upper-bout pickup switch that, in "She Loves You," for example, allowed him to feature his original chord-chiming technique through the very bright bridge pickup (0:26–0:31), but to elicit darker neck-pickup tones for his hand-sliding Chuck Berry-like riffs (0:11–0:13) and the low-register Duane Eddy-like motive repeated in the song's coda (1:52–1:54). (The Ed Sullivan videos are the best way to see how George manipulates the switch to achieve these tonal contrasts.) Although George used a single-pickup Rickenbacker 425 to record his lead part in "I Want to Hold Your Hand," he is filmed using his Country Gent to perform this song on stage at the Liverpool Empire on December 7, 1963, frequently switching between bright and mid-range pickups. Part of the reason for these changes is to simulate the chromatic bass overdub George recorded on "Hand," above the bent-note figure heard at 0:11 on the single, but never played live. In the hands of Pete Townshend and then Hendrix, the pickup switch would transform the colors of individual sustained pitches, a technique that George would later appropriate in turn to vary the feedback in the intro to "It's All Too Much" (at 0:09). George gave the Bigsby vibrato on his Country Gent a frequent workout, but most brazenly in solos for covers such as "Lucille," "Matchbox," "Leave My Kitten Alone," and "Bad Boy." "I Want to Hold Your Hand" is the only track on which George plays the Rickenbacker 425; this use is perhaps most notable for the unfamiliarly sweeping portamento slides that prepare the G-major chords at refrain endings.

With his Country Gent solo for the Beatles' June 1964 cover of "Slow Down," George opens school for would-be rockabilly soloists. Here, in a brief original piece that substitutes for the sax passage in Larry Williams's model recording, George displays an imaginative series of provocative guitar techniques, introducing hammer-ons at 1:41, legato slides at 1:43 (used in approaching dyadic thirds throughout the song and previously championed in "Hippy Hippy Shake"), half-step bends with releases at 1:55, a combination of all these at 1:57, then sliding into dyads at 2:00, crunchy half-step double-stops at 2:02, fingered and picked double stops on non-adjacent strings at 2:08, and a pull-off at 2:14.

George's third and final Gretsch model was the twangy Tennessean, with which he brings a down-home style to his playing in the solos for "I'm a Loser" and "I Don't Want to Spoil the Party" on *Beatles for Sale*. Note also in the "She's a Woman" solo how George plays slurpy bent notes both before and after an extended passage of sliding sixths, framing a rockabilly sound that contrasts sharply against John's quickly muted backbeat-stab-bing chords reminiscent of Steve Cropper's work with Stax in Memphis, combining for lots of varied Tennessee-based sounds in quick juxtaposi-tion. The Gretsch Tennessean was capable of a brilliant sound, partly because its treble pickup hugged the bridge more closely than it does on the Country Gent (which has two felt mutes in between its bridge and pickup), and thus features a higher ratio of upper partials. This quality may have reminded George of Holly's bright Stratocaster, for George resurrects "Words of Love," with its glittering arpeggiations and distinctive double-stopped solo, for the fall 1964 album. The glitter of the Tennessean will take on an original dissonant quality in a chromatic run of overdubbed arpeggiations that introduces each verse of "Help!" with an unusually stinging piquancy.

The electric twelve-string Rickenbacker 360 that George made famous in *A Hard Day's Night* was quickly adopted by Pete Townshend of the Who in London and Jim McGuinn of the Byrds in Los Angeles. Its six pairs of strings, four of them tuned in the octaves that George had worked assiduously to achieve on the Gibson, permitted glistening solo parts (as in the lead ostinatos of "What You're Doing" and "Ticket to Ride") and brightly chiming chords (as in the first turnaround in "If I Fell"). The "chiming" by which George had accented chord changes on downbeats with his Gibson in "P. S. I Love You" verses and the "Please Please Me" bridge (and on the Gretsch for the bridge of "Hold Me Tight"), and in broken chords in the verses of "A Taste of Honey" and the bridges of "Thank You Girl" (and then on his six-string Rickenbacker in the bridge of "I Want to Hold Your Hand") would significantly gain in coloristic impact when applied with the twelve-string, as in the harpsichord-worthy changes supporting John's aria-like bridge in "I Should Have Known Better."

This last example is not the early Beatles' closest borrowing of a classical sonority, which was instead furnished by George's nylon-string classical Ramírez guitar. Long before George Martin would add the string quartet to "Yesterday" and Paul McCartney would bring his avant-garde tape loops to "Tomorrow Never Knows," George Harrison adopted the classical guitar as played by his progenitor, Andrés Segovia. The Latin flavor thus conferred upon the Beatles' jazz-invoking cover of "Till There Was You" and original ballad, "And I Love Her," was accompanied in each case by Ringo's understated bongos. George's sensitive solo in the latter song is a vehicle for his elegant wrist vibrato (a classical and jazz technique always applied to sustained notes in Paul's bass playing), as seen in *A Hard Day's Night*.

Although Bob Dylan was not generally known for playing an acoustic twelve-string (but see the Traveling Wilburys' "Handle With Care"!), this was a common instrument among early folk (Pete Seeger) and blues (Lead Belly) players, and so John Lennon's Dylan pastiches featured his new Framus twelve-string in the *Beatles for Sale–Help!* era. John milked this folk guitar in the ametrically strummed intro to "I'm a Loser," and showcased it more famously in "You've Got to Hide Your Love Away" as well as the title song for the group's second film. The *Help!* album featured another new acoustic, the large Epiphone Texan with which Paul played "Yesterday." The song's foreboding quality comes from the long-repeated thirdless opening chords and a very unusual whole-step detuning that removes the strings' focus. As with one of his Höfner basses, this particular Epiphone continues to see near-daily work in Paul's new-millennium stage shows. Although acoustic guitars were played in many different styles through 1964, they were reserved mostly for folk strumming in 1965 and then given a new function with fingerpicking in 1968–69.

Two other important electric-guitar models were acquired at the end of 1964: Paul's hot hollow-body Epiphone Casino (a guitar also added to George's and John's arsenals), and (finally!) John's and George's matching Fender Stratocasters. But because the Beatles did not record with these before 1965, we will reluctantly hold off on further comment on them here. The Beatles would introduce many new guitar-playing ideas (as well as many new instruments) in their middle years and beyond: the ethereal volume-tone pedal in *Help!* tracks; the bottleneck slide, capos, and Maestro fuzz box in *Rubber Soul*; backwards guitar parts in *Revolver* and the Leslie cabinet in *Sgt. Pepper*, but these colorful innovations were to some degree icing on a cake fully baked in the unpretentious era of Beatlemania.

CHAPTER 7

The Beatles in Performance: From Dance Hall Days to Stadium Tours

Chuck Gunderson

Liverpool, England: one afternoon in November 1961, a well-dressed man arrived at the entrance of a wildly popular club. He carefully descended the narrow, precipitous steps to a dark, dank, smoke-filled cellar reeking of boiled hot dogs, rotting fruit, and cleaning fluid. Pushing his way across a crowded floor filled with the younger set on a lunch break, the man observed the band playing on a tiny illuminated stage.

Everyone at the Cavern Club[1] that afternoon was there for one thing: gritty, sweat-infused rock 'n' roll. The four young men delivering it were what had attracted that well-dressed man, Brian Epstein. He wanted to see for himself what was causing such a shaking underneath the city's Mathew Street. The raucous sounds he was hearing came from a group called the Beatles.

Epstein was no stranger to popular music, as he was running the most successful record shop in northern England, NEMS,[2] and was a regular contributor to Bill Harry's *Mersey Beat*,[3] a newspaper devoted to the local music scene. Epstein had heard of the Beatles from its pages and from posters around town that advertised the group. He wanted to see them up close to determine for himself what all the fuss was about.

Although he had never before managed any of the local "Beat groups,"[4] he immediately saw something on this November afternoon that captivated him. He later remarked, "I was immediately struck by their music,

---

[1] Located at 10 Mathew Street in Liverpool, England, the Cavern Club originally opened as a jazz venue on January 16, 1957. The Beatles made close to 300 appearances there over a two-and-a-half year period. From Mark Lewisohn, *The Complete Beatles Chronicle* (London: Hamlyn 2003), 118.

[2] NEMS was the acronym for North End Music Stores, owned by Brian Epstein's parents, Harry and Queenie Epstein. Young Brian was tasked with running the record department, among other responsibilities.

[3] Bill Harry was one of John Lennon's classmates at the Liverpool College of Art. He founded *Mersey Beat* in July 1961.

[4] Beat music was a fusion of rock 'n' roll, R&B, doo-wop, and skiffle.

their beat and their sense of humour on stage – and, even afterwards, when I met them, I was struck again by their personal charm. And it was there that, really, it all started."[5]

Epstein soon began discussions with the group about becoming their manager, and he signed them to a contract on January 24, 1962. Included in the soon-to-be legendary lineup at that time were John Lennon, Paul McCartney, and George Harrison, along with drummer Pete Best, who would be replaced by Ringo Starr in August 1962.

Thanks to Epstein's tutelage, to the group's sheer determination, and mostly to hard work by all, the Beatles would experience a level of success that most observers of the day would find difficult to believe.[6] The idea that a musical act from northern England could become more popular than Elvis Presley and his contemporaries seemed preposterous to most at the time, but Epstein thought differently: "I knew they would be bigger than Elvis. I knew they would be the biggest in the world."[7]

The Beatles' rise to fame began in 1963, after several years of relative obscurity playing the dance-hall circuit in their native Britain and the seedy clubs in the Reeperbahn of Hamburg, Germany. Beatlemania, as it was called, would explode onto the world stage and rapidly change not only the concert industry but also how popular music was bought, sold, and listened to. The group would have a huge influence on popular culture as well.

What the Beatles and Epstein accomplished in a few short years trig-gered a metamorphosis of the music and concert industry. Its business model was then so primitive that Elvis, its biggest star in the 1950s, still performed some concerts in high school gymnasiums. That said, Elvis's influence, and that of other rock 'n' roll pioneers, on the musicians of the day was immense – especially on the Beatles, who tried endlessly to lay down their own unique sound, different from those who inspired them.

Record companies, which lived and died on the sales of their little black lacquered discs by the "next big thing," also saw a major change in the 1960s, as their profits soared into the stratosphere – largely due to the Beatles' chart-topping hits and the many musical acts they inspired.[8] Beginning in 1964, particularly in the US market, the Beatles launched a

[5] *The Mersey Sound* (BBC TV documentary), 1963.
[6] The Beatles' impact has been immense. Their US record sales alone top 1.6 billion singles and over 175 million albums and they continue to hold the record for the most No. 1 hits. In addition, the group has had an enormous influence on the arts, fashion, and even politics.
[7] Mark Lewisohn, *Tune In: The Beatles – All These Years, Extended Special Edition* (London: Little, Brown, 2013), 991.
[8] The Beatles held the first five places on the April 4, 1964 *Billboard* Hot 100, a feat that has never been replicated.

musical revolution that other artists quickly embraced, to the delight of record company executives.

Indeed, during the 1960s John, Paul, George, and Ringo, along with manager Epstein, perhaps singlehandedly laid the blueprint for all who would follow in music, popular culture, fashion, and revolutionary thinking – one that remains intact today.

The rise of fandom during the Beatles' touring years was also significant, and it would have a lasting impact on the music industry. Thanks to the baby boom after World War II, masses of young people came of age in the early 1960s – perfectly positioned to usher in this phenomenon. Frank Sinatra had captured the hearts of teens and adults in the 1940s and 1950s, and Elvis's concerts took fan adulation a major step further. When the Beatles toured America in 1964, though, hardly a concert or appearance went by without uncontrollable mayhem.

* * *

Rock 'n' roll began in the mid-1950s with names like Chuck Berry, Little Richard, Elvis Presley, Gene Vincent, Buddy Holly, Jerry Lee Lewis, and Fats Domino. They made easy teenage converts with the music's simple tribal beat, words, and rhythm. From Elvis's gyrating hips to Little Richard's howling voice and Chuck Berry's duck walk, the music and its performance style effortlessly captivated its younger audience, who were yearning for something different from what their parents listened to. From the earnest wail of Gene Vincent's "Be-Bop-a-Lula" or the stomping intro to Little Richard's "Tutti Frutti" ("Wop bop a loo bop a lop bam boom!"), rock 'n' roll was much more enticing and rebellious than the slow, haunting, and very mature sound of Frank Sinatra's "All the Way."[9]

As the 1950s rolled into the 1960s, however, many of the musicians who had given birth to rock 'n' roll seemed to fade away. Buddy Holly perished in a plane crash; Little Richard turned to God; Chuck Berry got in trouble with the law; Jerry Lee Lewis married his 13-year-old first cousin; and 'The King', Elvis Presley, was delivering more movie lines than hit records. American music stagnated into a comfortable, palatable style dominated by teen idols named Bobby with Vaseline-laden hair. In December 1963, the No. 1 hit in America was the Singing Nun's "Dominique," and just a month into 1964 a singer named – yes – Bobby Vinton scored a No. 1 hit with "There, I Said It Again." Vinton's song resonated with parents rather

---

[9] "All the Way" was released by Capitol Records, the Beatles' future label, in 1957, at the height of the early rock 'n' roll era.

than teens, it was something they could hum while mowing the lawn or doing the dishes.

Meanwhile, the Beatles, who had started with a loyal local following in Liverpool, continued to perform relentlessly throughout the United Kingdom, culminating in an appearance on the popular television show *Sunday Night at the London Palladium* on October 13, 1963. Shortly thereafter, they accepted an invitation from the Queen to appear in the annual *Royal Variety Performance*, a televised program that raised money for royal charities. In America, the Beatles single "I Want to Hold Your Hand" was released in late 1963. The album that followed in January 1964, simply titled *Meet the Beatles*, began a headwind that swept the States the next month, when the Beatles made their first visit.

The Beatles went from playing small British dance halls and clubs to performing on the world's largest and most prestigious stages, in large part because America's teenagers embraced them. At no time was this more true than on the night of February 9, 1964 when the band first appeared on *The Ed Sullivan Show*, a popular Sunday night variety television show. (In fact, Sullivan booked them for three consecutive Sunday nights.) That first appearance was seen by a then-record 73 million people.[10]

In that moment, teenagers searching for something to get excited about found exactly what they were looking for. While parents scoffed at the Beatles' long hair, teenage girls enthusiastically proclaimed their devotion to their favorite member of the band. And suddenly teenagers who secretly wanted to play an instrument, sing and write songs did not have to aspire to be Elvis; instead, they could emulate the more affable Beatles. Soon after the Sullivan performances, sales of the instruments the Beatles played soared: Rickenbacker, Gretsch, and Höfner guitars, along with Ludwig drums.[11]

Just five days after the Beatles landed in America, a reporter asked Paul McCartney an overarching but prophetic question.

REPORTER: Paul, what place do you think the story of the Beatles is going to have in the history of Western culture?

---

[10] The program's Nielsen rating was a record-setting 45.3, meaning that it was watched in 45.3 percent of American households with televisions, or 23,240,000 homes. The show garnered a 60 share, meaning that 60 percent of the televisions turned on were tuned in to Ed Sullivan and the Beatles. From "The Beatles" page, Official Ed Sullivan Site, www.edsullivan.com/artists/the-beatles.

[11] Andy Babiuk, *Beatles Gear: All the Fab Four's Instruments from Stage to Studio* (Milwaukee, WI: Hal Leonard Corporation, 2001), 117.

PAUL: Western culture? Ah, I don't know. You must be kidding with that
    question. Culture – it's not culture.
REPORTER: What is it?
PAUL: It's a good laugh.[12]

A laugh? Hardly. Before the Sullivan shows, no British music star had
enjoyed significant success in America. But afterward, manager Brian
Epstein had a certifiable phenomenon on his hands. He was different
than most band managers, carefully grooming and crafting the image of
his "boys," as he called them. (It was Beatles PR Man Tony Barrow who
dubbed them the Fab Four.) Most music insiders thought the group to be a
flash in the pan and urged Epstein to take every offer presented before the
bubble burst.

Instead, he relied on the extensive experience of Norman Weiss, an
American entertainment agent he had met in Paris just a month before the
Sullivan shows, who counseled a more conservative approach. Epstein
contracted with Weiss's company, General Artists Corporation, to field
offers to present the Beatles on a whirlwind tour of North America
beginning in August 1964. Soon unprecedented offers came flooding in
from promoters eager to book enormous venues such as Detroit's Tiger
Stadium (50,000 seats), New York's Shea Stadium (60,000), and even the
Los Angeles Coliseum (80,000).

At that point in their career, the Beatles had never performed to an
audience larger than 12,000,[13] and just a year prior they had been playing
regular gigs at the Cavern Club. Epstein heeded Weiss's advice and chose
smaller venues, such as arenas and amphitheaters, with an average of
17,000 seats. This decision would prove critical in building momentum
for subsequent tours. If Epstein had greedily selected larger venues early
on in America, it could have proved disastrous. The press would have
vilified the group for attracting only 20,000 concertgoers to a 60,000-seat
venue despite the fact that this was still a sizeable crowd in 1964. Instead,
arenas, coliseums, amphitheaters and even fairground grandstands were
filled to capacity, and those who missed out were eager to see a return in
1965.

The resulting tour was legendary in concert history: thirty-two shows in
twenty-six venues in twenty-four cities in just thirty-three days, attended

[12] Bruce Spizer, *The Beatles Are Coming! The Birth of Beatlemania in America* (New Orleans, LA: 498
Productions, 2010), 208.
[13] The band's concert at Australia's Sydney Stadium on June 18, 1964 drew 12,000 fans, their largest
attendance before touring America. Interestingly, their largest show in Britain had only 8,000
attendees; the venue was the Empire Pool in Wembley, England.

by hundreds of thousands of fans. The revenues set records too: while tried-and-true American superstars such as Frank Sinatra, Liza Minnelli, and Judy Garland were garnering $10,000 to $15,000 a night, Epstein required upwards of $30,000 a night in guarantees and up to 60 percent of the gate receipts for a Beatles performance. Weiss would later comment, "In the more than fifteen years that I have been in this business, I do not know of any attraction that has come close to this sort of money in so short a tour."[14] Indeed, the 1964 tour was record-shattering, precedent-setting, groundbreaking, earth-shaking, and moneymaking.

And as if that were not enough, the 1965 tour was even bigger. The Beatles reached perhaps the pinnacle of their live-performance career with a massive sold-out show at New York's Shea Stadium on August 15, 1965. The concert smashed records for attendance (55,600) and gross earnings ($304,000), for a 30-minute show in which the group belted out twelve songs, earning a tidy $160,000 for their efforts.

Throughout their North American tours, the Beatles' concerts were sheer bedlam, beginning with the first strum of the guitar for the song that opened every show, the Isley Brothers' 1962 hit "Twist and Shout." After attempting to record a live concert at the 1964 Hollywood Bowl show for future release, producer George Martin likened the audience's screams to the sound of a 747 jet engine. Ringo Starr would later comment, "I never felt people came to hear our shows; I felt they came to see us, because from the count in from the first number, the volume of screams would just drown everything out."[15]

In 1966, during what would be the Beatles' last tour of America, a jaded New York television reporter tried his best to deflate the enthusiasm of the teenagers he was interviewing.

REPORTER: Don't you think this whole Beatle craze is sorta silly and strictly for girls?
MALE FAN: No, not really. I think they are very talented musicians and songwriters, and excellent showmen.

This New York fan may have said it best in replying to the reporter's questions.

FEMALE FAN: The Beatles bring joy into the world . . . we forget our cares when we hear Beatle records.

[14] Norman Weiss to Brian Epstein, April 1, 1964, Gunderson Collection, Carlsbad, California.
[15] The Beatles, *The Beatles Anthology* (San Francisco: Chronicle Books, 2000), 186.

REPORTER: Tell me this: How long do you think the Beatles will last?
FEMALE FAN: I wish they'd last forever. They could bring happiness to everybody.[16]

To the dismay of their adoring fans, after three tours of America and performances around the world, the Beatles grew weary of the screaming, the difficulty of recreating their new sounds on stage due to the technical limitations of the day, and the stresses of the road in general. In August 1966 they decided to stop touring forever. John Lennon once opined, "Beatles concerts are nothing to do with music anymore. They're just bloody tribal rites."[17]

By quitting the road, the Beatles freed themselves to spend more time in the studio, and they were no longer limited to writing only songs they could perform live. The results were stunning, including seminal albums such as *Sgt. Pepper's Lonely Hearts Club Band*, *The Beatles* (also known as *The White Album*) and *Abbey Road*.

After the band's acrimonious break-up in 1970, historians, music industry insiders, and fans began what became endless rounds of talk, study, and comparison of all subsequent musicians to the Beatles. Meanwhile, young people and other newcomers have continued to discover the magic of the Beatles that Brian Epstein found in the dank cellar of a club in Liverpool all those years ago.

Promoters with large talent agencies learned lessons from the Beatles. They quickly realized that concert tours had the potential to fill thousands of seats and generate profit beyond their wildest imagination. The success of the Beatles' 1965 Shea Stadium concert surely encouraged the large shows of the future, such as Woodstock, the Watkins Glen Summer Jam, and even Live Aid. Today the supergroups of rock fill stadiums on a regular basis, and the concert industry has become a multi-billion-dollar business, thanks in no small degree to the Beatles' pioneering success.[18]

Record companies as well saw a major transformation in their best-selling product during the Beatles era. The 45, a 7-inch vinyl record containing a single song on each side that was played at 45 rpm, was the gold standard of the 1950s. The 1960s saw the rise of the LP, a long-playing record album containing multiple songs on each side. No longer were artists relegated to two songs on a 45; now they could create a complete

---

[16] The Beatles, *The Beatles Anthology*, DVD.   [17] The Beatles, *The Beatles Anthology*, 229.
[18] The concert industry today generates billions of dollars in revenue. The largest promoters are Live Nation and AEG Live (Anschutz Entertainment Group). From Dave DiMartino, "Live Nation Leads the Charge in Concert Business' Booming Revenue," *Variety*, February 8, 2017, http://variety.com/2017/music/features/live-nation-concert-business-1201979571.

concept album – an innovation the Beatles mastered with the 1967 release of *Sgt. Pepper's Lonely Hearts Club Band*, consistently rated the greatest album of all time.[19] The transformation continues today, as digitization and downloading rule the music world. In 2010, when the Beatles allowed their catalog to be released on Apple's iTunes, sales soared and new fans discovered the band, to the delight of the music industry.[20]

Undoubtedly, from the dance hall to the stadium, the Beatles' stage career "was perhaps the most important ingredient of all in the make-up of their unprecedented fame."[21] They did not win over legions of fans by cutting records in a sterile studio, but rather seduced them one by one in live performances, beginning in 1957 on the rough-and-tumble stages of Liverpool, all the way to the bright lights of the world's largest venues in front of tens of thousands.

[19] "The 500 Greatest Albums of All Time" (poll), *Rolling Stone*, May 31, 2012.
[20] "Beatles Sell 2 Million Songs in First Week on iTunes," *Billboard*, November 23, 2010, www.billboard.com/articles/news/950355/beatles-sell-2-million-songs-in-first-week-on-itunes.
[21] Mark Lewisohn, *The Beatles Live!* (New York: Henry Holt, 1986), 9.

CHAPTER 8

Beatlemania

Melissa Davis

Beatlemania: biːt (ə) lˈmeɪnɪə/

From Gr (noun) mania (ma'-ni-a) mānēə meaning madness or frenzy. Extreme enthusiasm for the Beatles pop group, as manifested in the frenzied behaviour of their fans in the 1960s. Synonyms: madness, derangement, dementia, lunacy, delirium, frenzy, hysteria, wildness.[1]

A CBS documentary marking the 50th anniversary of the Beatles' arrival in New York on February 7, 1964 captured the scene: "Even half a century later, the sound is unmistakable. It is the sound of frenzied joy."[2]

Tom Wolfe called it, "rapturous agony."[3]

Origin of the Term

Tony Barrow, who served as the Beatles press secretary, credited the British press for coining the word, tracing it to news coverage of the audience reaction to the group's appearance on Val Parnell's *Sunday Night At The London Palladium* variety program on October 13, 1963. This was the first nationally televised live Beatles performance and after witnessing the screaming audience drown out the music, Fleet Street "discovered" Beatlemania.

The *Daily Mail* ran a feature by Vincent Mulchrone under the headline "This Beatlemania: Beatles Flee in Fantastic Palladium Siege": "more than 1,000 screaming teenagers" held the Beatles in a "day-long siege ... eventually fighting to break through a cordon of more than 60 police officers."[4]

---

[1] "Beatlemania," *Lexico*, https://en.oxforddictionaries.com/definition/beatlemania.
[2] "When the Beatles Changed Everything," *CBS News*, February 2, 2014, www.cbsnews.com/news/when-the-beatles-changed-everything/.
[3] Tom Wolfe, *The Kandy-Kolored Tangerine Flake Streamline Baby* (New York: Farrar, Straus & Giroux, 1965).
[4] The *Daily Mail*, October 21, 1963.

Figure 8.1 American television host Ed Sullivan smiles while standing with British
rock group the Beatles on the set of his television variety series, New York, February
9, 1964 . Photo by Express Newspapers/Getty Images

Barrow said he had "spent days that summer trying to get the London
papers to pay attention to them but they wouldn't take my calls." After the
Palladium show – the press contacted him.[5]

Scottish music promoter Andi Lothian claimed he used the term first
during the Beatles' tour of Scotland on October 7, 1963: "It was absolute
pandemonium. Girls fainting, screaming, wetting seats. I'd never seen
anything like it."[6]

The Beatles arrived in New York on February 7, 1964 to an estimated
crowd of 5,000 at John F. Kennedy International Airport. That night, they
watched coverage of their arrival on the national evening news program,
CBS Evening News with Walter Cronkite, as the venerable newsman

[5] Tony Barrow, *John, Paul, George, Ringo & Me: The Real Beatles Story* (New York: Da Capo Press,
2006)
[6] Dorian Lynskey, "Beatlemania: 'The Screamers' and Other Tales of Fandom," *The Guardian*,
September 28, 2013.

announced: "The British invasion this time goes by the code name Beatlemania."

In an article on the 50th anniversary of Beatlemania in Britain, Dorian Lynskey wrote in *The Guardian*: "Throughout 1963 there had been reports of teenage girls screaming, crying, fainting and chasing the band down the street; police escorts were already required. But catchy new words have a magical power in the media. Once it caught on, it seemed to cement the phenomenon in the collective imagination."[7]

The headlines from around the world speak for themselves.

BEATLEMANIA: IT'S HAPPENING EVERYWHERE – EVEN IN SEDATE CHELTENHAM (*The Daily Herald*, October 1963)

1,000 TEENAGE FANS STORM THEATER: POLICE LOSE HELMETS IN BATTLES (*The Daily Herald*, October 1963)

Britons Succumb to "Beatlemania" (*New York Times Magazine*, December 1, 1963)

YEAH! YEAH! USA! 5,000 scream "welcome" to the Beatles (*New York Daily Mirror*, February 8, 1964)

BEATLES ON TV WOW AMERICA (*New York Daily Mirror*, February 10, 1964)

"Beatlemania" SWEEPS U.S. (*National Record News*, 1964)

TEENS GO BUGGY OVER BEATLES (*Miami News*, 14 February 1964)

Beatles Leave L.A. Gasping (*Los Angeles Herald Examiner*, 24 August 1964)

55,000 Scream for Beatles (*Daily News*, New York, 16 August 1965)

300 Beatle Fans Taken to Hospital (*Houston Post*, 20 August 1965)

Archbishop Has Praise For Beatles (*Milwaukee Journal*, 9 October 1965)

WILD WELCOME AT KAI TAK FOR THE BEATLES (*South China Post*, Hong Kong, 9 June 1964)

E' IN ARRIVO UN CICLONE CHIAMATO BEATLES (trans. from Italian: A cyclone called Beatles is coming) (June 1965)

THE SECRET OF THE BEATLES: An intimate account of their American tour and a probing analysis of their incredible power to evoke frenzied emotions among the young (*Saturday Evening Post*, 21 March 1964)

---

[7] Lynskey, "Beatlemania."

Jet Magazine/What The Beatles Learned From Negroes (July 1, 1965)

For the Beatles, the excitement wore off quickly. The demands of touring, banal questions from the press, and lack of privacy soon outweighed the thrill of screaming fans. By 1966, the development and evolution of their music and international controversies leading to threats to their physical safety ended their live appearances on August 29, 1966.

Popular Manias

There had been manias before.

In seventeenth-century Holland, then the economic powerhouse of the globe, "Tulipmania" saw single bulbs trading for more than the annual income of most people at the time. The flowers were unique and became a status symbol – a single Viceroy Tulip sold at five times the cost of a family home.

The craze was short-lived, lasting from 1636 to 1637, ending when the market crashed and those stuck with a surplus of bulbs found themselves facing financial ruin.[8]

Two centuries later, Hungarian pianist and composer Franz Liszt inspired the type of frenzied behavior described by German poet Christian Heine as "Lisztomania" to illustrate the reaction of both adult men and women who became overwhelmed by the passionate style of the composer. According to folklore, a wealthy fan scooped up his discarded cigar butt from the gutter and fashioned it into a locket, wearing it next to her heart as a lifelong memento.

According to musicologist Dana Gooley, physicians believed the mania was a medical condition, hypothesizing that it was possibly a form of mass epilepsy, even seeking an immunization against the disease.[9]

By the time the next mania struck, well into the twentieth century, it would not be limited to live performances by artists, but extend to movie theaters and a New York mortuary.

Female fans of the 1920s silent film star Rudolph Valentino turned out in the thousands at the New York premiere of the film *The Son of the Sheik*: "The temperature was close to one hundred degrees, but a mob of thousands formed around the theater, and as Valentino

---

[8] Mike Dash, *Tulipmania: The Story of the World's Most Coveted Flower and the Extraordinary Passions It Aroused* (New York: Three Rivers Press, 1999).

[9] Dana Andrew Gooley, *The Virtuoso Liszt* (New York: Cambridge University Press, 2004).

tried to make his way out of Times Square they ripped at his clothes."[10]

When Valentino died suddenly at the age of 31, "more than 100,000 people gathered on the streets in chaos outside the Frank Campbell Funeral Home. Flappers tore at their own clothes, clutched at their chests, and collapsed in the heat. The New York Police Department tried to bring order to the mob, and there were reports of despondent fans committing suicide."[11]

A new type of fandom had emerged.

The Emerging Fan Cohort

There had also been teen idols before. The mid-twentieth century saw a new demographic – the teenager. Young people dressed differently than their parents and listened to different music. In the 1920s many young girls wore their hair and their skirts short, using rouge not only on their faces, but also on their knees. Young college men sported raccoon coats and took to swallowing live goldfish. Jazz emerged with solo artists and big bands dominating music in the 1930s and 1940s during the Depression and World War II.

Sinatra and "Bobby Soxers"

In the early 1940s, a singing waiter named Frank Sinatra became the favorite of teenaged girls who shrieked and swooned during his appearances. Their behavior, however, was initially the result of efforts by his publicist who handed out free tickets to the singer's first big shows and paid the then-enormous sum of $5-a-head to girls, giving them specific instructions on when and how loudly to scream.[12]

Evans's ploy worked and the reaction of the fans at Sinatra's appearance at the Paramount Theater on 12 October 1944 when 25,000 fans blocked traffic in Times Square and caused what the *New York Times* called "the Columbus Day Riot."[13]

[10] Gilbert King, "The 'Latin Lover' and His Enemies," *Smithsonian*, June 13, 2012, www.smithsonian mag.com/history/the-latin-lover-and-his-enemies-119968944/#8yOGrY6rxJDOA9kd.99.
[11] King, "The 'Latin Lover' and His Enemies."
[12] Howard Reich, "8 Things You Didn't Know about Frank Sinatra," *Chicago Tribune*, December 12, 2015.
[13] Reich, "8 Things You Didn't Know about Frank Sinatra."

Newspapers and newsreels spread the word with the sound and images of Sinatra's shows and soon fans around the country followed suit. Press coverage drew attention to the girls, labeling them "Bobby Soxers" after that ubiquitous clothing item so popular among them. "Not since the days of ... Valentino has American womanhood made such unabashed public love to an entertainer."[14]

New York photographer Arthur Fellig reported on the pandemonium: "Sinatra appeared on stage ... hysterical shouts of 'Frankie ... Frankie'; you've heard the squeals on the radio when he sings. Multiply that by about a thousand times and you get an idea of the deafening noise."[15]

The London-based *The Guardian* newspaper reported on Sinatra in language that, twenty years later, could be used to describe the reaction of Beatles fans: "The United States is now in the midst of one of those remarkable phenomena of mass hysteria, which occur from time to time ... Frank Sinatra is inspiring extraordinary personal devotion on the part of many thousands of young people, and particularly young girls between the ages of, say, twelve and eighteen."[16]

President Roosevelt said Sinatra had "revived the charming art of swooning," although the New York City Board of Education scolded, "We cannot tolerate young people making a public display of losing control of their emotions."[17]

But there was no "Sinatramania," per se; the craze was labeled and referred to by the most readily identifiable symbol of the fans, "Bobby Soxers," not the artist himself. Nor it did not extend beyond America.

Elvis

In the mid-1950s, girls had the same reaction to Elvis Presley that Valentino and Sinatra had generated, but many adults dismissed the truck driver from Memphis as "Elvis the Pelvis," attributing his appeal to his unique stage moves such as hip-swiveling while ignoring his distinctive singing style: "His one specialty is an accented movement of the body ... primarily identified with the repertoire of the blond bombshells of the burlesque runway."[18]

---

[14] *Time Magazine*, 1943.
[15] Jon Savage, "The Columbus Day Riot: Frank Sinatra is Pop's First Star," *The Guardian*, June 10, 2011.
[16] *The Guardian*, January 1945.   [17] Richard Setlow, *Variety*, November 5, 1992.
[18] Jack Gould, "Elvis Presley Rises to Fame as Vocalist Who Is Vituoso of Hootchy-Kootchy," *New York Times*, June 6, 1956, https://archive.nytimes.com/www.nytimes.com/partners/aol/special/elvis/early-elvis1.html.

Ben Gross of the *New York Daily News* wrote that popular music "has reached its lowest depths in the 'grunt and groin' antics of one Elvis Presley ... Elvis, who rotates his pelvis ... gave an exhibition that was suggestive and vulgar, tinged with the kind of animalism that should be confined to dives and bordellos."[19]

The Catholic diocese in La Crosse, Wisconsin sent a letter to FBI director J. Edgar Hoover calling Presley, "a definite danger to the security of the United States ... [His] actions and motions were such as to rouse the sexual passions of teenaged youth ... After the show, more than 1,000 teenagers tried to gang into Presley's room at the auditorium."[20]

Ed Sullivan vowed Elvis would never appear on his Sunday evening variety show, but after a Presley television appearance on another program beat his ratings, he relented, telling *TV Guide*, "As for his gyrations, the whole thing can be controlled with camera shots."[21]

As it unfolded, the Beatles did, in fact, become bigger not only than Elvis, just as he had become bigger than Sinatra, but also, in their case, the reaction of fans – crying, screaming, shrieking, fainting, losing bladder control, swarming their "getaway" cars as they left concerts, straining to touch them – crossed geographical, linguistic, and cultural boundaries spreading from the north of England to all of the UK, Europe, the USA, Australia, and Asia.

That fan reaction also had a name: Beatlemania.

Despite the seeming suddenness with which Beatlemania erupted, they had not been an overnight success, having spent what should have been their high school and college days playing at dances and family weddings in and around Liverpool. In 1960, aged 17 to 19, they spent almost four months playing in a raunchy and raucous Hamburg club, bunking behind the restroom of a porn theater, putting in the onstage hours that would hone them into a solid unit. By the time they returned from Germany, they not only looked different, but sounded unlike any other group in Liverpool.

Deported and dejected, four of the five Beatles arrived home without plans, unsure whether they would even continue to play together. But for a post-Christmas dance in Litherland in north Liverpool in December 1960,

[19] Peter Guralnick and Ernst Jorgensen, *Elvis Day by Day: The Definitive Record of His Life and Music* (New York: Ballantine, 1999).
[20] Thomas Fensch, *The FBI Files on Elvis Presley* (Woodlands, TX: New Century Books, 2001).
[21] Jake Austen, *TV-A-Go-Go: Rock on TV from American Bandstand to American Idol* (Chicago: Chicago Review Press, 2005).

the Beatles might have given up, broken up, or formed different groups with other lineups.

Chas Newby, home from college for the Christmas holidays, was recruited to substitute for the Beatles' bass player who had stayed behind in Hamburg (McCartney played guitar at that time). His memory of the night confirms other contemporaneous accounts of the audience's reaction.

> We are all on stage, behind the curtains. This is a large ballroom, so all three amplifiers are turned up to 10. The compere announces the band, "Ladies and Gentlemen, Direct from Hamburg, The Fabulous Beatles." The curtain opens and Paul screams, *"I'm gonna tell Aunt Mary 'bout Uncle John ... "* as we launch into *Long Tall Sally*. We follow with songs by Elvis, Buddy Holly, Carl Perkins, and Larry Williams. The audience goes bananas, the dancing fizzles out, and everybody closes in on the stage. The promoter thinks a fight has broken out, but it is just members of the audience enjoying themselves. We finish with the Ray Charles' song, *What'd I Say* and the audience joins in the "call back." Mayhem![22]

Their drummer at the time, Pete Best recalled, "you could physically feel the crowd gasp ... When we finished the first number the place went into rapture, it just exploded."[23]

Best remembered the screaming: "they stopped dancing when we played and surged forward in a crowd to be nearer to us ... and above all to scream. People didn't go to a dance to scream: this was news."[24]

Newby's career with the Beatles ended on New Year's Day 1961; within days he was back at college, but he had witnessed and played a role in the birth of Beatlemania.

The Litherland appearance marked not only a pivotal moment in the group's confidence, but also arguably the first instance of Beatlemania. Following the gig, the Beatles began to attract a dedicated fan base in Liverpool and the Merseyside area – and their number grew.

In late 1961, local businessman Brian Epstein became their manager, and began booking them into better venues, securing a recording contract with EMI. Their first record, "Love Me Do," was released in October 1962; their first No. 1 single, "Please Please Me," in January 1963. From then on, fans began queuing up for their performances.

---

[22] Newby to Davis personal communication, September 3, 2018.
[23] Roag Best with Pete Best and Rory Best, *The Beatles: True Beginnings* (New York: Thomas Dunne Books, 2003).
[24] Joe Gooden, *The Beatles Bible*, www.beatlesbible.com/1960/12/27/live-litherland-town-hall-liverpool/.

As their popularity grew, so did Beatlemania, spreading from Liverpool throughout Britain.

The Mania

The specifics – cities, dates, venues, crowd size, and descriptions of the pandemonium are more than adequately documented in thousands of books, articles, journals, documentaries, and magazines.

The mania followed the group wherever they went. Fans screamed and waved signs, surged through barriers, clutched at chainlink fences, and fainted in crowds at airports, hotels, and concert venues. According to a *New York Times Magazine* article printed just before the Beatles came to the United States, the Dublin police chief said the group's visit was "alright until the mania degenerated into barbarism."[25]

A huge crowd (estimates vary between 2,000 and 5,000) welcomed the Beatles at John F. Kennedy International Airport when the Beatles arrived on February 7, 1964, with crowds gathering on the sidewalks below their window at the Plaza Hotel. Reporter Larry Kane likened the sound of thousands of Beatle fans screaming to jet engines, which at the time ranged between 90 and 100 decibels; when the JFK crowd welcomed the group, the recording device was reported to have registered 112 decibels.[26]

An estimated "300,000 people lined the streets of Adelaide, the biggest Beatles crowd anywhere, any time," according to Peter Cox, the curator of "The Beatles in Australia" exhibition at the Museum of Applied Arts and Sciences.[27] "There was such a crush outside the hotel that Sunday afternoon that navy and army cadets were summoned to help the 300 police keep order."[28]

The scenes repeated in cities and countries around the world were all the same; a letter from George Harrison to his parents in June 1964 describes the mayhem:

[25] Barbara Ehrenreich, Elizabeth Hess and Gloria Jacobs, "Beatlemania: Girls Just Want To Have Fun," in *The Adoring Audience: Fan Culture And Popular Music*, ed. Lisa Lewis (London: Routledge 1992), 85.

[26] "The Beatles Arrive in America (Queens, New York, February 7, 1964)", *YouTube*, www.youtube.com/watch?v=aeswlOJEdQg.

[27] Peter Cox, *The Beatles in Australia Essay*, April 5, 2018, https://maas.museum/the-beatles-in-australia-essay/.

[28] Alan Howe, "The Beatles in Australia, 50 Years On: How Four Days Changed Melbourne," *Sunday Herald Sun*, May 24, 2014, www.heraldsun.com.au/news/victoria/the-beatles-in-australia-50-years-on-how-four-days-changed-melbourne/news-story/5de26eafc62b02396670d7aaf9615f59.

Dear Mum and Dad,

The shows have been going great with everybody going potty and everywhere we go we have about 20 police on motorbikes escorting us. We have
had two Cadillacs every place, but tonight when we finished the show and
ran out, the cars weren't there and had gone to another door so we went
back inside until we could get out. All the kids came out of the show and saw
the two cars around the side and stormed them, and jumped all over them,
and the drivers had to get out, and both cars were completely wrecked and
the roofs were right down on the seats inside. Some girl fell through the
skylight from the roof of a building and 45 more were put in hospital. In the
end, we escaped in an ambulance. Don't worry because no one can get near
us for all the police and security.[29]

Australian disc jockey Bob Rogers spoke of what it was like to travel with
the group. It "meant living every minute upside-down and inside-out. It
was mentally and physically exhausting. And everything the Beatles said or
did was of momentous importance, even if they'd said or done it many
times before. That was part of Beatlemania."[30]

News reports, like this one from the *Spokesman-Review*, continued to
put Beatlemania on the front pages in language that would both alarm
parents and excite fans: "Between 2,000 and 3,000 screaming teenage
Beatle fans rushed on to the field of Cleveland Stadium in an attempt to
mob the famous quartet, halting the show for about a half-hour. The
young fans leaped a small fence, raced past police, onto the field and to
the stage ... about 100 to 150 policemen on duty were on the field during
the rebellion."[31]

The Whittier Hotel in Detroit and the Hotel Muehlebach in Kansas
City found a ready market of eager fans for 1 inch square pieces of bed
sheets the Beatles supposedly slept on during the 1964 tour. The hotel
managers authenticated the squares, identifying which Beatle had slept on
the square. Young, trusting, and naïve fans bought the story – and the
squares.[32]

Successful and established artists capitalized on the mania releasing
cover versions of Beatle songs: *Love Songs to The Beatles* (Mary Wells),
which included "She Loves You" rephrased as "*He* Loves You"; Count

[29] *George Harrison: Living in the Material World*, Film film by dir. by Martin Scorsese, Grove Street
Pictures, 2011.
[30] Philip O'Brien, *The Beatles Let It Be in Australia: 1964*, *The Sydney Morning Herald*, June 3, 2014,
www.smh.com.au/entertainment/the-beatles-let-it-be-in-australia-1964-20140606-zrvui.html.
[31] *Spokesman-Review*, Spokane Washington, 15 August 1965, http://thebeatlesinthenews.blogspot.com/
2015/01/the-beatles-spokesman-review-wa-august_40.html.
[32] "Selling the Beatles Hotel Sheets (1964)," *YouTube*, www.youtube.com/watch?v=dfN_pCWBQWE.

Basie with *Basie's Beatle Bag*, and *The Chipmunks Sing the Beatles Hits*. Ella Fitzgerald had a hit in 1964 with a cover of "Can't Buy Me Love."

Following the release of *Beatles '65*, Sinatra recorded *Sinatra '65*, Duke Ellington released *Ellington '65*, and Sérgio Mendes came out with *Brasil '65*.

The Fans

Adolescent girls had been clipping pictures of matinee idols and singers out of magazines for a generation by the time the Beatles reached their goal to be "bigger than Elvis."

Surging hormones found their focus on attractive young men who were inaccessible and unattainable, and therefore vastly more intriguing and less threatening than the boys they knew and dated.

Arguably, the mania was contagious: peer pressure bonded them together with the only real dispute among them being which Beatle was "cuter." Fan clubs, including an official one sanctioned by the group, cropped up in the UK, the USA, and around the world.

Barbara Ehrenreich wrote of the kinship of Beatle fans, talking about the Beatles with other fans, speculating about their private lives: "What do you think Paul had for breakfast? Is John really the leader? Is George really more sensitive?" This was an integral part of the experience.[33]

The approval of adults did nothing to diminish their appeal to fans. Ed Sullivan said, "These youngsters and their conduct over here ... will leave an imprint with everyone who has met them" adding the accolades of composers Richard Rogers and Aaron Copland. Classical figures Dimitri Shostakovich and Leonard Bernstein openly praised the Beatles, with no effect on the rock 'n' roll bona fides of the group.[34]

The praise from respected adults extended far beyond the world of popular music. Their first film, *A Hard Day's Night*, received good reviews from surprised film critics, as well as two Academy Award nominations, but fans were not deterred and continued to fill the theaters and scream while the film was showing.[35]

---

[33] Ehrenreich et al., "Beatlemania: Girls Just Want To Have Fun."
[34] *The Ed Sullivan Show*, February 23, 1964, DVD, SOFA Entertainment, Inc.; see also, CBS Sunday Morning, www.youtube.com/watch?v=1eBQ3arZ4v0&t=1099s.
[35] "You Can't Do That: The Making of A Hard Day's Night," *YouTube*, www.youtube.com/watch?v=lQMr2BVlYOs.

In the watershed year 1964, John Lennon was honored at Foyle's Literary Luncheon for his collection of poems and drawings, joining the ranks of past honorees General de Gaulle and T. S. Eliot.

The Beatles played before the Queen Mother at the Royal Command Performance in November 1963. Queen Elizabeth II awarded them the MBE (Member of the Most Excellent Order of the British Empire) 18 months later, as fans gathered outside Buckingham Palace, straining against a line of bobbies who linked arms to create a barrier, climbing the gates, chanting, "We want the Beatles," mobbing their car, and as usual, screaming.[36]

Derision heaped on the Beatles and their fans only served to increase the Beatles' appeal. Reviews following the Sullivan appearances ridiculed their music, their style, and their fans in language reminiscent of that used to mock Bobby Soxers and Elvis fans.

The *Washington Post* attacked the fans directly: "Just thinking about the Beatles seems to induce mental disturbance."[37]

Science Newsletter dismissed the group by referencing previous teen idols: "The Beatles follow a line of glamorous figures who aroused passionate cries and deep swoons. Most prominent in the 1940s was Frank Sinatra and in the 1950s Elvis Presley. Their glory passed when they got too old to be teenagers' idols or when teenagers got too old to need them."[38]

In a *New Statesman* essay titled "The Menace of Beatlism," Paul Johnson did more than ridicule the fans, writing insultingly, "Those who flock round the Beatles, who scream themselves into hysteria, whose vacant faces flicker over the TV screen, are the least fortunate of their generation, the dull, the idle, the failures."[39]

Variety Magazine took a sinister view, suggesting that Beatlemania was "a phenomenon closely linked to the current wave of racial rioting."[40]

William F. Buckley simply hated them: "The Beatles are not merely awful ... they are so unbelievably horrible, so appallingly unmusical, so dogmatically insensitive to the magic of the art that they qualify as crowned

[36] "A Taste of Beatlemania in the 1960s," *YouTube*, www.youtube.com/watch?v=7mwiD3HTGng.
[37] Richard Harrington, "Remembering the Beatles' Debut in D.C.," *Washington Post*, February 9, 1982, www.washingtonpost.com/archive/lifestyle/1982/02/09/remembering-the-beatles-debut-in-dc/789b6d0b-b89e-4298-8eac-2a65113303a6/?utm_term=.50e7fb911d1d.
[38] Alan Rinzler, *Science Newsletter*, February 29, 1964.
[39] Paul Johnson, "From the Archive: The Menace of Beatlism," *New Statesman*, August 28, 2014, www.newstatesman.com/culture/2014/08/archive-menace-beatlism.
[40] Nicholas Schaffner, *The Beatles Forever* (New York: McGraw-Hill 1977).

heads of anti-music, even as the imposter popes went down in history as 'anti-popes.'"[41]

Mostly, critics tried to outdo each other with "witty" statements about the Beatles' hair: "With their bizarre shrubbery, the Beatles are obviously a press agent's dream combo ... the hirsute thickets project a certain kittenish charm which drives the immature, shall we say, ape."[42]

CBS reporter Alexander Kendrick disdainfully referred to "the epidemic called Beatlemania." Focusing on what he called "dish-mop hair style ... sheepdog hairdo," Kendrick said, "They symbolize the 20th century non-hero, as they make non-music, wear non-haircuts."[43]

Harkening back to the medical explanation for Lisztomania as a disease, the *Boston Globe* managed to disparage the Beatles' music, performance, accents, and hair while patronizing the fans:

> Don't let the Beatles bother you. If you don't think about them, they will go away, and in a few more years they will probably be bald ... teenagers, go ahead and enjoy your Beatlemania. It won't be fatal and will give you a lot of laughs a few years hence when you find one of their old records or come across a picture of Ringo in a crew cut. This Liverpool lunacy is merely the 1964 version of a mild disease ... characterized by excessive hair growth, an inability to recognize melody, a highly emotional state with severe body twitches and a strange accent ... The disease is at the height of its virulence, but the fever will subside and the victims may receive immunity for life.[44]

The *New York Times*, unable to resist insulting their hair, compared the Beatles to previous idols and a daytime kiddie TV show host: "The boys hardly did for daughter what Elvis Presley did for her older sister or Frank Sinatra for mother ... borrowing the square hairdo used every morning on television by Captain Kangaroo."[45]

---

[41] Buckley, William, "Yeah, Yeah, Yeah ... They Stink!!!," *National Review*, 1964.

[42] "What the Critics Wrote about The Beatles in 1964," compiled by Cary Schneider, *Los Angeles Times*, February 9, 2014, www.latimes.com/opinion/la-xpm-2014-feb-09-la-oe-beatles-quotes-2014 0209-story.html.

[43] "The Beatles on CBS News, 21 November 1963," *YouTube*, www.youtube.com/watch? v=UeolhjIWPYs.

[44] Cary Schneider, comp., "What the Critics Wrote About the Beatles in 1964," *Los Angeles Times*, February 9, 2014, www.latimes.com/opinion/la-xpm-2014-feb-09-la-oe-beatles-quotes-20140209-s tory.html.

[45] Peter Marks, "Recalling Screams Heard Round the World," *New York Times*, February 6, 1994, w ww.nytimes.com/1994/02/06/nyregion/recalling-screams-heard-round-the-world.html?mtrref=ww w.google.com&gwh=A80F26EE07F15CB3F75702B122793F50&gwt=pay.

What Were the Girls Thinking?

Girls may have wanted to marry a Beatle, but most realized their chances to achieve that goal were slim to nil; just meeting a Beatle seemed a more likely possibility, although a remote one. Video footage of the audience during Beatle concerts and airport arrivals shows girls waving at the group, as if their favorite would notice them among the sea of faces.

"All the girls talked about marrying their favourite Beatle . . . They were adorable, they were different, they were irreverent and our parents didn't approve of them, which made it even better," Linda Ihle, a 13-year-old Paul fan in 1964, told Dorian Lynskey. She still owns one of the blank pieces of paper that rained down on fans waiting outside the Plaza Hotel in New York that February 1964: "If they'd touched it, we wanted it."[46]

One New York fan, holding one of the many signs proclaiming love and allegiance ("I LOVE YOU, PLEASE STAY 4EVER; ELVIS IS DEAD, LONG LIVE THE BEATLES"), was asked what she hoped to achieve: "That they would see our signs from up there and make us their girlfriends."[47]

One Australia fan described what it meant to be a Beatle fan:

My whole life revolved around the Beatles, from my haircut down to my boots. My Beatle mug was the only thing I would ever drink my tea out of. I wore Beatle brooches and sweatshirts and kept big scrapbooks full of newspaper clippings. The day they arrived . . . I was glued to the TV screen hours before the plane landed. The moment they walked out onto the steps, I burst into tears. I did a lot of screaming and crying that week.[48]

An article from the *New York Daily News* in August of 1966 describes the extremity of the mania"

Beatle Fans Threaten Suicide: Gals Dare Death To See Beatles

Two teen-age girls, undergoing what a Roosevelt Hospital psychiatrist later described as an "acute situation reaction," attracted thousands of startled sidewalk gawkers yesterday afternoon by perching on the edge of the 23rd floor rooftop of the Americana Hotel.

"We must see the Beatles," they told emergency responders trying for 20 minutes to talk them in from the 18" ledge where they sat with their legs dangling. "I have a letter for Paul. I have to give it to him. You wouldn't understand. Nobody understands what they mean to us."

46 Lynskey, "Beatlemania."
47 "CBS Sunday Morning," *YouTube*, www.youtube.com/watch?v=1eBQ3arZ4vo&t=1099s.
48 Glen Baker, *The Beatles Down Under: The 1964 Australia and New Zealand Tour* (Glebe, New South Wales: Wild and Woolley, 1982).

After the sobbing girls said they wouldn't come down from the ledge unless they could see the Beatles, police resorted to a ploy – a squad car with siren blaring pulled up on the street below. "It's the Beatles, girls, they've got the Beatles and they're bringing them up here to see you," the cop told them.

"They combed their hair and put on fresh lipstick 200 feet above Seventh Avenue, preparing to meet the Beatles."

At the other end of the spectrum was a fan standing outside the Plaza Hotel holding the portrait of Paul McCartney she had painted for him. When a reporter asked what she would say to McCartney if she could meet him, she said simply, "I would talk to him like a decent person."[49]

More common were the fans who screamed in theaters during *A Hard Day's Night*, hiding in restrooms to watch the movie again throughout the remaining showings of the day.[50] One fan remembers being the only girl in her circle allowed to attend a Beatle concert; her friends wanted to cut her dress into pieces.[51]

So intense was the desire of the fans that even people tangentially associated with the group received offers of sexual favors from fans, promising at least one reporter to "do anything" to secure an introduction. Longtime Philadelphia newsman and anchor, Larry Kane, who experienced Beatlemania firsthand as the only American reporter covering all three of their US tours, recalls a woman offering herself to him so her daughters could meet a Beatle.[52]

Psychological Theories and Medical Explanations

Steven Baron, a child and adolescent psychologist and author, notes that Beatlemania was an extreme example of a phenomenon called Groupthink where the desire for group harmony or conformity results in an irrational or dysfunctional decision-making process. Any critical evaluation of alternative outcomes does not occur. With respect to Beatlemania, many fans succumbed to the point of putting themselves in potential physical danger. Being part of the moment, experiencing the exhilaration of that moment, in addition to feeling part of a bigger social network eradicated rationality,

---

[49] "Paul McCartney Sprout of a New Generation," *YouTube*, www.youtube.com/watch?v=jl8btUoEYno.
[50] "You Can't Do That," *YouTube*.
[51] Ehrenreich et al., "Beatlemania: Girls Just Want To Have Fun."
[52] Larry Kane, *A Ticket to Ride: Inside the Beatles' 1964 and 1965 Tours That Changed the World* (Philadelphia: Running Dog Press, 2003).

especially in large-scale demonstrations of the mania. It was as if the individual egos of the participants became a collective and the individual judgment of the participants evaporated.[53]

Londoner Bridget Kelly remembers her first Beatles concert as "a place between childhood and adulthood where you could let go and go mad. I would never dream of being cheeky to my parents, so that was our little outlet."[54]

Some of the responses have a rational medical explanation. Dr. Jordan Lewis, in *Psychology Today*, reasons that crying and fainting by female Beatle fans was a natural response of the body: "the neurological explanation for the tears is simple – the parasympathetic (rest-and-digest) branch of the nervous system, which is connected to tear ducts, reacts and for those fans relieved to finally see their Fab Four, tears were commonplace." The reaction of the parasympathetic branch also expands blood vessels and slows the heart rate – hence the fainting.[55]

Beatlemania in the United States

If the estimates of the crowd at JFK disagree as to the actual number, the sources were in agreement that the reception was unprecedented. The quote, variously ascribed to John Lennon or Ringo Starr, "So this is America – they all seem out of their minds!," describes the scenes they encountered.

In New York, the Beatles taped a rehearsal and performed on a top-rated television show before sold-out audiences with tickets at such a premium (50,000 requests for tickets for the 728 seats in the theater), that the wife and children of the governor were unable to attend. After a sold-out appearance in Washington DC, they performed two sold-out performances at Carnegie Hall with the demand for seats so high that the Beatles were boxed in by extra chairs placed on the stage.

Savvy marketers spotting a good thing quickly brought out a variety of products, some of which had only tangential ties to the Beatles, to exploit teenage fans. In February 1964, American fans alone bought more than records, spending $2.5 million in Beatle wigs, hats, T-shirts, pajamas, bubblegum cards, ice cream, hairspray, lunchboxes, lapel buttons, and paint-by-number portrait kits of their favorite Beatle.

---

[53] Baron to Davis, September 14, 2018.   [54] Lynskey, "Beatlemania."
[55] Jordan Gaines Lewis, "Beatlemania: Fainting, Crying, and Swooning? Neuroscience Can Explain Why," *Psychology Today*, February 6, 2014, www.psychologytoday.com/us/blog/brain-babble/2014 02/love-love-medulla-the-neuroscience-beatlemania.

Novelty records were rushed to the air to capitalize on the phenomenal popularity of the group, with four songs making the *Billboard* 100 chart in April 1964. Fans serenaded the group outside their hotels with, "We love you Beatles, oh yes we do. We don't love anyone as much as you. When you're not near us, we're blue. Oh Beatles we love you," an adaptation of "We Love You, Conrad" from the Broadway musical, *Bye, Bye Birdie*.

A particularly bizarre Beatle-related song, *Ringo for President*, nominated the Beatle as a presidential candidate; 1964 was an election year in the United States and some fans, probably too young to cast a ballot (the voting age was 21 at the time), reportedly went to the Republican National Convention bearing signs promoting their write-in candidate.

The sheer volume and magnitude of the reception in the USA outdistanced probably even their own wildest dreams and set the stage for summertime tours of the USA and beyond. As Steven Stark notes: "For all they had accomplished in England by the end of 1963, if things had stopped there they would be pretty much forgotten today . . . the madness really began in 1964 when [they] set forth for the first time from England to America to try to conquer the world."[56]

Beatlemania was not confined to the West: beyond the UK and the USA, they received manic receptions in Canada, Europe, Australasia, Hong Kong, Japan, and the Philippines. A proposed visit to Israel was abandoned when the government rejected their request for visas. They did not tour the USSR or the Soviet Bloc countries where listening to the Beatles was prohibited even to the point of being illegal.

What Did the Beatles Think of Beatlemania?

Mobs of screaming fans soon made normal life impossible for the Beatles and their families. On tour, massive crowds endangered the Beatles, as well as the fans. After fans destroyed cars in frenzied attempts to touch them, they were driven to appearances in Wells Fargo trucks and ambulances, and flown in on helicopters to avoid being crushed by fans.

At a press conference, Paul McCartney revealed, "We were told by the police as soon as we got here, don't look out of the windows and don't wave. And if we do that, we get the police chief coming up and saying, 'We're finished boys' and he goes away they won't look after us, so we can't

---

[56] Steven D. Stark, *Meet the Beatles: A Cultural History of the Band That Shook Youth, Gender, and the World* (New York: Harper, 2006), 8.

do anything."[57] In response to a reporter's question, John Lennon said the Beatles wanted to talk to the fans, "but if we wave to them, somebody always says, 'Stop that waving – you're inciting them.'"[58]

Despite appearing in capital cities around the world, they were unable to venture from their suite to visit landmarks or tourists spots. McCartney requested a tour of Denver's Brown Palace Hotel in 1976 while on tour with Wings, telling the landmark's historian that the Beatles had been confined to their two-bedroom suite during their stay in August 1964.[59]

Ringo Starr points to one positive effect – the increased closeness of the group:

> The Beatles only ever had one car and two rooms in any hotel between them. We got closer together the bigger it got, the closer we became because from the minute you left the security of your apartment, the heat was on. People wanted a piece, wanted to talk, wanted a photo . . . and so we sort of kept each other company. In New York, we had a whole floor at The Plaza and the four of us ended up in the bathroom . . . just to get a break from the incredible pressure.[60]

Eventually, the mania impacted the music. As Ringo told television host Ellen Degeneres:

> We couldn't hear us. It seemed to me that you came to see the Beatles, then Paul counted it in then you screamed and we bowed and then we left. What made us question all this round 1966 was that we were becoming mediocre players, musicians. I just had to keep time . . . I'd be watching Paul's foot or John's ass.[61]

Yet many live recordings of their appearances disprove those assessments, lending credence to their remarks made at other times that their music was becoming too complicated (the sitar in *Norwegian Wood*, electronics in *Tomorrow Never Knows*, violin and cello in *Yesterday* and *Eleanor Rigby*) to replicate live on stage.

The dark side of the mania emerged years later when psychologically disturbed fans whose obsession led to violent physical attacks, seriously injured George Harrison in his own home in 1999 and killed John Lennon in 1980.

[57] "The Beatles at The Ed Sullivan Theater," CBS News 50 Years Later, *YouTube*, www.youtube.com/watch?v=7mwiD3HTGng.
[58] "The Beatles at The Ed Sullivan Theater," *YouTube*.
[59] Koegel interview with Davis, April 2009.
[60] *George Harrison: Living in the Material World*, dir. Scorsese.
[61] "Ringo Starr on Life as a Beatle," The Ellen Show, *YouTube*, www.youtube.com/watch?v=HtG55zlN3L8.

Why Then?

In 'Why 1955? Explaining the advent of rock music,' Richard Peterson discusses three influences that 'either singly or in combination' contribute to a musical shift: The arrival of the artist, changes in the composition of the audience, and the transformation of the commercial culture industry. Writing of the advent of rock 'n' roll in 1955, Peterson names Elvis as the emerging artist, the large segment of the population born post-World War II as the emerging audience, and details a variety of factors, including law, technology, and marketing that formed the milieu in which the artist met.[62]

The coming together of the political, social, cultural, and technological strands at play at a given time provides a useful model in examining Beatlemania. To paraphrase Peterson: why 1964?

Because the Beatles had been honing their musicianship, composition skills, and stagecraft, as well as their interpersonal relationships long before the public heard of them, the timing of Beatlemania bears examination.

Various explanations have been sought for the massive success of the Beatles first in their home port of Liverpool, then throughout the north of Britain and south to London, on the European continent, then to America, Canada, and Australasia in 1964.

The 'Baby Boom' Generation

Not only were there more teenagers than ever before due to the post-war baby boom (generally dated from 1946 to 1964), but they enjoyed more free time and spending power than their parents had during the Sinatra years, during the depression and the war, or during the Elvis years. The Beatles hit at the precise time the first of the "boomers," mostly in families of three or four children, were turning 18. They had the time, money, and sheer numbers to fuel Beatlemania – buying records, posters, magazines, bubble gum cards, and tickets to *A Hard Day's Night*. If they were lucky enough to live in a major city, the cost of a ticket to see them live in concert ran from $3.50 to $6.00.

Kennedy Assassination

One theory, often put forth and only occasionally disputed, argues that the USA was ripe for distraction due to the national mood following the

---

[62] Richard Peterson, "Why 1955? Explaining the Advent of Rock Music," *Journal of Popular Music*, 9, 1 (Jan. 1990), 97–116.

assassination of President Kennedy in late November 1963. "The country was in a collective depression, essentially," writes Steven Stark, "and to have these incredible fun and funny guys show up ... was incredibly energizing for people."[63]

The theory has found support throughout the years: "Is it giving the Beatles too much credit, forty years later ... to imagine them coming to our wounded country in its time of trouble, wearing their Arthurian haircuts and singing their songs of love and joy ... restoring our emotional health and happiness?"[64]

Ian MacDonald cited the healing effect of the Beatles: "When Capitol issued *I Want To Hold Your Hand*, the record's joyous energy and invention lifted America out of its gloom."[65]

Although an intriguing theory, it fails to explain the spread of Beatlemania throughout the rest of the world, which had not suffered the loss of a leader as the United States had.

Still, it must be acknowledged that, other than a contract for a television appearance, the Beatles had no success in America prior to the Kennedy assassination; some shift had taken place between the failure of "She Loves You" in the fall of 1963 and the success of "I Want To Hold Your Hand" at the beginning of 1964.

Why Them?

Biographers, historians, sociologists, psychologists, journalists, and authors in music, cultural studies, and marketing have speculated whether it was timing, clever marketing, astute management, talent, demographics, technology, media exposure, hard work, luck, or a combination of the above that created Beatlemania. While each would have its place in a pie chart, it is arguable that all of them contributed to the phenomenon.

New and Different

When Elvis went into the army, benign and acceptable teen idols filled the vacuum. As Chas Newby recalls:

> Elvis, Buddy Holly, Little Richard, Jerry Lee Lewis, and Chuck Berry had been replaced by the sanitized 'Bobbys' – Vee, Vinton, and Rydell. This effect had been transported to our side of the pond in the form of nice

---

[63] Stark, *Meet the Beatles*.
[64] Martin Goldsmith, *The Beatles Come to America* (New York: John Wiley, 2004), 4.
[65] Ian MacDonald, *Revolution in the Head*, 2nd edn (Vintage Books, 2009), 77.

clean-cut guys like Cliff Richard, backed on stage by instrumentalists doing mincing little dance steps in time to the music.[66]

These post-rock 'n' roll singers failed to excite girls or alarm parents in the extreme way the Beatles did.

The Foursome

Unlike solo artists Sinatra and Elvis, four Beatles offered a choice of personalities and looks that appealed to a wide range of girls in many countries.

The four were quickly labeled by the press and fans: Lennon the "smart one," McCartney the "cute one," Harrison the "quiet one," and Starr the "cuddly one." That Harrison had been ordered not to talk by the Plaza Hotel doctor who treated him for a throat infection, did not matter; Harrison had been "the quiet one" and would remain so.

In 1988, Starr explained the difference between the fans. "I had the mothers . . . and the children . . . George had the mystics. John had the intellectuals, the college attitudes, and Paul had the teenies. I feel that was one of our strengths. We were a band that was appealing to children and grandparents."[67]

The sense of equality was appealing to fans, the Beatles were four equal, yet distinctive individuals, their easy camaraderie and perceived friendship so evident in press conferences formed the plot for their first film, *A Hard Day's Night*, and served as the premise for the fabricated television group, the Monkees, in 1966.

The Beatles were irreverent, witty, and cheeky, especially compared to the rougher, yet polite Southern boys like Elvis and Jerry Lee Lewis. Beatles did not use "Sir" or "Ma'am" when responding to questions from the press. They were also educated: Lennon had attended art college, and McCartney and Harrison had attended one of the most prestigious schools in Liverpool, while Starr had a gift for quick-witted bon mots.

The Look and Style

Of course it was their hairstyles, variously described by the press as "mop-top" or "pudding bowl" that drew the most attention from both outraged parents and teachers, and teenaged boys, who soon began brushing their hair forward.

---

[66] Newby to Davis personal communication, September 3, 2018.
[67] "George Harrison and Ringo on Aspel & Co. 1988", *YouTube*, www.youtube.com/watch?v=JQaqcLPAI_s&t=788s.

Their fashion choices – collarless suits, velvet lapels, tapered pants, Cuban heels – were in sharp contrast to other entertainers in the era of V-neck sweaters and crew cuts, and set immediate trends.

Male Fans

Teenage girls were not the only fans; boys also played truant to greet the Beatles at JFK, following them into the city in cars. Footage of the first Sullivan appearance shows boys in the audience already sporting fringe. In Amsterdam boys were among the crowds lining the canal; one boy was plucked out as he swam out to their sightseeing barge. Male fans were filmed climbing in the rafters of an arena high above the audience at a German concert. A year later, boys at the Shea Stadium concert stood next to screaming girls; one broke through the barriers and ran across center field toward the stage before being apprehended by police. "I memorized every Beatle song and went to Shea Stadium and screamed right along with all those chicks," says Joe Walsh.[68]

"We were so innocent and along come the four nutty boys who said the funny things and said the crazy things," Prof. William McKeen, who teaches the history of rock music at Boston University, remembered.

Even older male fans copied the hairstyle, purchased instruments, and studied chord progressions. David Crosby, 22 in 1964, said he went to see *A Hard Day's Night* multiple times with Roger McGuinn and Gene Clark, going home and standing "in front of a mirror trying to figure out how to hold an electric guitar and play rock 'n' roll."[69]

The Media

The American press went to the group's first press conference intent on exposing them as empty-headed "mop-tops." Instead, they came away charmed by the flippant answers to their inane questions: "How many of you are bald?" "All of us" (McCartney). "Can you sing something?" "No, we need money first" (Lennon). "Do you plan to get a haircut while you are here?" "I had one yesterday" (Harrison). The surprising wit and aplomb with which the Beatles handled their press conferences amounted to a public relations coup.

[68] Cameron Crowe, "Rolling Stone #181: Joe Walsh," *The Uncool*, February 27, 1975, www.theuncool .com/journalism/rs181-joe-walsh/.
[69] "The Beatles: When a New Generation of Musicians Discovered Themselves," *CBS*, February 2, 2014, www.cbsnews.com/news/the-beatles-when-a-new-generation-of-musicians-discovered-them selves/.

As Tony Barrow had learned, members of the media clamoring for an interview, a quote, or a photograph became a powerful publicity engine. Reporters were eager to give them positive publicity, withholding anything negative.

The Community of Fans

The communal nature of fandom – of being able to talk to other fans in ways only a fellow Beatle fan could understand – played an important role in the mania. Linda Ihle told Dorian Lynskey:

> The idea of community and collectivity is important. It makes you feel like part of something larger. You're not by yourself. Individually, teenagers are isolated and worried and scared all the time of whether or not they're doing the right things and wearing the right clothes, but everybody liked the Beatles so everybody was equal. It didn't matter what your clothes were or where your parents worked; we were all in it together.[70]

Jan Myers, a Londoner writing about her experiences as a hardcore Beatles fan, told Lynskey: "We could stand outside Abbey Road for 16 hours and as long as one of them came and smiled or said something it was fine . . . I didn't smoke, I didn't drink, I was just obsessed. All I could think about was them."[71]

Emerging Feminism

Critic Barbara Ehrenreich posited a deeper meaning in a 1992 essay: "To abandon control – to scream, faint, dash about in mobs – was, in form if not in conscious intent, to protest the sexual repressiveness, the rigid double standard of female teen culture. It was the first and most dramatic uprising of women's sexual revolution."[72]

In a few years, the girls who screamed and fainted would be in college, protesting the Vietnam War, and a few years later, burning their bras.

Management and the Luck Factor

Shrewd management decisions alone cannot explain Beatlemania, nor can promotional efforts of Capitol. Vince Gilmore, vice president of Capitol

---

[70] Lynskey, "Beatlemania."   [71] Lynskey, "Beatlemania."
[72] Ehrenreich et al., "Beatlemania: Girls Just Want To Have Fun."

Records notes, "All the hype in the world isn't going to sell a bad product."[73]

Starr put particular emphasis on luck: "Things used to fall right for us as a band. We couldn't stop it. The gods were on our side ... things just fell into place."[74]

The Music

It started with the music and, for some, it all comes back to the songs. Of course, their talent cannot be ignored, nor can the contribution of EMI producer George Martin be overlooked.

Popular music in America was wide open and ready to receive new types of sounds and music in 1964. Rock, surf, folk, ballad, R&B, country, comedy, foreign language, and instrumental records all found a place at the top of the charts in 1963; no single genre was dominant when the Beatles had their first success in 1964.

The Grammy Award for Best Rock and Roll Record of the Year in 1963 was "Deep Purple," a Big Band-era tune reincarnated by a brother and sister duo; it also reached No. 1 on the Adult Contemporary Chart. The Grammy Association often misreads music trends, but it speaks volumes about the state of music for teenagers that the rock record of 1963 would also figure so prominently on the adult chart as 1964 dawned.

Popular music in America was not strictly American in 1964. A Belgian nun singing French, and a Japanese actor singing in his native tongue finished in the Top 10 best-selling records of 1963. Audiences were apparently ready, willing, and able to receive new artists, even those from as distant a place as a seaport in the northwest of England and with such a diversity of genres on the air, there could have been every reason to believe that "yeah, yeah, yeah" would find an audience. The range of artists having success in 1963 meant music was open to anyone – even an art college dropout and his mates.

Personal Lyrics and Joyful Music

"I was amazed the sheer musicality and The Beatles' ability to project what a confident, joyful and beautiful band they were. I'd never seen anything

---

[73] Hunter Davies, *The Beatles*, updated edn (New York: W. W. Norton, 2010).
[74] The Beatles, *The Beatles Anthology* (San Francisco: Chronicle Books, 2000).

like them before – or since. But, you know, it's always about the music. Those guys could really play and sing. They had the goods."[75]

By the time they finally made it, the Beatles were writing many of their own songs and lyrics in songs like "From Me To You," "I Want to Hold Your Hand," "Please Please Me," "If I Fell," "Thank You Girl," and "I'm Happy Just to Dance with You" created the perception of a personal connection for their female fans. Songs about rejection strengthened the bond as teenage girls found it impossible to believe anyone fortunate enough to actually meet, let alone date, a Beatle would reject them, imagining themselves as the perfect girl for their favorite Beatle.

Post-mania

Parents, teachers, and other adults, appalled by the scenes they saw on television and at home, assured themselves that Beatlemania would be a short-lived fad. They were wrong.

Beatlemania continued through at least three years of the group's massive exposure from 1963 through 1966 – avoiding overexposure despite countless television appearances, two films, and worldwide touring. It even survived boycotts and record burnings in the American south after John Lennon was quoted out of context noting that the group's popularity exceeded that of Christ, or at least organized religion. There had been death threats – among others, French-Canadian separatists threatened Starr and police sharpshooters were posted at the Forum in Montreal[76] and the deliberate manhandling of the Beatles' party by police and soldiers in Manila at the direction of the Marcos regime the same summer as the boycott served as the final straw and put an end to their touring.

After the Beatles stopped performing in 1966, the mania subsided, but did not abate altogether and any illusions the Beatles themselves may have had that it would be the end of Beatlemania eventually proved unfounded. Beatle sightings still drew attention and elicited excited reactions.

George Harrison's surprise appearance on the *Smothers Brothers Comedy Hour* television program on November 17, 1968 was received with shrieks and screams from the audience at the mere mention of the word "Beatle," as he was introduced. Only moments before, they had applauded politely

[75] Joe Bosso, *Guitars*, February 8, 2014.
[76] "Live: Forum, Montreal, Canada," *The Beatles Bible*, September 8, 1964, www.beatlesbible.com/1964/09/08/live-forum-montreal-canada.

at the announcement of Dion and Donovan, both at the top of the charts at the time.

More than two years after the Beatles had stopped touring, nearly five years after the first Sullivan appearance, fans who might have been thought too mature and "cool" to react as they had during the days of Beatlemania continued wild applause and screams until Harrison finally put his hands up, saying, "Quiet now, quiet please."

As the Beatles began their "studio years," some fans took on a near-reverential attitude toward the group. Dubbed *Apple Scruffs* by George Harrison in a song on his first solo album, *All Things Must Pass*, fans began taking up posts at Beatle locations – EMI Studios on Abbey Road, Paul McCartney's home nearby, and the Apple offices on Savile Row in the posh business area. These fans were a calm, Praetorian guard who, according to Harrison's lyric, stood "in the fog and in the rain," "flowers in hand," occasionally walking McCartney's dog, Martha, and even warning the Beatle when his fiancée, Jane Asher, drove up the street even as he was entertaining a female guest in the house.

Conclusion

More than fifty years later, interest, if not hysteria, continues, although audience reaction to sold-out Paul McCartney concerts around the world and across three generations are still loud, albeit without fainting. His appearance on James Corden's *Carpool Karaoke* in June 2018 drew so many viewers, CBS showed an expanded version in prime time. David Bianculli of National Public Radio wrote, "Fifty-four years after appearing on *The Ed Sullivan Show*, Paul McCartney is still making exciting, unforgettable television."

Ringo Starr's All Star Reviews are popular, as are numberless tribute bands and the long-running Cirque du Soleil production, LOVE, in Las Vegas.

Remastered and expanded issues of their albums *Sgt. Pepper's Lonely Hearts Club Band* and *The Beatles (The White Album)* are eagerly pre-ordered in the millions. Books, including this one, are published even after it could be presumed that everything there is to be said about the Beatles and Beatlemania has already been printed.

The Final Word

In criticizing the mania and the fans, Paul Johnson wrote, "The teenager comes not to hear but to participate in a ritual." Lynskey agrees, but offers a better definition of Beatlemania – the fans' screams were a "celebration of themselves, their freedom, their youth, their power. Screaming didn't drown out the performance: it was a performance."[77]

Perhaps it is best to give the final word to someone who experienced Beatlemania "in the eye of the hurricane." When asked how he would define Beatlemania, John Lennon said, "I couldn't define it. A lot of people have tried, I'm not going to try. Leave it to the psychologists and let them get it wrong."[78]

---

[77] Lynskey, "Beatlemania."
[78] "Beatles Los Angeles Press Conference 1966," *YouTube*, www.youtube.com/watch? v=O8MgItRRaTo&t=6s.

CHAPTER 9

The End of the Road: The Beatles' Decision to Stop Touring

David Venturo

On Monday, August 29, 1966, the Beatles performed before about 24,000 fans at Candlestick Park, home of the baseball Giants and football Forty-Niners, in San Francisco, California. Sales were brisk but demand was not as great as during the 1965 North American tour. Approximately 8,000 tickets went unsold. As the concert closed, John Lennon told the crowd, "See you again next year." When the Beatles' chartered American Airlines flight left San Francisco for Los Angeles later that evening, however, George Harrison remarked to the band's publicist, Tony Barrow, "That's it. I'm not a Beatle anymore." Harrison, of course, remained a member of the group until it disbanded in April 1970. Still, the Beatles' circumstances had changed in the spring and summer of 1966. Though none of them would have predicted it that night, the band had just finished its last paid, public concert. When the Beatles returned to London on Wednesday, August 31, John, Paul, George, and Ringo were all planning to spend time apart, pursuing individual projects. Never before had the Beatles sought such a respite from each other. When they returned to EMI Studios in St. John's Wood on November 24, though, they seemed eager to regroup. What happened that spring and summer to shake the Beatles' previous camaraderie and how had their experience changed them as they began recording the songs that evolved into *Sgt. Pepper's Lonely Hearts Club Band*?[1]

   The year 1966 was a time of musical growth and critical acclaim for the Beatles punctuated by a series of unsettling confrontations. The acclaim, of course, arose from the recording of *Revolver*. Bob Dylan, listening in May 1966 to acetates of songs (including "Tomorrow Never Knows") from the in-progress album quipped to John and Paul, "Oh, I get it. You don't want to be cute anymore."[2] Dylan, though perhaps speaking bitingly, was right.

[1] Steve Turner, *Beatles '66: The Revolutionary Year* (New York: HarperCollins, 2016), 309–12.
[2] Turner, *Beatles '66*, 175–77.

Instead of the joys and sorrows of teenaged love, the Beatles now addressed everything from Britain's graduated income tax ("Taxman") to a physician known for injecting celebrity patients with amphetamine "speedballs" ("Dr. Robert") to the moral emptiness of everyday life and institutions ("Eleanor Rigby"). Tying the album together were music and lyrics inflected by psychedelic experience ("I'm Only Sleeping," "She Said She Said," "Got to Get You Into My Life," "Tomorrow Never Knows") and doubts about Western values ("Love You To," "I Want to Tell You"). The confrontations occurred during the Beatles' tours of Japan, the Philippines, and North America in June, July, and August 1966. By 1966, the lovable mop-tops of 1964 and 1965 – "the boys" as depicted in the films *A Hard Day's Night* and *Help!* – no longer existed. Instead, the Beatles had become avatars of an emerging counterculture, which questioned traditional attitudes toward religion, authority, the family, work, and gender roles. Consequently, they began to be viewed by the political and religious right as threats to established order who had to be put in their place. Extreme Japanese nationalists, an authoritarian Philippine president and his wife, and American evangelicals and their rather surprising allies-of-the-moment in the mainstream US media, all challenged the Beatles in 1966. Despite the buffetings, however, and a three-month retreat from public view, the Beatles reappeared late in the year stronger and more creatively invigorated than ever.

From the beginning, the Beatles' manager, Brian Epstein, assiduously urged them against publicly expressing political and other controversial opinions that might alienate fans and depress record and ticket sales. For the most part, the Beatles complied. They said little to reporters about opposing the Vietnam War, for example, though they made known their support of the American civil rights movement as early as August 1964, insisting they would not perform that September at the Gator Bowl in Jacksonville, Florida, unless the city government desegregated the seating.[3] By 1966, however, the Beatles were more forthcoming. That winter, Maureen Cleave, who wrote the "Disc Date" music column for the London *Evening Standard* newspaper, interviewed the four band members and Brian Epstein for a series of one-page sketches to be titled "How Does a Beatle Live?" and published on consecutive Fridays from March 4 through April 1. John, George, and Ringo had all recently moved to the wealthy stockbroker belt in Surrey County, and it was rumored that the

---

[3] Larry Kane, *Ticket to Ride: Inside the Beatles' 1964 Tour That Changed the World* (Philadelphia: Running Book Press, 2003), 39–40, 110–12.

Beatles and their interests were maturing. Paul had purchased a townhouse near EMI Studios in north London, after living for years in a room in his fiancée Jane Asher's parents' house on Wimpole Street. Cleave was born in India in 1934, where her father was a major in the British Indian Army. Her mother was Irish, and she was raised primarily in Ireland. She read history at St. Anne's College, Oxford, and worked as a features writer for the *Standard* after her hiring in 1959. Cleave had known the Beatles since 1963, and liked them, especially John, whom she had challenged (successfully) to rewrite some of the lyrics to "Help!"[4]

The essay on Lennon is sympathetic and psychologically astute. Cleave spent a whole day with him, first at his mock Tudor mansion in Weybridge, then riding to London with him in his chauffeur-driven, amenities-filled Rolls-Royce, and finally at several city venues including the high-end store Asprey's and Brian Epstein's office, where Cleave and Lennon bantered with Epstein's assistant, Wendy Hanson, before heading back to Weybridge. Cleave's tale of John Lennon could have been inspired by Samuel Johnson's little eighteenth-century storybook, *Rasselas, Prince of Abissinia, or, The Choice of Life.* Like Johnson's Rasselas, a son of the king of Abissinia, Lennon is faced with the challenge of filling up the vacuities of his existence. Rasselas, at 26, almost the same age as Lennon, lives in a kind of secular Eden called the Happy Valley, where his every need is instantly met. Though he has everything, however, he still suffers from what Johnson calls "that hunger of imagination which preys incessantly upon life."[5] He is a man whose fertile, restless mind always longs for more – for something beyond the material satisfactions of life. The same is true of Cleave's Lennon. Taking her on a tour of his house, he shows her some of his favorite possessions: a suit of armor (named Stanley), a room full of tiny, scale-model electric racing cars, eight little green boxes lit with flashing red lights, a fruit machine, a full-sized gorilla suit, a huge altar crucifix, an enormous Bible. Next come bigger items: tape recorders, five television sets, telephones with numbers Lennon does not know, a Rolls-Royce, a Mini-Cooper, a Ferrari, and, finally, a grand swimming pool. None of these things satisfies, even the beautifully bound books (kept in a special room) that John enjoys reading. Although "[f]amous and loaded" (his words), Lennon confesses an emptiness: "You see, there's something else I'm going to do, something I must do – only I don't know what it is.

---

[4] Steve Turner, *The Gospel According to the Beatles* (Louisville: Westminster John Knox Press, 2006), 18–21; Turner, *Beatles '66*, 75–77.
[5] Samuel Johnson, *Rasselas and Other Tales*, vol. 16 of the *Yale Edition of the Works of Samuel Johnson*, ed. Gwin J. Kolb (New Haven: Yale University Press, 1990), 118.

That's why I go round painting and taping and drawing and writing and that, because it may be one of them." This is the essence of John's character – what makes him tick.

Less central to Cleave's chief point are two paragraphs that appear early in the essay. In the first, Lennon praises Indian music, to which George Harrison had introduced him: "Are you listening? This music is thousands of years old; it makes me laugh, the British going over there and telling them what to do. Quite amazing." The succeeding paragraph seems to take up the same theme, contrasting the ancient East and the Johnny-come-lately West. Lennon expresses his doubts about the staying power of Christianity, which he may have been comparing to the much longer-lived Hinduism: "'Christianity will go,' he said. 'It will vanish and shrink. I needn't argue about that; I'm right and I will be proved right. We're more popular than Jesus now; I don't know which will go first – rock 'n' roll or Christianity.'" Lennon then opines, "Jesus was all right but his disciples were thick and ordinary. It's them twisting it that ruins it for me." Cleave closes the paragraph matter-of-factly, "He is reading extensively about religion."[6]

The essay caused little stir in Britain. The following Monday, biographer John Grigg in his *Guardian* column wryly noted that Christianity had been "in the charts" for two millennia, and one *Evening Standard* reader in a letter to the editor groused that he was "nauseated" by John's opinions – but mostly by Lennon's revelation that he did not like his grifter-drifter father Fred, who had opportunistically reappeared in his son's life after deserting the family twenty years before.[7] When Maureen Cleave rewrote her four Beatles interviews, including John's Jesus comment, for a longer feature published in the Sunday, July 3, *New York Times Magazine*, no outrage ensued, either.

Lennon later revealed that his thoughts about Jesus and the "thick and ordinary" disciples were inspired by reading Hugh Schonfield's *The Passover Plot* (1965), which speculates that Jesus purposely tried to fulfill the prophecies in the Hebrew Bible in order to become a real-world messiah.[8] Aided by Joseph of Arimathea, he tried to fake his death by crucifixion. Unfortunately, according to Schonfield, a British-Jewish

---

[6] Maureen Cleave, "How Does a Beatle Live? John Lennon Lives Like This," *London Evening Standard*, March 4, 1966, 10. Repr. in *Read the Beatles: Classic and New Writings on the Beatles, Their Legacy, and Why They Still Matter*, ed. June Skinner Sawyers (New York: Penguin, 2006), 87–91.

[7] Turner, *The Gospel According to the Beatles*, 21.

[8] Hugh J. Schonfield, *The Passover Plot: New Light on the History of Jesus* (London: Hutchinson, 1965).

religious scholar who had worked on the Dead Sea Scrolls, a Roman soldier speared Jesus in the side and he bled to death. John identified with the notion of Jesus as a real man, probably with a charismatic personality, forced into a messianic role by adoring disciples. (In 1978, George Harrison funded the production of Monty Python's comedy *The Life of Brian* about a similarly reluctant messiah, after EMI Films withdrew support just as filming was to begin.) On their 1964 and 1965 world tours, Lennon incorporated a messianic-papal benediction into the repertoire of gestures that he delivered to adoring crowds from hotel and city hall balconies.[9] Moreover, he was rattled by people who regarded him and his fellow Beatles as faith healers, who could, with a touch, cure the sick and disabled. (The British Crown had ended its practice of faith healing when Queen Anne died in 1714.) Indeed, the Beatles and their two roadies, Neil Aspinall and Mal Evans, developed a code when they wished to avoid such encounters. "Crips," short for "cripples," someone would whisper, and the Beatles would scatter.

Beatles' management so liked Cleave's Lennon essay that, the day after the *Evening Standard* ran it, NEMS publicist Tony Barrow mailed a clipped copy to Art Unger, editor and publisher of the American teen magazine *Datebook*, hoping that he would reprint the series. *Datebook* had a good reputation; it featured thoughtful articles on topics such as Ku Klux Klan violence, the struggle for civil rights, and interracial dating, as well as more conventional ones on pop performers and teen life. Unger accepted the invitation.[10]

While these events unfolded, few people on either side of the Atlantic connected with the Beatles seemed to notice that on Friday, April 8, *Time* magazine published a cover story, its headline boldly printed in large red letters on a black background: "Is God Dead?" The story questioned the relevance of a traditional God in the contemporary world. Such concerns were widespread in the revolutionary 1960s. Even the Roman Catholic Church, that most conservative of religious institutions, had recently faced the scrutiny of the Second Vatican Council (1962–65), under the auspices of Popes John XXIII and Paul VI, the most sweeping review of that church since the Council of Trent (1545–63). The *Time* story with its provocative cover attracted 3,421 replies, the most in the magazine's history, many of them outraged and indignant.[11]

* * *

---

[9] Jonathan Gould, *Can't Buy Me Love: The Beatles, Britain, and America* (New York: Random House, 2007), 341.

[10] Turner, *The Gospel According to the Beatles*, 23–24.

[11] Lily Rothman, "Is God Dead? At 50," *Time*, http://time.com/isgoddead/.

The Beatles' 1964 and 1965 international concert tours were remarkably friendly affairs. The band and its small entourage were welcomed virtually everywhere they traveled. Sometimes, as in Adelaide, Australia, the reception bordered on adulation. That changed in 1966 with visits to Japan, the Philippines, and North America, where the Beatles' cheerful, cheeky indifference to tradition and convention met resistance. In Hamburg, the Beatles received a telegram, warning them not to fly to Tokyo, where they were scheduled to perform five concerts between June 30 and July 2. It turned out that not all young people liked John, Paul, George, and Ringo. Student extremists – right-wing nationalists – regarded the Beatles as a sink of foreign decadence, a threat to traditional Japanese values. Some hoped to kidnap the Beatles and cut their hair. Others wanted to shoot them. Many were offended because they considered the Nippon Budokan, built for the 1964 Summer Olympics and site of the concerts, a shrine to Japanese martial arts. Western rock 'n' roll, they believed, desecrated the place. The police kept the Beatles bottled up for their own safety in the Tokyo Hilton. John and Paul each managed to sneak out briefly with a roadie, only to be returned to the hotel. The police, fearing snipers, patrolled the concerts with binoculars; they kept the fans seated and the band on a stage atop an eight-foot-high podium. The Beatles spent most of their free time between concerts in the hotel, painting pictures.[12]

Things got worse in the Philippines. Although the Beatles were there only from July 3rd to 5th – just over 48 hours – the whole visit was fraught. The band was scheduled to play two concerts – at 4:00 pm and 8:30 pm – at Rizal Memorial Stadium on July 4, the twentieth anniversary of Philippine independence from the USA. Filipino First Lady Imelda Marcos and her husband, President Ferdinand Marcos, had invited the Beatles to a reception for 300 children (including their own three) at 11:00 am on Independence Day at Malacañang Palace, the presidential residence. Brian Epstein had declined on behalf of the band when they were in Tokyo, but Mrs. Marcos refused to take no for an answer. Indeed, the Manila *Times* newspaper published an article on July 3 anticipating the event. On the morning of July 4, uniformed men from the presidential palace demanded that the Beatles come with them: "This is not a request. We have our orders." Epstein and the Beatles refused, even when confronted by the concert promoter and ranking representatives of the Manila Police and Philippine Constabulary.

---

[12] See Turner, *Beatles '66*, 222–40.

Although Ferdinand Marcos was not yet known as a ruthless autocrat who murdered political opponents (such as Benigno Aquino), or Imelda Marcos as the profligate owner of thousands of pairs of shoes, the repercussions against the Beatles were swift and harsh. By late afternoon, television news reports featured footage of crying children stood up by the Beatles. Brian Epstein filmed an apology for the state-owned television station, but the broadcast signal was jammed when the apology aired. No one could understand what Epstein said. Epstein and his NEMS colleague Vic Lewis were compelled, it seems, to hand over the Beatles' concert fees to government officials. The next day, the Beatles and their small entourage had to carry their own equipment through Manila Airport and up escalators that the airport manager had ordered turned off. Epstein, Lennon, and Starr were punched and thugs beat and kicked roadie Mal Evans and chauffeur Alf Bicknell. The plane was then stopped on the tarmac and Mal Evans and Tony Barrow were ordered off because their passports were not in order. Evans, in tears, told the Beatles to tell his wife, Lil, that he loved her: he was afraid the authorities might kill him. When Barrow and Evans returned to the plane, the KLM flight departed for Delhi, India, on the way back to London. Lewis and Epstein quarreled loudly about the concert fees. After the Beatles left, Ferdinand Marcos publicly lied, denying any role in harassing them.[13]

The worst, however, happened a month later in the USA. Art Unger, *Datebook* editor and publisher, in late July sent advance copies of the September "Shout-Out" issue, featuring Maureen Cleave's John Lennon and Paul McCartney interviews, to conservative disc jockeys in the Deep South. Lennon's comment, "I don't know which will go first – rock 'n' roll or Christianity!" and Paul's deploring that "anyone black" in the United States is regarded as "a dirty nigger," were on the cover. Doug Layton and Tommy Charles, morning DJs and owners of thousand-watt Birmingham, Alabama, AM radio station WAQY (Wacky Radio) took the Lennon bait. (No one touched McCartney's racism charge.) On the air on Friday, July 29, Layton told Charles that John Lennon had said, "We're more popular than Jesus." Charles replied, "Oh, that does it for me. I'm not playing the Beatles anymore." Both hosts encouraged fans to drop off Beatles records at WAQY for a huge bonfire on August 19, when the band was scheduled to perform in Memphis. (The bonfire never occurred.) So began the American John Lennon–Jesus controversy, with an impromptu exchange and proposal. It might have died in Birmingham, however, if Alvin Benn,

---

[13] See Turner, *Beatles '66*, 240–54; Gould, *Can't Buy Me Love*, 338–39.

Birmingham's young bureau chief for wire service United Press International had not heard the exchange. He knew Layton and Charles and their "abrasive skits" and called them for comment. Sunday, July 31, his story on the Beatles bonfire and boycott ran. On August 2, Benn filed a second story. The Associated Press picked it up on August 4. The UPI report spread to Atlanta, then to New York and overseas.[14] On Friday, August 5, the Beatles boycott made the front page of the *New York Times*. Meanwhile, radio stations around the country heard of the Birmingham boycott. A smattering of stations nationwide joined.

The resulting echo chamber magnified the story. Evangelicals outraged by criticism of Jesus, their souls' gateway to eternal salvation, coupled with expanding press, radio, and television coverage of the story, meant that when the Beatles arrived in Chicago for the start of their North American tour on Thursday, August 11, a large contingent of reporters met the band at the Astor Towers Hotel in Chicago. The reporters, most of them quite cosmopolitan and with no personal investment in evangelicalism, repeatedly pressed a shaken Lennon, who felt that he had nothing for which to apologize, to apologize for his comment. A second news conference extracted a second apology the next day. Reporters did not pursue McCartney, whose new song, "Eleanor Rigby," expressed sentiments similar to John's about the state of Christianity. As Father McKenzie wipes the dirt from his hands after Rigby's burial, we learn that the ritual was empty: "No one was saved." Over the next few weeks, the reaction to John's comment continued, capped by a Ku Klux Klan demonstration outside the Memphis Arena where the Beatles performed twice on August 19, and a frightening moment during the second show when a concertgoer threw a firecracker on the stage. The Beatles at first thought that someone had shot at them. Around the world, some of the most authoritarian countries banned Beatles records: Franco's fascist Spain, apartheid South Africa, and one-party, right-wing Mexico. Oddly, the American media mostly found itself on the wrong side of a free speech debate.[15]

* * *

When the band left San Francisco on August 29, it is no wonder that they sought time off. The summer of 1966 had tried the Beatles and their

---

[14] On Alvin Benn's role in the controversy, see his memoir essay Alvin Benn, "First Person: John Lennon's Jesus Comments 50 Years Ago Sparked Blaze," *UPI*, www.upi.com/Top_News/US/2016/03/04/First-person-John-Lennons-Jesus-comments-50-years-ago-sparked-blaze/3351456764892/.

[15] See Turner, *The Gospel According to the Beatles*, 24–36; Turner, *Beatles '66*, 263–312; Gould, *Can't Buy Me Love*, 336–47.

entourage. When John left for Almería, Spain, for the filming of Dick Lester's anti-war satire, *How I Won the War*, he acquired a Spanish acoustic guitar. In Spain, far from home, with time on his hands between scene takes, Lennon soothed and reoriented himself by working on a song grounded in his Liverpool childhood. Return by memory to one's childhood was a familiar Romantic artistic gesture. Poets such as William Wordsworth and W. B. Yeats, and novelists including James Joyce had done so before. John began his song by trying to recapture the innocence and confusion of childhood. He called it "Not Too Bad," and set it in a special place where he had played as a boy, scrambling over the walls with friends, where he could hide from Aunt Mimi, smoke "ciggies," and indulge his imagination.[16] The place? A Salvation Army orphanage named Strawberry Field.

---

[16] Barry Miles, *Paul McCartney:Many Years From Now* (New York: Henry Holt, 1997), 306–07.

PART III

The Beatles on TV, Film, and the Internet

From Juke Box Jury to The Ed Sullivan Show: Radio and TV – the Beatles' "Star-Making Machinery"

Al Sussman

In the twenty-first century, there are myriad ways for a fledgling rock band to gain exposure and promote itself. The band can set up its own website or take advantage of the new world of social media. If the band is signed to a record company, a grand strategy may be explored, in the hope of getting the band exposure on radio stations whose formats are compatible with the band's music and on streaming services like Spotify or Google Music, among many others, as well as visual exposure via YouTube and hopefully even cable or network television and more.

Virtually none of this "star-making machinery" existed in early 1962, when a young band from Liverpool, England, called the Beatles was trying to become known beyond its home while the band's new manager, Brian Epstein, was trying to secure the group a recording contract. For instance, the only national television vehicle in the UK for what was generally called "pop music" in 1962 was *Thank Your Lucky Stars*, produced by ABC (Associated British Corporation) Television for the country's only national commercial outlet, ITV (Independent Television). The Beatles would not make it to *Thank Your Lucky Stars* until January 1963.

Opportunities for exposure via radio were only marginally better. Unlike the USA and Canada, with their many local Top 40 stations and popular disc jockeys, the only venue for hearing popular music in the UK was the staid, venerable British Broadcasting Corporation's Light Programme network. In his definitive book on the Beatles' performances for the BBC, *The Beatles: The BBC Archives*, Kevin Howlett describes the UK radio listening landscape:

> Satisfying a teenage desire for rock 'n' roll was not seen by the BBC as "raising public taste." Instead, it ignored what it considered primitive music in the hope that it might go away. Only the Light Programme occasionally

allowed rock 'n' roll into your home. Perhaps a request for The Crickets' "That'll Be The Day" would be selected for *Two Way Family Favorites* – if you were lucky. When the Light did feature a whole programme of popular music, because of Musician Union restrictions, records were usually side-lined for emasculated renditions of hits performed by old-fashioned dance bands. There was no local radio, no land-based commercial radio. The only alternative to the BBC was a crackling, phasing Radio Luxembourg trans-mitted from that country at night.[1]

By early 1962, the Light Programme had added a weekday half-hour spot for pop and rock 'n' roll at 5:00 pm called *Teenagers Turn*, which was made up of five individual shows. The Beatles, who had just recently been turned down for a recording contract by Decca Records, were able to secure a BBC audition that February, which led to a spot on the Thursday *Teenagers Turn* show *Here We Go*. The Beatles' radio debut came on the March 8, 1962 edition of *Here We Go*. On a show that also included Brad Newman, The Trad Lads, and the Northern Dance Orchestra (under the direction of no less than Bernard Hermann), the Beatles performed three songs, recorded the day before at Manchester's Playhouse Theatre. All were cover versions, Chuck Berry's "Memphis Tennessee," The Marvelettes' recent hit "Please Mr. Postman," and Roy Orbison's then-current release "Dream Baby."

Following their third extended season of dates in Hamburg, this time at the Star-Club, the Beatles returned to *Here We Go* on June 15, performing a John Lennon–Paul McCartney composition, "Ask Me Why," for the first time on radio, as well as Joe Brown's then-current hit "A Picture Of You" and the pop chestnut "Bésame Mucho." By October 1962 much had happened to the Beatles. They had secured a recording contract with EMI but had also dropped their drummer, Pete Best, replacing him with the more-capable-and-personable Ringo Starr. A crew from Granada Television had filmed the group at the Cavern in Liverpool just a few days after Starr joined the band, though the film would not be aired for over a year. And a pair of early September sessions at EMI's London studios produced the Beatles' debut single, "Love Me Do"/"P.S. I Love You."

Here is where the meager star-making apparatus of that era comes into play. To promote the single to a hopefully wide audience, the Beatles appeared before a studio audience on the EMI-sponsored *The Friday Spectacular* on Radio Luxembourg, recorded on October 8 at EMI House in London's Manchester Square, the scene of the photo shoot for

[1] Kevin Howlett, *The Beatles: The BBC Archives* (London: BBC Books, 2013), 21.

their first album a few months later, for broadcast that Friday night. The group was interviewed and both sides of the single were aired before the Beatles left for a round of interviews with freelance journalists and the pop weeklies to promote the single. Five days after the EMI broadcast, the Beatles made a belated TV debut on *People and Places,* a Granada TV show recorded in Granada's Manchester studios and aired in the north of England, performing "Love Me Do" and also Richie Barrett's "Some Other Guy," which they had performed at the Cavern for the unaired Granada filming in August.

On October 25, the Beatles were back at the Playhouse Theatre in Manchester for their first BBC radio appearance since recording their first single. They performed both sides, plus the recently popular film and stage title song "A Taste Of Honey" and Tommy Roe's current hit "Sheila." Four days later, it was back to Granada's *People and Places* and performances of "Love Me Do" and "A Taste Of Honey," which the group would soon record for their first LP. After another two weeks at the Star-Club in Hamburg, the Beatles returned to EMI House in London for another appearance on EMI's *The Friday Spectacular,* another interview, and another airing of both sides of their single. And, on November 27, they recorded another BBC radio appearance, this one in London and for the Tuesday afternoon *The Talent Spot,* once again performing both sides of their single and their rocked-up cover of the '62 Isley Brothers hit that would climax their first LP and become the band's live showstopper, "Twist And Shout." In December, they made three more local TV appearances to promote the single: on Television Wales/ITV's *Discs a Gogo* on December 3, Associated Rediffusion/ITV's *Tuesday Rendezvous* the next day, and a third appearance on Granada's *People and Places* on December 17.

For all of that activity, plus the group's usual round of gigs at the Cavern and other venues, primarily in the north of England, "Love Me Do" squeaked into the Record Retailer Top 20, peaking at No. 17, and the Beatles received a "don't call us, we'll call you" response to a November 23 audition for BBC-TV. Not exactly a harbinger of things to come.

Three days later, though, they recorded their second single, "Please Please Me"/"Ask Me Why," which would be released on January 11, 1963, after the Beatles had returned from a final two-week Hamburg engagement at the Star-Club and a very short, wintry tour of Scotland, shortly before embarking on their first national tour, albeit at the bottom of a bill headed by teenage hit-maker Helen Shapiro. Two days after the release of "Please Please Me," the Beatles lip-synced the record for their national TV debut on *Thank Your Lucky Stars*, which aired across most of England six nights later, and mimed both sides of the single on January 16 for a fourth appearance on Granada's *People and Places*. The same night, the band recorded another appearance on the BBC's *Here We Go* that would air on January 25. For that show, they performed both sides of the new single, plus the Cookies' recent Gerry Goffin–Carole King-written US hit "Chains."

With the Helen Shapiro tour fast approaching, radio promotion for "Please Please Me" began in earnest in late January. On January 21, they made a third visit to London's EMI House for a taping of EMI's *The Friday Spectacular*, which would air on January 25. The next day, they made a similar promotional stop at the BBC Light Programme's *Pop Inn* and then recorded their first appearance on the Beeb's very popular Saturday morning pop music show *Saturday Club*, hosted by Brian Matthew, who also MC'd *Thank Your Lucky Stars* and would host more Beatles radio and TV appearances than anyone else, in England or America. Over the course of the two-hour show, which aired on the morning of January 26, the Beatles could be heard performing both of their singles, plus "Some Other Guy," Little Eva's recent hit "Keep Your Hands Off My Baby," and a rocked-up treatment of Stephen Foster's "Beautiful Dreamer," none of which would be recorded for the Beatles' original EMI catalog. Following the *Saturday Club* session, the group also recorded an appearance for January 29 on, once again, *The Talent Spot*, on which they would perform both sides of their new single, plus, once again, "Some Other Guy."

The payoff for all of this radio/TV activity was much better than for "Love Me Do." In its fourth week on the pop paper *Melody Maker*'s chart, "Please Please Me" reached the Top 10 and, by the first week in March, had fulfilled producer George Martin's prediction and had become the Beatles' first No. 1 record, on all the charts except for Record Retailer's. Even as "Please Please Me" was climbing the UK charts, on February 11, the Beatles and George Martin convened in EMI's Studio Two for what would be a ten-hour session to record the ten non-singles tracks for the group's first LP, an album that would be released on March 22 and spend much of the spring, all of the summer, and most of the fall of 1963 as Britain's No. 1 album.

Meanwhile, on February 7, Vee-Jay Records in Chicago released the single of "Please Please Me"/"Ask Me Why," albeit crediting the record to "The Beattles" in the first ads for the disc and on the first pressings. Hollywood-based Capitol Records was EMI's US subsidiary and so had right of first refusal on any EMI releases and the man who made those calls at Capitol was Dave Dexter. The big bands/jazz-bred Dexter had already rejected "Love Me Do" for US release on Capitol in the fall of 1962 and did the same with "Please Please Me" so, through counsel Paul Marshall, Vee-Jay was pitched "Please Please Me." Since the mainly R&B-based label had enjoyed recent pop success with the Four Seasons and Frank Ifield, it really had nothing to lose in releasing this single by a British rock band.

In America, this was the era when the nighttime DJ on Top 40 radio stations wielded a good amount of power, though not as much as before the 1959–60 payola scandal, and was something of a tastemaker. On Chicago's leading Top 40 station, WLS, the nighttime personality was Dick Biondi and, not surprisingly, one of his Chicago record business friends was Vee-Jay's president Ewart Abner. Abner pitched the Beatles record to Biondi. Better than half a century later, Biondi is still on the air in Chicago and recalls that he may have played "Please Please Me" as early as the day after its US release. Just over a month later, in the week of March 15, "Please Please Me" reached its peak on WLS's survey at No. 35 and got a smattering of airplay in some smaller markets but did not make any of the national charts.

Meanwhile, back in the UK, the Beatles were still promoting "Please Please Me," which they lip-synced for their second appearance on *Thank Your Lucky Stars*, though they were third on the show's bill this time. That appearance was recorded on February 17 for telecast on February 23. In between, on February 20, they performed their two A-sides at London's Playhouse Theatre for the BBC Light Programme's *Parade Of The Pops*. With "Please Please Me" having just hit No. 1 on most charts, the Beatles and Epstein did a lengthy live interview for the UK news magazine *ABC At Large* on March 2, three days before the band recorded its third single and, very soon, second No. 1, "From Me To You"/"Thank You Girl."

In 1963, the single was still the music business' currency of choice, while albums were often treated like bad pennies. The Beatles would be at the vanguard of permanently changing that attitude as the 1960s progressed but album showcases on radio and TV were still years, if not decades, away. To promote their debut LP, then, the Beatles had to resort to the broadcast vehicles they had been using to promote their first two singles. Thus, the day after recording their third single, they were back at London's Playhouse Theatre for their fifth and final appearance on the BBC Light Programme's *Here We Go*, performing three tracks from the *Please Please Me* LP, plus the title song, though the album's leadoff track, "I Saw Her Standing There," was clipped from the broadcast on March 12. Next up was the beginning of a new tour, headed up by the recent American hit-makers Tommy Roe and

Chris Montez and a fourth and final appearance on EMI's *The Friday Spectacular* on Radio Luxembourg, once again promoting their chart-topping second single.

With that No. 1 single in hand and with their formerly lengthy sets from their club and ballroom dates now whittled down to a few songs as part of a package tour show, the Beatles began using their increasing number of BBC radio appearances not only to promote their new records but also to stretch out and dip into their club repertoire. For instance, for the band's live appearance on *Saturday Club* on March 16, they performed three songs from the *Please Please Me* LP, including the title song, plus Chuck Berry's "Too Much Monkey Business" and "I'm Talking About You" and Chan Romero's "The Hippy Hippy Shake," a Liverpool beat club standard that the Merseyside band the Swinging Blue Jeans would take into the UK Top 5 and the US Top 25 nearly a year later. That was followed by a more mundane three-song LP promotional spot the following Thursday for the Beeb's *On The Scene*.

On April 1, the same day the Beatles were awarded a Silver Disc for sales of "Please Please Me," they did a lengthy session to record a pair of guest spots on the popular BBC Light Programme show *Side By Side*. Besides performing the pop standard show theme with the show's band, the Karl Denver Trio, the Beatles performed five songs from the new LP and, for the first time, "From Me To You," which was slated to be released eleven days before the show's April 22 broadcast. The second taping was for a May 13 broadcast of *Side By Side*, with the group performing three songs from the *Please Please Me* LP, plus both "From Me To You" and "Thank You Girl" and Little Richard's "Long Tall Sally," a longtime favorite from their club repertoire and a song that would become the show-closer for Beatles concerts for much of their touring career. For a third *Side By Side* taping on April 4, the group performed "Love Me Do," "From Me To You," and Ringo Starr's *Please Please Me* solo track "*Boys*," plus Chuck Berry's "Too Much Monkey Business" and a Lennon–McCartney song that they had given to Billy J. Kramer but which the Beatles never recorded or performed again, "I'll Be On My Way."

On April 3, they were back at the Playhouse Theatre for a taping of the Beeb's *Easy Beat*, for which the band performed "Please Please Me," "From Me To You," and the LP track "Misery" for broadcast on April 7. In addition, Lennon and McCartney participated in a record review segment not unlike the very popular BBC TV show *Juke Box Jury*. This flurry of advance tapings was done with the Beatles' accelerating touring schedule in mind. Next came appearances to promote "From Me To You," on the

BBC's *Pop Inn* and Rediffusion TV's *Tuesday Rendezvous* on April 9, the national BBC TV program *The 6:25 Show* on April 13 (for broadcast three nights later), their third appearance on *Thank Your Lucky Stars* on April 14 (for airing on April 20), and Granada TV's *Scene At 6:30* on April 16.

The payoff for this round of promotional work was swift and spectacular. By the first week in May, the Beatles had the No. 1 single on all of the charts with "From Me To You" and the No. 1 LP with *Please Please Me*. A band that had begun 1963 in virtual anonymity in much of England was now top of the pops throughout the nation. An indication of how popular the Beatles were becoming was their inclusion in one of a series of BBC concerts at the prestigious Royal Albert Hall called *Swinging Sound '63*. Part of a crowded bill, they appeared in each of two halves of the show, performing "Please Please Me" and "Misery" in the first half and "From Me To You" and "Twist And Shout" in the second. An even bigger indicator came on April 21. The Beatles had barely placed on the *New Musical Express* year-end poll but, with one No. 1 single and about to have a second and a No. 1 debut LP, they were added to the annual *NME* Poll-Winners' Concert before a crowd of 10,000 at Wembley's Empire Pool. Interestingly slotted just before the headlining Cliff Richard and the Shadows, they performed their two hit singles plus their two most popular live numbers, "Twist And Shout" and "Long Tall Sally." The Beatles would be the *NME* concert headliners the next three years. And, on May 11, the band taped their first headlining appearance on *Thank Your Lucky Stars,* lip-syncing "From Me To You" and "I Saw Her Standing There" for the telecast the following Saturday evening.

That evening, the Beatles began their third nationwide tour of Britain, this time second on the bill, ahead of Liverpool's Gerry & the Pacemakers but behind the headlining Roy Orbison, one of the group's great musical heroes. Quickly, though, despite Orbison's onstage magnetism, the growing fan hysteria during the Beatles' seven-song set caused them to be made the closing act and Orbison to begin talking up the group as a potential star act in America. Unfortunately, in the United States, there was no indication that Orbison might be right in his feelings about the possibility of the Beatles making it in America. On May 6, Vee-Jay released "From Me To You" as a single and it took some two months before the record struggled to No. 116 on *Billboard*'s singles chart. Another American hit-maker, Del Shannon, had taken a liking to "From Me To You" when he saw the group perform it at the BBC's *Swinging Sound '63* show. Shannon would soon record the song, the first American to cover a Beatles song, and his version, which would reach No. 77 on *Billboard*'s Hot 100 and No. 67 on Cash

Box's singles chart in July, may have helped the original to reach the "bubbling under" regions of *Billboard*'s chart.

Another assist in the relative American "success" of "From Me To You" came from Dick Biondi, who had been fired by WLS in May but was soon picked up by the popular Los Angeles Top 40 station KRLA. Once there, Biondi talked his new program director into adding the Beatles' version of "From Me To You" to the station playlist and it spent six weeks that summer on the KRLA survey, peaking at No. 32 at the end of August. Back in England, though, it was a very different story. On May 25, in a show recorded the previous Tuesday, the Beatles topped the bill for the first time on *Saturday Club*, playing three songs from their LP, plus "From Me To You," "Long Tall Sally," and the band's rocked-up version of Barrett Strong's early Motown hit "Money (That's What I Want)."

That same week, a band that, as the year began, had only one single to its credit and not much of a reputation outside of the north of England had its first recording session for its own radio series. *Pop Go The Beatles* was greenlighted as a limited-run half-hour series to be heard late on Tuesday afternoons over the BBC's Light Programme. The Beatles hosted the show along with a professional Beeb MC (Lee Peters for the original four shows, Rodney Burke later on in what turned into a fifteen-week run) and would have a Beeb-selected guest band each week, the Irish light pop harmony group the Bachelors being the best-known on the first several shows and the Swinging Blue Jeans, Searchers, and Hollies on later episodes. But the focus was clearly on the Beatles, who would banter with the MC, read listener requests, and perform several songs on each episode (six on the premiere). Again, this gave the band the chance to musically stretch out and reach into its deep repertoire of songs.

The Beatles performed fifty-six songs on the fifteen *Pop Go The Beatles* shows. Thirty-nine of them were new to most of the listening audience (save for their longtime fans in Liverpool) and twenty-six never made it to the group's original EMI/Apple catalog. Many of those performances can be found on the two official Apple collections of the Beatles' BBC performances, with the balance to be found on the numerous underground Beeb collections.

On June 29 came another milestone. John Lennon appeared solo, as part of the panel on BBC TV's *Juke Box Jury*. On a panel with three British show business, but not music, personalities, Lennon gave "Miss" verdicts to each of the records played on that episode, including the Tymes' US No. 1 hit that summer, "So Much In Love," and Elvis Presley's "(You're The)

Devil In Disguise," clearly showing Lennon's disenchantment with the post-army Elvis.

Even with the weekly exposure of their own radio series, the Beatles still were able to head a June 29 all-Liverpool episode of the *Thank Your Lucky Stars* sort-of summer replacement, *Lucky Stars (Summer Spin)*, which aired just hours after the band made another headlining radio appearance on *Saturday Club*. With their popularity rapidly escalating, the Beatles had a very busy summer of 1963 – continuing to do increasingly frenzied one-nighters, recording episodes of *Pop Go The Beatles* and other BBC radio shows, and squeezing in recording sessions for the second Beatles LP and, on July 1, the recording of their next single, the one that would become the band's first million-selling record and launch them into superstardom, "She Loves You."

"She Loves You" b/w "I'll Get You" was released on August 23 and, the next night, the Beatles lip-synced both sides of the single for a nearly national TV audience on a second appearance on *Lucky Stars (Summer Spin)*. They spent the last week in August being filmed by producer Don Haworth for a BBC TV documentary on the Liverpool beat scene but heavily concentrating on the Beatles. The film, *The Mersey Sound*, aired regionally on John Lennon's 23rd birthday, October 9, and nationally on November 13, and would be a source for Beatles documentaries for decades to come.

On September 7, the Beatles made their first guest appearance on ITV's *Big Night Out*, hosted by Mike and Bernie Winters, with whom the Beatles developed a fine and funny rapport over their four appearances on the show in the next two years. A week later, the band recorded its participation in the fifth birthday episode of *Saturday Club*, for which they even recorded a rocked-up "Happy Birthday." On September 16, after further work on their second album, the Beatles finally got some hard-earned vacation time, their first since the spring. George Harrison and his brother Peter journeyed to America for a two-week visit with their sister Louise in Benton, Illinois. During the summer, Louise had been trying to drum up interest in the Beatles via local radio stations. First, she tried KXOX in St. Louis by sending the station a copy of "From Me To You," but the station had already been playing the Del Shannon version and turned her down. She was able to get the group some exposure on a small West Franklin, Illinois, station, WFRX, through the station owner's daughter, Marcia Shafer, who played the Beatles' UK singles on her *Saturday Session* teen music show that summer. Marcia also interviewed George Harrison during his visit and wrote about the band for her high school newspaper. It would not be the only time that year that a teenage girl would influence US radio airplay for the Beatles.

Back home, "She Loves You" had crashed into the singles charts at the end of August and spent five weeks at No. 1 in the *Melody Maker* chart and a total of six on *Record Retailer*'s chart, four in September and an additional two in November. In America, though, with both Capitol and Vee-Jay passing on the record, it ended up being released by the small Philadelphia label Swan. Dick Clark had a business relationship with Swan so he put "She Loves You" on the Rate-A-Record feature on *American Bandstand* in September, but it got a mediocre response from the musically unadventurous *Bandstand* audience. The very popular New York disc jockey Murray "The K" Kaufman, the flamboyant prime time, nighttime DJ on NYC's WINS, had been made aware of the Beatles by his wife Jackie, who had seen write-ups about the group in European fashion magazines because of the collarless Cardin jackets they frequently wore onstage. Murray put "She Loves You" on his Record Review Board feature in October but it received much the same middling response as on *Bandstand*.

The Beatles reconvened in London to begin the most crucial period in their career arc. It began with the group recording an interview for a November 3 examination of the Liverpool beat scene for the BBC radio magazine *The Public Ear*. On October 4, they made their first appearance on the new ITV Friday evening pop/rock showcase *Ready, Steady, Go!*, on which they lip-synced three songs and were interviewed by MC Keith Fordyce and soon-to-be-star Dusty Springfield.

Nine nights later came the next great turning point in the Beatles ascension to superstardom. *Sunday Night at the London Palladium* was Britain's top-rated television show, a Sunday night institution similar to *The Ed Sullivan Show* in the United States, with a guaranteed audience of some 15 million viewers. As would be the case the following February in America with Sullivan, the Beatles were given top billing for their debut at the Palladium and closed the show with a four-song set ("From Me To You," "I'll Get You," "She Loves You," "Twist And Shout") before a rapturous audience in the fabled theater. What set this night apart, though, from previous Beatles live shows and TV appearances was the pandemonium that was reigning outside the theater on London's Argyll Street. The scenes of fan hysteria got the attention of the London-based Fleet Street press and legend has it that the word "Beatlemania" appeared for the first time the next morning in the front page coverage of the Beatles' Palladium appearance. Indeed, there had been a feature on the ITN news after the

Palladium show, a sure sign that the Beatles had moved on from just being a hit group to a pop phenomenon.

Two days after the Palladium telecast, on October 15, it was announced that the Beatles had been invited to perform at the annual *Royal Variety Show* at the Prince of Wales Theater on November 4. The next day, October 16 (for a show that would air that Sunday), the band performed before a theater audience for the last time on a BBC radio program for *Easy Beat*. On October 17, the Beatles recorded their fifth single, the one that would finally launch them in America, "I Want To Hold Your Hand." And, that Sunday, October 20, they made another bill-topping appearance on *Thank Your Lucky Stars*.

Three days later, the Beatles flew to Sweden for their first professional international trip since becoming stars and, once again, it was radio and TV that provided them the vehicle to bring them to much of the potential Swedish audience. First came a radio appearance on which they performed seven songs before a receptive, but not manic, audience, and that performance is among the best examples of the Beatles as a live act beyond their beat club apprenticeship, as would be their appearance on the TV show *Drop In*, taped on the last night of a very successful Swedish engagement.

The next day, October 31, the Beatles flew back to London and were greeted at the airport by thousands of fans. Legend has it that one of the witnesses to the tumult at the airport was Ed Sullivan, who is said to have asked what all the fuss was about and he was told the Beatles. Whether this actually happened is open to question but Sullivan would find out about the group in short order. On November 4, the Beatles appeared before Princess Margaret and the Queen Mother as part of the nineteen-act *Royal Variety Show*. Appearing seventh on a bill with talent as famed and diverse as Marlene Dietrich and Tommy Steele, the Beatles, as on the Palladium show, performed four songs ("From Me To You," "She Loves You," "Till There Was You," "Twist And Shout" – preceded by Lennon suggesting that "the people in the cheap seats clap . . . The rest of you just rattle your jewelry"). Along with Lennon's cheekiness, the group again made the front pages of the next day's papers because of the pandemonium outside the Prince of Wales Theater and, as had become customary in the videotape era, the entire Royal Command Performance was televised on Sunday, November 10.[2]

---

[2] "Royal Beatles," *The Guardian* (London), November 5, 1963, 8, www.newspapers.com/image/2598 61865/?terms=Beatles.

The dual displays of mass hysteria in the heart of London had by now gotten the attention of the London bureaus of the American media. A short piece on the October 31 airport fan reception ran in the *New York Times* on November 4 and, by mid-November, articles on the Beatles had run in *Time* magazine and *Newsweek*. In addition, film of a Beatles concert with voiceover by Edwin Newman ran on NBC News' *Huntley-Brinkley Report* on November 16. Meanwhile, Brian Epstein flew to New York and was able to secure a commitment from Sullivan for two headlining/co-head-lining appearances (soon expanded to three) by the group on his show in February. And, by the end of November, Capitol Records had finally come around and committed to backing the new Beatles single, "I Want To Hold Your Hand."

On the morning of November 22, even as the Beatles' second LP was being released in England, a report on the group and Beatlemania filed by CBS News' London bureau chief Alexander Kendrick ran on *The CBS Morning News with Mike Wallace* and was scheduled to run on that evening's *CBS Evening News with Walter Cronkite*. That afternoon, though, President John F. Kennedy was assassinated in Dallas and Cronkite's news program was folded into the network's continuous cover-age of the assassination. Cronkite, who was the managing editor of his newscast, finally aired the Kendrick piece on December 10, feeling that the time was right for a lighter piece to end that night's newscast. And here's where sheer happenstance turned into "star-making machinery."

Watching the Kendrick report that evening in Silver Springs, Maryland, was a 15-year-old girl named Marsha Albert. She was impressed with what she saw and, especially, the little bit of Beatles music in the report. She then wrote a letter to her favorite disc jockey at her favorite radio station, Carroll James, the nighttime DJ on WWDC in Washington, DC, requesting that James play some Beatles music on his show. Not only was James the station's most popular air personality, but WWDC had a policy of trying to fill any listener request. James had a friend who worked for BOAC airlines and had her obtain a copy of "I Want To Hold Your Hand." On the evening of December 17, one week after Marsha Albert saw the Kendrick report, James had her come to the WWDC studios and intro-duce what was probably the first play in the United States of the Beatles' new single. And, like something out of a bad Hollywood film script, the request lines lit up like a Christmas tree and the record was immediately added to the station's playlist, much to the displeasure of Capitol Records, which was not planning on releasing the single until the second week in January. In what can only be described as twisted logic, Capitol, in effect, ordered WWDC to stop playing "I Want To Hold Your Hand" but, with James in the lead, the station refused, saying that its listeners wanted to hear the record. In addition, James had made copies of the record for DJ friends of his and, with airplay in Chicago and St. Louis, "I Want To Hold Your Hand" was beginning to spread like a prairie fire. Even though virtually nothing ever gets released during the holiday season, Capitol moved the date for the release of "I Want To Hold Your Hand" up to December 26. And, that day, the record made its New York debut on WMCA, with WABC and its 50,000-watt clear channel signal and high-energy Top 40 format adding it to its playlist by New Year.

While all this was happening in America, British Beatlemania also kept building. On November 20, the Beatles were filmed on stage in Manchester for a Pathe newsreel featurette called *The Beatles Come to Town*, which showed the group performing "She Loves You" and "Twist And Shout," color footage that would be used extensively in coming decades, right up to the 2016 feature film documentary *Eight Days A Week* (albeit with the Manchester audio replaced by the more raucous 1964 Hollywood Bowl performances).

Two days later, the Beatles' second LP, *With The Beatles*, was released and, with advance orders in Britain of 300,000 and an attention-getting (and soon to be iconic) album cover, it was a newsworthy story until the bad news from Dallas hit England that evening. On December 7, the Beatles were back in Liverpool for their first concert there in months, a special show for 2,500 members of the Northern Area Beatles Fan Club at the Liverpool Empire, a half-hour of which was shown that night on BBC TV as a special called *It's The Beatles*. A similar concert with a meet-and-greet for some 3,000 members of the Southern Area Fan Club was held a week later at Wimbledon. Following the Liverpool show, the group served as the entire panel for a special episode of *Juke Box Jury*. Unlike Lennon's previous appearance as a panelist, the group gave "Hit" votes to the majority of the eleven discs they sampled, including Liverpool's Swinging Blue Jeans' version of "The Hippy Hippy Shake." Among the records they gave "Miss" marks to was Bobby Vinton's "There! I've Said It Again," which would go to No. 1 in the United States in January and be knocked from the top by "I Want To Hold Your Hand."

Mid- to late December saw the Beatles make their sixth appearance of the year on *Thank Your Lucky Stars* and another top-billed appearance on *Saturday Club*, plus their own two-hour Boxing Day special for BBC radio, *From Us To You*. A year that saw the Beatles leap from relative obscurity in their home country to the cusp of international superstardom ended with a

2½-week engagement that extended into mid-January at the Astoria Cinema in Finsbury Park for *The Beatles' Christmas Show*. With "I Want To Hold Your Hand" officially released in the United States, Capitol rolled out a massive (for that time and for a group with no American track record) promotional push called "The Beatles Are Coming!" In the first week of the New Year, the record took off like a rocket in a number of major radio markets. For instance, it entered the weekly survey for WABC in New York at No. 35. By January 7, it had leaped to No. 1, nearly a month ahead of the national trade magazine charts. On Friday night, January 3, Jack Paar ran a short segment on the Beatles on his prime-time NBC TV show, showing British Beatles concert film from that fall and making fun of the fan hysteria for his "more adult" viewing audience, while also putting in a plug for the group's February appearances with Ed Sullivan.

With "I Want To Hold Your Hand" finally breaking the Beatles in the United States, Vee-Jay and Swan had quickly re-released their Beatles singles by mid-January, with Vee-Jay making a new single of the two A-sides with which the Chicago label had little success during 1963, "Please Please Me"/"From Me To You." Vee-Jay also belatedly issued its US version of the first Beatles album, *Introducing The Beatles*, on January 10. Ten days later, Capitol released its *Meet The Beatles* LP on January 13, containing both sides of their single, plus its UK B-side, "This Boy," and the core of the British *With The Beatles* album. Even MGM Records got into the act by releasing "My Bonnie," the 1961 German single by Tony Sheridan on which the Beatles backed him up and the record that first brought the Beatles to the full attention of Brian Epstein. With demand for any Beatles music suddenly at fever pitch, radio stations added all of this material to their playlists, creating saturation level Beatles programming by the end of January and the approach of the group's first visit to America. Murray The K, who had quickly dropped "She Loves You" after it failed to get much of a reaction back in October, was called back from a post-holiday vacation to helm WINS' Beatles coverage.

With Beatlemania exploding in America and with the Beatles about to embark on their first visit as a group to France, the group's second head-lining appearance on *Sunday Night At The London Palladium* on January 12 did not take on nearly the legendary status of their October 13 debut appearance.

It was late on their first night in Paris that Epstein received a cable informing him that, in its issue dated January 25, *Cash Box*, *Billboard*'s main competitor among the US music industry trade publications, would have "I Want To Hold Your Hand" as the new No. 1 song on its pop singles chart in its January 25 issue, setting off a wild celebration at the exclusive George V hotel and making for a great start to the Beatles' eighteen-day stand, with Sylvie Vartan and Trini Lopez, at the Olympia Theatre in Paris. The engagement ended on February 4 and the group returned to England the next day, just in time to prepare to fly to New York two days later.

New York's Idlewild Airport had been renamed for the assassinated president in a somber Christmas Eve ceremony at the airport's International Arrivals Building. Forty-five days later, that building was the focus of another media event. News crews from both local and network TV and radio outlets were there, as well as Murray The K and, from WABC, "Cousin" Bruce Morrow and Scott Muni, who had piloted the launch of a WABC Beatles fan club a month earlier. WMCA's nighttime host B. Mitchell Reed was a holdout but, between the three local Top 40 stations, enough interest had been whipped up that several thousand teenagers showed up at the airport, creating a riotous scene that hit fever pitch when the flight from London landed and the Beatles disembarked.

After a lengthy photo op on the tarmac and going through customs, the group appeared before the gathered American media for the first time and, instead of being "four Elvis Presleys," as one question inferred – looking pretty and saying nothing – the Beatles proved themselves to be smart, irreverent, and nothing like the archetypal teen idols. That earned them some grudging respect from the overwhelmingly male and middle-aged news media and the coverage of the group's arrival in America, while certainly condescending, was not nearly as totally dismissive as had been expected of coverage of a sudden teen sensation that most Americans were unfamiliar with on New Year's Day.

Two nights after their arrival in America came the main event – the Beatles' live US debut on *The Ed Sullivan Show*. Sullivan's long-running show was the ultimate viewing for the whole family, generally watched on the one living room TV that most American families had by 1964. The show was hosted by a round-shouldered, marble-mouthed man with little stage presence. But Sullivan was a longtime newspaper columnist and he knew a big story when he saw one. With all of the excitement that had built up over the last month and especially the Beatles' first two days in America, he instinctively knew all this was leading up to a "really big shew."

It turned out to be very big. Something approximating half of the available TVs in the country that night were tuned to Sullivan's show. The official figure was 73 million viewers in a country with a population of about 194 million. It was the highest-rated entertainment program in TV's still-young history and, over fifty years later, it is still one of the highest-rated episodes of a continuing series. But it was more than that. Along with the teenage girls who had flipped for the Beatles on first hearing "I Want To Hold Your Hand," there were teenage boys who saw their future that night. Bruce Springsteen, Billy Joel, Tom Petty, David Cassidy and many others watched the show and immediately knew that they wanted to be musicians and play in a rock 'n' roll band and have girls scream for them. Springsteen's E Street band comrade Steven Van Zandt called it "rock 'n' roll's Big Bang."

The Beatles' Sullivan show sets seemed tailor-made for this massive audience. They began with not a single but an album track, "All My Loving," from the new US *Meet The Beatles* LP. Then, another track from that album, their version of the hit song from Meredith Wilson's *The Music Man*, "Till There Was You," sung by the most mom-friendly member of the group, Paul McCartney. That short-circuited any of the kind of parental outrage that swirled around Elvis Presley's 1956 TV appearances. Add in "She Loves You," with the "yeah yeah yeah" that was becoming a Beatles trademark and America was theirs.

The Beatles came back as the penultimate act on that night's Sullivan show, with a pre-taped tumbling act incongruously closing the show. They performed both sides of the No. 1 single in the USA, a rocking "I Saw Her Standing There" and "I Want To Hold Your Hand," with most of the audience in ecstasy. At the end of the song, the group bowed, left their instruments, and walked over to greet Sullivan and accept the screams of the crowd. Watching that moment five decades later, one can easily sense that something important just happened, that a page in at least the pop culture history book had just turned. Just short of two years after emerging from Liverpool with their first tentative appearances on radio in the north of England, the Beatles had used the star-making apparatus of their time to reach, as they would say, "the toppermost of the poppermost."[3]

---

[3] John Lennon and Yoko Ono, *All We Are Saying: The Last Major Interview with John Lennon and Yoko Ono*, interview by David Sheff, ed. G. Barry Golson (New York: Griffin, 2000), 159.

Projecting the Visuality of the Beatles: A Hard Day's Night and Help!

David Melbye

In our increasingly mediated visual culture, we have acquired a tendency to *see* before we listen. And looking back on the evolution of the Beatles as a serious topic for cultural study, it is fair to say American university visual arts courses, at least, recognized Beatles films for their own sake *before* the group's musical contributions to popular culture were deemed worthy of academic attention. Even the critically denounced *Magical Mystery Tour* (1967), on campuses, was treated as an important cultural product or as "art" beyond any entertainment value (or dearth thereof). But such recognition really begins with the Beatles' first two filmic endeavors, *A Hard Day's Night* (1964) and *Help!* (1965), which, taken together, anticipate the mid-1960s seismic shift from Beatlemania to the Beatles as a *Gesamtkunstwerk* or, rather, from an outlet for "incorrigible" teenagers to the irrefutable, all-encompassing voice for an entire generation of progressive-minded young adults on both sides of the Atlantic – and around the world. But this "voice" was cinematically *seen* in these films before it was musically heard on forthcoming albums, namely *Rubber Soul, Revolver,* and, of course, *Sgt. Pepper's.* And precisely what was seen must be understood as a confluence of creative and industrial forces working well beyond the collaboration of four talented, hardworking Liverpudlian musicians. If we are, then, to really examine the Beatles *in context*, we must consider a number of these "contexts" causing the group to impact the world through visual means. Proceeding from the general to the specific, these include the rising presence of television in the average household, post-war British film culture (especially in terms of Hollywood's impact upon it), the expat American director Richard Lester (and his own influences), and, of course, the Beatles and *their* particular circumstances. And there were certainly a number of other visionary personalities contributing to this process, not least of which was manager Brian Epstein. Just as American rock 'n' roll evolved across the 1950s from a teenage dance craze into a cultural phenomenon moreover to be looked at on stages, in films, and especially on TV sets, the Beatles and their music were rapidly

Figure 11.1 A poster for the British release of Richard Lester's 1965 comedy, *Help!*,
starring the Beatles. Photo by Movie Poster Image Art/Getty Images

propelled into visual media where their *visuality*, per se, would not only be
exploited to reinforce the influence of radio on their record sales, but would
make them become *the* iconic arbiters of global popular culture and con-
sumerism (when, really, they were, as initially, four talented, hardworking
Liverpudlian musicians). And, indeed, the "context" of what impelled (and
impels) the world to put a precedent on *looking at* the Beatles is what
increasingly got the better of them.

At this point, *A Hard Day's Night* and *Help!*, apart from the Beatles'
career and legacy, have been treated upon rather amply since the group
(officially) disbanded in 1970. Let's survey some of the more recent and
laudable efforts. As a point of entry, Bob Neaverson's *The Beatles Movies*
(1997) is perfectly thorough in providing both production specifics and
cultural insights for his stated topic. For *A Hard Day's Night*, he explores
the film's essential ingredients: "humour"[1] (already established through the

---

[1] Bob Neaverson, *The Beatles Movies* (London: Cassell, 1997), 22.

Beatles' televised press interviews), "working-class provincialism"[2] (i.e., their British ordinariness), and "individualism"[3] (while a collaborative entity, they were also John, Paul, George, and Ringo). Neaverson concludes, "the crossover into film helped to furnish the Beatles with a total mass appeal hitherto unprecedented in pop."[4] In other words, their assembled visualization established an accessibility beyond what their music could achieve. Their personal identities were now sufficiently palpable – as moving image – for anyone (especially older generations) to embrace. Steven D. Stark's historical account, *Meet the Beatles* (2005), echoes this notion, claiming about the film's release, "Walt Disney had fashioned an entertainment imprint for children through various media – an 'image in the public mind,' he called it – and the Beatles were doing something similar."[5] And, in their edited volume, *Reading the Beatles* (2006), Kenneth Womack and Todd F. Davis reinforce this notion, asserting:

> In addition to marketing the band as a happy-go-lucky group of unthreatening young men, *A Hard Day's Night* concretized the Beatles' individual images for the current generation, and – thanks to videocassettes, DVDs, and cable television – generations to come. Henceforth, Lennon became known for his sarcastic intelligence; McCartney for his boyish charm and good looks; George Harrison for being the "quiet one"; and Ringo Starr for his affable personality and good-natured humor.[6]

In 2007, alone, at least three more Beatles histories emerged, though offering varied accounts of the group's film forays. Bob Spitz's *Yeah, Yeah, Yeah*, closer to a fanzine narrative, only touches on the films as passing elements of the larger experience of the Beatles' meteoric fame, and so dispenses with any mention of their cultural impact. A more detailed and rewardingly observational history is Jonathan Gould's *Can't Buy Me Love*, which also points toward the primacy of the moving image so thoroughly mobilized in *A Hard Day's Night*, stating, "Dick Lester's efforts to present the Beatles as comedic and cinematic archetypes gave the picture a universality that easily bridged any problems of cultural translation."[7] Of

---

[2] Neaverson, *The Beatles Movies*, 22.   [3] Neaverson, *The Beatles Movies*, 24.
[4] Neaverson, *The Beatles Movies*, 27.
[5] Steven D. Stark, *Meet the Beatles: A Cultural History of the Band That Shook Youth, Gender, and the World* (New York: HarperCollins, 2005), 159.
[6] Kenneth Womack and Todd F. Davis, "Mythology, Remythology, Demythology: The Beatles on Film," in *Reading the Beatles: Cultural Studies, Literary Criticism, and the Fab Four*, ed. Kenneth Womack and Todd F. Davis (New York: State University of New York Press, 2006), 101.
[7] Jonathan Gould, *Can't Buy Me Love: The Beatles, Britain, and America* (New York: Harmony Books, 2007), 246.

particular relevance along these lines is Gould's coverage of the film's
critical reception, wherein one critic, Elizabeth Sutherland for *The New
Republic*, dismissing their music, nevertheless appreciates the film as a
testament to a notion the band members "will not try too hard to be
funny or angry or poetic."[8] Such a testament is, of course, to be located in
the visual aspects of the film. Third among these books is Michael R.
Frontani's *The Beatles: Image and the Media* (2007), embarking on its close
examination of the film's elements from the notion that, "at this point in
the band's career, their status as teen idols was still being cultivated within
the image."[9] And this pattern of (mostly) intensive scrutiny paid to both *A
Hard Day's Night* and *Help!* would continue in three recent film studies:
Neil Sinyard's *Richard Lester* (2010), Stephen Glynn's *The British Pop
Music Film* (2013), and, most recently, David James's *Rock 'n' Film*
(2015). Well beyond the scope of the ensuing chapter, these latter single-
authored analyses also offer detailed accounts in considering how the mid-
1960s Beatles films explore, celebrate, and propagate their visuality.

Ironically, the germination of a Beatles movie, or, rather, what would
become the release of *A Hard Day's Night* in 1964, proceeded not from any
grand or prescient vision of the image's power to captivate the teenage
Beatlemaniac listener beyond her listening. It was simply a contractual
means through which United Artists could, in turn, release a soundtrack
album – and partake of profits Capitol Records and other Beatles labels
were enjoying. Across the 1950s, soundtrack LPs had already proven
themselves extremely profitable, especially Hollywood musicals and films
featuring Doris Day and other popular actor-singers. And rock 'n' roll
musicals had already gone some distance to popularize (and pasteurize) the
"sound" of teenage recalcitrance on both sides of the Atlantic, with Elvis
films in America and Tommy Steele and Cliff Richard films in Britain, so
that, ultimately, more records by these artists would sell. And United
Artist's less-than-abundant allocation of £200,000 for the film's production affirms this ulterior motive on their part. Nevertheless, the primacy of
Beatles' visuality was a steady evolution from the group's own beginnings,
and so well anticipates even a low-budget film's potential to exploit the
moving image toward this end. Even before there was any indication of a
profitable career path, the Beatles themselves can be credited for their own
sense of pursuing a collective "look" on stage, which, in their Hamburg

---

[8] Gould, *Can't Buy Me Love*, 245.
[9] Michael R. Frontani, *The Beatles: Image and the Media* (Jackson: University Press of Mississippi,
     2007), 73.

period, became Parisian mop-top haircuts and "Wild One" black leather jackets. The latter 1950s rocker fashion choice, of course, would be "cleaned up" and/or *mod*ified by manager Brian Epstein to become gray suits and ties, and this visual presentation, minus their former onstage antics, would propel the four of them as an instantly recognizable "whole" toward Beatlemania. As for the potential for this wholeness to become just as recognizable moving and speaking images, this also evolved steadily (from wiggling their mop-tops on stage).

The Albert and David Maysles 1964 documentary, *What's Happening! The Beatles in the U.S.A.*, covering the group's triumphant arrival to America, should be treated moreover as pivotal to what fulfilled United Artists' contract for a Beatles film. Even if producer Walter Shenson, director Richard Lester, and screenwriter Alun Owen never watched the footage for ideas, this hour-long film certainly appears as a "study" for the subsequent feature, particularly for featuring its own Ringo dance sequence and the band members variously fooling about in train cars. Well beyond its inclusion in the film, the airport press interview with the four Beatles has long been celebrated as introducing the Beatles' Liverpudlian knack for ironic wit and clever repartee (in their endearing Scouse accents) to the American masses. But early on in the film, the Beatles are rather apparently unaccustomed to a camera also following them into their limousine and hotel room – places normally treated as private or simply transitional between appointed limelight. In the backseat of the car, Paul and the others struggle to appear unaware of the camera staring at them from the front seat especially as they run dry with conversation to fill the void. And then in the hotel room, their collective stiffness persists as they watch themselves on TV, Lennon hiding behind his sunglasses. Later in the film, however, and certainly after they had accomplished their pressured first American TV performance on *The Ed Sullivan Show*, the Beatles commence performing impromptu comic relief for the Maysles' camera, each of them intermittently smirking directly into the lens. For the group, at least, this film's offstage spaces were a screen actor's training ground, and similar scenes would be performed again back in England that same year to become *A Hard Day's Night*.

Even if the hardworking Beatles and their ambitious manager had already honed and fashioned a readymade onstage moving image for the camera to simply capture and present to the masses on television, an enormous potential remained for the cinema and its aesthetic arsenal to transform them even further. The Maysles documentary, if not deliberately treated as a prototype for Lester, certainly conditioned the Beatles toward their potential to entertain just as much offstage as on. But beyond *A Hard Day's Night*'s similar "day in the life" narrative of the Beatles traveling by train to an eventual TV appearance, including an attendant press party and hotel room interludes, Lester's particular barrage of cinematic choices took the film well beyond merely a "mockumentary" response to the Maysles' effort. The emerging director, noticed by the Beatles for his work with Peter Sellers and the Goons, embarked from a screenplay penned by Alun Owen, who toward this end had been hired to accompany the Beatles on a string of shows in Ireland the previous year. An established Welsh play-wright also from Liverpool, Owen was recruited for his well-anticipated ability to recreate the comedic side of the group's personalities and dialo-gue faithfully. Lester, in turn, furnished the appropriate realism for Owen's script through location shooting and oft-handheld cinematography, closer to the direct cinema approach of the limousine backseat scene in Maysles' documentary, where the camera is (barely) ignored, as opposed to the *cinéma vérité* approach we see later in their film, where the Beatles playfully engage with the camera.[10] Also, as Sinyard's study points out, Lester's editing was less aggressive than many would have it, with "fewer" shots "than in the average film of that time."[11] And Lester certainly restrained himself from overindulging the visual effects rampant in the musical sequences of his previous rock 'n' roll film, *It's Trad, Dad!* (1962). So, all told, it is perfectly reasonable to encapsulate the director's cinematic style as a "French New Wave" approach, especially akin to that of Jean Luc Godard for *Breathless* (1960), with its definitive use of street locations, handheld camera, jump cuts, and episodic narrative.[12] Less productive, as Frontani's study affirms,[13] is associating Lester's style with the British Free Cinema and/or Kitchen Sink Realism movements, since these were the-matically propelled by a social critique of living conditions in the industrial North, and, anyway, also took much of their aesthetic inspiration from *nouvelle vague* films. Situating *A Hard Day's Night* firmly within a French New Wave "mode" of visual narrative, then, accomplishes an

---

[10] Many Beatles studies attribute the term "*cinéma vérité*," "*cine-vérité*," or simply "*vérité*" to Lester's approach in *A Hard Day's Night*, but "direct cinema" is more accurate, since a non-invasive "fly-on-the wall" use of camera was a tenet of Robert Drew and other documentarians affiliated with the latter movement. The Maysles brothers, on the other hand, with an interactive film like *Grey Gardens* (1975), gravitated decidedly toward the *cinéma vérité* approach.
[11] Neil Sinyard, *Richard Lester* (Manchester and New York: Manchester University Press, 2010), 12.
[12] An effective jump cut can be found in *A Hard Day's Night* when the group are shown playing cards on the train, crosscut with the girls watching them from the other side of the cage, and, abruptly, the boys are then singing and playing their instruments.
[13] See Frontani, *The Beatles: Image and the Media*, 74.

understanding of the film as a departure from musical and rock 'n' roll films coming before it, and goes some distance in explaining why audiences and critics immune to the "sound" of Beatlemania were nevertheless impressed with Lester's expression of its visuality.

Beyond his formalist, *nouvelle vague* approach to cinematic expression, Richard Lester, at this early stage of his career, was also deeply invested in the comedic moving image as derived from the content itself. The absurd situations, specifically ridiculous in terms of their visual physicality, are traceable back, of course, to the director's first short, *The Running Jumping & Standing Still Film* (1959). Closer to a silent era comedy (especially Buster Keaton's work) as a "showcase" of theatrics in wide outdoor spaces, this film's narrative comprises a number of characters whose various agendas in a public park encroach upon each other physically in silly ways. (And that is really it.) For example, a portrait painter's sitter finds a convenient seat upon the back of an athlete doing sit-ups, much to the latter's chagrin. So, in addition to Alun Owen's perfectly believable scenes of snappy dialogue between the Beatles and those in their "daily" midst, Lester contributes an array of absurdist visual gags, such as when the lads suddenly appear running along outside the window of the very train car where they had just been wrangling with a disgruntled elder, or, later in the film, when wandering Ringo, in an attempt to take a portrait of himself near a river, yanks the camera abruptly into the water by its shutter release cord. And Lester's comedic vision finds its purest realization in the absence of any dialogue – in the oft-celebrated outdoor athletic field scene wherein the four band members indulge in their own "running jumping & standing still" antics, as the only available escape from the smothering monotony of their Beatlemania grind. Previous analyses have already deconstructed this scene as a standalone example of the Beatles *as* art, but, suffice it to say, it is moreover important to recognize the group's music here as *subsidiary* to the moving image, and not the other way around, as in other scenes in the film where the Beatles are performing their songs. (And this example should also be singled out from other non-diegetic uses of music as score, namely George Martin's instrumental versions of Beatles music, since the sound-less physicality of the lads' romp on the field would scarcely entertain without its musical accompaniment.) Thus, it is a still-appreciable harmony of what at the time were freshly avant-garde approaches to cinematic expression, propagated by Godard and his peers, along with absurd situations (all too often effected by Paul's mischievous "grandfather" in the film's otherwise authentic environments) that becomes formulaic in *A Hard Day's Night.*

But, alas, whatever was carried over from the previous film's "formula" for visuality contributed far less in establishing the Beatles as a universal artwork, and so this task would remain for their subsequent studio recordings (and *their* visual components). And we must admit that *any* imaginable Beatles film appearing in the immediate wake of *A Hard Day's Night's* all-approving reception would be a surefire hit at the box office. What was decidedly removed from its formula for success may account for its execrable departure from anything artful, entertaining, or redeemable on any level, even in fifty years' hindsight. (The single exception among the several surveyed Beatles scholars who actually "prefers" *Help!* to its predecessor shall go unnamed here, *à chacun son goût*.) For one, the Beatles are no longer the four hardworking onstage and live-television performers struggling through an entertainingly frenzied day in their lives. In other words, the meticulously honed and established visuality of Beatlemania, from the band members in their collective suits to their mitigating sense of humor, is here absent. And, for that matter, *any* semblance of realism, achieved through authentic locations and/or black-and-white documentary camerawork, is here exchanged for the pure cinematic fantasy derived from a remedial, Hollywood-sized budget. The occasionally absurd situations the lads encounter (or bring about on their own) in the previous film become the absurd comic-book *world* of this entire film, reinforced through its aggressive use of elaborate sets and exotic locations, color filters, and just about everything else Godard would have ascribed to the decadence of major Hollywood studios, as well as to the French Tradition of Quality. And, of course, the pages of this particular "comic book" are literally turned for us through the onscreen appearance of narrative blurbs, as if to admit the plot's threadbare logic would otherwise crumble. What's more, the authenticity of Alun Owen's screenplay is here traded out for Marc Behm and Charles Wood's flat and unfunny attempt at (oft-mumbled) Beatle-banter. All this would also serve to remove the Beatles themselves from any sufficiently familiar environment in which their limited acting skills would allow them to be convincing visually as characters in this fantasyland. (Even their lip-syncing during non-sequitur song sequences is clumsy and only contributes to the larger artificiality of the film.) Finally, as an intended James Bond send-up, the film's mere repetition of the nefarious "Indian" cult's attempts, initially, at retrieving their sacrificial ring, and, subsequently, at sacrificing Ringo whilst it remains stuck on his finger is insufficient to sustain any intrigue. And the film's nevertheless over-the-top antics scarcely approach the modest physical comedy of Lester's fledgling short. Indeed, the fundamental problem with this follow-up feature is its attempt to cinematically render the Beatles "out of" context, but, as such, the four of them are no longer recognizable or even desirable.

No Beatles scholar would argue the follow-up film, what ended up as *Help!*, "should have" attempted again to accomplish what was accomplished in *A Hard Day's Night*, and this chapter is no exception. The confluence of creative forces simply did not extend the visuality of the group any further than had the first. Rather, these forces broke from Beatlemania's particular visuality altogether and attempted something completely different that had very little to do with the Beatles and their reality, or with the reality of the culture surrounding their fame. Nevertheless, a very profitable number of tickets *was* sold, allowing many listeners to hear new songs by the Beatles, which these listeners could, in turn, purchase subsequently on a 45 single or LP record. And because these songs maintained the consistency of the Beatles' unparalleled songwriting talent and innovativeness, the film's stake in *any* visuality could be overlooked ultimately and even immediately after the film's release in theaters. The previous film, anyway, had achieved something only needing to be achieved once – the establishment of the Beatles as a listenable *and* watchable, *total* artwork – and moreover a comprehensively *human* artwork capable of expressing the entire range of human experiences, from the excesses of love to those of loss – and the sense of humor essential to mitigating either. And, indeed, if we have been trained to look at the Beatles before we listen to them, then we must not allow ourselves to be carried away too soon by visualities both in *and* out of context – and miss the point of their music.

CHAPTER 12

Beatletoons: Moxie, Music, and the Media

Mitchell Axelrod

On Saturday morning September 25, 1965, at 10:30 am EDT, the Beatles cartoon series premiered on ABC TV in the USA. Thirty minutes of Beatles music and fun. Two five and a half minute shorts with a sing along segment sandwiched in between. They were simple, uncomplicated stories of the Beatles interacting in society in all regions of the world. All stories were based on the lyrics of a Beatles song. Now often considered a forgotten piece of Beatles lore, the series was an immediate ratings success, lasting three seasons in its original run, with numerous re-runs in syndication. As the Beatles were considered pioneers in the music industry, having been credited with many "firsts" in their field, the cartoon series would be another feather in their pioneering cap as it was the very first weekly series to feature animated versions of living people. The trend continued in animation as many other entertainment acts were to be the subject of cartoon series for the foreseeable future, none of which would garner the ratings success of "The Beatles." How did this popular series come to be? And if it was such a success, why is it considered forgotten? The answers lie in the moxie of a man named Al Brodax, the music of the Beatles, and the perceptions of the worldwide media.

"Ladies and gentlemen, the Beatles." Thanks to those five words spoken by TV host Ed Sullivan, the world was never the same. A reported 73 million Americans were glued to their television sets as "The Fab Four," a term coined by their own press officer Tony Barrow, lit up the screen with music that sounded exciting and new. The American music scene just prior to the explosion of the British Invasion was becoming a bit dull and saccharin with artists such as Paul Anka, Bobby Vinton, and Frankie Avalon. On their way out were guitar groups. Some very exciting music was coming out of Motown, but it was considered "black music" and was considered forbidden in many homes in the early 1960s. American pop was doing just fine with the music of Phil Spector, Sam Cooke, and the Beach Boys, but the Beatles jolted the whole scene like a bolt of electricity. John,

Figure 12.1 The Beatles pose in front of animated cartoons of themselves in London on November 11,1964 . Photo by Mark and Colleen Hayward/Redferns

Paul, George, and Ringo were four long-haired kids from Liverpool, England who were rocking a new look and sound and America took notice.

One of the people taking notice of this different look and sound from the lads from across the pond was Al Brodax. A decorated war veteran, Brodax was working for King Features Syndicate (KFS) as the head of their newly created film and television development department. Having served in World War II, Brooklyn-born Brodax had a lot of self-confidence, or "chutzpah." From 1960 to 1962, Al and his team had been involved in producing 220 successful Popeye cartoons for KFS. His team and he developed a system for simplifying and streamlining the production process to produce in two years what had previously taken Paramount Studios twenty-four years to complete. This was an incredible pace which would serve them well in the future.

Brodax not only took notice of the Ed Sullivan show, but of how the media had begun to bow down to all things Beatle. The American newspapers, particularly the local New York tabloids, were reporting the daily

Beatles frenzy, garnering increasing readership. He knew when something was hot, and Al wanted to strike while he thought the group was still newsworthy. Using some of that "chutzpah," Brodax found out where the Beatles were staying and phoned the hotel direct in order to speak to their manager, Brian Epstein. Brian's secretary Wendy Hanson answered the phone and the first thing Al Brodax said to her was, "Hi, my name is Al Brodax and I can help the Beatles." Help the Beatles? The group had just played to a record-breaking television audience and had America in the palm of their hands and this brash, fast-talking New Yorker was offering them help. In the end, Al Brodax was right. He *did* help the group, and their relationship continued long enough for team Brodax and KFS to produce the animated classic film *Yellow Submarine.* But that's a whole other story.[1]

Months passed and after several meetings with Epstein, Al was able to secure the rights to animate the Beatles. It was now mid-1964 and Al wanted to ensure that the cartoon series would be on the television schedule as soon as possible. After all, nobody in America thought or could know that the group would remain as hot a commodity as they were when they were seen on the Ed Sullivan Show. If their popularity faded before the premiere of the cartoon show, KFS would lose money and the Brodax name would lose a bit of luster in the industry. Al was not about to let that happen. Having perfected the art of producing a cartoon series quickly, team Brodax set the wheels in motion to secure financing, commercial sponsors, production studios, a television network willing to take a chance on a much unknown commodity, and voice-over actors to portray each member of the band. There was no way that the group themselves could take the time to voice a cartoon when they were trying to establish themselves worldwide. Their popularity was still going strong and their busy schedule of television shows, concerts, films, and other personal appearances just would not afford them the time to sit for cartoon recording sessions. There was much to be done in a very little time.

Getting sponsors for a show like this was no easy task but Al spoke with Anson Issacson, president and chief operating officer of the A.C. Gilbert Company. The A.C. Gilbert Company was famous for their line of Erector sets and American Flyer trains. The company had steadily declining sales in previous years and had hopes that sponsoring 'the Beatles' would lead children to their products after viewing the

[1] Mitchell Axelrod, *BeatleToons: The Real Story Behind The Cartoon Beatles* (Pickens, SC: Winn, 1999), 22.

commercials. Other commercial sponsors were Quaker Oats and the Mars candy company. But Anson Issacson spoke with the ABC television network executives and convinced them that the Beatles would still be going strong until at least September 1965, so ABC green-lighted the cartoon series for the fall of 1965. Time was really growing short but team Brodax knew they could make it happen despite the tight time constraints. The potential revenue stream for KFS was a motivating factor as well.

Al secured TV Cartoons (TVC Studios) in London to be the main studio to produce the series. As quickly as they worked, it soon became apparent that in order to meet the fall deadline they would need to sub-contract out some work to other studios. They had connections to studios in Holland, Australia, and Canada, with TVC producing the bulk of the thirty-nine half-hour programs. Exactly what they had to work with was, initially, a mystery to all of the studios. The animation industry had not yet caught up to the rest of the world in regards to the popularity of the Fab Four so animating them became quite a chore. In fact, when Al Brodax approached one of the animation directors about directing some episodes of the new television series about the Beatles, the response was, "Al, you know insects do not make good characters in a cartoon show." Yes, it seems the beetles were still more significant than the Beatles to many people at that point in time.[2]

From the start the appeal of the Beatles was first and foremost, the music. Their music exploded out of their instruments and into your soul. It was fresh, ambitious guitar driven rock 'n' roll. Influenced by early rock pioneers such as Buddy Holly, Elvis Presley, the Everly Brothers, Chuck Berry, and Little Richard, the Beatles music expanded upon what their forefathers had produced and took it to new heights that had not been heard before by the youth of the period. But in the beginning of the production process, only a handful of albums and singles had been released by the group, which explains why a lot of album "filler" tracks were used in the series. Songs such as "Misery," "Chains," "Little Child," to name just a few became more popular due to the series. The deeper into production, the more songs were released and the deeper into the catalog the studio could delve. Although most of the "hits" had been used in the episodes, more and more "filler" tracks also had to be used, which made for some clever storylines for songs such as "When I Get Home," "Tell Me What You See," and "What You're Doing." It did not matter to the kids whether

[2] Axelrod, *BeatleToons*, 22.

they heard the hits or not, as long as they were constantly hearing the Beatles music, the kids, and adults, were happy and ratings remained high.

How were the Beatles going to be portrayed in animated form? By the time production was due to begin, the Beatles had completed several TV appearances, concerts, and even a major motion picture, *A Hard Day's Night*. Worldwide media had begun noticing certain characteristics of each Beatle and had nicknames for each: John was "the witty one"; Paul, "the cute one"; George, "the quiet one"; and Ringo was dubbed "the sad (clown) one." The job of designing the cartoon characterizations of the Beatles at TVC was given to 21-year-old Peter Sander. Sander had a mop-top haircut and looked like he would fit right in as a member of the group. Sander created model sheets of each Beatle to be handed out to each animation team in all countries to maintain continuity throughout the world. This proved unsuccessful because each studio added their own nuances to the series and the differences were easily discernable upon viewing. Peter Sander took the media stereotypes of the group and added a bit more depth to each character. He described John as "really looking like the leader." Paul was described as "poised and stylish." Although Sander could not really keep George as the quiet one because each char-acter needed to speak in the cartoons, he described him as "awkward and angular." Sander repeated Ringo's stereotype by stating "He is a nice gentle Beatle. Always deadpan and looks rather sad." In fact, Ringo became the center of the Beatles cartoon universe and became the fall guy for most of the episodes and sing-along segments following the premise of *A Hard Day's Night*, and later their second motion picture, *Help!* But even with the model sheet descriptions, the animation teams had trouble telling each Beatle apart and often had to ask the assistance of young Beatles fans who were near the studio in order to correctly animate to the voice soundtracks. As the series went on, the animators were a bit more versed in the idiosyncrasies of each Beatle after watching more of their filmed perfor-mances. Not being able to tell each Beatle apart was far from the headaches that were to come.[3]

Choosing voice actors to portray the Beatles was a decision made by Al and his team, which would prove to be a most controversial one, and the main reason the series has been forgotten and, in some cases, never seen by most Beatles fans. The series was targeted for an American audience. But the intention was that if the show were successful, it would be seen worldwide. Early in the production process, Al decided that children in

[3] Axelrod, *BeatleToons*, 28.

America would have difficulty understanding any type of Liverpudlian accent. Voices for the group would have to be an "Americanized" version of a Liverpool accent. To accomplish this feat, Brodax hired American voice actor Paul Frees to portray John Lennon and George Harrison. Frees was already a very established and accomplished voice actor in Hollywood. He was known as "The Man of a Thousand Voices," having voiced characters in commercials, movies, and cartoon series such as Boris Badenov (*The Rocky & Bullwinkle Show*), Inspector Fenwick (*Dudley Do-Right*), countless Rankin Bass holiday specials and he is even the voice of the "Ghost Host" in the Haunted Mansion in Disneyworld. For the voices of Paul McCartney and Ringo Starr, Brodax hired British actor Lance Percival. Percival was known for his appearances on the UK show *That Was the Week That Was*. Percival would go on to voice the "Old Fred" character in *Yellow Submarine*.

Although an accredited voice actor, Frees voiced John Lennon to sound much older than his actual 24 years of age and ended up sounding like British actor Rex Harrison. For George Harrison, Frees sounded much more like Peter Lorre than the youngest Beatle. Reaction to the voice choices, especially Frees, was swift and quite negative by the public and the Beatles themselves.

With all of the process pieces firmly in place, production on the Beatles cartoon series began. The animation teams throughout the world were like well-oiled machines. There were no computers to aid in the animation process and each 5½ minute cartoon took four to six weeks to produce. Having four studios working simultaneously ensured that the show would be ready for its premiere. There was only one thing left to do, show the cartoons to the group.

July 29, 1965 was a long day for the Beatles. They were scheduled to attend the world premiere of their new movie, *Help!* They were rehearsing for their August 1 appearance on the TV show *Blackpool Night Out*, and they were tired, or as John told one of the animators "completely knack-ered [exhausted]." It would seem the last thing they needed to be doing on that date was to be ushered into a small animation studio to see the progress of the cartoon series. But that is just what happened. The Beatles' cars pulled up to 38 Dean Street in London where a camera crew from ABC TV was waiting, as well as a few reporters and a lot of the UK animation team including Paul Frees and Lance Percival. Each Beatle and their personal minder (bodyguard) entered into a flash of camera bulbs. They posed in front of a mural with their cartoon counterparts on it and settled in for a screening of the first two episodes ever shown on TV, *A Hard Day's Night*, and *I Want To Hold Your Hand*. Lance Percival was seated in between the two Beatles he voiced and could hear every reaction as the screening continued. Paul would quip, "Do I really sound like that with such a high squeaky voice?" while Ringo would add, "They made me the dum-dum." Lance wanted to slither down in his seat and crawl away, but kept his composure throughout the 15-minute screening. Reactions from John and George were equally negative with John allegedly telling Brodax "You've made us into the bloody Flintstones." The screening turned into a drinking party and John Lennon even went under a buffet table with a bottle of wine to escape the craziness of the event. Years later Lance Percival told me that the guys told him that they really did admire being honored with a cartoon series, but did not exactly enjoy how they were portrayed.[4]

The Beatles series premiered to a very impressive 52 percent share of the television viewers. Families rocked and rolled to Beatles music each week, and although the group did not exactly enjoy the series, they certainly did not complain when cashing the checks from King Features. As time moved on, so did the Beatles. They quickly outgrew the young mop-top image, venturing into more ambitious music and more mature comments about society. In the fall of 1966, the live action show *Batman* premiered and the youth of America became fixated on super heroes. Rival network CBS quickly amended their Saturday morning schedule to focus on super heroes like *The New Adventures of Superman*, *Space Ghost*, and *Frankenstein Jr. and The Impossibles*. Although the Beatles were still performing respectably, the new trend of super heroes were out-rating the lads from Liverpool. Having thirteen half-hour shows a season did not help. It meant that in a fifty-two week span, each half-hour would be shown four times. Seeing an episode for the first time was great. Seeing it a second time was okay, but by the time they got around to a third or fourth showing in re-runs, children were turning the channel. As the Beatles themselves matured, the cartoon counterparts did not. The last songs from the group to be animated were "Penny Lane," and "Strawberry Fields Forever." Seeing the clean cut mop-top Beatles singing "Strawberry Fields" while the real Beatles had moustaches and beards was a shock to some viewers who knew better. Unfortunately for the series, when the Beatles grew up, so did their audiences and the cartoon ratings slipped tremendously. Being a savvy businessman, Al was ready to move on as well and had already convinced Brian Epstein to let his team produce the feature film *Yellow Submarine*. In

---

[4] Axelrod, *BeatleToons*, 124.

1968, the Beatles cartoon series was moved to the ABC Sunday schedule, and in 1969 the series was canceled.

The Beatles cartoon series was a success in spite of itself. For three years it made money for all parties involved with the exception of the A.C. Gilbert Company. Their hopes of kids rushing to buy their toys after seeing the commercials during the Beatles show never came to fruition. In fact, the shows only led to children buying more Beatles records and the company ceased operations in 1967. And reaction within the Beatles' organization to the voice choices was so negative that Brian Epstein made a deal with Al Brodax that ensured the cartoons would not be seen on UK television. This remains the biggest reason that the cartoon series to date has never been released on any format for home viewing. The success of the cartoon series was always due to one thing: the music. It brought smiles to children's faces while watching their musical heroes in cartoon form. And while more than fifty years after its premiere that cartoon has been confined to history, Beatles music still lights up the faces of all who hear it.

CHAPTER 13

Documentary, Rockumentary: Let It Be *and the Rooftop Concert*

Steve Matteo

The Beatles' place in the annals of popular music is secure and untouchable. They are unquestionably the most influential artists of all time, eclipsing even Frank Sinatra and Elvis Presley. As recording artists they have no rival. While Bob Dylan is perhaps the single most important songwriter of post-war popular music, collectively, the songs of Lennon and McCartney (and George Harrison) may have a more universal and lasting appeal. There are certainly many who outstripped the Beatles as live performers in rock music history, but that may be the only area where others eclipse the group.

One area, though, where the Beatles were at the forefront of innovation and musical influence is in the films they appeared in during their brief time together. Of course, the Beatles did not make the films themselves, but their personas and the new pop aesthetic they gave birth to demanded a new film language to accurately capture their essence on celluloid.

Much has been written about how influential the Beatles' first film, *A Hard Day's Night*, released in 1964, was, not just on film, but also on what would become the 1980s video music revolution. Much of the success and innovation of the film was actually due to the film's director, Richard Lester. Lester was an American living in England who worked with members of England's celebrated comic radio troupe the Goons and specifically on the short film *The Running, Jumping, and Standing Still Film*, released in 1959, starring Peter Sellers with co-screenplay credit by Spike Milligan and Sellers, who along with Harry Secombe and Michael Bentine, comprised the Goons. The film foreshadowed some of the elements of *A Hard Day's Night* in its cheeky English sketch comedy format with interconnecting storylines. It exhibited an anti-establishment irreverence and a youthful exuberance that drew a sharp contrast to the button-down, English reserve of the period.

Figure 13.1 The Beatles performing their last live public concert on the rooftop of the Apple Organization building for director Michael Lindsay-Hogg's film documentary, *Let It Be*, on Savile Row, London, UK, January 30,1969. Lennon's wife Yoko Ono sits at right. Photo by Evening Standard/Hulton Archive/Getty Images

Lester was the perfect director to capture the energy of the Beatles' music and the British Invasion movement. Enlisting help from Alun Owen, who wrote a script that reflected who the four boys from Liverpool really were, as opposed to creating fake screen personas that were commonplace after the first flush of the rock 'n' roll explosion in American films, Lester unleashed on screen for a mass audience many of the key aspects of Beatlemania and the new British youth-quake.

After that point, Beatles films were unfortunately flawed at best or outright flops at their worst. In retrospect, however, some of the initial overheated criticism has been tempered with time and all the group's films fare much better when evaluated far from the glare of the prism of 1960s culture and the Beatles' place at the red hot center, particularly when compared to *A Hard Day's Night*, which is not simply a great pop music film, but one of the best and most influential films of the 1960s.

The group's next film, *Help!*, released in 1965, was, like *A Hard Day's Night*, a feature. Unlike *A Hard Day's Night*, however, it did not project a feeling of naturalism. It was instead more of a spoof on the then-current craze for British spy films such as the James Bond movies. The cartoonish color film (*A Hard Day's Night* was in black and white) featured great Beatles music, but it left out what was the most important element of the first film: the Beatles' outsized personalities.

After *Help!* there was probably too much of the Beatles in the group's next film, *Magical Mystery Tour*, released in 1967. Made to be shown on television, the 52-minute film was essentially conceived and directed by the Beatles with help from veteran British film and television director Bernard Knowles. Knowles had worked extensively as a cinematographer with Alfred Hitchcock in the 1930s and with others, including on the film classic *Gaslight* in 1940. *Help!* was actually his last project before his death in 1975.

Magical Mystery Tour debuted on British television on Christmas Day, but was not well received. Those that watched the surreal color film on their tiny black and white televisions, hoping for some light holiday fare, were treated to a disjointed, obviously drug-inspired psychedelic journey, which failed to capture either the unique, yet changing personalities of the Beatles, or the hippie traveling adventures of a few of the film's influences, such as Ken Kesey's *Merry Pranksters* and, to a lesser degree, the characters in Jack Kerouac's *On The Road*. Again, there was some great music and some sequences would have an influence on the future of music videos, but for the most part the film was a flop. For years, however, it had an afterlife at midnight cult film showings and was reissued and viewed with fresh eyes on VHS, DVD, and Blu-Ray.

The group's next film, *Yellow Submarine*, released in 1968, barely includes the Beatles at all. While their songs obviously populate the movie, the animated film features the four Beatles as characters, but actors supplied the voices. The real Beatles do not appear until a short sequence at the end. The film was a success, though, as the innovative psychedelic animation, trippy images, and subliminal anti-establishment theme resonated with the culture of the time. It was shown in glorious color in cinemas around the world and benefited by the sure-handed direction of veteran animation producer George Dunning. Dunning also oversaw the ABC television cartoon series *The Beatles*, which ran from 1964 to 1967.

What would turn out to be the Beatles' last official film while they were together was the documentary *Let It Be*. This would be the first documentary from the group. While it was primarily filmed in 1969, it did not come out until 1970. The documentary film genre was going through a transformation in the 1960s, as the counterculture was exerting a growing influence on the culture, particularly in films on music, such as *Don't Look Back* (1967), *Festival* (1967), and *Monterey Pop* (1968), as well as *Woodstock*, which actually would not be released until 1970, and *Celebration at Big Sur*, which would not be released until 1971. Films like *Festival Express* and *Message of Love: The Isle of Wight Festival*, while both filmed in 1970, would not be released until decades later.

The Rolling Stones filmed many movies in the 1960s that fit into the documentary genre, including the incendiary *Gimme Shelter*, which came out in 1970, and the more obscure *One Plus One (Sympathy for the Devil)* (1968); there were also two films, *Charlie is My Darling* and *The Rolling Stones Rock 'n' Roll Circus*, which were filmed in the 1960s but did not come out until 2012 and 1996, respectively. Directors with extensive documentary experience such as D.A. Pennebaker and Murray Lerner were involved in several of the major music documentary films of the 1960s, and such high-profile international directors as Jean Luc Godard and emerging filmmakers such as Michael Lindsay-Hogg and Martin Scorsese were involved in others.

None of those documentary films were blockbusters at the box office, as was the case with documentaries in general, with the exception of one of them. *Woodstock*, produced on a budget of roughly $600,000, grossed $50,000,000 and was the sixth-highest grossing film of 1970. The documentary format of the film provided an accurate reflection of a moment in cultural history that was emblematic of a generation, yet for many it also signaled the end of not just the 1960s, but the counterculture. The hippie generation was no longer an amorphous underground subculture and the marketplace appropriated the hippie ethos, making all the accoutrements of the counterculture – sex, drugs, long hair, hippie fashions, and related lifestyle totems – ripe for monetary exploitation. The rock album, probably more than any other goods, propelled the rock music business into the entertainment stratosphere, monetarily eclipsing film. Oddly enough, as the 1970s moved along, more musical artists would be drawn to film and for many film scholars, the 1970s would be a watershed decade for American film.

For the Beatles, their entry into the documentary film genre with *Let It Be* would, like *Woodstock*, chronicle the end of the 1960s. Moreover, it also essentially heralded the end of the Beatles. Like *Magical Mystery Tour, Let It Be* would be perceived by critics as somewhat of a failure, although the film's climax, the group performing together on the roof of Apple Records, its London headquarters, rescued the film from being a complete failure. This would be the last time the group would perform together and, surprisingly, *Rolling Stone* magazine picked it as the greatest concert in the history of rock. In fact, in retrospect, the film has gone through a revaluation, with the group's fans clamoring for it to be re-released. The film was originally released on VHS and laserdisc in the early 1980s and has never had an official release on DVD or Blu-Ray. It was remastered in 1992 and again in 2003, with the intent of reissuing it with the Beatles' *Let It Be ... Naked* CD. Beatles scholars have long contended that the film has never been reissued because Paul McCartney and Ringo Starr do not want their fans to see the group in such a dark light, although McCartney has more recently warmed to the idea of allowing the film to be reissued at some point. Also, when George Harrison was alive, he was reportedly even more opposed to having the film reissued than McCartney and Starr.

For a film that has been out of official circulation since the early 1980s, a surprising amount of film and audio of the making of it and the album has continued to pour out into the bootleg market for years. Through Apple, the Beatles themselves include scenes from the film in their *Anthology* DVD box set and some of the previously un-issued audio surfaced on *Let It Be ... Naked*. The film unfortunately does reflect the sad end of the Beatles as a group. The soundtrack became the last official group album, even though *Abbey Road*, released in 1969, was technically the last album they recorded together.

Let It Be became the sole Beatles documentary film produced during the group's short time together and came about after a long twisted process that began when the group taped a promotional video for its track "Hey Jude." Filmed for the David Frost television show in September 1968, the performance was live in front of an audience. The group actually sang live to the musical backing track of the recording, but it was the closest thing to a live performance the group had done since its last official concert in San Francisco in August 1966.

The group had happily abandoned the road, tired of the screaming girls, poor sound, and circus-like atmosphere. However, the "Hey Jude" taping re-energized the group and all four of them enjoyed the performing experience, as limited as it was under the circumstances. Many live-concert performing ideas were tossed around for months, with the group finally deciding to start filming what was seen as rehearsals for whatever the live show(s) would become. They enlisted Michael Lindsay-Hogg, who had worked with them on several successful promotional videos. He was an American, who made his name producing various British rock television shows. The other decision they made was that producer/engineer Glyn Johns would handle the sound, as opposed to their long-time producer George Martin.

The four members of the group, the film crew, and various assistants spent most of the first half of January 1969 holed up on a soundstage at Twickenham film studios in London. In the end, that filming took up a large portion of the first third of the film. Film cameras were turned on any time any of the Beatles were on the premises, making for a *cinéma vérité*, unscripted hodgepodge of snippets of performances, people standing around talking and the group presented in a totally uncensored way. The film was a rare glimpse of the group at work, but was also for many boring or depressing. It was obvious that the members were unclear about what they were trying to do and had grown weary of each other at times, which sparked friction and made for an overall dour mood.

Fortunately, the group decided Twickenham was not working out and adjourned to their corporate headquarters, Apple Records. After George Martin helped them set up proper recording equipment, the group relied less on jamming on old songs and goofing around and set about trying to make progress on new songs, such as "The Long and Winding Road" and the title song "Let It Be." What also helped the sessions coalesce was the addition of keyboardist Billy Preston. With their admired guest the members were on good behavior. Some of the "performances" from these sessions would be used in the film as a complement to the live finale.

The next phase of the film would be the famed rooftop concert, which provided much of the end of the film and the climax (or some would say anti-climax) of the Beatles' time together. For an entire generation that grew up on the Beatles, the four Beatles (and Billy Preston) performing on the roof of Apple Records on that gray January day in London would be the last image of the Beatles as a group. Performing on the roof was not how the group originally envisioned its return to a live concert experience when the idea was first floated back after the David Frost taping in September 1968. Many elaborate ideas were discussed, including performing near the pyramids in Egypt or on the QE2. After all, it was the 1960s and they were the Beatles.

Finally deciding on the rooftop came about more out of necessity and as a means of finding a way to bring what was increasingly an unhappy experience to a conclusion. Even minutes before they were to perform, the members of the group were not sure if they were going to see it through. It was actually John Lennon who finally said they should go through with it and play live together again. The set was a loose and casual, at times spirited performance, punctuated by nervous jokes and asides that provided glimpses of the special camaraderie the group had in its halcyon days.

The way the concert finally ended provided the only cinematic tension in the film, as the noise from the concert brought the London police to Apple to shut the concert down. The metaphor of "the man" (the police) trying to stop the most visible figures of the 1960s counterculture was not lost on those that viewed the film looking for any final messages the group might have wanted to leave its fans at the end of the 1960s. As great as some of the performances in the film were, including most of the rooftop concert, the film and the resultant soundtrack album were mostly savaged in the press. The film did not artistically escalate what was essentially a moribund film genre (the documentary) in any way. While Murray Lerner, D.A. Pennebaker and others captured the new vitality of the counter-cultural musical movements of the 1960s, *Let It Be* was more a funereal and dark chronicle of the near-end of the greatest rock group in history and the sad end to the most revolutionary decade of the twentieth century.

For all its problems, the shortcomings of the film were not the fault of the film's director Michael Lindsay-Hogg. Lindsay-Hogg had been through much of the same experience with the Rolling Stones while working on the group's *Rock and Roll Circus*. That film was also delayed in being released and was not viewed with pleasure by the Rolling Stones, as *Let It Be* was not viewed with pleasure by the Beatles. It would be easy to dismiss the film *Let It Be* as one of those rare instances where the Beatles failed, but in retrospect the film has been viewed less harshly. It also was partially responsible for setting a template for the music film that chronicles the end of a group, with the most obvious example being *The Last Waltz*, the farewell concert by The Band at Winterland in San Francisco on Thanksgiving night, 1976. That film also chronicled not only the end of a group but also the end of a musical era. That concert reflected the more North American side of 1970s acoustic folk-rock and country rock and featured such artists as Neil Young, Joni Mitchell, Emmylou Harris, Bob Dylan, and others.

While *Let It Be* will most likely never make its way onto any list of best documentaries or best music films of all time, it is still significant as the final cinematic document of the Beatles. Film and of course music scholars will dissect, evaluate, and re-evaluate the film for years to come. New generations of music and movie fans will discover it for themselves and use it as part of their way into understanding and appreciating the Beatles' music and their times. Probably the best parody of the film was the Rutles' performance of "Get Up and Go." The song was so similar to "Get Back" that ATV, who owned the song publishing rights, sued and won. The video for the song is a pitch-perfect duplication of one of the songs from the rooftop segment of the film. Like *A Hard Day's Night, Help!, Magical Mystery Tour,* and *Yellow Submarine, Let It Be* will be watched by Beatles fans for generations to come. It is hard to know what film and music fans will say about film in the future, but for better or worse it will be viewed as the end of the group's long and winding road and, by some, as the end of the 1960s.

It was announced in January 2019 that Peter Jackson, director of the *Lord of the Rings* trilogy, is working with 55 hours of unreleased footage of the *Let It Be* shoot to create a new film that will be a companion to a reissue of the original film. No release date has been announced, but the 50th anniversary of the album and film occurs in May 2020.

CHAPTER 14

The Beatles Redux: The Anthology Series and the Video Age

Walter J. Podrazik

By design and coincidence, the Beatles exploited the reach of television in the USA. They used the medium to introduce themselves to American audiences and subsequently to renew that connection over the decades, individually and on behalf of the group.

Television allowed the Beatles to reach beyond their ardent music fan base to become an accepted part of the US national conversation and American popular culture. They successfully navigated the world of US variety and talk shows in the 1960s and 1970s, leveraged music video programs in the 1980s and 1990s, and found twenty-first century online opportunities, epitomized by the embrace of *Carpool Karaoke* (with James Corden in 2018) which went from broadcast network television to viral video.

Yet it was all of a piece that built on an approach executed by Beatles manager Brian Epstein, who recognized the value in cross-platform promotion, first in Great Britain and then on a far greater scale in the USA.

In 1963, Epstein brought the group from Liverpool to a national UK stage on a year-long ascent as he judged potential appearances beyond booking fees. He used strategic opportunities to leverage their growing reputation, especially through press and media buzz.

That reached a milestone in Great Britain in 1963 when the British press coined the term "Beatlemania" in the wake of their October 13 appearance on the television program *Sunday Night At The London Palladium*. There was a rapturous crowd of cheering and screaming fans who were captured in photos and on film, not only inside at the concert, but also in front of the venue itself.

Less than a month later, the Beatles cemented this image when they appeared as part of the prestigious *Royal Variety Performance*. The group had earned a spot in the lineup with their year-long sales success. On November 4, 1963, as seventh on the nineteen-act bill, the Beatles stole the show (including Lennon's "rattle your jewelry" quip). When that event was televised to a national British audience on Sunday, November 10, it was as if the whole country had jammed into the theater and been charmed by their banter and music.

Brian Epstein leveraged such moments as he ventured to where no other British band had ever achieved success: the US market. He used the twin tracks of their success. On the one hand, the story in Great Britain in 1963 had been the emerging musical talent of John Lennon, Paul McCartney, George Harrison, and Ringo Starr, touted as hit recording artists from Great Britain. When the Beatles became a sales phenomenon in the USA in advance of their landing in February 1964, there was curiosity to see these previously unknown stars who had managed such a rapid and impressive Stateside ascent.

The charismatic stage presence of the Beatles and the resulting frenzied crowds were equally important to the story, and perfect for television. To fans there was no mystery. The Beatles were a personal experience to be embraced and enjoyed again and again. That is why they tuned in.

For others, it was an intriguing puzzle. These less ardent observers felt like outsiders sneaking a peak, even those who enjoyed their music, just not as intensely. There was straightforward deep curiosity: What was this all about? What was the group's secret? Where did they come from? What was going on? Why these reactions?

The timing of the premiere appearance by the Beatles on the February 9, 1964, *Ed Sullivan Show* was perfect, drawing one of the largest viewing audiences to that point in US TV history. It set the stage for showcasing the two powerful draws of Beatlemania.

US viewers tuned in to observe the hit tunes by this new act and, in the process, experienced first-hand the charismatic performances that touched off the screams and shouts and outright adoration by the audience. Somewhere in those television images was the tease of possibly under-standing it all.

There was no better place for their promotional quest to unfold than US television. By good fortune, Brian Epstein hit a booming American broadcast medium in 1964. Following a decade of rapid growth, there were more than 600 individual over-the-air broadcast television stations throughout the country as well as about 5000 AM and FM radio stations. This was an increase of some 40 percent in TV numbers from the era of Elvis Presley and Ed Sullivan in 1956.

National nightly news programs in the USA had only recently doubled in length (from 15 to 30 minutes) on the two leading networks, CBS and

NBC, and they also offered morning news programs. In conjunction with those expanded showcases, the network news departments had grown with additional news bureaus, domestically and internationally. News operations covered the headlines of the day, but they also took opportunities to go further afield. For example, late in 1963 the CBS morning news had already offered a brief report on the phenomenon of the Beatles in Great Britain.

Thriving local stations throughout the USA were similarly situated, having upgraded the scope and quality of their local news programs that aired apart from the network offerings. When the Beatles embarked on their first US concert tour in 1964, they held press conferences at each stop. These gave local curious press the chance to see the Beatles phenomenon for themselves, creating opportunities for light entertainment news clips and human interest fan features.

That was the formula through three years of tours, with cinematic reinforcement provided by their feature films in 1964 (*A Hard Day's Night*) and 1965 (*Help!*). Yet also during that time the Beatles began generally to downplay in-studio live television musical performances and instead dispatched creative films of themselves and their latest songs. (Other British groups at the time also did the same.) With "Paperback Writer" and "Rain" these films from the Beatles began to display increasingly sophisticated cinematic sheen.

After the Beatles ended live concert touring in 1966 and immersed themselves in the studio for *Sgt. Pepper*, they used a pair of promotional films to kick off this new phase. Videos for the "Penny Lane" and "Strawberry Fields Forever" tracks found ready TV showcases (most notably in the USA with Dick Clark's *American Bandstand*). More than ever, the aura around the group remained, and the Beatles still benefited from the public's fascination, even down to interest in their new beards, sideburns, and mustaches, visible in the videos.

The plan to substitute films for touring seemed to work through the balance of the 1960s, although there were no guarantees. The *Magical Mystery Tour* special for British television (essentially a collection of music videos, led by "I Am The Walrus,") did not find a venue in the US market at the time either in cinemas or television.

Notable Beatles promotional videos from 1967 through 1970 included accompaniment to "Hello Goodbye," "Lady Madonna," "Hey Jude," "Revolution," "The Ballad of John and Yoko," "Get Back", and "Let It Be" (the latter two plucked from production footage for the *Let It Be* feature film documentary). These turned up on US television on such variety shows as *The Smothers Brothers Comedy Hour, The Glen Campbell Goodtime Hour, Music Scene,* and *The Ed Sullivan Show.*

When the Beatles broke up in 1970, they further added to their mystique with two new questions for public speculation: 1) How well would the individual Beatles perform as solo artists? and 2) When would the Beatles get back together?

With no new Beatles group performances, and no new Beatles albums, this would have been the perfect time to consolidate the promotional films they had produced to that point in their career, including footage that had never aired publicly (such as "A Day In The Life" from the *Sgt. Pepper* sessions).

That did not happen. Home video recording was not yet common. There were no ongoing US television video showcases and no practical way to see such footage repeatedly. Cost recovery was uncertain. As a result, after these films had their TV debut, they essentially took a bow and quickly disappeared from public view. Their subsequent limited availability added yet another layer to the Beatles legend.

Yet deep behind the scenes in the 1970s, Apple manager Neil Aspinall informally began a rough video scrapbook history of the group (dubbed *The Long and Winding Road*). He started to assemble bits from concerts, interviews, and TV appearances, but there was no new involvement by the principals. That effort stayed unfinished.

Instead, through the 1970s, John, Paul, George, and Ringo quickly incorporated their own new video performances into their respective solo careers. While there were still limited television showcases in the USA for video, the former Beatles were able to use portions of such films to ward off requests for a live performance in a TV talk show chat.

John Lennon most aggressively embraced video, starting with experimental films created with Yoko Ono before the Beatles split. Lennon's most polished and ambitious work was a video version of his second album, *Imagine,* in 1971. That film consisted of intimate performances of the *Imagine* album's songs, as well as tracks from Yoko Ono's companion release, *Fly,* accompanied by documentary and dialogue sequences.

On US television, ABC talk show host Dick Cavett gave John and Yoko the greatest airtime exposure and conversational leeway. In this venue, Lennon effectively demonstrated how each of the individual Beatles would continue to tap the public's fascination with them. Similar to Brian Epstein's original templates, the now seasoned and increasingly media savvy former Beatles would allow for a few "Beatles moments" such as a "What was it really like?" question or simply a moment of gratitude by the host for their past music. That was the informal trade-off. Then, it would be all about their new work.

Until Lennon stepped away from the entertainment industry in 1976, he also turned out standalone short promo videos (such as the 1972 "Power to the People"). He put aside these projects, though, during his hiatus. By the time Lennon and Yoko Ono returned with *Double Fantasy* in 1980, video promotion was an increasingly assumed element, as the medium had better established itself. Lennon and Ono had already recorded video footage for the song "Woman" at the time of his murder.

Following Lennon's death, additional videos were crafted posthumously, often drawing from the extensive *Imagine*-era film archive to accompany newly released *Double Fantasy* outtakes such as "Nobody Told Me" or reissues of past material such as "Love" (from the 1970 *Plastic Ono Band* album). Such offerings continued to allow them a musical presence in contemporary media.

Music video had grown in stature during the 1970s because artists and record labels came to embrace the form as a viable promotional tool, even underwriting the productions. That effectively provided television with flashy, inexpensive programming at little cost to the outlets. New TV ventures promoting rock music in that era included *The Midnight Special* and *Don Kirshner's Rock Concert* (both begun in 1973) and NBC's new comedy-variety series *Saturday Night Live* in 1975.

Beginning in 1981 on US cable, the new MTV network built its schedule around a continuous stream of video music films, like a video jukebox. In 1983, NBC added the late weekend broadcast showcase, *Friday Night Videos*.

As part of this process, artists and labels also significantly elevated the production quality of videos, sometimes turning them into mini-movies. The 1982 Michael Jackson album *Thriller* validated these investments when its videos helped to turn *Thriller* into the all-time best-selling album.

The Beatles as solo artists took advantage of these platforms to continue to distinguish themselves, including their own mini-movies. Even before the emergence of MTV, George Harrison had taken inspiration from his Monty Python friends for playful song videos. His 1976 *Thirty-three & 1/3* album generated a courtroom parody ("This Song"), a goofy tour of his estate ("Crackerbox Palace"), and an exaggerated courtship farce ("True Love"). Ringo Starr, who primarily pursued feature film acting roles during this period, also created promotional music videos. For "Only You" he was depicted as he landed a flying saucer at the Capitol Records Tower in Los Angeles.

Two of George Harrison's most effective music videos were with his low-key superstar group the Traveling Wilburys. "Handle With Care" introduced the assemblage of Harrison, Bob Dylan, Tom Petty, Jeff Lynne, and Roy Orbison with a joyful sense of onscreen camaraderie. "End of the Line" bookended that, with a loving nod to Orbison at his death. As with John Lennon, Harrison's own passing led to posthumous matchings of selected songs to archive video.

As a solo artist, Paul McCartney most consistently turned to music on film, not only for multiple promotional videos but also as its own art form, sometimes in collaboration with his wife Linda. The film of her song "Seaside Woman" won the Short Film Palme d'Or at the 1980 Cannes Film Festival. Another animation short, *Rupert and the Frog Song* ("We All Stand Together"), was fashioned as a bright children's cartoon.

Some of McCartney's mini-movie videos included the fantasy staging of a famous World War I Christmas battlefield truce (to "Pipes of Peace") and a traveling "medicine show" act with Michael Jackson (to "Say Say Say"). He also offered interpretive visuals such as striding the black and white keys of a piano with Stevie Wonder for their "Ebony and Ivory" duet.

McCartney's one major misstep in the genre was the 1984 feature-length film *Give My Regards to Broad Street*, which was heavily promoted as a first run theatrical offering rather than a more modest collection of new music video performances, strung together with a barebones story. Even then, the video for the song "No More Lonely Nights" was extracted from the film and became a hit.

Yet as the individual Beatles built their own solo video histories, the Beatles group videos remained unavailable, a low priority for official release. At last in the early 1990s, following settlement of internal ongoing legal matters, Apple re-emerged with a renewed focus representing the interests of McCartney, Starr, Harrison, and Yoko Ono. That included video.

The company struck a deal with the US ABC television network to produce a multi-part documentary history, *The Beatles Anthology*, to contain a mix of clips from concerts, films, songs, media appearances, and news coverage. Most important, there was to be involvement by the principals, including newly filmed interviews with Paul, George, and Ringo – with John Lennon's comments taken from archive footage.

This was the story of the Beatles as told by the Beatles, filtered through the decades. Paul, George, and Ringo even embraced how the passage of time sometimes left them with different memories of the same events. While there were also selected new interview comments by a few members of their inner circle (including producer George Martin), there was no third person/narrator to provide historical context and outsider perspective.

With a healthy production budget, vintage concerts and promotional videos were located and remastered. The black and white television footage of the "All You Need Is Love" live world broadcast from June 25, 1967, was vividly and painstakingly colorized. Arcane detail permeated the production, creating a polished, high-gloss scrapbook of the group's career, ending at the 1970 public break-up. No solo stories. John Lennon does not die.

There was a contemporary coda, though. Paul, George, and Ringo pulled off what they had repeatedly said could not be done: they got back together in the studio and turned out new recordings, using John Lennon solo demos to make it a foursome. The songs "Free As A Bird" and "Real Love" were both accompanied by new interpretive video productions.

The Beatles Anthology aired on ABC over three non-consecutive nights across two separate Nielsen ratings weeks: November 19 (Sunday), then November 22 and 23. Leading up to the premiere, the ABC network heavily promoted the series, dubbing itself "A-Beatles-C." Parts 1 and 2 won their respective nights in the ratings, with Part 1 number 6 for its week. However, these were not record-setting 1964 *Ed Sullivan Show* numbers. The *Chicago Tribune* called *The Beatles Anthology* "A ratings boomlet, but not a bombshell." The final part, on Thanksgiving night, lost to reruns of the feature film *Home Alone* and the series *ER*.[1]

Part 1 probably scored highest in part because it went back to the questions of where the Beatles came from. Equally important, the episode answered the question: Will the Beatles get back together? Paul, George, and Ringo introduced the affirmative answer with the video of their new song "Free As A Bird." While *The Beatles Anthology* did not dominate the US TV ratings, it did very well as a cross-platform media property that spawned a hefty tie-in book, three multi-disc audio collections, and, later, home video releases on tape and disc.[2]

Oddly, even after *the Beatles Anthology*, some promotional song videos still remained without a home, having aired only as excerpts in that special, or not at all. That situation did not change until the twenty-first century success of the Beatles *1*, a collection of their No. 1 songs which became the

[1] Harry Castleman and J. Walter Podrazik, *Watching TV: Eight Decades of American Television*, 3rd edn (New York: Syracuse University Press, 2016).
[2] Nielsen Ratings for *The Beatles Anthology* on US broadcast television cited from reports that appeared in the newspaper *USA Today* (November 1995).

top-selling album of the new century's first decade. That led to the DVD *1+* in 2015, which at last gathered not only the videos for the No. 1 hits, but also twenty-three additional tracks on a bonus disc. In the twenty-first century, the decades of Beatles group and solo video productions provided them with the material to enrich their group and individual websites. This catalog helped to boost them as viable artists for yet another age of music.

Still, the success of the 2018 *Carpool Karaoke* video harkened back to the original reason for the synergy between TV and the Beatles: their personal charisma. The 23-minute intimate visit with Sir Paul McCartney was irresistible. More than half a century after the Beatles first arrived on the pop culture scene, this was the medium's most powerful contribution. Video continued the opportunities to see and hear John Lennon, Paul McCartney, George Harrison, and Ringo Starr on the screen of choice, anytime, in ongoing access to an invaluable cultural legacy.

CHAPTER 15

Pop Goes the Internet

Allison J. Boron

Brian Epstein Could Not Fathom the Internet

The Beatles' manager died nearly a quarter of a century before the first website was born.[1] He never had a Facebook account, an email address, or a Twitter handle. In Epstein's lifetime, "bandwidth" was how much brain power and energy you could spare, superhighways connected major cities, and "Spotify" sounded like a great name for a dalmatian. Yet, he was steadfast in one conviction.

When asked by journalist Larry Kane in 1964 how long the Beatles "would last," Epstein responded with, "The children of the 21st century will be listening to the Beatles."[2]

Today, we know that Epstein's prediction came true – and then some. But for all of his foresight in so many ways, he probably could never have imagined just *how* those children (and teenagers, and adults, and ...) would listen to the Beatles. He did, however, know about virality, masterful marketing concepts, and the important role fans played in the success of his "artistes." After all, these are not new concepts, even though they have been retooled, enhanced, and digitized for today's music industry, where worldwide phenomena blow up instantly and burn out just as fast.

Because this chapter is talking about what are, right now, at this very second, as I am writing this, pretty modern concepts, by the time you read this, they will probably be obsolete. Such is the nature of the Internet, digital marketing, and music itself – landscapes where attention is at an ever-elusive premium – and most everything else is merely "freemium." And where some "stars" are guiding lights and some are supernovas.

---

[1] "The First Website Ever Celebrates Its 20th Birthday – Newsfeed," *Time*, August 6, 2011, http://newsfeed.time.com/2011/08/06/the-first-website-ever-celebrates-its-20th-birthday/.
[2] "Larry Kane Examines the Early Beatles," *Philadelphia Style Magazine*, September 3, 2013, https://phillystylemag.com/larry-kane-the-beatles-when-they-were-boys.

A Brief History of (Music's) Time (on the Internet)

Once upon a time, the only way to buy a song or an album was by trekking to the local record shop, laying down cash, and carting a vinyl 7- or 12-inch, CD, eight-track, or cassette home. That is, until 1997 when Derek Sivers introduced the world to CD Baby. While it might not have been the web's first online record shop, it has proven to be the longest lasting. And, most importantly for artists and consumers alike, it cut the red tape to sell music from independent artists without a distributor or major label pushing their music to record stores (in-person or online).[3]

Back then, the CD was king; its cheap manufacturing cost and ever-rising prices flooded the music industry with cash. By 1992, annual global sales surpassed one billion, then two billion in 1996.[4] It seemed too good to be true. Because it was.

The advent of modern computers' "ripping power" made it possible to transform music files from CDs into digital ones. Now, all listeners needed was a way to swap and download these files, especially as the Internet invaded American households. Enter Napster. On June 1, 1999, the pre-eminent file-sharing giant was born, and just nine months later, it boasted 20 million users.[5]

The music industry was, in technical terms, freaking out. Online piracy threatened its cash cow (CDs, which many consumers felt were too expensive anyway). Meanwhile, Napster's numbers kept climbing. The Recording Industry Association of America (RIAA)'s knee-jerk reaction was to sue the bastards who were stealing music; in one case, after the defendant (a grandfather of three named Larry Scantlebury) died, the RIAA then pursued charges against his family, generously allowing them sixty days to grieve before proceeding. (Ultimately, and thankfully, the lawsuit was eventually dropped.[6])

Napster's original incarnation shuttered in July 2001, and other looka-like platforms (LimeWire, Kazaa, BitTorrent, etc.) did not last long either. Among the ashes of the file-sharing giant stood around 35,000 of its users

[3] "Derek Sivers Interview January 2009," *The Music Entrepreneur HQ*, February 6 2009, www.musicentrepreneurhq.com/derek-sivers-interview-january-2009/.
[4] "How the Compact Disc Lost Its Shine," *The Guardian*, May 28, 2015, www.theguardian.com/music/2015/may/28/how-the-compact-disc-lost-its-shine.
[5] "15 Years After Napster: How the Music Service Changed the Industry," 6 June, 2014, *The Daily Beast*, www.thedailybeast.com/15-years-after-napster-how-the-music-service-changed-the-industry.
[6] "RIAA Drops Suit Against Grieving Family," *Ars Technica*, August 15, 2006, https://arstechnica.com/uncategorized/2006/08/7507/.

still embroiled in lawsuits brought by the RIAA that continued through 2008.[7]

The bubble had burst – big time. The music industry had made a fatal error; instead of realizing that file-sharing was heralding the next wave of music distribution (digital), it fought to keep the most profitable and historical format in play to its own detriment. Between 1999 and 2009, US music sales and licensing plunged from $14.6 billion in revenue to a paltry $6.3 billion.[8] It looked like things would never get better.

Well, until streaming became a thing.

The Savior

While the music industry was initially (and understandably) hesitant to embrace streaming as its savior, the numbers do not lie: in 2016, the industry reported $15.7 billion in revenue, thanks in large part to the 112 million paying users of services like Spotify, Apple Music, and Tidal.[9] (Though $15.7 billion 2018 dollars is still less than $14.6 billion 1999 dollars – about $22 billion today.)

In the beginning, there was Apple's iTunes, ready to pick up the digital-download torch just as Napster went offline. Finally, the industry could monetize those pesky files in a way that was positioned as a deal to customers. Who could argue with $0.99 per track?

Turns out, a lot of people over the ensuing fifteen years or so. "Owning" music, whether on CDs, cassettes, or as files living on computers, just was not that important. (A caveat: vinyl, in shocking turn of events, is still experiencing a renaissance – sales were up 10 percent in 2017, hitting a 25-year high,[10] and both CDs and vinyl outsold digital downloads.[11]) Instead, the almost laughably cost-effective (free, in some cases) streaming platforms including Spotify, Apple Music, and Tidal rose up.

---

[7] "The Music Industry's Digital Reversal," *The Star*, January 12, 2009, www.thestar.com/business/2009/01/12/the_music_industrys_digital_reversal.html.

[8] "Music's Lost Decade: Sales Cut in Half in 2000s," *CNN Money*, February 2, 2010, https://money.cnn.com/2010/02/02/news/companies/napster_music_industry/.

[9] "How Streaming Saved the Music: Global Industry Revenues hit £12bn," April 25, 2017, www.theguardian.com/business/2017/apr/25/2016-marks-tipping-point-for-music-industry-with-revenues-of-15bn.

[10] "End of Owning Music: How CDs, Downloads Died," *Rolling Stone*, June 14, 2018, www.rollingstone.com/music/music-news/the-end-of-owning-music-how-cds-and-downloads-died-628660/.

[11] "CDs, Vinyl Are Outselling Digital Downloads for the First Time Since 2011," March 23, 2018, www.washingtonpost.com/news/morning-mix/wp/2018/03/23/cds-vinyl-are-outselling-digital-downloads-for-the-first-time-since-2011/.

Today, Americans consume more music than ever before,[12] over half of which is delivered via on-demand streaming.[13] At the end of 2016, it was reported that 750,000 tracks are streamed around the world every minute on Spotify alone – and that number is projected in the millions now.[14] One hundred days after the Beatles' catalog debuted on Spotify in early 2016, the 50+-year-old band had racked up a staggering 24 million hours of streams.[15] In context, that is 24 million hours of songs listeners had heard before and probably owned in at least one other format.

That is the beauty of music in the digital age: the whole of music history is available not just at fingertips, but also on multiple devices and on multiple streaming platforms – and people are gobbling it up voraciously. Which means that artists from Mozart to the Beatles to Beyoncé are not only in demand, but also actually competitors for market share, buzz, and, of course, ears.

The Magical, Musical Internet Marketing Machine

Here is a (probably not) hypothetical: you "like" the Beatles on Facebook and you spend a decent amount of time listening to them on Spotify. The amount of Beatles-related content that makes it into your newsfeed probably does not surprise you, especially if you activated notifications or whatever system *du jour* is overriding the social-media algorithm when you are reading this.

What might surprise you, however, is when ads related to the Beatles, or interests marketers determine you might also like based on your love of the Fab Four, begin popping up everywhere from Instagram to Amazon. Such is the super-intelligent, highly targeted, and sometimes-creepy landscape of modern Internet marketing.

What used to be a fun and frivolous way to kill time posting pictures and leaving innocuous comments on friends statuses is now a key marketing component for everyone from the Beatles to Beyoncé. Quantitatively,

---

[12] "US Music Mid-Year Report 2018," *Nielsen*, July 6, 2018, www.nielsen.com/us/en/insights/reports/2018/us-music-mid-year-report-2018.html.

[13] "2017 US Music Year-End Report," *Nielsen*, January 3, 2018, www.nielsen.com/us/en/insights/reports/2018/2017-music-us-year-end-report.html.

[14] "Let's Play a Guessing Game: How Many Songs Are Streamed Each Minute on Spotify?," *Happy*, April 11, 2017, https://hhhhappy.com/lets-play-a-guessing-game-how-many-songs-are-streamed-each-minute-on-spotify/.

[15] "24 Million Hours Of Beatles Music Has Been Played In Their First 100 Days on Spotify," *Forbes*, April 8, 2016, www.forbes.com/sites/hughmcintyre/2016/04/08/in-their-first-100-days-on-spotify-24-million-hours-of-beatles-music-has-been-played/.

social media advertising is a must as a relatively easy, inexpensive, and engaging way to get music, concert promos, or merchandise in front of consumers; in 2017, ad spending totaled a whopping $40 million on Facebook alone.[16]

Beyond the science and numbers, however, social media's primary (and, some would say, more important) role is connecting fans and artists in a more personal way. For the first time in history, instant communication between the two is possible, and engagement is everything. A third of Twitter users follow and engage with social media celebrities and influencers.

The group with the highest reach, though? Musicians and actors, who are followed by more than 50 percent of Twitter users.[17] And, of the Top 10 most-followed accounts on Instagram, half are musical artists, all with over 100 million followers.[18] (In comparison, as of this writing, the Beatles have 1.8 million followers on Instagram, and Paul McCartney is the most highly followed Beatle with 2.1 million.)

Gaming the Charts

Where those "vanity" metrics like likes and follower numbers hit IRL (in real life, of course) is when those followers impact chart data, streaming numbers, and, ultimately, payouts from digital service providers (DSPs), record labels, publishing companies, and more. Though it is tricky as methods for measuring how and what streams count toward chart progress change on the reg, audio-streaming data accounts for somewhere between 40 and 50 percent of a song's *Billboard* Hot 100 each week.[19]

Of course, music-industry executives have tried to implement fraud-detection systems. For instance, if one user from one IP address plays a song or album repeatedly on Spotify for a straight week, it might raise a bit of suspicion. But this type of "chart gaming" is really nothing new – in the Beatles' heyday, record-label bigwigs would routinely buy up copies of

[16] "Facebook Reports Fourth Quarter and Full Year 2017 Results," *Investor Relations*, January 31, 2018, https://investor.fb.com/investor-news/press-release-details/2018/facebook-reports-fourth-quarter-and-full-year-2017-results/default.aspx.

[17] "New Research: The Value of Influencers on Twitter," *Twitter Blog*, May 10, 2016, https://blog.twitter.com/marketing/en_us/a/2016/new-research-the-value-of-influencers-on-twitter.html.

[18] "Most Followed Instagram Accounts 2018," *Statista*, 2019, www.statista.com/statistics/421169/most-followers-instagram/.

[19] "Fans to the Front: How Internet Fandoms Are Gaming the Music Industry," *Rolling Stone*, May 5, 2017, www.rollingstone.com/music/music-news/fans-to-the-front-how-internet-fandoms-are-gaming-the-music-industry-194067/.

singles or engage in payola, a now-hedonistic pastime of "pay to play" radio. (Speaking of the Beatles, stubborn rumors persist that Brian Epstein purchased 10,000 copies of the band's first hit, "Love Me Do," to drive it up the charts [to No. 17 in the UK], but it has never been proven.[20])

I'm Famous on the Internet

As music streaming became the norm, "freemium" made many platforms and services available to a wider swath of people, and as digital media became synonymous with just "media," the Internet also morphed into a breeding ground for famous (and infamous) pop-culture icons. While the part it plays is sometimes purely circumstantial, in many cases, the Internet is the genre-agnostic common denominator from which viral music is both created and consumed.

Case in point: the career of rapper and songwriter Austin Richard Post (better known as Post Malone) skyrocketed after his 2015 track "White Iverson" went viral on SoundCloud.[21] Soon after, Post landed a label deal with Republic Records and released his first full-length album, *Stoney*, in 2016, which debuted at No. 6 on the *Billboard* 200.

It would be his follow up, 2018's *Beerbongs & Bentleys*, however, that proved the staying power of some Internet-born artists: not only did the album debut at No. 1 *and* have the biggest-ever streaming week for an album, but also each of its eighteen tracks ranked on the *Billboard* Hot 100 singles chart.

And, most significantly, nine of those tracks landed in the Top 20, breaking the record for most simultaneous entries in the Top 20. A record previously held by – you guessed it – the Beatles, who claimed the title after putting six songs in the Top 20 between April 11 and April 18, 1964.[22] The only artist to challenge the Fabs was J. Cole, who tied the Beatles' record just a week before Post Malone cracked it wide open.

Now, Post Malone's unique path to the top is not to say he (and artists like him) were beneficiaries of pure, dumb luck. Post honed his chops as a guitarist, auditioned for bands, and even recorded and released a mixtape

[20] "BBC News – Eyewitness Account Says Epstein Bolstered Beatles Sales," *BBC*, October 4, 2012, www.bbc.co.uk/news/uk-england-19714392.
[21] "5 Big Artists Who Started On SoundCloud," *SoundCloud Reviews*, January 7, 2017, http://soundcloudreviews.org/5-big-artists-started-on-soundcloud/.
[22] "Post Malone Breaks Hot 100 Record For Most Simultaneous Top 20 Hits," *Billboard*, May 7, 2018, www.billboard.com/articles/columns/chart-beat/8454957/post-malone-breaks-hot-100-record-most-top-20-songs-beerbongs-and-bentleys.

prior to his SoundCloud breakthrough. But he had one thing that artists, even those who have spent years on labels, who have worked the touring circuit for decades, and who count Grammys and gold records in their accolades chase with often-unsuccessful fervor: a viral hit.

Going Viral

The definition of virality is akin to something like the definition of pornography in the eyes of the law: we cannot put our finger on it, but we know it when we see it. In the case of viral content, sometimes literally.

Virality relies on lightning-fast sharing, pop-culture saturation, and a degree of buzz from tech-savvy millennials, of course, and also familiarity from their grandparents with flip phones. In other words, virality in the digital age ushers in newer and newer "household names" – the way the Beatles became an instant part of greater America's lexicon on February 9, 1964, regardless of generation, economic status, or gender.

So, what is it about a song or video that makes it go viral on the Internet? Experts cite a few uniting factors[23] among tracks that experience this rare and beautiful honor:

- **Emotional resonance:** particularly, songs that are funny, shocking, sexy, or random and that are relatable to listeners.
- **Effort:** believe it not, content does not go viral by accident. In most cases, there is an extensive and elaborate marketing plan full of gimmicks and clever placements to thank for a viral hit.
- **Creativity:** the concept needs to be unique, something the public has not quite seen before. Think the Mannequin Challenge or the Harlem Shake, both of which boasted tracks that also rode the wave of virality ("Black Beatles" by Rae Sremmurd and "Harlem Shake" by Baauer, respectively).[24]
- **Quality:** let's face it – a terrible song with abysmal quality will not get far. At the very least, it needs listener-friendly production, but ear-wormy lyrics and melody serve a purpose, too.

When it comes to music, it is possible for a track (especially one heating up the streaming charts) to go viral, but an eye-catching video certainly helps. In 2012, K-Pop star Psy invaded America with his dance track,

[23] "Behind The Scenes of Viral Music," *Visual.ly*, April 2, 2013, https://visual.ly/community/info graphic/entertainment/behind-scenes-viral-music.
[24] "Case Study: How Artists and Songs Go Viral," *EDMProd*, November 9, 2017, www.edmprod.co m/case-study-how-artists-and-songs-go-viral/.

"Gangnam Style," which, to date, has earned over 3 billion views on YouTube, and held the title of most-viewed video (not just music video) on YouTube for a full four and a half years.

Today, Luis Fonsi's Latin-pop-crossover anthem "Despacito" claims that honor after it broke records[25] to become the fastest music video ever to reach 1.5, 2, and 2.5 billion views. As of September 2018, the video accounted for more than 5.5 billion views in total.

Virality and fame (no matter how fleeting) is great, but how do artists actually make money to, you know, live? Artists like Justin Bieber, Rihanna, and Adele generate millions from fans watching and sharing their content, but what about your middle-of-the-industry heatseeker trying to sculpt a bona fide music career?

In 2017, digital music revenue grew by 19.1 percent to $9.4 billion according to IFPI,[26] although per-song payouts remain fractions of a cent: streaming giant (with a 51.1 percent market share) Spotify pays just $0.00397 per stream.[27] And with a meager $0.00074 per-stream artist-revenue rate, YouTube has the lowest payout of all digital platforms, which means artists should not count on it for actually making a living.

Unless, of course, you are Psy.

For all its buzz, the actual numbers behind "Gangnam Style," are a bit murky. It is estimated that Psy earned around $12 million from commercial deals, downloads, and streaming, but earnings from YouTube (i.e., his viral video) are somewhere in the range of $750,000 to $4 million.[28] (The actual figure might lie somewhere around the $2 million mark, although it has also been rumored at around $8 million.)

The Holy Trinity: Artists, Their Fans, the Internet

So far, we have seen that the Internet changed virtually everything about how artists make, release, and market music. But on the opposite side of the coin, it also revolutionized the fan experience like nothing else in

[25] "YouTube Trends: 'Despacito' Is Now the Most Viewed Video in YouTube History," *YouTube Trends*, August 4, 2017, http://youtube-trends.blogspot.com/2017/08/despacito-is-now-most-viewed-video-in.html.

[26] "Global Music Report 2018," *IFPI*, www.ifpi.org/downloads/GMR2018.pdf.

[27] "2017 Streaming Price Bible! Spotify per Stream Rates Drop 9% . . .," *The Trichordist*, January 15, 2018, https://thetrichordist.com/2018/01/15/2017-streaming-price-bible-spotify-per-stream-rates-drop-9-apple-music-gains-marketshare-of-both-plays-and-overall-revenue/.

[28] "Behind The Scenes of Viral Music," *Visual.ly*; "How Much Money Does 3 Billion YouTube Views Actually Bring In," *Forbes*, September 18, 2017, www.forbes.com/sites/hughmcintyre/2017/09/18/how-much-money-does-3-billion-youtube-views-bring-in/.

history. Reaching back to primitive forums and message boards, email mailing lists and chat rooms, the digital age is the first time in history that artists started following the fans' lead; they now are able to home in on what consumers love, want, and will buy. Fans are architects of communities, artisanal creators of merchandise, and tastemakers and influencers with incredible power.

The Internet offers something for everyone at any level of fandom. Casual fans can absentmindedly Google Dave Matthews' name to see his latest tour dates; hardcore fans can create special social-media accounts dedicated to obsessing over every outfit Katy Perry has ever worn onstage. The beauty of this sometimes ugly digital landscape is there is a place for all; that ugliness takes the form of trolls, and know-it-all armchair experts who spread misinformation while condescending to anyone they deem lower on the fandom totem pole.

And, interestingly, fans are not just interested in engaging with celebrities and their fellow peers in the same fanbase – they are also dedicated to taking up the cross when they see unsavory behavior, including trolls of all sizes.

Beyoncé is one of the most-followed people, period, on social media, and when Queen Bey announced her new activewear line in 2016, yoga-wear clothiers Lululemon tried to climb on the party bus, tweeting that Beyoncé must love their products so much, she decided to copy them.[29]

> They do say imitation is the best form of flattery. Maybe Beyoncé is so Crazy In Love with our brand, she made her own. (Lululemon's later-deleted tweet)

But a barrage of Beyoncé's hardcore fans (mobilized as "the BeyHive") immediately put the publicly traded company on blast for insinuating that their goddess would ever deign to rip off Lululemon. As a result, Lululemon hastily deleted tweets and worked feverishly to backpedal. One fan tweeted, "RIP Lululemon," to which the brand said, "Hey now, you won't find us six feet under. We love a little competition, especially with the Queen B."

Just as Brian Epstein had no idea how the people of 2018 would consume Beatles music (just that they *would*), he could not have had any idea just how rampant instant celebrity would become, how streaming would revolutionize the music industry, and how the seemingly endless twists

---

[29] "Beyoncé Fans and Lululemon Trade Snarky Tweets . . .," *CNN Money*, March 31, 2016, https://money.cnn.com/2016/03/31/news/companies/lululemon-beyonce-ivy-park/index.html.

and turns of social media and marketing would turn everything he knew on its head.

Though today's technology has turned pop culture into something vastly different than the Beatles' experienced in the 1960s, there is a bottom-line lesson here: people have never, and will never, stop loving music. Whether it is heard on vinyl or Spotify, which flash-in-the-pan Internet celebrity is singing it, or who is spreading the word via what social media platform is just all arbitrary. What survives is that love.

And, as someone once said, "Love is all you need."

PART IV

The Beatles' Sound

CHAPTER 16

Abbey Road Studios

Brian Southall

It is a sad and disappointing fact that the Beatles did not name the last album they made together in tribute to the place where they learnt and mastered their recording skills over eight years during the glorious, swingin' 1960s.

The title *Abbey Road* came about, according to Paul McCartney, because it was "the simplest thing to do" after deciding against the name Mount Everest. And, as the group's bassist further explained, it might "imply something kinda mystical – Monastery Avenue sorta thing."[1]

However, by bringing the location of the recording studios owned by the giant EMI company to the attention of every music lover, the Beatles honored an anonymous Georgian house built in the north London district of St John's Wood and turned it into a musical shrine.

Although the studios were never officially christened 'Abbey Road' – the sign on the door of number 3 Abbey Road NW8 read EMI Recording Studios – it is likely that is what the two-studio complex was called from the time it opened its doors in November 1931 to welcome Sir Edward Elgar and the London Symphony Orchestra for the first recording session.

In fact Abbey Road studios came about just months after the landmark merger of the Gramophone Company and the Columbia Graphophone Company, which signaled the birth of Electric & Musical Industries Ltd – EMI. Among the early producers working in the new studio complex were Fred Gaisberg, who discovered Enrico Caruso for the company's HMV label, and David Bicknell, while the likes of Sir Thomas Beecham, Yehudi Menuhin, Arturo Toscanini, Artur Schnabel, Joe Loss, Jack Payne, Al Bowlly, Noel Coward, and American stars such as Fred Astaire and Paul Robeson all made the journey to what was the world's largest building dedicated to recording.

---

[1] Brian Southall, *Abbey Road: The Story of the World's Most Famous Studios* (Wellingborough: Patrick Stephens, 1982), ch. 7.

Figure 16.1 The entrance to Abbey Road Studios, London, September 21, 2010.
Photo by Kevin Nixon/Future Music Magazine via Getty Images

In the lead-up to World War II, Britain's prime minister-in-waiting, Sir
Winston Churchill, paid a brief visit to Abbey Road and, noticing that the
staff all wore white coats, observed, "It looks like a hospital." In many
ways the studio was an institutionalized place with a regulation dress

code – collars and ties with white coats – and strict three-hour recording sessions of 10 am to 1 pm, 2 pm until 5 pm and 7 pm through to 10 pm – and there were no exceptions.[2]

Legendary American bandleader Glenn Miller was another visitor to the studio when, in September 1944, he recorded with Dinah Shore and an Allied Forces band. A few weeks later Miller's plane was lost over the English Channel and, bizarrely, the recordings remained unreleased for fifty years until the expiry of copyright restrictions in 1994.

However, it was classical music that took pride of place in Abbey Road's recording schedules. Producer Bicknell was joined by Walter Legge and Lawrance Collingwood and between them they added artists such as Tito Gobbi, Carlo Maria Giulini, Wilhelm Furtwängler, Herbert van Karajan, and Elisabeth Schwarzkopf to the HMV and Columbia rosters.

With the arrival of 33⅓ rpm long-playing records and 45 rpm singles, and the resulting replacement of wax cylinders by lacquer discs, records became more popular and "pop" music heralded in the 1950s and a new chapter in the Abbey Road story.

The emergence of pop music required Abbey Road to recruit a team of new non-classical producers including Norman Newell, Ray Martin, Wally Ridley, Norrie Paramor, and a 24-year-old named George Martin. This new breed of producers was charged with finding and recording pop talent for EMI's three pop labels – Columbia, HMV, and Parlophone – which would compete with the records coming from America.

EMI's UK licencing agreements with RCA Victor and CBS meant that they were responsible for releasing records by the likes of Guy Mitchell, Eddie Fisher, Johnnie Ray, Paul Anka, and Elvis Presley but when those deals expired the British company had to find home-grown artists to record in Abbey Road and compete in the new pop singles chart introduced by the *New Musical Express* in 1952.

The first British No. 1 record to emerge from Abbey Road was a trumpet instrumental titled "Oh Mein Papa" by Eddie Calvert which was produced by Ray Martin. His colleagues (or rivals) soon followed suit with Ridley taking Ronnie Hilton and Alma Cogan to No. 1, Paramor emerging with Ruby Murray and Newell adding pianist Russ Conway to the list of Abbey Road's first seven chart toppers between 1954 and 1959.

---

[2] Southall, *Abbey Road*, ch. 2.

As pop music grew in popularity so Abbey Road's team of producers
created more and more chart-topping records from the likes of Cliff
Richard, the Shadows, Adam Faith, Johnny Kidd, Ricky Valance,
Helen Shapiro, the Temperance Seven, Shirley Bassey, Danny
Williams, and Frank Ifield. At the same time the studio continued to
produce major classical works from conductors such as Sir Thomas
Beecham and Sir Malcolm Sargeant, alongside musicals and a host of
popular comedy records which came mainly from George Martin and his
Parlophone label.

Creating hit records made Abbey Road more popular and the need
to invest in new technology became apparent as George Martin
recalled following a trip to America in late 1957 to see Frank Sinatra
record in the studios of EMI's sister company, Capitol Records: "I was
impressed with the techniques used over there and realised we were
terribly way behind. The people at the top (in EMI UK) were reluctant
to buy better equipment, however we slowly managed to change the
studios and progress."[3]

New developments with echo chambers, overdubbing, acoustics,
two-track and stereo recording were taking place in the studios as
the 1960s arrived to herald an extraordinary and unique period in the
history of Abbey Road which was led by four young men from
Liverpool.

The Beatles – John Lennon, Paul McCartney, George Harrison, and
eventually Ringo Starr, who replaced original drummer Pete Best – came
to George Martin's attention after the group's manager, Brian Epstein, had
gone to EMI's HMV record store in London's Oxford Street to have a
demonstration tape transferred to disc.

One of the people in the store who heard the tape recommended the
group to Martin and on June 6, 1962 the Beatles sat with their new
producer in Abbey Road for what in those days was called an artist test –
a simple recording session to assess an act's ability and talent. That first
two-hour evening session involved the Beatles performing four songs: a
cover version of "Besame Mucho" and three of their own Lennon/
McCartney compositions – "Love Me Do," "P.S. I Love You," and "Ask
Me Why."

Before deciding whether to sign the Beatles to his Parlophone label,
Martin had to consider whether to change the group's title to feature a
leader. The arrival of rock 'n' roll brought with it groups such as Cliff

[3] Southall, *Abbey Road*, ch. 3.

Richard and the Shadows, Johnny Kidd and the Pirates, Adam Faith and the Roulettes and it was left to the producer to decide whether Lennon or McCartney should front the Beatles. Deciding that they were best left as they were, he offered the Beatles a standard EMI recording contract which was backdated to June 4 to include the four tracks recorded during the original session.

The Beatles returned to Abbey Road on September 4, 1962 and came with new column amplifiers and a selection of American records including Carl Perkins and early Motown releases in an effort to show their new record label the sort of sound they wanted to reproduce. According to Abbey Road technical engineer Ken Townsend, the newly dubbed 'fab four' were instrumental in changing the way the studio worked: "They very soon moved from two track to four track recording and began to revolutionise the way in which Abbey Road had worked for 30 years."[4]

As they grew ever more successful, the Beatles had a greater influence on the workings within Abbey Road. They turned the studios – mainly studio 2 – into a workshop, rehearsing and composing songs while at the same time putting pressure on Martin and his colleagues to keep up with their creative demands.

By the end of 1965 the Beatles had released six albums and every one of them had topped the charts in the UK, while they could claim eight No. 1 collections in America where the titles and track listings were changed for the US market. However, other acts were treading the boards in the studio and the likes of Gerry and the Pacemakers, Cilla Black, the Hollies, Manfred Mann, the Seekers, Peter & Gordon, and Ken Dodd all notched up chart-topping singles in the first half of the glorious 1960s.

At the same time, while acts such as comedy duo Morecambe & Wise, organist Reginald Dixon, jazz diva Ella Fitzgerald, and rock 'n' roll legend Gene Vincent recorded in Abbey Road, a host of stars were recorded "on the road" by the studio's mobile unit, including Scottish singer Sandy Stewart and Judy Garland and her daughter Liza Minelli at the London Palladium.

In April 1966 the Beatles set about recording a song called "Mark I," which by the time it appeared as the closing track on the album *Revolver* had been titled "Tomorrow Never Knows." It represented a new peak in the group's creativity on an album that took them to new heights as

---

[4] Southall, *Abbey Road*, ch. 6.

they prepared to put their touring years behind them and focus on working in the studio.

In order to produce *Revolver*, the Beatles needed help from the technical staff at Abbey Road and Townsend was at the forefront of the team as he created Artificial Double Tracking (ADT), which revolutionized the laborious process of double-tracking vocals. John Lennon was so impressed with Townsend's invention that he dubbed it "Ken's flanger" and "flanging" stands today as an accepted recording phrase.[5]

Just a week after the release of *Revolver* on August 5, 1966, the Beatles began their last ever concert tour and when they returned from America at the end of the month, they went into Abbey Road and set about creating their next album which in turn became another recording watershed, even though their producer George Martin had ended his 15-year career at Abbey Road and left to set up his own AIR Studios.

The rules at Abbey Road had always insisted that only acts signed to EMI could record there and only staff employed by the studio could work on recordings, but things changed after Martin left as the Beatles insisted he be allowed to return to Abbey Road to work on their recordings. Music entrepreneur Mickie Most was another who benefited from the changes as the white coat rule disappeared and the strict three-hour sessions became a thing of the past: "The Beatles changed all that because they began all-night recording – they lived in the studios and just experimented."[6]

In the light of their enormous global success nobody at EMI or Abbey Road was going to try to influence the Beatles' recording timetable and the making of *Sgt. Pepper's Lonely Hearts Club Band* showed why, as John, Paul, George, and Ringo plus producer Martin and engineer Geoff Emerick created what would turn out to be the group's best-selling album during more than 700 hours of studio time over a five month period – at a record cost of £25,000.

All four Beatles, together with their partners, visited India in the early part of 1968 to study meditation with the Maharishi Mahesh Yogi and ended up with enough new songs to make their first ever double album. When they returned to Abbey Road in May to begin recording, the studio was about to embrace a new innovation – eight-track machines.

The new Studer machines would make ADT a thing of the past and allow the Beatles and other artists to record in a revolutionary new way. However, according to Townsend, the studio's most famous customers did not take to the new technology as they embarked on their album *The*

[5] Southall, *Abbey Road*, ch. 4.   [6] Southall, *Abbey Road*, ch. 8.

Beatles (known forever as *The White Album*): "They did have the new toy but they didn't take to eight track straight away because the machines couldn't do what they wanted."[7] As a result, much of *The Beatles* was created using two four-track machines.

Tensions were high during the six months spent making their ninth studio album as the group members often recorded separately the songs they had each created. McCartney described it as "the tension album" before explaining, "We were all in the middle of the psychedelic thing or just coming out of it. It was weird."[8]

The Beatles were without a manager following Epstein's death, there was a level of resentment at the arrival of Lennon's new girlfriend Yoko Ono, a falling out with engineer Emerick meant he left mid-way through recording, individual production issues had to be dealt with and finally there was a difference of opinion with their long-time producer. Martin believed *The White Album* would make "a very, very good single album" while the Beatles insisted on a thirty-track collection filling four sides.[9]

Despite all the issues, *The Beatles* was yet another worldwide hit album and another feather in the cap of both Abbey Road Studios and producer George Martin.

Even though Abbey Road had become a second home to the Beatles for over six years, they decided to create their own studio in the basement of their Apple offices in Savile Row in London's Mayfair district. Created by Alexis "Magic Alex" Mardas, who ran Apple Electronics, the new studio, he claimed, would have seventy-two tracks compared to Abbey Road's eight-track facility.

The ill-fated project was eventually rescued when Martin ordered equipment from Abbey Road and the Beatles set about recording the songs that would eventually appear on the album *Let It Be* via an abandoned TV project entitled *Get Back*. However, during the making of *Let It Be* in their Apple Studio – with visits to Abbey Road to work on at least three tracks – the group also embarked on another project, which would turn out to be the last album they would ever record together.

The album *Abbey Road* brought the group and producer Martin back "home" to St. John's Wood to record, according to McCartney, "the way we used to." Despite concerns about their most recent time in the studio together, Martin agreed but insisted that the Beatles themselves had to be "the way they used to be."[10]

---

[7] Southall, *Abbey Road*, ch. 8.   [8] Southall, *Abbey Road*, ch. 8.   [9] Southall, *Abbey Road*, ch. 9.
[10] Southall, *Abbey Road*, ch. 10.

The resulting *Abbey Road* album, recorded over seven months in 1969, was a fitting finale to the Beatles' career in Abbey Road Studios and included the group's final session together on August 20 when they mixed and arranged the running order for *Abbey Road*.

Despite the departure of the Beatles, who confirmed they were splitting up April 1970, Abbey Road Studios continued to flourish with the likes of Pink Floyd, Sky, Kate Bush, Sade, Take That, Blur, Radiohead, Sting, Kanye West, and Adele continuing the hit-making tradition established by the Beatles during the 1960s.

If the group known as the Beatles was gone forever, the four individual members were not lost to Abbey Road as each of them returned to further their solo careers. George Harrison recorded his 1968 effort, *Wonderwall*, in both EMI's studio in Bombay, India and Abbey Road and his best-selling double album, *All Things Must Pass* – the first solo No. 1 by an ex-Beatle – was also produced there.

John Lennon chose Abbey Road when he came to make the *Wedding Album* in 1969 and his *John Lennon/Plastic Ono Band* collection a year later. While the 1971 album *Imagine* was mainly recorded at Ascot Sound, his home studio in England, it is possible that some mixing took place at Abbey Road before Lennon left Britain for the last time that August.

While Ringo Starr only returned to Abbey Road to record his 1970 album *Sentimental Journey*, Paul McCartney maintained a close, long-term relationship with the studios. Since recording his debut solo album *McCartney* in 1970, he has returned time and time again to make albums such as *Wild Life, Back To The Egg, Give My Regards To Broad Street*, and *Flaming Pie* through to the 2013 release *New*.

His love of the studio was highlighted in 1977 when he was unable to book time in studio two because Shadows' guitarist and producer Bruce Welch was booked in – "we didn't throw anyone out, not even for the Beatles," explained Townsend. Keen to mix his new album in studio two, McCartney decided to re-create the famous control room in the basement studio in his London office: "The great thing was that we had a picture of the studio on the wall with a clock that worked."[11]

When I spoke to the former bass player with the Beatles in 1981 for the book *Abbey Road – The Story of the World's Most Famous Recording Studio*, McCartney was glowing in his praise for the building, which was granted English Heritage Grade II listing in 2010.

---

[11] Southall, *Abbey Road*, ch. 7.

Talking to me in the place where he used to go for peace and quiet during the heady days of Beatlemania – the studio's boiler room – McCartney explained, "I would just say that Abbey Road is the best studio in town; town being the world." Seated on an up-turned beer crate, he went on to explain, "Obviously there are more modern studios, more technological; studios, places where you can park your car but there's a kinda of nostalgia for me whenever I come back into the place."[12]

And as it closes in on ninety years as Britain's most prestigious and famous recording studio, Abbey Road, although no longer part of the great British EMI company – it was acquired by Universal Music in 2011 – continues to attract artists and producers plus fans from all around the world who are drawn there by the unforgettable music that John, Paul, George, and Ringo created in a converted nine-bedroomed "desirable residence" built in 1830.

---

[12] Southall, *Abbey Road*, Foreword.

CHAPTER 17

Producing Sound Pictures with Sir George Martin

Kenneth Womack

The most widely acclaimed record producer of his generation, George Martin enjoyed unparalleled success during a fifty-year musical career in which he oversaw the production of some thirty No. 1 hits and more than 700 recordings. For many rock historians, he truly deserves the title of being the "Fifth Beatle," despite Murray "The K" Kaufman's well-known comments to the contrary. Martin not only transformed the Beatles into popular music's most influential recording artists, but also handled key duties involving the musical arrangement and orchestration of their mid- to late period recordings, including a spate of landmark albums – *Rubber Soul* (1965), *Revolver* (1966), *Sgt. Pepper's Lonely Hearts Club Band* (1967), *The Beatles* (*The White Album*, 1968), and *Abbey Road* (1969). It is difficult to imagine a more prestigious output.

In spite of his posh-sounding accent, Martin had far more in common with the Beatles' working-class origins than they could have possibly imagined when they first came into his orbit at EMI's Abbey Road Studios in June 1962. Martin was born on January 3, 1926, into a north London household without benefit of electricity or running water. As the Great Depression exerted its awful toll, Martin's father Harry worked sporadically as a craftsman carpenter, while his mother Bertha took odd jobs as a maid and a seamstress. The sound of music pierced young George's world at an early age, as he toyed with an old upright that the family had acquired via an uncle, who worked at a piano factory. At the tender age of eight, he wrote his first composition, "The Spider's Dance," after half a dozen lessons. His great moment of epiphany occurred several years later when his school played host to the BBC Symphony Orchestra. Under the direction of Sir Adrian Boult, the orchestra performed Debussy's *Prélude à l'après-midi d'un faune* and 15-year-old George fell under the music's spell. "I thought it was absolutely heavenly," he recalled. "I couldn't believe human beings made that sound." But even at that early

Figure 17.1 The Beatles pose for a portrait in the studio with their producer George Martin in circa 1964. Photo by Michael Ochs Archives/Getty Images

moment, George found himself enrapt with the *making* of music as much as with its aesthetic beauty: "I could see these men in their monkey-jackets, scraping away at pieces of gut with horsehair and blowing into funny instruments with bits of cane on their ends. But the mechanical things I saw simply didn't relate to the dream-like sound I heard. It was sheer magic, and I was completely enthralled."[1]

Not long afterwards, Martin and his friends organized a dance band called the Four Tune Tellers. Before long, they developed a steady following and a standing musical repertoire. "We played the standards by Jerome Kern, Cole Porter, and so on, things like 'The Way You Look Tonight,'" he later recalled. "Quicksteps were always the most popular, and we always ended with 'The Goodnight Waltz.'"[2] But as with so many young men of his day, Martin's ambitions began shifting toward the omnipresent military effort that galvanized the nation. With World War II in full swing, he joined the War Office's non-uniformed ranks before enlisting in the Royal Navy's Fleet Air Arm. While Martin never saw combat, his training took him from the English coast to New York City and Trinidad and back

[1] George Martin with Jeremy Hornsby, *All You Need Is Ears* (New York: St. Martin's, 1999), 30.
[2] George Martin, *Playback: An Illustrated Memoir* (Guildford: Genesis Publications, 2003), 18.

again. Along the way, he began to self-consciously refine his unsharpened
north London accent with the posh tones of the gentlemen-officers whom
he chose to emulate. Paul McCartney credits Martin's military service with
the leadership abilities that assisted the producer in shaping the Beatles as
his musical protégés: "I think that's where George got his excellent bedside
manner. He'd dealt with navigators and pilots. He could deal with us when
we got out of line."[3]

After the war, Martin enrolled in the Guildhall School of Music and
Drama, where he specialized in piano and oboe. Three years later, he
landed a plum job as Assistant A&R man for EMI's Parlophone label,
which was under the supervision of Oscar Preuss. In 1955, Martin was
promoted to label head at the youthful age of 29. By the mid-1950s, he had
salvaged the struggling label from the scrapheap after developing an
eclectic stable of artists, including comedy acts like Peter Sellers and the
Goons, with whom Martin recorded several strong-selling records. There is
little doubt that his newly acquired "cut-glass voice," in the words of
Beatles historian Mark Lewisohn, played a role in his ascent in the class-
conscious UK. In the ensuing years, Martin served as producer for a variety
of artists, ranging from Cleo Laine and Stan Getz to Humphrey Lyttelton
and Judy Garland. He also made a name for himself producing comedy
records by Peter Ustinov, Peter Cook, Dudley Moore, and members of the
Goons.

In the early 1960s, Martin planned to expand Parlophone's catalog by
venturing into the evolving world of pop music. He came into the Beatles'
orbit via their manager Brian Epstein. Having been rejected by Decca
Records, among a host of other British record firms, Epstein cut an acetate
from the band's Decca audition tapes. With the demo in hand, he made a
circuitous route through London's music publishing offices, eventually
coming into contact with Martin at Parlophone, the bottom of the
proverbial barrel amongst EMI's numerous subsidiary labels. While
Martin listened to Epstein's increasingly tiresome pitch that the Beatles
were bigger than Elvis, he held firm on his resolve not to offer them a
contract without auditioning them first. A few months later, in May 1962,
Epstein made one last effort to win a contract from Parlophone. During a
morning appointment with Martin at EMI Studios in St. John's Wood,
London, Epstein toned down the overconfident approach that he had
employed earlier in the year. To Epstein's genuine surprise, Martin agreed

---

[3] Kenneth Womack, *The Beatles Encyclopedia: Everything Fab Four* (Santa Barbara, CA: Greenwood, 2016), 327.

to provide the Beatles with a recording contract without having met them, much less auditioned them.

During the Beatles' historic first visit to Abbey Road Studios in June 1962, Martin was initially unimpressed with their musicianship. "They were rotten composers," Martin decided, and "their own stuff wasn't any good." After an introductory session, Martin launched into an unvarnished critique of their performance. When Martin concluded his diatribe, he asked the Beatles if there was anything they did not like, to which George Harrison famously responded, in perfect deadpan: "Well, for a start, I don't like your tie." Quite suddenly, the room, which had lapsed into an unearthly silence, erupted with laughter. "During that one conversation," Assistant Producer Ron Richards recalled, "we realized they were something special."[4]

At first glance, Martin's partnership with the Beatles seemed like an unlikely pairing; the classically trained, 36-year-old producer seemed to have little in common with four North Country lads from Liverpool. As Beatles biographer Ray Coleman observes, though, their relationship "began as record producer and young pop stars and developed into that of a wise uncle, and eventually to friendship."[5] By the time the Beatles entered his world in the summer of 1962, Martin had developed a keen ambition to work with a beat group, preferably, one with hit-making potential. After his initial efforts to reshape the band in the image of the day – as "John Lennon and the Beatles" or "Paul McCartney and the Beatles," he could not quite decide which way to go – he soon began to afford them with the artistic space to chart their own creative destiny, an unusual move in a recording industry that frequently treated pop singers and musicians like so much chattel.

After producing the band's first No. 1 hit, "Please Please Me," and assisting them in crafting the sound that flowered into the global phenomenon known as Beatlemania, Martin challenged the Beatles as both songwriters and musicians by introducing them to classical influences and encouraging the experimentation that characterized their artistic heights in the late 1960s. By this point, Martin's initial misgivings had all but vanished. "They learned so quickly how to write a hit," he recalled. "They were like plants in a hothouse. They grew incredibly fast."[6]

As Martin later reflected on his time with the Beatles:

---

[4] Bob Spitz, *The Beatles: The Biography* (Boston: Little Brown, 2005), 318.
[5] Womack, *The Beatles Encyclopedia*, 330.   [6] Martin, *Playback*, 88.

A two-way swing developed in our relationship. On the one hand, as the style emerged and the recording techniques developed, so my control – over what the finished product sounded like – increased. Yet at the same time, my need for changing the pure music became less and less. As I could see their talent growing, I could recognize that an idea coming from them was better than an idea coming from me, though it would still be up to me to decide which was the better approach. In a sense, I made a sort of tactical withdrawal, recognizing that theirs was the greater talent.[7]

But that is not to say that he did not leave his mark on their music – however subtle that imprint may have been. He frequently prompted the bandmates to revise their musical structure in key ways – witness "Can't Buy Me Love," which began, quite arrestingly, with the chorus at Martin's suggestion. And then there's "A Hard Day's Night," which the producer launched into the stratosphere via his varispeed "wind-up piano" technique via a solo duet with George Harrison. But for Martin, "the turning point" emerged during the June 1965 sessions for "Yesterday," the most covered composition in the Lennon–McCartney songbook. Martin later wrote:

> It was on "Yesterday" that we first used instruments or musicians other than the Beatles and myself (I had often played the piano where it was necessary, as on *A Hard Day's Night*). On "Yesterday" the added ingredient was no more nor less than a string quartet; and that, in the pop world of those days, was quite a step to take. It was with "Yesterday" that we started breaking out of the phase of using just four instruments and went into something more experimental, though our initial experiments were severely limited by the fairly crude tools at our disposal, and had simply to be molded out of my recording experience.[8]

In addition to providing them with nuggets of recording artistry such as the "wind-up piano" technique, he shared his own musical performances with the band – most notably, the piano solo on "In My Life" – while also composing such classical arrangements on their behalf as the groundbreaking "Yesterday" and "Eleanor Rigby" orchestrations, among a host of others. In terms of his own professional career, he eventually severed his relationship with the EMI Group after the conglomerate refused to increase his paltry salary despite his considerable role in the Beatles' international success. In 1965, he left EMI and established AIR (Associated Independent Recordings), an independent production company.

---

[7] Martin, *All You Need Is Ears*, 167.   [8] Martin, *All You Need Is Ears*, p166–67.

Peter Asher, the brother of McCartney's erstwhile fiancée Jane Asher and one of the stars of 1960s pop duo Peter and Gordon, and later a talented musical producer himself, lauds Martin for his significant role in shaping the Beatles' astounding musical development:

> The Beatles were brimming over with brilliant ideas and radical concepts, but it took extraordinary diplomacy, exceptional musical expertise, limit-less patience, and visionary clarity to bring these ideas to fruition and greatness. Sometimes, George's genius was knowing when to jump in and offer musical advice; sometimes, it was knowing when to go down to the canteen and have a cup of tea, letting them get on with whatever they were up to.[9]

Martin and the Beatles' penchant for experimentation would take them on an incredible musical journey from *Revolver* (1966) and *Sgt. Pepper's Lonely Hearts Club Band* (1967) through *The Beatles* (*The White Album*, 1968) and *Abbey Road* (1969), their incredible swansong. But for George's money, the "Penny Lane" b/w "Strawberry Fields Forever" single was "the best record we ever made."[10] With its crisp production and rich sense of melody, the single had all the hallmarks of a George Martin production. On the one hand, it required a fair amount of studio trickery to pull off – especially "Strawberry Fields Forever," which consisted of two parts with conflicting time and key signatures that George skillfully grafted together. On the other hand, the listener can scarcely ascertain the producer's fingerprints on the "Penny Lane" b/w "Strawberry Fields Forever" single at all.

During his post-Beatles career, Martin produced albums by a variety of different artists, including Jeff Beck, America, Elton John, Celine Dion, the Little River Band, and Cheap Trick. In addition to producing McCartney's celebrated *Tug of War* (1982) album, he supervised the Beatles' *Anthology* series during the mid-1990s, as well as the production of their remarkably successful compilation, *The Beatles 1*, in 2000. His career includes a number of noteworthy milestones. In 1963, for instance, recordings produced by Martin spent an unprecedented thirty-seven weeks in the No. 1 position on British record charts. In 1995, he was honored with a knighthood. In 1996, he directed an acclaimed benefit concert starring McCartney, Eric Clapton, Elton John, and Sting on behalf of the volcano-ravaged island of Montserrat, the former home of one of AIR's recording studios.

---

[9] Womack, *The Beatles Encyclopedia*, 330.   [10] Martin, *All You Need Is Ears*, 168.

He produced his last No. 1 single, John's "Candle in the Wind '97," to commemorate the tragic death of Princess Diana. In 1998, he memorialized his musical career with the release of *In My Life*, an album of Beatles songs performed by several world-renowned musicians and actors, including Phil Collins, Celine Dion, and Sean Connery. Over the years, he has written four books about his experiences: *All You Need Is Ears* (1979), *Making Music* (1983), *With a Little Help from My Friends* (1994), and *Playback* (2002). His later years were punctuated by the international acclaim associated with *Love* (2006), the Cirque du Soleil show that featured innovative Beatles musical pastiches produced by Martin and his son Giles. Martin died at age 90 in March 2016.

The Beatles, of course, would mark the lion's share of Martin's contributions to music. As fledgling musicians, they benefited from his highly sophisticated manner in dealing with artists. He was truly the ultimate producer in the sense that he could make people feel relaxed by taking himself out of the equation and succeed in getting the performance from virtually anyone. That was his genius. A great producer is like the greatest of film directors in that you cannot glimpse their imprint on the finished product. For his part, Martin remained largely invisible, having disappeared into the background of the act of creation.

And that final aspect, in and of itself, defines the whole of Martin's work. As he well knew, the act of production should be invisible. It should be so effective and evocative that you do not even know the producer is somewhere there in the back of the recording, behind the curtain, bringing the whole effort into tantalizing Technicolor and real life. For all of his accolades, a "Phil Spector" production is always inalienably by Spector. Whether it involves the Beatles or the Chiffons, the echo chamber is right there, front and center, reminding us who is standing behind the control board. But a George Martin production is both less and more. It is decidedly *less* because George's identity in the music is latent – he has guided the artist to the moment in which the art comes to fruition without noise or fanfare. But it is also *more* because he is able to facilitate the release of the magical germ inside the artist's head over and over – so much so, in fact, that Martin's skills as a producer emerged as a kind of fifth instrument for the Beatles: it was always there for the playing, for making the track brighter and, more often than not, better. And with George Martin and the Beatles, brighter and better usually translated into a new classic for the ages.

CHAPTER 18

Rock 'n' Roll Music! The Beatles and the Rise of the Merseybeat

Anthony Robustelli

When George Martin first heard the Beatles he was not that impressed. Manager Brian Epstein had secured a meeting with the Parlophone record producer due to the fact that EMI's publishing company, Ardmore & Beechwood, was interested in securing the publishing rights to John Lennon and Paul McCartney's original material. While some of the duo's early songs were simplistic such as "Hello Little Girl," "One After 909," and "Too Bad About Sorrows," there were others that were more sophisticated and should have impressed Martin. Oddly enough, Martin initially did not think the duo had much to offer as composers.

While they did not have the plethora of material that McCartney has claimed they had, they had written a number of songs with striking melodies and unique chord progressions including "Love Of The Loved," "Like Dreamers Do," "I Call Your Name," "I'll Follow The Sun," "Ask Me Why" and "P.S. I Love You." The latter two in particular are strong examples of the early Lennon-McCartney writing style and although Martin might not have thought that a mid tempo, Latin-tinged song was the best way to introduce the group to the record-buying public, it's puzzling that he failed to acknowledge the fact that they were at least competent songwriters at this early juncture. By claiming that "Love Me Do" was the best they had at the time, the B-sides of the first two Beatles songs were automatically discounted as having any artistic merit. Ron Richards, who handled most of the rock 'n' roll acts for Parlophone, did like "P.S. I Love You," but since there was a recent song of the same name, it was passed over as an A-side. Although they were in no position to demand anything from George Martin or EMI, the Beatles were adamant that their first single be an original composition. Unbeknownst to them they had the publishing men at Ardmore & Beechwood on their side from the very beginning. To Martin's credit he did see something in the group at their initial session on June 6, 1962 that other label executives had failed to recognize.

The thing that set the Beatles apart from their contemporaries was the fact that they incorporated various genres of music into their live performances and later, into their compositions. While other groups such as the Rolling Stones and the Yardbirds relied heavily on the blues and 1950s rock 'n' roll pioneers for their inspiration, the Beatles ventured further back, integrating the music of their youth before rock 'n' roll took over Britain.

It's been said that necessity is the mother of invention, and in the Beatles case this could not be any truer. When the group initially arrived in Hamburg in August 1960, they had only two hours of material, but they soon realized they needed more than double that. Although it would require more work, they had no desire to repeat material. In order to fill their sets, and keep it interesting for themselves, they pulled from every musical genre. They had no problem playing a Chuck Berry potboiler such as "Roll Over Beethoven" followed by Hoagy Carmichael's "Up a Lazy River," or a song with a country and western bent like Carl Perkins "Honey Don't" alongside show tunes like a "A Taste of Honey" and "Till There Was You." This open-minded attitude was pervasive in their songwriting as well and this quest for original sounds guided them on their journey as songwriters. McCartney explained it best:

> The reason why we started writing our songs was because if you were playing on a bill with maybe three or four other bands, and you were possibly going on third, the other bands before you had often played your whole act . . . So we started thinking, "We had better look for obscure tracks or just start writing tracks for ourselves."[1]

When the two future Beatles first met on that fateful day in July 1957, Lennon was impressed with McCartney's ability to play and sing Eddie Cochran's "Twenty Flight Rock," and McCartney by the fact that Lennon was the leader of his own band. While this initial meeting led to Lennon inviting the younger musician to join his group, the Quarry Men, it was their interest in songwriting that would have the greatest impact on their future. Many teenagers loved skiffle and the relatively new style of music, rock 'n' roll, but few wrote their own songs. Once McCartney played Lennon one of his earliest compositions written about the loss of his mother, "I Lost My Little Girl," Lennon felt comfortable enough to

---

[1] Keith Badman, *The Beatles Off the Record: Outrageous Opinions and Unrehearsed Interviews* (London: Omnibus, 2001), ch. 4.

show his future partner some of his own compositions. Soon after they began writing together, McCartney was always eager to label each song "Another Lennon–McCartney original."[2]

Initially the duo wrote separately because Lennon believed that McCartney was more advanced than he was. As Lennon described it, McCartney was "always a couple of chords ahead," but they were quickly writing "eye to eye," and while their initial compositions were simple, they developed over time.[3]

McCartney's father had played the piano and led Jim Mac's Jazz Band in the 1920s. The house was filled with music and the aspiring musician was influenced by everything he heard, including the pop and jazz standards of the day. While Lennon often stated in public that he hated jazz, this could not be further from the truth. His chord changes on "Ask Me Why," "All I've Got To Do," and "Do You Want To Know A Secret," his comping on "Till There Was You," or his guitar solo and jazzy voicings on "Honey Pie" paint quite a different picture for the listener.

Learning chords initially presented a challenge for Lennon, so his mother taught him banjo and ukulele chords, which were simpler to finger, and eventually, taught him how to play the piano accordion. Although she played Elvis Presley records on her record player, he also was exposed to the pre-rock 'n' roll standards of the day. While Lennon had no formal training, his tendency to move his hands around the fretboard looking for a certain chord change led him to stumble upon many treasures, often unorthodox but nonetheless brilliant; an ear that was raised on more than just rock 'n' roll at work.

While the Who's chief songwriter, Pete Townshend, could at times be dismissive of the Beatles' recordings, his observation of the group as composers could not be more appropriate: "The Beatles brought song-writing to rock 'n' roll."[4] Quite a bold statement, but true in many ways. From the 1920s through to the 1950s big band and swing music was considered the "popular" music of the day and could simultaneously be quite complex. By contrast, when rock 'n' roll swept over America in the mid-1950s, the music was basically blues with a backbeat. The songs, including those by the artists the Beatles worshiped, were often based on a twelve-bar blues or the I–vi–ii–V doo-wop progression, of which the Beatles were so fond. A major component of Lennon–McCartney's

[2] Barry Miles, *Paul McCartney: Many Years from Now* (New York: Holt, 1997), 36.
[3] Mark Lewisohn, *Tune In: The Beatles – All These Years* (New York: Crown, 2013), 214.
[4] Dominic Pedler, *The Songwriting Secrets of the Beatles* (London: Omnibus, 2010), ch. 3.

songwriting, however, comes not from their love of rock 'n' roll but from their internalization of a treasure trove of stylistically varied music that was a part of their lives before rock 'n' roll came into being.

One has to imagine the world they lived in as children and the songs they were exposed to pre-rock 'n' roll. This appreciation of other types of music led to a sophistication absent from many previous rock 'n' roll records. By incorporating elements from these varied sources, the Beatles elevated what a pop song could be in the early 1960s. But rock 'n' roll was always the backdrop for the Beatles, and with it they created some of the most groundbreaking music of the twentieth century.

Lennon and McCartney's uncanny ability to pair interesting, innovative chord progressions with stellar melodies put them in a league of their own, and the idea that a "beat group" could write their own material was not wasted on the managers of the day that prodded their groups to do as the Beatles had done. But Beatles songs always had a twist, whether it was a borrowed or non-diatonic chord to spice up an A section or a key modulation to take a middle eight in a new direction. They were able to use songwriting techniques that were not heard in pop music in the 1960s and simultaneously change the expectations of the pop music that was to come. Many of these modernisms are what propelled the evolution of pop music into the rock music we know today, but Lennon and McCartney were not always as prolific as they would become.

After an exuberant start between 1958 and 1959, their songwriting slowed down considerably with little being written until late 1961. Once Brian Epstein learned that Lennon and McCartney wrote songs, he encouraged the pair to make their songs a part of their set list. Few, if any, bands wrote their own material and Epstein saw this as a selling point that should be exploited. At the end of 1961, the Beatles added three originals to their Cavern Club set lists, John's "Hello Little Girl" and Paul's "Like Dreamers Do" and "Love of the Loved." Once they had secured their first EMI recording session, which was scheduled for June 6, 1962, Epstein instructed them to "rehearse new material." The band took this as a cue to compose more songs.[5]

Although they had been writing sporadically for years, the excitement of a record deal with EMI rekindled the flame that had led them to quickly fill a school exercise book with Lennon and McCartney originals in 1958. They had been extremely self-conscious about playing their own compositions

---

[5] Kenneth Womack, *The Beatles Encyclopedia: Everything Fab Four* (Santa Barbara: Greenwood, 2016), 329.

during their shows at the Cavern and in Hamburg, but Brian encouraged them to explore this avenue from the start. For this reason, they included "Hello Little Girl," "Like Dreamers Do," and "Love of the Loved" in the set list for their failed Decca audition on January 1, 1962.

Once they revived their songwriting partnership in 1962, their song-writing ability accelerated at an incredible pace. They had figured out a way to inject a "moment" into their hit singles, as well as many album tracks, that would make the crowds go wild. A well-placed "oooo" sung in falsetto, a hooky "yeah, yeah, yeah," or one of many long, slow build-ups proved to be key to a successful song. By creating these moments, Lennon and McCartney would write some of the most striking and memorable material of the twentieth century.

The development of Lennon and McCartney as composers, and the Beatles as a band, from late 1962 to early 1964 is astounding. There were a few originals that stood out on their debut album, *Please Please Me*, as rather sophisticated harmonically, notably the title track, "Ask Me Why," and "P.S. I Love You." Their second single, "Please Please Me" was worlds apart from their first, "Love Me Do," not only as a song but also by its sheer execution. The energy that jumps off the record is astounding and the attack of this performance is what propelled the Beatles to their first taste of true recognition by their record producer and the record-buying public. Clever songwriting, impassioned vocals, and a dynamic, driving rhythm put this song at the top of the charts, as Martin had predicted at the end of the session and while "Please Please Me" was the second official single, it can be argued that it is the first that really counts. The growth seen in two and a half months is remarkable. This fast-paced evolution would be evident throughout the Beatles' career and is a key reason for their longevity. The ability to morph from one record to another, while still maintaining an identifiable "sound," has rarely been seen on this level.

For lesser artists this rapid progression might have waned soon after, but this was not the case for the Beatles. By their sophomore LP, released eight months after their debut, they were for all intents and purposes quite a different band. Songs such as "All My Loving," "It Won't Be Long," "All I've Got to Do," and "Not a Second Time" show a more mature approach to composition and hint at the mid-1960s, post-mop-top Beatles that would be fully formed by *Rubber Soul*. Even Harrison's first foray as a fully fledged songwriter is impressive, and is by far the darkest song, both musically and lyrically, in the Beatles canon up to that point.

The fact that there was no filler on *With The Beatles*, a rarity for 1960s pop albums, is a testament to the band's integrity and talent. Most albums in the 1960s capitalized on the fact that a group had a hit single and put together a long player that had one or two successful singles and a number of lackluster songs, often composed by the producer, to fill in the gaps. While *Please Please Me* had featured the Beatles' first two singles and was released in order to take advantage of their current popularity, it contained four additional Lennon–McCartney originals and six choice covers. But *With The Beatles* contained no singles, a formula they would repeat throughout most of their career, creating what was essentially the first Beatles songbook album, as it was referred to by producer Martin. The album was not about hits; it was about music. Even their cover choices had been elevated. Smokey Robinson and the Miracles' "You've Really Got a Hold on Me," Chuck Berry's "Roll Over Beethoven," and "Till There Was You," from the musical *The Music Man*, were examples of the musical palate from which the group chose to paint and the results were stellar.

But before they began recording songs for *With the Beatles* they first needed to follow up the success of their first No. 1 single, "Please Please Me." Their third single, "From Me to You," was interesting, especially the middle section, but it is what followed that demonstrated the unique powers of the Lennon–McCartney songwriting team and the Beatles as a band. "She Loves You" was arguably their best song at that point with an infectious hook, innovative chord changes, impassioned vocals, and a rock solid rhythm section. The fact that it was recorded less than five months after the marathon session that produced the majority of the tracks for their debut LP is miraculous in and of itself. Within the confines of a 2-minute pop song the Beatles interjected more ideas than ever into a song that would point toward the future of rock music.

The band continued to raise the bar with each single and album release. "I Want to Hold Your Hand" was the song that finally introduced them to an American audience and things were never the same. It sounded like nothing else on the airwaves at the time and was different from any previous Beatles record. One contributing factor that is rarely discussed when speaking of the differences between "I Want to Hold Your Hand" and their prior singles is the slower tempo. "Love Me Do," "Please Please Me," and "From Me To You" hovered between 140 and 150 bpm, and "She Loves You" topped them at a lively 160 bpm. "I Want To Hold Your Hand," however, rocks along at 132 bpm and this slightly slower tempo allows the song to breathe and groove harder than any previous single. Add to this the mean, heavily compressed sound of Lennon's persistent eighth-note rhythm guitar and Starr's full out assault on the open hi-hat, and one hears what seems to be the future of rock, not pop, music.

"I Want To Hold Your Hand" also gave the band their first taste of four-track recording. Until that day the group's output had been recorded on a twin-track machine offering them only two tracks on which to record. They did, however, bounce tracks from one machine to another to open up additional tracks and truly discovered the art of double-tracking their vocals while recording *With The Beatles*, something that was used to great effect throughout their career.

During the recording of their sophomore album, the band and Martin began to use the studio as a workshop, finessing songs more frequently in the studio. Other than Martin's keyboard overdubs on their debut LP and the overdub of harmonica on "Thank You Girl," the group had never spent more than one session on a song. Although *With The Beatles* was recorded in only seven separate sessions over three months, it was not uncommon to start a song and return to it at a later date for a remake or for overdubs, an occurrence that would become commonplace as the group developed throughout the decade.

This approach to recording was only enhanced with their introduction to four-track recording. It opened up new opportunities production-wise and led to some of the most forward-thinking recordings of the 1960s. With their new found worldwide success their schedules grew even more hectic, but their output remained steady as their songwriting chops developed.

The year 1964 brought new challenges: their first feature film, their first World Tour, and their first album comprising solely original material. While McCartney wrote three of the album's most impressive songs, "Can't Buy Me Love," "And I Love Her," and "Things We Said Today," Lennon was the primary songwriter on nine of the album's thirteen tracks. *A Hard Day's Night* was a leap ahead from *With The Beatles*. Gone was the "yeah, yeah, yeah" and the Little Richard-infused "ooo." The band was already a bit world-weary and the lyrical content showed this. They rarely sang directly to the fans anymore and instead explored more adult themes in their songs.

The music had changed as well. Although it was released less than sixteen months after *Please Please Me*, the opening chord of the title track could not be farther from the exuberant count-in of their debut LP. It was a modernist album that proved that the Beatles were more than a teeny-bopper sensation; they were a band to be taken seriously. The songs were harmonically challenging, melodically nimble, and the instrumentation was fresh and new. Harrison's use of his newly acquired Rickenbacker twelve-string electric guitar was a major factor in creating this new sound and added a sparkle to numerous songs. It also helped spawn a new electric folk sound in the USA led by groups such as the Byrds.

They explored new avenues stylistically as well with the country and western influenced "I'll Cry Instead," the R&B funk of "You Can't Do That," and the Dylanesque feel of "I Should Have Known Better." Although Lennon and Harrison used their Gibson J-160E acoustic-electric guitars on the first two albums, they were often plugged into their Vox AC15 or AC30 amplifiers, giving them a more "electric" sound. For *A Hard Day's Night*, Lennon's J-160E was captured with a microphone, more frequently giving the album a more acoustic guitar-driven feel.

Because the album was in essence a soundtrack album with seven of the thirteen songs featured in the film, the two singles were lifted from the album to promote the film as well. "Can't Buy Me Love" brings back the swing of McCartney's "All My Loving" and was deemed so catchy that it was used twice in the film when director Richard Lester decided that the melancholy lyrics of "I'll Cry Instead" did not fit the mood of a particular scene. It was also novel being the first single to feature a solo vocal with no backing.

There was always competition between the primary songwriters of the Beatles, and it led them to heights they might not have reached had it not been for this healthy competition. For all its innovations "Can't Buy Me Love" is a fantastic song, but "A Hard Day's Night" set the bar higher for the group and for all that followed. Musicians, authors, and critics still cannot agree as to what the opening chord is. Lennon wrote the lyrics based on one of Starr's malapropisms and the story he tells is not one of holding hands or pleasing a partner. It addresses the fact that the Beatles were being run ragged and the bluesy inflections in the melody articulate this feeling perfectly.

By the end of 1964, the Beatles were no longer the fresh-faced mop-tops that had graced the covers of magazines for nearly two years. The photo chosen for their fourth LP, *Beatles For Sale*, demonstrates this fact clearly. Under pressure their eighth single did not fail to surprise. The B-side, "She's a Woman," finds McCartney channeling his inner Little Richard flawlessly, but the feedback heard at the beginning of the A-side, "I Feel Fine," is what announced to the world that the Beatles were not done pushing the envelope as to what a pop record could sound like.

Had the group been given more time in the fall of 1964, they had the makings for what might have been considered one of their greatest accomplishments: an insightful, mature record that charted their development as songwriters and performers. With songs such as "No Reply," "Baby's in Black," "I'm A Loser," "I'll Follow the Sun," "I Don't Want to Spoil the Party," and "Eight Days a Week," *Beatles For Sale* could have been a fantastic album. But due to time constraints the band had to revert to the formula of their first two albums: eight originals and six covers. So what we ended up with was an album that was both forward thinking and regressive at the same time. Covers notwithstanding, one thing was certain: the Beatles had proven that they were game changers within the first eighteen months of their recording career and would continue to grow and develop for five more years. For many fans, some of their most creative and groundbreaking music was yet to come, but the music released in 1963 and 1964 was far more advanced than many realize and set the stage for a revolution.

CHAPTER 19

Positively Bob Dylan: The Beatles and the Folk Movement

Kit O'Toole

John Lennon: "I realized that we were poets but we were really folk poets, and rock & roll was folk poetry – I've always felt that. Rock & roll was folk music.[1]

While the folk revival movement traces back to the 1930s, the 1960s saw a new phase: the combination of traditional folk and rock, two seemingly dichotomous genres. Bob Dylan remains the primary symbol of 1960s folk, and American artists such as the Byrds, Buffalo Springfield, Crosby, Stills and Nash, and Simon and Garfunkel continued the charge. In the UK, musicians such as Donovan, the Searchers, and Fairport Convention added British folk traditions to the movement. During this folk-rock boom, the Beatles released the acoustic guitar-heavy album *Rubber Soul*, often cited as their venture into the genre and heavily influenced by Dylan. However, the Beatles and folk-rock had a reciprocal relationship, with the Beatles' early work shaping the movement and, in turn, the music transforming John Lennon and Paul McCartney's songwriting. A close examination of three Beatles albums – *Beatles for Sale*, *Help!*, and *Rubber Soul* – reveals this symbiotic relationship.

"We Were Cross-Pollinating Each Other": Beatles and Dylan

By 1964, Dylan had become the voice of folk, with *The Freewheelin' Bob Dylan* and *The Times They Are A-Changin'* earning virtually universal acclaim from purist folk fans as well as peers such as the Beatles. *Freewheelin' Bob Dylan* contained mostly original material, a rarity for a folk artist at that time and a signal that he would not rely solely on folk traditions. As Richie Unterberger notes, "Dylan nudged folk closer to the

---

[1] Pete Hamill, "Long Day's Journey into Day: A Conversation with John Lennon," *Rolling Stone*, June 5, 1975, www.beatlesinterviews.org/db1975.0605.beatles.html.

mainstream of popular culture – and hence, though no one could have foreseen it, rock music – by writing both personal songs that tapped into his generation's zeitgeist."[2] "Masters of War," "Blowin' in the Wind," and "A Hard Rain's A-Gonna Fall" perfectly captured the political and cultural turmoil of the 1960s. His poetic language also deviated from that of the more straightforward Woody Guthrie and Pete Seeger, and ushered in a new era of folk that broke away from the constraints of traditional folk such as that based on nineteenth-century English and Scottish popular ballads.

Yet a year later Dylan would transition from a purely political songwriter to a highly personal one. *Another Side of Bob Dylan* would alienate some fans with his tales of broken love, rejection of social conformity, and discomfort with his own protest songs. As Tim Riley argues in *Hard Rain: A Dylan Commentary*, "My Back Pages" served as "a thorough X-ray of Dylan's former social proselytizing ... Dylan renounces his former over-serious messianic perch, and disowns false insights (he calls teachers 'mongrel dogs')."[3]

The Beatles took notice of Dylan's poetic and highly personal style. During Lennon's 1971 *Rolling Stone* interview with Jann Wenner, he expanded upon Dylan's impact on his songwriting. Through hearing Dylan's work, he explained, he realized "I'd have a separate song-writing John Lennon who wrote songs for the sort of meat market, and I did not consider them – the lyrics or anything – to have any depth at all." After listening to Dylan's lyrics, Lennon said, he began treating words more seriously: "I started being me about the songs, not writing them objectively, but subjectively."[4]

While Dylan's influence on the Beatles has been frequently dissected, the group's impact on his work receives less attention. The Beatles' revitalization of rock 'n' roll reignited Dylan's interest in the genre; according to Ian MacDonald, this led to the troubadour's highly influential album *Bringing It All Back Home.*[5] As Howard Sounes explains, the album "integrated what he had learned from the success of British bands like the Beatles with his own, more poetic lyrics."[6]

In May 1964, Dylan would travel to England for a concert tour, and artists such as Eric Burdon, the Rolling Stones, and the Beatles attended his

---

[2] Richie Unterberger, *Jingle Jangle Morning: The Birth and Heyday of 1960s Folk-Rock*, Kindle edn (Richie Unterberger, 2014), ch. 10.
[3] Tim Riley, *Hard Rain: A Dylan Commentary*, Kindle edn (New York: Vintage, 1992), ch. 2.
[4] John Lennon, *Lennon Remembers*, interview by Jann Wenner (New York: Verso, 1970), 84.
[5] Mark Hertsgaard, *A Day in the Life: The Music and Artistry of the Beatles* (New York: Delacorte, 1995).
[6] Howard Sounes, *Down the Highway: The Life of Bob Dylan* (New York: Grove, 2001), 166.

shows. Energized by records such as the Animals' "House of the Rising Sun," Dylan would cease recording explicit protest songs and move toward literary prose, abstract imagery, introspective lyrics, and the all-important electric guitar. Groups and electric rock were the future, and Dylan needed to change with the times. "You better start swimmin'," Dylan explains in "The Times They Are A-Changin'," "or you'll sink like a stone."

Just a year after Dylan and the Beatles met in New York, Dylan would shock the audience at the Newport Folk Festival, strapping on an electric guitar and performing with a five-piece group. The Beatles most likely admired Dylan for risking his career to move in this bold direction. As Devin McKinney writes in *Magic Circles: The Beatles in Dream and History*: "They had jarred an older generation's sense of what was true and false, but they had not risked their supremacy among pop fans by daring real controversy, a radical move, a non sequitur."[7] Nevertheless, the Beatles' soundtrack for *A Hard Day's Night* provided the template for the folk-rock movement through its acoustic-tinged songs.

Groundbreaking: *A Hard Day's Night*

Crucially, the twelve-string opening of "A Hard Day's Night" sparked what became the folk-rock movement. As Howard Hampton wrote in his essay for the Criterion Collection release of the film, "you have only to look at the loving shots of George Harrison playing his Rickenbacker twelve-string electric guitar – no one had seen or heard anything like it (it was only the second one ever manufactured)." When Roger McGuinn saw the film, "he had a veritable religious experience: thus were born the Byrds, folk rock was launched, and a thousand chiming, eight-mile-high tunes went chasing after Harrison's sound."[8]

Another song that played a key role in the development of folk-rock is "You Can't Do That," the first time Harrison played a twelve-string guitar on record. In *The Complete Beatles Recording Sessions*, Mark Lewisohn describes the first take of "I Should Have Known Better" as starting with a Dylan-sequel harmonica solo by Lennon.[9] The moody "I'll be Back,"

[7] Devin McKinney, *Magic Circles: The Beatles in Dream and History* (Cambridge, MA: Harvard University Press, 2003), 107.
[8] Howard Hampton, "*A Hard Day's Night*: The Whole World Is Watching," *The Criterion Collection*, June 24, 2014, www.criterion.com/current/posts/3205-a-hard-day-s-night-the-whole-world-is-watching.
[9] Mark Lewisohn, *The Complete Beatles Recording Sessions: The Official Abbey Road Studio Session Notes, 1962–1970* (New York: Harmony, 1988).

with its prominent acoustic guitar arrangement and lush harmonies, would inspire the tight blend of the Byrds and the Mamas and the Papas. In addition, "Things We Said Today" made heavy use of acoustic guitars and its complex tale of an affair that may not stand the test of time.

Delving Deeper: *Beatles for Sale*

From its album cover to the songs' darker overtones, *Beatles for Sale* presents the Beatles at a crossroads. Their weary faces adorning the cover illustrates the personal toll that Beatlemania took on them, and their exploration of deeper subject matter suggests a readiness to move on from their earlier work. Certain tracks illustrate Dylan's influence on Lennon's songwriting; in turn, Lennon reveals a vulnerability not present on previous LPs.

Like no other *Beatles for Sale* track, "I'm A Loser" bears Dylan's fingerprints in both Lennon's nasal delivery, the introspective lyrics, and acoustic guitar-driven sound. Lennon even admitted that the song represented his "Dylan period," and the lyrics perfectly illustrate this fact. He uses the analogy of the sad clown: "Although I laugh and I act like a clown / Beneath this mask I am wearing a frown," he sings, his voice dropping lower on the word "frown" as Dylan might. Lennon later admitted that the word "clown" definitely emulates Dylan's songwriting. "I objected to the word 'clown,' because that was always artsy fartsy, but Dylan had used it so I thought it was all right, and it rhymed with whatever I was doing," he said.[10] Lennon describes his tears as "falling like rain from the sky" but asks "is it for her or myself that I cry?" Underscoring the idea of living behind a mask, he repeats "And I'm not what I appear to be" three times throughout the song. Dylan's "Masters of War" explores similar themes, although he alone sees underneath leaders' war-mongering: "I just want you to know / I can see through your masks."

Interestingly, Peter, Paul, and Mary member Noel Stookey told *Melody Maker* that he views "I'm a Loser" as a protest song: "Lennon is saying we are all losers. You can be a loser in life, by not being involved in it," he said.[11] During his 1980 *Playboy* interview, Lennon somewhat supported Stookey's thesis: "Part of me suspects I'm a loser and part of me thinks I'm God almighty," he said.[12] With its brooding subject matter, "I'm a Loser"

---

[10] The Beatles, *Anthology* (San Francisco: Chronicle, 2000), 160.
[11] Unterberger, *Jingle Jangle Morning*, ch. 2.
[12] William J. Dowlding, *Beatlesongs* (New York: Fireside, 1989), 82.

touched folk musicians and fans and paid respect to the leading voice in folk music by 1964.

Similar to "I'm A Loser," Lennon's lead vocals on "No Reply" possess a nasal quality, and the harmonies play a key role in the song's storyline. The words may not contain Dylan's typical abstractness and opaqueness – the narrator's anguish over his lover's infidelity is communicated in a straightforward manner. However, the line "I saw the light," accentuated by Harrison, Lennon, and McCartney's tight harmonies, suggests more than just discovering the lover's transgressions. "The light" could refer to seeing the truth in a general sense, similar to Harrison's composition "Think for Yourself" in terms of the story representing more than just the literal storyline. The acoustic guitar-dominated sound (powered by Harrison and Lennon) predates the folk-feel of *Rubber Soul*, while Lennon's darker examination of love signals the deepening maturity and complexity of his lyrics.

"No Reply" stands as a track that folk-rock artists would relate to in terms of personal subject matter, stellar harmonies, and that crucial acoustic guitar sound. As for Lennon's vocals, producer George Martin repeatedly coached Lennon to not sing so obviously in Dylan's style: "He wasn't doing it deliberately. It was subconscious more than anything," he said.[13] Through lyrics and voice, "No Reply" tells a darker story of betrayal and questionable redemption.

While McCartney penned the track "I'll Follow the Sun" in 1959, the group altered the lyrics and sound for *Beatles for Sale*. Early Lennon–McCartney compositions typically addressed listeners in the second person ("From Me to You," "P.S. I Love You," "She Loves You," "I Want to Hold Your Hand") – in this case, McCartney tells the story chiefly from his perspective. He understands his relationship may wither, but that life will go on: "Tomorrow may rain, so I'll follow the sun," he sings, indicating he expects an ultimately positive outcome. Jonathan Gould compares "I'll Follow the Sun" to Dylan's "Don't Think Twice, It's All Right" in that both feature nomadic, restless characters who will most likely never settle down. "With its symmetrical melody and acoustic instrumentation, ['Sun'] has the simplicity of an old folk song, combining a spirit of musical innocence with a pessimistic view of human relations that is almost perversely the standards of pop romance."[14]

[13] Kenneth Womack, *Maximum Volume: The Life of Beatles Producer George Martin* (Chicago: Chicago Review Press, 2017), 250.
[14] Jonathan Gould, *Can't Buy Me Love: The Beatles, Britain, and America* (New York: Harmony, 2007), 259.

Beatles for Sale serves as a bridge between the early Beatles and the emerging "new" Beatles. The music proved a turning point in the Beatles' artistic development, and indicated that the group's mission was not only to change their sound, but also to prove that rock should be considered a valid art form. In turn, aspiring folk-rock artists further understood that rock and folk did not stand as far apart as previously thought.

Partial Immersion: *Help!*

The Beatles' second soundtrack offered a potpourri of pop, rock, and folk elements. At this point, Lennon was fully immersed in Dylan, with "You've Got to Hide Your Love Away" the most obvious example. As Steve Turner writes, Lennon "began to write songs in which his state of mind became the immediate starting point."[15] Lennon's nasal vocals, the acoustic guitar, and sophisticated wordplay illustrate that Lennon was still in his so-called "Dylan period." McCartney described the "hey" interjection in the lyrics as "a very Dylan impression."[16] The first lines signal a change from previous ballads, as Lennon half-moans "Here I stand head in hand / Turn my face to the wall." He uses the unusual metaphor of feeling "two foot small," stating that the world is laughing at his expense. People advise him to mask his feelings (as he attempted in "I'm a Loser") and restrain his emotions. He follows with the lyric "gather round all you clowns," a Dylan-esque image. The ending presents a twist, however. Listeners would usually expect a Dylan harmonica solo; instead, a delicate flute weaves through the tune, the last note slowly fading away.

Gould compares the track to one of the Beatles' favorite cuts off *Another Side of Bob Dylan*: "I Don't Believe You (She Acts Like We Never Have Met)." In that track, Dylan begins with the lines "I can't under*stand* / She let go of my *hand* / And left me here facing the *wall*." Lennon penned similar lyrics, his voice emphasizing similar syllables and words as Dylan: his song: "Here I *stand*, head in *hand*, turn my face to the *wall*."

Interestingly, Riley argues that "You've Got to Hide Your Love Away" bears Dylan's general influence rather than his specific style. While Dylan might cloak deeper meanings in poetic language, literary references, and abstract images, Lennon's forthright lyrics leaves no doubt as to the narrator's anguish. "Although Lennon's delivery here is detached and

---

[15] Steve Turner, *The Beatles: A Hard Day's Write* (New York: MJF, 1994), 118.
[16] Paul Du Noyer, *Conversations with McCartney* (London: Hodder and Stoughton, 2015), 62.

somewhat restrained, it's still more personally revealing than most of the masks Dylan wore," Riley posits in *Tell Me Why*.[17]

The iconic twelve-string Rickenbacker also reappears on *Help!* Harrison plays it on his composition "I Need You," and uses it to power the main guitar riff of "Ticket to Ride." McCartney's composition "Yesterday" encompasses the highly confessional, personal style that he had not used on previous albums. The classical arrangement may not resemble a Dylan song, but the lines "Suddenly, I'm not half the man I used to be / There's a shadow hanging over me" recall the harsh self-examination of "My Back Pages" or "It Ain't Me, Babe."

While not immediately evident, the title track reveals Lennon's increasing comfort with introspection. The arrangement may have been relentlessly up-tempo pop, but the lyrics tell a different story. As Unterberger writes, the song "was an illustration par excellence of Lennon taking cues from Dylan's verbose, cathartic writing, although the Beatle put a more confessional, self-doubting tilt on the style, as well as melodies that Dylan couldn't hope to match."[18] The irresistible song became a massive hit, but a close examination of the lyrics exposes Lennon's weariness with fame. "When I was younger, So much younger than today," Lennon sings with a slight rasp.

Lennon's lyrics belie the upbeat sound of the track, the words mimicking Dylan's increasingly confessional topics. Mark Hertsgaard adds that "artistically he was increasingly stimulated by the young American troubadour's practice of inserting real poetry into the framework of popular song."[19] In other words, just as Dylan had been inspired by the Beatles' reinvigoration of rock 'n' roll, Lennon reshaped his composition style thanks to Dylan's thoughtful, poetic lyrics.

Full Immersion: *Rubber Soul*

Perhaps trying to capitalize on the folk-rock craze, Capitol Records marketed the US release of *Rubber Soul* as the Beatles' entry into the genre. While that label fails to capture the album's entire character, the other tracks further explore the acoustic sound present on *Beatles for Sale* and *Help!*

One of Lennon's finest works, "Norwegian Wood" best approximates Dylan's poetic style. A description of a love affair – cleverly disguised to

---

[17] Tim Riley, *Tell Me Why* (New York: Alfred A. Knopf, 1988), 142.
[18] Unterberger, *Jingle Jangle Morning*, ch. 4.   [19] Hertsgaard, *A Day in the Life*, 126–27.

avoid specific details – the narrator tells the tale of going home with a mysterious woman. MacDonald deems the track "the first Beatles song in which the lyric is more important than the music."[20] Lennon's mysterious woman may also borrow from Dylan's "She Belongs to Me" (*Bringing It All Back Home*, 1965), as Dylan paints a portrait of a dominant, seductive lover: "She's a hypnotist collector, you are a walking antique," he sings. Compare the lyrics to Lennon's lead character in "Norwegian Wood": "I once had a girl, or should I say, she once had me."

Clearly Dylan recognized Lennon's homage; he returned the favor by writing and recording "4th Time Around" in 1966. At first Lennon believed it was Dylan's parody of "Norwegian Wood"; eventually he decided it was essentially a good-natured tribute.

While not a folk song on its face, "I'm Looking through You" possesses some folk-rock qualities beyond the acoustic guitar. As Unterberger writes, the track remains "as thoroughbred folk-rock as anything recorded by anyone in 1965."[21] Perhaps the lyrics were partially inspired by "I Don't Believe You (She Acts Like We Never Have Met)" from *Another Side of Bob Dylan*. McCartney bemoans that "you don't look different, but you have changed" and that "I thought I knew you, what did I know?" Similarly, Dylan remains stunned at a transformation in his lover: "Yet it's hard t' think on / That she's the same one / That last night I was with," he sings. As McCartney cries "you're not the same," Dylan also wails that "But now something has changed / For she ain't the same." While McCartney has never explicitly stated that "I Don't Believe You" specifically inspired "I'm Looking through You," the lyrics and themes strongly resemble each other.

"You Won't See Me" continues McCartney's progression as a songwriter as well as the group's growing interest in an acoustic sound. McCartney attempts to emulate the nomadic figures in Dylan's work in lines such as "I won't want to stay / I don't have much to say." He admits that he "can't turn away" because he knows the love he would miss. McCartney's traditional romantic side peeks out through a facade of indifference, a key difference from tracks such as "It Ain't Me, Babe."

Straying from the Beatles' previous subject matter, "Nowhere Man" represents what Unterberger calls "a sympathetic ode to a man adrift without purpose, marking the first Beatles original to tenure into lyrical territory with no ties to man/woman romance whatsoever."[22] Lennon may

---

[20] Ian MacDonald, *Revolution in the Head: The Beatles' Records in the Sixties* (New York: Henry Holt, 1994), 131.
[21] Unterberger, *Jingle Jangle Morning*, ch. 4.   [22] Unterberger, *Jingle Jangle Morning*, ch. 4.

have been inspired by Dylan's tales of everyday people, with these three-dimensional character studies serving as cautionary tales. In *Highway 61 Revisited*'s "Desolation Row," Dylan portrays great figures in history and literature as people fallen on hard times due to drugs, depression, madness, and hubris. Through comedic images, Dylan strips these figures of their romantic qualities and reveals them to possess the same weaknesses as everyone. Lennon's tale of the "nowhere man" portrays the main character as a fool, but suddenly the lyrics directly address the listener: "Isn't he a bit like you and me?"

"Girl" exudes folk in that it invokes acoustic arrangements and tight harmonies. In their "100 Greatest Beatles Songs" list, *Rolling Stone* claims that Dylan clearly inspired "Girl," but "Lennon surpasses him here – 'Girl' makes 'Just Like a Woman' sound like kid stuff." Indeed, the girl holds sexual power and control over the narrator, similar to Dylan's "She Belongs to Me." That title misdirects the listener, as the lyrics portray a woman in complete control: "You will start out standing / Proud to steal her anything she sees / But you will wind up peeking through her keyhole / Down upon your knees," he sings. The woman in "Girl" similarly controls the narrator, as Lennon laments that "When I think of all the times I tried so hard to leave her / She will turn to me and start to cry / And she promises the earth to me and I believe her." The line "Was she told when she was young that pain would lead to pleasure" suggests a masochistic relationship. Like in "You Belong to Me," the narrator may appear to dominate the relationship, but the lyrics suggest the opposite.

"We're Both Going Towards the Same Thing, I Think": Folk and Rock Converge and Capture the 1960s Zeitgeist

The year after *Rubber Soul*'s release saw the Beatles move in yet another direction, this time diving into the avant-garde and psychedelia. Dylan would also transition into a new phase, moving beyond his acoustic, protest-based folk and into fusing rock with intensely personal lyrics. By 1966, Dylan would complete his trio of electric albums – *Bringing It All Back Home*, *Highway 61 Revisited*, and *Blonde on Blonde* – all pioneering works. His combination of rock and folk was at least partially inspired by the Beatles' blending of various genres, particularly the seemingly diametrically opposed folk and rock genres. In turn, as Peter Yarrow told Unterberger, the Beatles "were writing songs with great mystery, content, and poetry, and vision that was directly evolved from folk music, via the contemporary singer-songwriters ... I think that [Dylan] was the most pervasive influence in terms of converting to another perspective."[23]

Ultimately the Beatles both shaped and were shaped by folk-rock; the same could be said for the two-way creative relationship between the Beatles and Dylan. As Hertsgaard asserts, "if the Beatles influenced Dylan toward a more rock 'n' roll future he in turn influenced them toward a more poetic approach to songwriting."[24] This reciprocal relationship is encapsulated by Riley in *Tell Me Why*: "The untold story of 1960s rock is how these artists admired each other without ever stooping to imitation."[25]

McCartney may have best summarized the Beatles–Dylan relationship during an August 22, 1966 press conference at Manhattan's Warwick Hotel. A reporter asked a pointed question: "You seem to be doing a Bob Dylan in reverse. That is, you became popular playing rock 'n' roll and now you seem to be doing a lot more folk rock. Would you care to comment on that?" McCartney responded diplomatically, stating "that thing about Bob Dylan is probably right, in reverse, because we're getting more interested now in the content of the songs, whereas Bob Dylan is getting more interested in rock 'n' roll. It's just, we're both going towards the same thing, I think."[26] Folk-rock may have had a relatively brief time occupying the charts, but the Beatles' journey into the musical form greatly expanded the band's lyrical and structural content.

---

[23] Unterberger, *Jingle Jangle Morning*, ch. 4.   [24] Hertsgaard, *A Day in the Life*, 50.
[25] Riley, *Tell Me Why*, 155.
[26] "Beatle Press Conference: New York City 8/22/1966," *Beatles Bible*, www.beatlesinterviews.org/d b1966.0822.beatles.html.

CHAPTER 20

"Listen to the Colour of Your Dreams": The Beatles Writ Psychedelic

Jason Kruppa

> I suppose I brought two major influences to bear on Beatles music: my formal training in classical music, and my love of experimental recording techniques.[1]

October 1959: George Martin and recording engineer Stuart Eltham are at EMI Studios editing a tape of comedians Peter Sellers and Irene Handl. Removing sections of the recording, taking a sentence, a phrase, or a word at a time, producer and engineer are reshaping a mostly ad-libbed 11-minute dialogue between the two actors into a more streamlined 6½ minutes. Once they complete the editing, they will add a few sound effects to create the illusion that these two odd characters are talking in an open-air park.

The completed track will be one of the highlights of *Songs For Swinging Sellers*, the second LP Martin has produced with the actor. The success the year before of their first album together, *The Best of Sellers*, vindicated Martin's sense that there was a niche for comedy records in Britain that he could fill, and his natural inclination for experimenting in the studio drove him to apply a variety of sound effects to these recordings, conjuring vivid scenes with just a few well-placed flourishes.

A third Sellers LP followed in 1960, amid an ongoing stream of albums and singles on which Martin distinguished himself in an industry where he had otherwise struggled to succeed. He was pioneering not only a particular genre of record, but also a style of production that was very much his own.

February 1962: Martin and Eltham are putting the finishing touches on an album with comedian Michael Bentine, whose anarchic, absurdist television show *It's a Square World* they are distilling into a series of deftly

---

[1] George Martin, with William Pearson, *With a Little Help from My Friends: The Making of Sgt. Pepper* (Boston: Little, Brown, 1994), 48.

executed audio recordings. The LP, which they have taped sporadically in sessions since July the previous year, is notable for its technical ingenuity, using EMI's four-track machine to overdub Bentine into multiple performances with himself, fleshed out with sound effects to create a distinct sense of place. Sketches are punctuated by fake commercials without any pause between segments, creating a free-flowing work complete with a framing concept, prefiguring the pacing and structure of *Sgt. Pepper's Lonely Hearts Club Band* and *The Who Sell Out* (both 1967). There is arguably no better example of the creative use of four-track recording in Martin's pre-Beatles *oeuvre*.

April 1962: working with the BBC Radiophonics Workshop, Martin releases an instrumental single under the name "Ray Cathode." The Workshop, established in the late 1950s to create sound effects and music for radio and television programs, used a variety of avant-garde techniques to fulfill its mission, including tape loops, extensive and painstaking editing, speeding up or slowing down recordings, and manipulating the sound of instruments to change their character completely. Martin's brainchild, the Ray Cathode single combines the producer's recordings of studio musicians with the Workshop's tape loops and electronic alterations. Always commercially minded, Martin was trying to work out how to integrate these avant-garde techniques within a pop framework.

May 1962: Peter Sellers is at the microphone in Studio 2, reading from a script by his *Goon Show* co-conspirator Spike Milligan, who stands at another microphone. Also present, at their own mics, are Dudley Moore, Peter Cook, and Jonathan Miller, three-fourths of the *Beyond the Fringe* revue, which had initiated a "satire boom" in Britain the previous year, and which George Martin had released to great success on LP. The occasion for this gathering of the top comic talent in England was a droll, absurdist send-up of the film *The Bridge on the River Kwai*, led by Sellers's deadpan impersonation of Alec Guinness.

That fall, Martin and Stuart Eltham would gather over forty sound effects Eltham had compiled, and weave them together with the voice recordings from May and a film score-style orchestral backing Martin had commissioned for the project. Martin would release the LP as *The Bridge on the River Wye* – the title changed to avoid a potential copyright dispute, while the contents remained essentially the same. A detailed, carefully choreographed and visually evocative recording sustained over the length of an entire album, the *River Wye* LP would be the most ambitious production of George Martin's career to date. He completed this wholly immersive and convincing "sound picture" just as he was drilling a young band from Liverpool on the basics of working in a recording studio.[2]

• • •

The story of the Beatles as recording artists is, at its core, the story of an always growing, always changing collaboration with their producer, George Martin. The most intense period of that collaboration, where artist and producer were contributing equally to the process of shaping and discovering the essence of each recording while re-writing the rules of the studio, was during the Beatles' so-called psychedelic period, from 1966 to 1967. Martin had always been an essential, if largely invisible, part of the Beatles' music, but here his approach to the studio-as-instrument becomes ascendant, and is deeply embedded in the DNA of these recordings.

When George Martin met the Beatles in 1962, he was only a moderately successful producer of commercial hit records. The comedy albums and singles had gotten him noticed, and with them he had established a particular kind of production that was uniquely his own. He had had a steady run of respectable hits with these records, too, but real pop success had eluded him. His only No. 1 at this point, The Temperance Seven's authentic arrangement of a song from 1930, "You're Driving Me Crazy," had taken advantage of a brief craze for trad jazz in Britain, but did not point to a sustainable future.

Once the Beatles exploded and the subsequent flood of artists from Liverpool gave Martin unprecedented dominance of the British charts in 1963 (his artists famously held the No. 1 spot for thirty-eight out of fifty-two weeks), he largely abandoned that experimental course simply for lack of time. By 1964, having crashed the uncrashable gates of America with the Beatles, Martin was the most in-demand producer in Britain, but Martin's experimental spirit was merely dormant. Throughout 1963 he used his "wind-up piano" technique (where the piano is overdubbed at half speed and played back at normal speed to alter the sound of the instrument) in different settings for different results.

The Beatles quickly absorbed the lessons Martin taught them about the studio. Most of these studio lessons in the first year and a half were practical, guiding them through the recording process and the construction of a recording through editing and overdubbing. His suggestion of a string quartet for "Yesterday" in June 1965 opened up a whole new musical palette, however, and the Beatles had no doubt taken note of the instances

---

[2] George Martin, *Playback: An Illustrated Memoir* (Guildford: Genesis Publications, 2002), 48.

of wind-up piano Martin had used on their songs, culminating with "In My Life" during the *Rubber Soul* sessions. Here, as the lessons of the previous years coalesced and their confidence in recording led them to take control in the studio, in John Lennon's words, the Beatles witnessed George Martin's recording technique dramatically change the sound of the piano to something like a harpsichord. Martin's mastery of the studio had long been self-evident, a part of his persona, and as the Beatles followed their end-of-year tour with an unscheduled three-month break, they gathered ideas with the confidence that their producer could match their new ambitions.

* * *

By April 1966, when the Beatles returned to EMI to begin recording their new album, they had already been dropping hints in the press about what was to come. John had been most direct, telling the *New Musical Express* in March that "the next LP is going to be very different." Paul had been spotted at a lecture by *musique concrète* composer Luciano Berio, and Maureen Cleave's concise, intimate profiles of each Beatle for the *Evening Standard* had made clear that, among other things, they were restless, endlessly curious, and electrified by new ideas.[3]

Within this atmosphere, Martin's experimental spirit stepped up. His vision of the studio as a creative workshop had long been underplayed – notable but still marginalized under the aegis of "comedy records." Paired with the most popular band in the world, these techniques would now, in a new context, transform the way producers and artists alike approached the recording studio.

The recording that kicked off the *Revolver* sessions would set the tone not just for the album, but also for much of the rest of the Beatles' career. Untitled at first, listed only as "Mark I" on the recording sheet, what would become "Tomorrow Never Knows" resulted in both a literal and a figurative rearrangement of the studio. Responding to the Beatles' desire to use tape loops, Martin drew on an idea he had first used in 1951, on the song "White Suit Samba," and also the A-side of the Ray Cathode single "Time Beat," both of which used a rhythmic sound on tape to cue the tempo of their recordings. This did not quite work to everyone's satisfaction, and instead Paul and Ringo laid down a bass-and-drum pattern so deliberately repetitive that it functioned as a tape loop itself.

---

[3] Kevin Ryan and Brian Kehew, *Recording the Beatles: The Studio Equipment and Techniques Used to Create Their Classic Albums* (Houston: Curvebender, 2006), 408.

After John overdubbed his vocal, they returned to the idea of the tape loops, now with the intention of weaving them in and out of the mix over the driving rhythm track. To get the loops onto the four track tape, Martin had to upend normal studio operations completely. First, engineer Geoff Emerick needed the four-track machine in the control room (it was normally housed in another room) and then engineers had to set up five reel-to-reel tape machines running Paul's loops, with five people holding the tension with various objects (pencils, a mason jar) fed into the mixing board. At that board, Paul faded the loops in and out of the track – the *artist*, not an engineer, was working the faders. In 1966, no other band would have asked for this kind of power, and no other producer would have granted it.

Emboldened by the success of this recording, the Beatles subsequently appeared at nearly every session with a new idea, forcing Martin to find creative solutions for the problems they presented him.[4] Some problems were familiar ones, where Martin could draw directly on work he had done on comedy records. The most direct descendant of those records is "Yellow Submarine," which uses a series of perfectly choreographed sound effects to conjure a vivid soundscape around the Beatles' simple recording to bring the song to life. The use of sound effects themselves was a hallmark of those comedy recordings, but the expert timing of the effects recalls two specific earlier Martin productions: Charlie Drake's 1961 hit "My Boomerang Won't Come Back," where a collection of bizarre effects – the frog-like croak of an instrument called a flappaphone, "Aborigines" chanting like beatniks, etc. – are positioned as "hooks," that is, memorable song elements; and Bernard Cribbins's recording of "Right Said Fred" where Martin arranged effects against the lyrics to punctuate the humorous story of three men laboring unsuccessfully to move a piano. There's an even more direct line in another 1962 Cribbins recording, "Sea Shanty," in which Martin used the same sloshing-of-waves sound effect that appears in "Yellow Submarine."

Other problems required more abstract solutions. John's request to sound like the Dalai Lama at the top of a mountain for "Tomorrow Never Knows" yielded the idea of running his voice through a Leslie speaker. Paul's request for the double string quartet on "Eleanor Rigby" to be "doing a rhythm" led Martin to write a score inspired by Bernard

---

[4] Ironically, when he was still a struggling producer, Martin had long wished for an artist that would be easier to produce than the comedy records, which required a new idea and new techniques each time out. But in 1966 and 1967, when they were in full experimental mode, he had to do this with nearly every Beatles song.

Herrmann's music for the shower scene in *Psycho*. After John accidentally played a test mix of "Rain" backward at home, he presented the idea to Martin, who took a section of John's vocal, turned it round, and laid it into the coda of the song. This in turn inspired Paul and George to add backward guitars to "Tomorrow Never Knows" and "I'm Only Sleeping," respectively.

These are also the sessions during which engineer Ken Townsend invented Artificial Double Tracking (or ADT), which reduced the need for manual double tracking, and also resulted in the ability to record at various speeds. The next logical step from Martin's half-speed "wind-up" technique, "varispeed" allowed for changes of smaller increments in tape speed, and as the Beatles wrestled with the new sensations that marijuana and LSD had brought them, they used varispeed as a tool for altering the textures of their voices and instruments to reflect these sensations. They recorded "Rain," for instance, at a fast tempo and had Martin slow the recording down more than a semitone for playback, thickening the sound of the guitars and drums; they similarly slowed down the rhythm track for "I'm Only Sleeping" to reflect the languid mood of the song. Martin used this technique himself to once again change the sound of the piano, this time dropping the recording of "Good Day Sunshine" two semitones to play his piano solo, which had more of the desired honky tonk sound when sped back up to normal speed. ADT and varispeed would color the sound of Beatles recordings for the next two years.

Martin's background in comedy obviously was not the only thing that prepared him for these challenges. As head of Parlophone Records since 1955, he had had to oversee everything the label recorded: classical, jazz, Scottish dance music, spoken word, pop vocal, children's records, and show tunes, all the while cultivating his own experimental recordings. When the Beatles' own wide-ranging sensibilities manifested full force on *Revolver*, Martin's comfort with a broad variety of genres allowed him to navigate (and combine) seemingly disparate elements with ease. With *Revolver*, Martin and the Beatles laid down a template that showed how popular music could be a completely democratic art form, expansive enough to embrace any style, any idea, any sound. The next sessions would expand upon this template even further.

* * *

On June 16, 1967, *Time* magazine ran a piece on *Sgt. Pepper* that began, "George Martin's new LP was out last week," going on to assert that, although the album had the Beatles' name on it, this was primarily

Martin's work. Over twenty-five years later, this perception still troubled Paul McCartney, who said in his 1994 memoir, "It was a piss-off for us because we'd put our heart and soul into it, all this work, and not to detract from George, but it was not good enough that he should get the credit . . . Ok, he was the producer, fine, and you have to give the producer credit, but he couldn't have made this album with Gerry and the Pacemakers." While *Time* and others certainly overstated the case for Martin's impact, oblivious to the collaborative nature of his work with the Beatles, the converse of McCartney's defense is also true: the Beatles could not have made *Sgt. Pepper* with anyone other than George Martin.[5]

As anyone in the studio during the making of *Revolver* would have seen, Martin and the Beatles were engaged in an ongoing five-way conversation. And just as with *Revolver*, *Sgt. Pepper* did not appear out of a vacuum, but was the continuation of five years of close work between producer and artist. Still, Martin's studio aesthetic is imprinted deeply upon *Sgt. Pepper*. The Beatles were now working squarely in the domain Martin had established. The studio was now their workshop, and no one knew that workshop better than Martin.

Having retired from live performances after their brutal summer 1966 tours, the Beatles were now free to explore that workshop fully, and they sought to push past what they had done on *Revolver*. There would be more of everything: more orchestral instruments – a full orchestra for the first time, in fact – more dramatic use of varispeed, more effects, more manipulation of sounds and voices. They would take great pains to get each song just right, beginning with "Strawberry Fields Forever," which required three different recordings to master, and a very lucky, varispeeded edit to combine the second and third recordings seamlessly.

In 1982, Martin contended that, "Technically, *Sgt Pepper* was not particularly innovative – I've heard it described as a watershed but I don't agree ... The innovation of *Sgt Pepper* – which began with 'Strawberry Fields' and 'Penny Lane' – was more artistic than technical." Just before this comment in the same interview, he said, "I mean, working on *Sgt Pepper* was very much like working on *Swingin' Sellers* or the *Best of Sellers*, we used the same kind of techniques."[6]

The techniques may have been the same, but as Martin indicated, the Beatles' ambitions were much greater, and they knew they were heading

---

[5] Barry Miles, *Paul McCartney: Many Years from Now* (New York: Holt, 1997), 346.
[6] Brian Southall, *Abbey Road: The Story of the World's Most Famous Studios* (Wellingborough: Patrick Stephens, 1982), 174–75.

into uncharted waters. And although Martin's point above about *Sgt. Pepper*'s artistic innovations outweighing its technical ones is valid, in rendering the orchestra for "A Day in the Life," the challenges were both artistic *and* technical. First there was the score. Martin translated the Beatles' desire for the orchestra to "freak out" into a form trained musicians could understand, but even then, the score itself required forty conservatory-trained instrumentalists to improvise and play completely independently from each other – the exact opposite of an orchestra's goal. If this was not enough of a tightrope to walk, Martin wanted to record the orchestra four times over. Only having one track of the four-track tape open, Martin asked engineer Ken Townsend on the day of the session to synchronize two four-track machines, in effect giving him an eight-track tape. Townsend's last-minute fix worked, but it was unreliable.

Only a few years before, four-track had seemed like such a luxury. On *Revolver*, the Beatles had regularly begun applying so many overdubs to a track, often with three or four Beatles performing on *each* track, that Martin would have to do reduction mixes, literally reducing the tracks by mixing down to another four-track tape to add more overdubs, *again* with several Beatles performing at once. Eleven of the sixteen songs taped during the *Revolver* sessions saw these kinds of reductions and overdubs.

The orchestral overdub for "A Day in the Life" may have been the worst of it, but this problem of too-few tracks ran through the *Sgt. Pepper* recordings. Fifteen of the sixteen songs taped during the sessions required a reduction mix, and several songs, like "Penny Lane," called for *more* than one reduction mix. This meant lots of planning. What overdubs could be recorded together? What tracks could be combined in the reductions? And then for the overdubs, which parts could be recorded together on each track of the tape, and who would play what? To manage this recording process, Martin and the Beatles had to collaborate even more closely than before.

All this intense collaboration produced an unexpected result. Whereas on *Revolver* the typical producer–artist relationship had evolved into a balanced exchange, on *Pepper* that balance began to shift. Emblematic of this shift was a session for "Being For The Benefit of Mr Kite," where the Beatles in the control room directed Martin in perfecting a harmonium part, playfully pushing him to do take after take until he collapsed on the floor in exhaustion. Although good natured, and a moment Martin would later call one of his fondest memories of working with the Beatles, this scene is as good a signpost as any for how the Beatles' proficiency in the studio now matched their producer's. Martin may have originated the idea of the studio-as-workshop, but on *Sgt. Pepper* the Beatles developed that idea in new ways that pushed Martin well past what he had previously achieved. Just as Martin had pushed the Beatles early on to write better songs and had taught them the fundamentals of studio recording, in meeting the challenge of each new problem the Beatles presented him, Martin had in turn expanded his skills as a producer.

To the world in 1967, none of this registered. *Sgt. Pepper's Lonely Hearts Club Band* would be the most scrutinized, most written about and most widely praised work of Martin and the Beatles' careers, and the picture it presents of producer and artist working in perfect harmony endures to this day. What none of them could have known is that they would never be so focused by a unified concept again.

* * *

Less than a month after *Sgt. Pepper's* 1 June release, the Beatles were on television in front of an estimated 350 million people for the first ever international satellite broadcast, performing "All You Need Is Love." But well before *Pepper* was in the shops, back in April, Paul had dreamed up the *Magical Mystery Tour* television film project and the band had taped the title track, followed soon by various stray recordings that would eventually see release in connection with other projects. In the glow of their greatest triumph, they scarcely took a breath.

Martin recalled in 1994: "One of my main jobs with the Beatles, as I saw it by 1967, was to give them as much freedom as possible in the studio, but to make sure that they did not come off the rails in the process." Now that they had total control of their career, free of the need for live performances and the expectations that encumbered other pop groups, the Beatles could do whatever they wanted, which is exactly what they did: whatever they wanted. More power, however, resulted in less structure and, once the "All You Need Is Love" broadcast was over, precious little urgency. Limited in how much he could prescribe any project – he had learned how futile *that* was when he tried to get them to record "How Do You Do It" back in 1962 – Martin had only so much ability to direct the Beatles' creative energies. For all of July and most of August the Beatles were not filming or recording, and not until Brian Epstein's death in late August did they begin working on the *Magical Mystery Tour* project with anything close to intention.[7]

---

[7] Martin, *Playback*, 68.

The film shoot was a mess, owing to the Beatles' lack of organization and inexperience with filmmaking, but at least the recordings, under Martin's careful supervision, were more controlled. Still, the *MMT* sessions show the Beatles giving less attention to songwriting than to exhausting the studio of all its potential. Paul did not bother writing more than a single verse for "Your Mother Should Know," but packed the arrangement of "Hello Goodbye" with so many overdubs that the recording required an unprecedented *four* reduction mixes. George Harrison indulged himself on "Blue Jay Way" with a variety of effects, from backward recordings to extreme flanging, investing the kind of time and effort normally reserved for one of John or Paul's songs. If *Revolver* was filled with the sense of discovery at what was possible in the studio and *Pepper* was driven by the desire to see just how far they could push those ideas, the recordings of the second half of 1967 find the Beatles simply at play in the kaleidoscopic world they had discovered.

"I Am the Walrus," reflecting like a funhouse mirror the disarray and excess of this period, is arguably the one song that benefits from the ornate production and pushes forward to break new ground. Even Martin's score was reportedly (intentionally) overwritten, with John at the session requesting the removal or change of certain parts before recording began. With pronounced *glissandi* rendering a woozy effect in the strings, as if the recording itself has been drugged, and sixteen vocalists singing swoops and such nonsense as "Umpa, umpa, stick it up your jumper" (a completely left-field reference to a 1935 record of that title by British Variety performers the Two Leslies), Martin's score matched Lennon's absurd, picturesque lyrics with an arrangement just as absurd and picturesque. John's random incorporation of a BBC radio broadcast of *King Lear* at the end of the mono mix escorted the recording into its fade out, a final brush stroke in the most abstract of Martin's sound pictures.

Appropriately, it was in the wake of this hypnotic chaos that Martin's collaborative dream began to unravel. After the triumph of *Pepper*, he had hoped they could all come together on a more cohesive work, one where each song really was connected in some way to the next. *Magical Mystery Tour* would not be that project, he knew, but perhaps in the new year things would be different. As Martin would eventually realize, though, too much had changed. Though they turned away from Martin's classical aspirations, the Beatles pushed the expansiveness of their 1966–67 work even further. But with the power they now wielded and their understanding of the studio matching Martin's, the Beatles would become collaborators with their producer as it suited them, rather than by necessity. The close working relationship Martin had fostered with them from the start, which had blossomed into full collaboration and partnership during *Revolver* and *Sgt. Pepper*, was changing, and the Beatles, now increasingly in control, were about to move collectively in another direction.

CHAPTER 21

Getting Back

Robert Rodriguez

The Beatles – which is to say John Lennon and Paul McCartney – dabbled in songwriting individually, prior to their joining forces in the Quarry Men in 1957. Paul had famously composed a ditty called "I Lost My Little Girl," a skiffle-styled number that may have been influenced by the recent death of his mother when he was fourteen. John less famously wrote a song of which no record exists, titled "Calypso Rock." In both instances, the two aspiring tunesmiths employed current styles as models for their compositions. (Calypso, embodied by Harry Belafonte, was a popular musical style in the USA and UK, coinciding with the nascent – and more popular – skiffle and rock 'n' roll eras.) It was quite natural for aspiring songwriters to draw upon styles of the day that drew their interest, distinct from the prevailing pop and jazz sounds.

But if all they ever did as songwriters was craft their takes on what was popular, we would not still be studying every nuance of their careers. Instead, they evolved. The music world they entered into marked a clear distinction between performers and songwriters. While a handful of notable exceptions wrote their own material – Chuck Berry, Eddie Cochran, Buddy Holly, Carl Perkins, Smokey Robinson – the majority of rock 'n' roll artists relied on music created by professionals. It is hard to imagine where Elvis would have been without the contributions of Leiber and Stoller or Pomus and Shuman, or likewise the Everly Brothers without Felice and Boudleaux Bryant. Being discerning students of the music they loved, John and Paul became aware of the work of the craftsmen and women who operated out of New York's Brill Building, and by the time they took up songwriting seriously, beyond their teenage dabbling, it was their stated goal to become "the Goffin and King of England."

In so declaring, they were asserting an intention to craft material of universal Top 40 appeal. The husband-and-wife team of Gerry Goffin and Carole King were responsible for scores of hits for dozens of artists, beginning in 1961 with "Will You Still Love Me Tomorrow" by the

Shirelles. The Beatles included several Goffin–King songs in their club repertoire:

> "Take Good Care of My Baby," recorded by Bobby Vee
> "Don't Ever Change," recorded by the Crickets
> "Keep Your Hands Off My Baby," recorded by Little Eva
> "Chains," recorded by the Cookies.

In time, the Lennon–McCartney songwriting team achieved their stated objective in the sense of producing radio-friendly music that could be successfully recorded by artists across a spectrum of styles. But what made the Beatles exceptional was their consistent drive to push the parameters of their art. Repeating a triumph was anathema; having mastered the hit single (and the evergreen composition), their growth led them to absorb influences around them that transcended the established boundaries, all the while maintaining the easy accessibility and commerciality that defined virtually their entire body of work.

Their recordings had, by 1965, increasingly taken on characteristics of both personal self-expression and sonic experimentation. Songs like the 1964 single "I Feel Fine" – compositionally a variation on the kind of romantic trifles that defined their genre – introduced deliberate feedback to the masses, while material crafted to flesh out albums like "I'm A Loser" and "Norwegian Wood" took a page from Bob Dylan stylistically, expressing the inner life of their composer (in both cases, John Lennon) and presenting it with enough ambiguity for listeners to not immediately recognize how personal a narrative was being presented. One could make the case that it was the Beatles' response to the influence of artists that they respected (which included Dylan, the Beach Boys and the Byrds) that in turn drove them into the era of *their* highest influence: 1966–67. As there existed between John and Paul a self-described "sibling rivalry" creatively, so too was there a friendly commercial and artistic rivalry between the Beatles and their peers, one that frequently developed into personal friendship.[1]

The 1965 *Rubber Soul* and 1966 *Revolver* put the world on notice that, like hothouse flowers, the Beatles were developing at a rate far faster than their peers, presenting material rich in sophistication and experimentation with every release, and raising the bar for all who followed. (The Beach Boys' Brian Wilson famously declared that *Rubber Soul* was the impetus for

---

[1] Mark Lewisohn, *Tune In: The Beatles – All These Years* (New York: Crown, 2013), 13.

his digging deeper to produce the landmark *Pet Sounds*.) That the Beatles managed to advance their art while staying connected to their audience was no small feat. While influences on some of their recordings were readily apparent (the Byrds on "If I Needed Someone," the Beach Boys on "Here, There and Everywhere"), other material had no real precedent within their peer group.

It was with *Revolver* that the Beatles' penchant for spawning sub-genres within the rock tapestry became manifest: electronica ("Tomorrow Never Knows"); "raga rock" (George Harrison's "Love You To"), and baroque (Paul's "For No One"), among others. Perhaps it was telling that, for the first time since their debut single, the 1962 "Love Me Do," the Beatles issued a single alongside a non-soundtrack album that was *not* a standalone release. "Yellow Submarine"/"Eleanor Rigby" was released simultaneously with *Revolver*, the parent album; in the normal course of things, single material had been judged by criteria separate from the songs comprising their album material. While it had been their practice from Day One to populate their long-players with material every bit as good as their singles, the Beatles were signaling something different here: where the currency of the rock marketplace had been the hit single, it was rapidly shifting to the album-length statement. It was an evolution led by the Beatles themselves.

Nowhere did this become more clear than with their next release, the post-touring *Sgt. Pepper's Lonely Hearts Club Band*. While critics and fans to this very day debate its place within their canon (or all of rock, for that matter), there is no denying its impact. Practitioners of the genre who took themselves seriously as artists were challenged to produce weighty expressions of their own, while the Establishment media, at long last, accepted that what had been largely regarded as a transient teenage fad was, in fact, capable of producing lasting art. By the end of 1967, the Beatles were arguably at the height of their influence: receiving validation from mainstream press as the face of the counterculture and recognized by the burgeoning rock press as catalysts for expansion of their idiom.

The period of 1966 through the end of 1967 coincided with the Beatles' heightened drive to fully utilize the capabilities the studio offered – with both technological advances and instrumental adventurism. Freed from any self-limiting obligation to replicate their recordings live onstage, all options were open: from tape manipulation (slowing down, speeding up, reversing) to populating their recordings with instrument voices largely unheard by a mainstream act (Indian tamboura, Mellotron, clavichord, and so forth). But it was their excursions into psychedelia during this same time that perhaps caught the imagination of the public most vividly.

Though the Beatles did not invent psychedelic rock per se, they certainly popularized it and by the sheer weight of their ubiquitous presence in the public consciousness, wielded the most influence.

Their earliest explorations came in 1966, with the exotic drone of "Rain," B-side to "Paperback Writer," as well as a number of songs issued on *Revolver*. Though much of *Sgt. Pepper* was permeated with a vibe of nostalgia (Edwardian and otherwise), the psychedelic overtones were unmistakable. Much attention was focused on "Lucy in the Sky with Diamonds," due in no small part to the purportedly deliberate initials of its title (Lennon denied this was conscious, and there is reason to believe him), but also with the grand orchestral crescendo twice featured in the album's finale, "A Day in the Life." Further refinement of their stylistic experimentation came with the songs recorded later that year for the *Magical Mystery Tour* film, most notably "I Am The Walrus" but also George's atmospheric "Blue Jay Way." The former tune included as innovation a live BBC radio feed of Shakespeare's *King Lear*, adding to the controlled chaos of the coda, while the latter recording was fed through a spinning Leslie organ speaker, enhancing the song's inherent trippy ambience.

Freedom from performing live liberated the Beatles from their self-imposed limitations in terms of where they could go compositionally and production-wise in the studio. But by the end of 1967 and the *Magical Mystery Tour* recordings, their innovation-for-innovation's-sake approach came to an end. What could have caused them to abruptly shift stylistic gears as they pivoted into 1968 and their last years as a collective unit? Three possibilities suggest themselves: first, such was the reception and accolades they had received in 1967 for *Sgt. Pepper* that the last thing they wanted to do was repeat themselves and offer up *Sgt. Pepper II*. This would have been wholly keeping in character. Seen within the whole of their career, *Sgt. Pepper* represented a one-off: a self-consciously crafted collection of tunes tied to an alter ego that the Beatles moved on from without looking back, married to groundbreaking studiocraft that caught everyone's ears, presented in grandiose packaging that no one could ignore. It was a one-of-a-kind *event* – just as fans could recollect the moment they first heard (or saw) the Beatles back in 1963–64, everyone of age in 1967 could recall the moment they first heard *Sgt. Pepper*. It was a singular achievement that they dared not ever attempt to contrive a sequel to.

The second possibility is that once their LSD experimentation ran its course in 1967 and they moved toward Transcendental Meditation as a benign replacement for it, their interest in exploring this musical direction curtailed accordingly. To a man, the Beatles expressed a positive take on their acid experience, at the same time concluding that its value to them had been played out. It is no coincidence that their embrace of the hallucinogen dovetailed utterly with the start of their psychedelic period, musically. By the time they had publicly renounced their need to use it further (while extolling the virtues of Transcendental Meditation), their last batch of tunes that fit the psychedelic paradigm had been written and were about to be recorded for a film project that gave them the latitude to explore the psychedelic experience *visually* (while maintaining a nostalgic air, not unlike *Pepper*). But like all trends, the world having caught up to a style that was outré when the Beatles first took it up, they risked becoming unfashionable by holding on to it.

One other possibility is that being the shrewd listeners to what was going on in their musical world, they picked up on an early clue to the new direction. Unlike most every peer artist (the Beach Boys, the Byrds, the Rolling Stones) that the Beatles held in high esteem, Bob Dylan never succumbed to the allure of psychedelia. Following the release of *Blonde on Blonde* in mid-1966, he spent well over the next year recouping from a motorcycle accident and staying out of the public eye, sidelined while psychedelia reached full flower during the so-called "Summer of Love." When he did return to releasing new material, *John Wesley Harding* – recorded in Nashville and issued in December 1967 – featured a stripped down, back-to-basics sound bordering on rustic. Ever the avid fans, the Beatles would have been aware of and doubtless familiar with Bob's new direction. If their next batch of recordings was anything to judge by, Bob's influence was as potent as ever: the acoustic guitars they had all but abandoned throughout their 1967 recordings would return with a vengeance. Setting aside production innovation, their focus shifted back to songcraft.

It wasn't just Dylan that was pointedly eschewing the era's prevailing vogue. Though psychedelia in rock remained a viable sound for any number of recording artists, newer ones especially (Pink Floyd's sophomore effort, *A Saucerful of Secrets*; the Moody Blues' *In Search of the Lost Chord*; debuts from Spooky Tooth, Iron Butterfly, the Steve Miller Band, and the Move, among others), some of the most compelling sounds of 1968 were far removed from the excesses of the previous year. The Rolling Stones, perhaps stung by the near-universal disdain for their "answer" to *Sgt. Pepper, Their Satanic Majesties' Request*, regrouped and came up with a solid collection of rootsy songs, drawing from their early blues and country influences: *Beggar's Banquet*. The Beach Boys, having seen their efforts to craft a "response" to *Revolver* collapse (along with Brian Wilson's creative reign) with the stillborn *Smile* (emerging as the disjointed *Smiley Smile*) shifted toward an R&B sound with *Wild Honey*. The Byrds, weathering stability issues as attrition took its toll, bounced back with a pair of releases that split the stylistic difference: one (*The Notorious Byrd Brothers*) being a sonic blend encompassing psychedelia; the other (*Sweetheart of the Rodeo*) that represented McGuinn and company going all in with their fusing of country and rock.

Two of the biggest acts to gain traction in 1968 evoked styles reminiscent of rock's earliest days. Creedence Clearwater Revival would in time become the masters of the 3-minute (or less) single, offering a sound that simultaneously recalled Sun Records and a mythical "swamp" that existed only in bandleader John Fogerty's head. While their earliest singles re-framed 1950s songs ("Suzie Q" and "I Put A Spell On You," originally recorded by Dale Hawkins and Screamin' Jay Hawkins, respectively) as extended jams with psychedelic overtones, Fogerty quickly became known for his concise, razor-sharp writing, encompassing everything from feel good skiffle ("Down on the Corner") to blistering polemics ("Fortunate Son").

The Band arrived on the scene with the prestige accorded Dylan associates. Their debut, *Music From The Big Pink*, displayed an organic eclecticism, seamlessly weaving elements of folk, blues, R&B, country, and gospel together and presenting it with an earnest collaborative spirit. Their pre-Dylan iteration as the Hawks – backing band of 1950s rock pioneer Ronnie Hawkins – underscored their ties to the genre's beginnings. That the Beatles took notice, there is no doubt: not only did George spend some quality time with them at years' end (bringing back to London a renewed band spirit that would go sadly unrequited), but Paul quoted "The Weight" in his semi-live vocal performance of "Hey Jude" presented for the cameras in September that year.

In a year that saw a rock pioneer – Fats Domino – issue a comeback album (produced by future Ringo's colleague Richard Perry) that was not only a return to form, but also featured a pair of recent Beatles compositions, a demonstrable synergy between rock's leading lights and the genre's earliest hitmakers was readily apparent. Though the concept of "Get Back" – returning to rock's basics while presenting a rawer, less produced product – was fully realized (or at least attempted) with the Beatles' January 1969 film project, eventually emerging as *Let It Be* (the album and the film), this style of personal nostalgia, drawing upon their earliest influences, was manifest on the sprawling, stylistically boundless self-titled double album issued by the Beatles in November 1968.

In so producing such a stylistically diverse collection of songs, the Beatles were simply reflecting back the influence they exerted over artists like the Band *and* the (notorious) Byrds, going back as far as *Revolver*. There was no explicit "concept" as had been suggested with *Sgt. Pepper*; instead, all unity was implicit, with the same core group of musicians presenting their work within varied musical settings. Another aspect of commonality between these artists suggests itself: despite the perception that *The Beatles* was an ironic title for a release comprising tunes revealing fault lines within the ranks, it is becoming clearer at this fifty-year distance how much the Beatles were in fact working together as a performing band on *The White Album* in a way that they had not since 1966, laying down the backings live rather than piecemeal. Furthermore, like the aforementioned releases by the Byrds and the Band, their 1968 album served as a showcase for individual artistry within the band, each sharing a turn in the spotlight but with the full support of their bandmates. This runs counter to the perception voiced by John Lennon that it was "me and a backing band, Paul and a backing band" and so forth, accepted uncritically through the years by writers ever since without ever really questioning how valid an observation this was.[2] Session tapes that have leaked out through the years reveal that even in recordings not requiring full band participation, another Beatle was usually nearby, offering support, encouragement, and input.

It was in early 1968 that the Beatles took their famous retreat in Rishikesh, India; studying Transcendental Meditation with Maharishi Mahesh Yogi. Removing themselves from the stresses and distractions of life in London would have marked a unique change in environment informing the songwriting that took place here, but so too would have the declared intent to drop all the self-medicating that had sustained them at least as far back as Hamburg. For the first time in their career, there would be no alcohol, weed, amphetamines, LSD or any other illicit refreshment to impact their perceptions as they created. (While no one can know with absolute certainty whether or not the Beatles managed to allow for some flexibility on the self-imposed restrictions, once can safely assume that it was drastically curtailed, at least, for the time of their stay, which ranged from two weeks in Ringo's case to two months in the case of John and George.)

What emerged from the group's three principal writers was a flood of new material. When one adds up all of the compositions written in

---

[2] Craig Cross, *The Beatles: Day-by-Day, Song-by-Song, Record-by-Record* (New York: iUniverse, 2005), 445.

Rishikesh, demoed at Esher in May, recorded and issued in the group's official releases or given away to other artists, 1968 stands as their most prolific year for crafting new songs. Even Ringo managed to finish up what would be recorded that year as his first self-penned tune, "Don't Pass Me By." Given that the song's origins went back several years, one can conclude that the environment at the ashram was conducive to creativity on a profound level. There was also the forced proximity, unseen since the touring years. Though the songwriting partnership between John and Paul never really ended – at the very least, they still acted as each other's editors – developments suggest that the situation they found themselves in lent itself to renewed productivity.

While the narrative that *The White Album* was the sound of the group's pending dissolution took hold for years following the Beatles' break-up, examination of the evidence both overlooked and newly emerged supports the conclusion that the band was far more unified this year than has been popularly supposed. The band performances and support of each other's contributions reinforces this thesis. That said, one could detect certain tendencies that would define the characteristics of their solo careers: George displayed his growing spirituality with songs like "Long, Long, Long" and "While My Guitar Gently Weeps"; Paul showed his flair for mastery of every genre, from sweet ballads ("I Will") to screaming rockers ("Helter Skelter") and everything in between, and John's contributions ran the gamut from deeply personal ("Julia") to political ("Revolution 1") – themes that would define his work outside the Beatles.

Despite setting aside the overt sonic and technological explorations that had defined their work in the last two years especially, *The Beatles* retained the group's sense of adventure and discovery. Certainly, nothing ever issued under the group's name was as great a departure from their established sound as the *musique concrète* of "Revolution 9." But elsewhere, their testing new approaches to their work is evident, with several songs evoking a "live performance" feel ("Yer Blues" being but one example); others featuring light production touches (the bird sounds and tapping heard in "Blackbird," for instance) that proved to be just what was needed, while deft use of outside musicians tailored to the specific song revealing their exquisite judgment in how best to enhance their work. (Compare the brass heard on "Mother Nature's Son," for example, to that heard on "Savoy Truffle.") If anything, the Beatles scaling back the production excesses of 1967 so drastically for the follow-up release signaled a statement unto itself: having taken the deliberate innovation as far as they cared to, they were revealing a return to the values of simplicity and direct communication.

From now on, the emphasis would be on the songs and the performances, not on crafting heretofore unheard sounds.

As if to emphasize this new philosophy, John – apparently speaking on the behalf of the band – told George Martin to his face, "I don't want any of your production shit," in the name of keeping the resulting product "honest."[3] He was speaking of what became known as the "Get Back" (or *Let It Be*) sessions of January 1969, and their desire to nail release-worthy takes without any "cheating" – editing or overdubbing. Fresh off the heels of the grueling gestation process and release of their double album, the Beatles committed themselves to the goal of crafting an entirely *new* set of songs; intended to be performed live at an as-yet-not-settled-upon venue for a televised broadcast. As new compositions emerged from John, Paul, and George, a number of characteristics were readily apparent. First, Paul was as prolific as ever, rolling out guitar-based and piano-based tunes in equal measure, all of which were readily adaptable to live performance without much need for outside augmentation. (Keyboard savant Billy Preston came aboard about halfway through the project, providing an element of versatility to the proceedings.) "Let It Be" and "The Long and Winding Road" proved to be classic McCartney evergreens; one may make the case that each possessed more universal appeal than anything he contributed to their swan song, *Abbey Road*.

George was not far behind, bringing in a passel of fully realized, high-quality compositions, many bearing spiritual or philosophical themes. Unfortunately, his vision of acceptance and validation from the group's two senior members was not as he had hoped, leading to frustration and his walk-out one week in. John struggled to come up with his quota of new material, having spent himself on the last sessions. In time, he did come up with "Don't Let Me Down," "Dig A Pony," and the rollicking throwback "One After 909." But his use of heroin at this time not only tamped down his creativity but also impacted his judgment and affected the band dynamic. Though the Beatles were, on the whole, as hardworking as ever in January 1969 and nearly as productive (George brought in far more songs than the group would ever record together at this time; other tunes unveiled by Paul and John during these sessions were only recorded and issued after the group's split), it was the disfunction and breakdown in the *esprit de corps* at this time that stayed with the individual group members for years ever after, not the actual moments of camaraderie and

---

[3] Hunter Davies, *The Beatles Book* (London: eBury, 2016), sec. 4.

productivity caught on tape and film that made this a far more positive epoch than they ever remembered it as.

The defining characteristic of the songs the Beatles recorded and released in 1968 was their stylistic diversity. From the 1950s throwback single "Lady Madonna" that they began the year with, to the quasi-gospel of "Hey Jude," to the bouncy ska of the single-that-never-was, "Ob-La-Di, Ob-La-Da," the Beatles could not be pigeonholed. Every *White Album* track was a new stylistic excursion: some (like "Back in the USSR," "Helter Skelter," or "Long, Long, Long") directly inspired by the work of others, while most seemed to be idiom explorations that encapsulated the unique artistry of their creators: John's "Happiness is a Warm Gun" or George's "Savoy Truffle," for examples. The former song was a mini-suite of styles, ending with a warped vision of 1950s doo-wop, while the latter was a horn-driven R&B-style exercise that sounded nothing like its Memphis antecedents.

The songs the Beatles produced for their next project (which ended up as the *Let It Be* album) continued this very basic approach, being more or less crafted for live performance. This was in keeping with the pared down sound shared by their peer group: albums released in 1969 by the artists most tied to the Beatles in the preceding years shared this approach: *20/20* from the Beach Boys; *Nashville Skyline* from Dylan; *Let It Bleed* from the Rolling Stones. (The Byrds, still in flux personnel-wise, issued the suitably schizophrenic *Dr. Byrds and Mr. Hyde*.)

But with albums outselling singles for the first time in 1968 in the USA and 1969 in the UK, the ground was shifting. The Top 40 commerciality essential for groups to compete, survive and thrive as they had for most of the years of the Beatles' existence had given way to a different paradigm. Along with it, the expectations and tastes of an audience that had grown up along with the Beatles likewise evolved. The year 1969 was when work that would define entire sub-genres in the coming decade was embraced by the masses: hard rock, as represented by Led Zeppelin's first two albums; singer-songwriter, embodied by Crosby, Stills and Nash, who issued their debut album that year, and Joni Mitchell, with *Clouds*; jazz-rock fusion, with the best-selling sophomore effort from Blood, Sweat and Tears, as well as Chicago's double album debut (as *Chicago Transit Authority*); progressive rock, with debuts from King Crimson, Yes, and Genesis; art rock, typified by Pink Floyd with *Ummagumma*, and funk, with popular releases by the Isley Brothers, Isaac Hayes, and Sly and the Family Stone. Unclassifiable albums were issued by Santana (his debut), Spirit, Captain Beefheart, and Jethro Tull. (Ironically, the best-selling album of 1969 was Iron Butterfly's *In-A-Gadda-Da-Vida*: a psychedelic classic that has not aged particularly well.)

Where the Beatles fit into this marketplace is not really clear. They were a genre unto themselves by then, and if *Abbey Road* was, as they saw it, the natural follow-up to *Sgt. Pepper*, it came on a much more subdued basis, minus the sense of event and attention-drawing presentation. A new Beatles album was always going to be a joyous experience to be sure, and *Abbey Road* was no exception. In terms of innovation, the most attention-grabbing aspect of the new release was the side two suite of unfinished songs, welded together to create a greater-than-the-sum-of-its-parts listening experience. While this was new for the Beatles, it was not particularly groundbreaking: among their peers, the Who had done this back in 1966 with *A Quick One*. Furthermore, 1969 was the year of *Tommy* – a popular (if not the first) "rock opera" that proved to be nearly as acclaimed as *Pepper* had been two years earlier in terms of, again, showing that rock might even be capable of producing "high art."

More groundbreaking on *Abbey Road* was their use of the Moog synthesizer purchased by George. He had issued an experimental LP of synth doodlings that year (*Electronic Sound*), but the use of his machine on *Abbey Road* was restrained and tasteful, unlike other artists who tended to use the Moog as a novel noisemaker. On *Abbey Road*, it was relegated to touches of color on "Maxwell's Silver Hammer," as a white noise generator on "I Want You (She's So Heavy)" and as a suitably compatible embellishment alongside an electric harpsichord on "Because." That last song also featured the impeccable and unmistakable three-part harmonies of John, Paul, and George, layered exquisitely for the last time on a Beatles record. Besides the Byrds and the Beach Boys, the only act operating on a Beatles level that was doing this kind of thing was Simon and Garfunkel, also slated to disband in 1970. While it is relatively easy to pick up on where S&G were influenced directly by the Beatles, it is harder to say where the synergy worked in reverse. (John declared that he believed that Paul was trying to write a "Bridge Over Troubled Water"-type of song with "Let It Be," but the chronology does not support this.) The work of both collectives did intersect with their superb craftsmanship in support of sterling songwriting.

It is easy to see that the Beatles worked toward expanding the rock 'n' roll palette, incorporating innovation and technological advances into the presentation of their songs from the very beginning. Also manifest was their habit of dropping "gimmicks" (such as harmonica) rather than flogging a successful attribute. They took cues from artists they liked, drew non-rock elements into their sound, and with considerable facilitat-ing from their producer and the production team, worked hard at creating a unique array of sounds that led the way as they broke down the limita-tions of their idiom. This practice reached its culmination in 1967, and by the year's end, they apparently reached the apex of sonic innovation for its own sake. They did not build on *Sgt. Pepper* in the sense of extending the experimentation to new sounds or forms; they instead returned to their back-to-basics roots, throughout all of 1968 and into the beginning of 1969. Following the wrap-up of the *Let It Be* film project, they regrouped for their final joint project, putting it together like the professionals that they were.

During the period between the end of 1967 going into 1970 and secure in their place within rock's pantheon, the Beatles ceded the leading edge: alongside their peer artists, they focused on producing optimum perfor-mances of well-crafted songs from this point on. Of the albums released during this period long-held to be groundbreaking (in terms of influence wielded on what followed), arguably only three – *John Wesley Harding*, *Sweetheart of the Rodeo*, and *Electric Ladyland* – came from artists on a peer level with the Beatles. Everything else came from artists who were not mega-sellers: names like the Velvet Underground, King Crimson, Black Sabbath, Fairport Convention, Isaac Hayes, the Stooges, Van Morrison. Their work in these years was every bit as paradigm-shattering as the Beatles' had been earlier.

But to quantify art on a track-by-track, album-by-album basis is to miss the greater point. It was not only for the music they produced that the Beatles are revered and carry untouchable status as artists, but also for the blueprint they gave the world. We study every aspect of their story today not just because we love their music so much, but also because they projected possibilities that everyone could understand. They came from nowhere (Liverpool being widely regarded as the province of hicks); they lacked any sort of formal musical education (not being able to read music, they operated intuitively, populating their material with innovative pro-gressions and harmonies – "aeolian cadences," to the educated);[4] their work ethic was astonishing (consider the volume of classic material they produced while touring the world, shooting films, and appearing steadily on TV and radio), and they showed the world what doing what you loved with friends could result in. Though their story is really a series of minor

---

[4] Kenneth Womack, *The Beatles Encyclopedia: Everything Fab Four* (Santa Barbara, Greenwood, 2016), 362.

miracles – meeting the right people in the right place at the right time – what they projected was that *anyone* could do what they did. They came off as approachable and down-to-earth, belying the magnitude of what true revolutionaries they were. In leading by example, these four musicians taught all the bands that followed how to play.

CHAPTER 22

On the Record! (Dis)Covering the Beatles

Jerry Zolten

You Say You Want a Revolution

The arrival of sound recording in the mid-nineteenth century radically changed how people experienced music. Physical presence at a performance was no longer necessary. Performances by specific artists were now preserved for playback in a personally ownable form – initially wax cylinders, then brittle shellac disks, and by the mid-twentieth century, more convenient magnetic tape and vinyl disks. Records over the radio broadcasted musical styles and genres across the land. Performances now had a life beyond the actual moment. Artists could now be appreciated and influential well beyond their active years as performers. And when the Beatles entered in the early 1960s, in a short span they helped expand what it meant to be a "recording artist" by creating music reliant on studio craft to the extent that their performances could not be exactly replicated live on stage, and could in essence exist only on record.[1]

The Beatles – and for that matter rock 'n' roll itself – could not have existed or persisted without the vinyl record and its modern-day equivalent, the electronic sound file. How so? By mid-twentieth century, vinyl records were the pollinators that spread around rhythm and sound. Vernacular musical styles once confined to region or community were now set free to inspire a new aesthetic about what could be considered musical. Rock 'n' roll in its earliest incarnation was rhythm and blues in disguise, primarily the music of black America available through records across demographic lines, and as such, vinyl vignettes of what really mattered to people engaged in struggle to transcend social stigma and status. For post-World War II baby boomers, those records, that music,

---

[1] "History of Recorded Music Timeline," *EMI Archive Trust*, www.emiarchivetrust.org/about/history-of-recording/.

could be illuminating, for that generation it heralded the beginning of a breakdown in racial and cultural divides.

That was certainly my experience as a white teenager growing up near Pittsburgh in the late 1950s. I heard African American R&B, blues, jazz, and gospel on local low-frequency stations at the bottom of the AM radio dial, and the music changed me, how I thought and who I was. More so, late night manipulation of the radio dial pulled in exotic sounds from stations as far away as Chicago, Memphis, and New Orleans. I got to know the music, and that turned me into a fanatic record collector. It was not enough to hear a song on the radio. I needed to own the physical record so that I could brag about having a copy and so that I could play it at will. Vinyl records – especially singles – were *that* emblematic, and, as I came to understand, also were for the adolescent Beatles and our generation world-wide. By the early 1960s, records had become a clear focal point of an unfolding international cultural dynamic.

A short aside. Records in those days were not the perfect music medium. They could not technically replicate the full sonic experience of a live perfor-mance. Absent were room ambience, stage spectacle, and audience/performer connectivity. Nonetheless, vinyl records did play a vital role in the launch and glide of many a rock artist career. The artist "brand" got out there and, though notoriously shortchanged by the powers that be, records did generate new income streams for artists, as in "go see the performer, now buy the record," or vice versa. When the Beatles entered the fray, vinyl singles ruled and, in fact, the group had already been influenced by singles that had come before them. Over the span of their roughly seven-year recording career, the Beatles in turn produced singles that would be equally influential to later artists, and also, through the sheer brilliance and appeal of their recorded performances, managed to shift the focus from singles to graphically stunning packages that offered a dozen tracks and more per album. Records, then, were not only a crucial influence on the Beatles, but also essential to their establishment as artists and ultimately the forwarding of their cachet into the future.

Good Day Sunshine

Because of records, the Beatles continue to shine beyond their active performing life as a group. What John Lennon said that outraged so many all those years ago – "We're more popular than Jesus now" – seems no longer to be quite so hyperbolic.[2] At this juncture, the Beatles

---

[2] Maureen Cleave, "The John Lennon I Knew," *Daily Telegraph*, October 5, 2005.

still have their passionate and loyal disciples along with a hallowed song-book of biblical proportion. Their recordings are indelibly imprinted in the collective cultural consciousness, but like any great record, have a flipside worth considering. The Beatles have given as they have received. Back when they were figuring out who they were as musicians, the Beatles pieced together a style by "covering," imitating, or otherwise repurposing what they had heard on records by artists who preceded them.

During the Beatles formative years in the late 1950s and early 1960s, the 7-inch 45-rpm (revolutions per minute) single, one song per side, was the primary delivery platform. Popular records were heard on the radio, but the passionate collectors wanted their own copies and sought out hard-to-find records by the more obscure artists. Rock critic Parke Puterbaugh, quoting another contemporary writer, described the Brit scene in a 1988 *Rolling Stone* article. "In the 1950s the UK had little more to offer than pallid imitations of American rock & roll singers. British pop was 'pure farce,' according to ... Nik Cohn. 'Nobody could sing, and nobody could write,' he said, 'and in any case, nobody gave a damn.' ... A handful of powerful managers groomed a stable of homegrown singers in the mold of Elvis Presley and Buddy Holly," but, Puterbaugh points out, "a movement of musical purists, enamored of black American music ... would indirectly lead to the Beatles and an indigenous British rock & roll sound."[3]

Early on, the Beatles and their UK contemporaries did not record much original material. Instead, they "covered" not just the song, but also the actual record with the aim of copying the sound as closely as possible. An earlier operative example is Brit proto-rocker Lonnie Donegan, who in 1955 recorded covers of African American blues artist Huddie "Leadbelly" Ledbetter's "Rock Island Line" and "John Henry." The style was branded "skiffle," and as Puterbaugh notes, the early Beatles' sound was "a souped-up form of beat music – essentially amplified skiffle with a heavy R&B influence, a style inspired by the records imported from the USA by Liverpool's merchant seamen."[4]

Keith Richards of the Rolling Stones tells a similar story about approaching a then stranger – Mick Jagger – on a train platform because Jagger was holding two hard-to-find record albums, Chuck Berry's *Rockin' at the Hops* and *The Best of Muddy Waters*. "It was, always, all about

---

Parke Puterbaugh, "The British Invasion: From the Beatles to the Stones, the Sixties Belonged to Britain," *Rolling Stone*, July 14, 1988, www.rollingstone.com/music/music-news/the-british-invasion-from-the-beatles-to-the-stones-the-sixties-belonged-to-britain-244870/.

Puterbaugh, "The British Invasion."

records," Richards wrote in his 2010 biography. "From when I was eleven or twelve years old, it was who had the records who you hung out with. They were precious things . . . Mick and I must have spent a year, while the Stones were coming together and before, record hunting. There were others like us, trawling far and wide, and meeting one another in record shops."[5]

American records steered the musical and philosophical direction of many early British rockers, including and most certainly the Beatles. As working-class teens, they related to both content and sound. They connected to these musical expressions from American outsiders, renegades, or socially marginalized. They were hearing real-life unfiltered and ill-mannered; sounds and structures that broke the rules of conventional music making; ungrammatical lines and rhymes; gritty unschooled vocals; amped-up instruments including electric bass, distorted wailing guitars, pounding piano, or the rhythm of drums punched way out front. George Harrison memorably embraced it all in his jubilant shout out in "For You Blue" to a Chicago blues legend he knew only from records, "Elmore James got nothin' on this, baby!"[6]

The most telling examples of records that shaped the Beatles are on the portable jukebox John Lennon carried on their mid-1960s world tours. The machine was a suitcase-sized British KB Discomatic that held forty vinyl singles, fully loaded weighing in at fifty pounds. That the Beatles chose to carry it on tour is an indication that they never wanted to be too far from their favorite records.

Those records reveal song ideas, instrumental licks, song constructions, and rhythmic feel that inspired or were outright sampled by the Beatles. Among the rock 'n' roll and R&B records that the Beatles covered were "Twist and Shout" (1962) by the Isley Brothers and "Please Mr. Postman" (1961) by the Marvelettes. There were records by the prominent pioneering black rock 'n' rollers such as Little Richard, Chuck Berry, and Larry Williams and their rockabilly progeny Elvis Presley, Jerry Lee Lewis, Buddy Holly, and Gene Vincent. Also among the jukebox selections, Motown and soul artists Smokey Robinson and the Miracles, Wilson Pickett, and Otis Redding.[7]

---

[5] Keith Richards with James Fox, *Life* (New York: Little, Brown, 2010), 80–88.
[6] "For You Blue," *Let It Be*, 1969.
[7] Tyll Hertsens, "John Lennon's 1965 Portable KB Discomatic Jukebox," blog, *Inner Fidelity*, www .innerfidelity.com/content/john-lennons-1965-portable-kb-discomatic-jukebox-page-2#HcDieiDSmWpBjj6l.99.

Less obvious influences are also present. For one, Bob Dylan's single "Positively 4th Street" (1964), and while the Beatles did not cover or imitate Dylan, he did have a decided impact on their lyrical direction. Said John Lennon, there had been a "separate songwriting John Lennon who wrote songs for the meat market" who did not consider the lyrics "to have any depth at all . . . Then," says Lennon, "I started being me about the songs . . . thinking about my own emotions, . . . what I felt about myself . . . It was Dylan who helped me realise [sic] that."[8]

More fascinating are the records the Beatles wholesale borrowed from in one way or another. Pee Wee Crayton's R&B hit "Do Unto Others" (1954) provided the opening power chords that launch "Revolution" (1968). The signature lick for the Beatles' "I Feel Fine" (1964) was lifted from Bobby Parker's "Watch Your Step" (1961). "Well, yeah," said John Lennon, "this is one of them oldies but goldies, as it were . . . which I call son of 'What'd I Say,' . . . the great record . . . by Ray Charles . . . The lick you'll recognize, 'cause I've used it, all the Beatles have used it, sort of in various forms."[9]

The Beatles were always forthcoming about their desire early on to copy American records. Speaking for the group, John Lennon said, "I'd like to make a record like 'Some Other Guy' [Richie Barrett, 1962] . . . Or 'Be-Bop-A-Lula' [Gene Vincent and the Bluecaps, 1957] or "Heartbreak Hotel" [Elvis Presley, 1956] or "Good Golly, Miss Molly" [Little Richard, 1958] or "Whole Lot of Shakin'" [Jerry Lee Lewis, 1957] . . . I mean we're still trying it. We sit there in the studio and we say, how did it go, how did it go? Come on, let's do that."[10] Ringo Starr launched his solo career with covers of Johnny Burnette's "You're Sixteen" (1961) and Buck Owen's "Act Naturally" (1963).

Paul McCartney acknowledged Buddy Holly" "John and I started to write because of Buddy Holly. It was like, 'Wow! He writes and is a musician.'"[11] The Beatles even took the cue for their group name from Buddy Holly's Crickets. "I remember," said McCartney, "talking to John about this. 'Cricket. What a fantastic idea . . . but we were turned on like nobody's business by the idea of the double meaning, so with our wit and wisdom and whatever . . . Beetles . . . little insects . . . but with an "a" it became something to do with beat.'"[12]

[8] The Beatles, *The Beatles Anthology* (San Francisco: Chronicle Books, 2000), 158.
[9] Jeff Burger and John Lennon. *Lennon On Lennon: Conversations With John Lennon* (London: Omnibus Press, 2017),326.
[10] Jonathan Cott, *Rolling Stone*, 22, November 23, 1968, 1–4.
[11] The Beatles, *The Beatles Anthology*, 22.
[12] Barry Miles, *Paul McCartney: Many Years from Now* (New York: Henry Holt, 1997), 52.

Then You Will Remember Things We Said Today

What goes around comes around. As much as records influenced the Beatles, so too have Beatles records influenced artists who followed. Important to note, though, is a factor that makes the Beatles different from their forebears. Unlike them, original recordings by the Beatles are ubiquitous and easily accessed, and in part because of that now roughly fifty years on from their last group-recorded releases, *Abbey Road* and *Let It Be*, the Beatles remain in play and subsequently relevant. Beyond ubiquity and access, though, there are a myriad of collective reasons why that includes reimagined or sonically improved remixes, renewed interest in vinyl collecting, high media visibility, cross-genre covers by other artists, family relationships in the twenty-first century, and in the end, what to date seems to be a timeless sound and lyrical appeal.

In terms of access, everything the Beatles ever recorded – albums, singles, outtakes, alternates, studio chatter, remixes, and literally every recorded interview – is available via delivery platforms that were not imaginable in the era of strictly vinyl, tape, or radio. Beatles fans, unless they want to, are not required to seek out hard copies of long out of print or obscure recordings. The CD (compact disk) eliminated the physical contact of a diamond needle cutting through a vinyl groove, and "the record" became an obsolete or at least a greatly diminished technology. Today, digitalization makes any Beatles track readily available via download, and beginning in the late 1980s, the technological shift from analog to digital gave impetus to the music industry to repackage the whole sweep of popular music and most certainly the entire Beatles catalog.[13] By 1986, the Beatles catalog had begun to be digitized.[14] Beatles tracks were now downloadable via the Internet. The first online sound recording "store" Napster was launched in 1999 with a peak of 80 million registered users before it collapsed under the weight of copyright and royalty legalities. Other sites took Napster's place and today streaming is the prevailing means of song acquisition.[15] In 2019, 75 percent of music industry revenue came from streaming.[16] The electronic availability of the Beatles catalog has been a vital factor in their sustained popularity, maybe even more so

---

[13] "Revolution's Brief History of Digital Music," *Campaign*, www.campaignlive.co.uk/article/revolutions-brief-history-digital-music/904234.

[14] Guy Massey, Paul Hicks and Steve Rooke, "Remastering The Beatles," *Sound on Sound*, www.soundonsound.com/techniques/remastering-beatles.

[15] "The History of Music Distribution," *mn2s*, November 18, 2015, https://mn2s.com/news/label-services/the-history-of-music-distribution/.

[16] *Rolling Stone Magazine*, 1323, January 2019, 73.

than later cover versions of their songs by other artists. Since nothing was any longer real, physical recordings no longer necessary, there was nothing to get hung about. Why listen to Beatles covers when you could have the real thing?

Covers, nonetheless, have played a role in sustaining the Beatles. There were some memorable cross-genre covers early on, such as Ray Charles's "Eleanor Rigby" (1968) and Joe Cocker's eccentric take on "With a Little Help from My Friends" (1969). Wilson Pickett had some success with "Hey Jude" (1969), Elton John with "Lucy in the Sky with Diamonds" (1975), and bluegrass/country artist Alison Krauss with "I Will" (1995). None eclipsed the originals, but interpreted in other stylistic approaches, they reminded how appealing Beatles' songs could be.

Beatles' songs have also been kept in the pop culture loop and reintroduced to younger generations through cover versions in movie soundtracks or as integral to entire storylines. The film *Sgt. Pepper's Lonely Hearts Club Band* (1978) about the struggles of a fictional band had moderate success, its best quality the soundtrack of Beatles' covers by pop artists of the day including the Bee Gees, Aerosmith, Peter Frampton, Alice Cooper, and Earth, Wind & Fire.

Along the same lines almost a decade later but without performances by high profile "hitmakers" (Bono, Jeff Beck, and Eddie Izzard excepted) is the film *Across the Universe* (2007). Originally screened in theaters the film, through digital streaming services, has become a cult classic with a soundtrack that draws from across the entire Beatles catalog, thirty-two songs in all. Characters take their names from Beatles songs – Jude, Prudence, Maxwell, Lucy, and so on. The storyline, about young people dealing with life and love in the 1960s Vietnam era, has resonated enough with millenials and gen-Xers to give the songs new traction within those age groups. Along with the title track, cover songs include "Helter Skelter," "I Want to Hold Your Hand," "Let It Be," "Why Don't We Do It in the Road?," "If I Fell," "I Am the Walrus," "Something," "Strawberry Fields Forever," "Revolution," "While My Guitar Gently Weeps," "Blackbird," "Hey Jude," "All You Need Is Love," and "Lucy in the Sky with Diamonds."[17]

The trend of keeping the Beatles and their songs alive via compelling film stories continues to unfold as evidenced in the 2019 hit film *Yesterday*. The premise is simple. A talented bar singer is knocked unconscious in an

[17] Nathan Charness, "BeatleBoomers: The Beatles in their Generation," thesis, Wesleyan University, 2010, 102, wesscholar.wesleyan.edu/cgi/viewcontent.cgi?article=1557&context=etd_hon_theses.

accident and comes to in a reality where rock 'n' roll reigns but somehow impossibly the Beatles are unknown. Realizing this, the singer works out from memory as many Beatles' songs as he can and wows crowds, becoming an artist on the brink of colossal fame. Without going further into the plot line, the film charms as a vehicle to revisit favorite Beatles' songs scattered throughout, pure nostalgia for the Sixties generation, but by casting contemporary artists such as Ed Sheeran, a connection to a younger generation of fans who might be hearing some of these Beatles' songs for the first time.

Original Beatles' recordings are also frequently used in film and television soundtracks. "Twist and Shout" appears in *Ferris Bueller's Day Off* (1986), "Come Together" in *A Bronx Tale* (1993), "Fool on the Hill" in *Dinner for Schmucks* (2010), and "Baby, You're a Rich Man" in *The Social Network* (2010).[18] TV commercials have capitalized on "Hello Goodbye" in a 2007 ad for Target stores or "Help" in a 2018 ad for Google.[19]

Most central to keeping the Beatles' legacy alive, though, is introducing the songs and original recordings to the youngest generations, television often the best medium. *Kids Incorporated* (1984–86), for example, was a Disney Channel series featuring a "kid" musical group that performed covers of "Paperback Writer," "We Can Work It Out," "All You Need Is Love," "In My Life," and "Ticket to Ride," the program syndicated well into the 1990s.[20] The 2016 Netflix animated series *Beat Bugs*, on air for three seasons and still available through streaming, told of five animated "kid" insects, the narrative propelled exclusively by Beatles songs, both original recordings and covers.[21] Nickleodeon's *Big Time Rush* (2009–13) featured real actors as four Minnesota friends trying to make it as a "boy band," the storyline propelled by covers of, among others, "I Want To Hold Your Hand," "We Can Work It Out," "A Hard Day's Night."

Popular reality television talent shows have also contributed to keeping the Beatles in the national spotlight. In 2008, for example, *American Idol* (based on the British program *Pop Idol*) featured a round that required contestants to perform songs from the Lennon–McCartney songbook. Covers included "Michelle," "If I Fell," "She's a Woman," and "I've Just

[18] "The Best Uses of Beatles Songs in Movies and TV," *Hollywood.com*, July 16, 2014, www.hollywood.com/movies/our-favorite-uses-of-beatles-music-in-pop-culture-57373531/.

[19] "Beatles and Advertising," *Beatles Blog*, April 11, 2012, https://beatlesblogger.com/2012/04/11/beatles-and-advertising/.

[20] "Kids Incorporated," *IMDb*, www.imdb.com/title/tt0086744/.

[21] "Beat Bugs," *Netflix*, www.netflix.com/title/80057611.

Seen a Face," with a performance of John Lennon's "Imagine" by series runner-up, 17-year-old David Archuleta.[22]

TV awards and ceremony shows also contribute. On the 47th Grammy Awards telecast in 2005, Billie Joe Armstrong performed "Across the Universe," and at the 82nd James Taylor performed "In My Life." A particularly memorable "gone viral" television moment was Prince's performance of "While My Guitar Gently Weeps" at the 2004 posthumous induction of George Harrison into the Rock and Roll Hall of Fame. The band included George's son Dhani along with Tom Petty, Jeff Lynne, and Steve Winwood.[23] In 2012 at the internationally televised *London Olympic Games Opening Ceremony*, the Arctic Monkeys performed "Come Together."[24]

Late night talk show TV has also introduced young fans to the Beatles, most notably through an episode of late night talk show host James Corden's *Carpool Karaoke*. In 2018, Corden and Paul McCartney drove through the streets of Liverpool visiting historic Beatles sites while a dashboard cam caught them unabashedly singing Beatles classics such as "Penny Lane," "Drive My Car," "Let It Be," and "Blackbird." According to Corden:

> I sort of just prodded him that it would be fun and it would be worthwhile and that he absolutely wouldn't ever regret doing it. I felt on the day that we captured something quite special. But in truth we were all kind of blown away by the response and the reaction to it, because I think across the Internet now, across Facebook and YouTube and stuff, it's been watched like 140 million times or something ... People have watched it on their phones or their laptops or whatever for 23 minutes, and yet it's testament to him really. It's testament to what he means to people; it's testament to what that music means to people.[25]

In the face of all the advanced technology, though, old-fashioned vinyl still has to be factored in to keeping the Beatles in play. In 2019, there is a robust cross-generational market for original vinyl pressings, prized like rare books in first or early original editions, but also in the form of new

[22] "American Idol Season 7 – David Archuleta – 'Imagine,'" *YouTube*, www.youtube.com/watch?v=5YoPkJZkDxI.

[23] Finn Cohen, "The Day Prince's Guitar Wept the Loudest," *New York Times*, April 28, 2016, www.nytimes.com/2016/04/28/arts/music/prince-guitar-rock-hall-of-fame.html.

[24] Jenny Stevens, "Arctic Monkeys Play London 2012 Olympics Opening Ceremony," *NME*, www.nme.com/news/music/nme-786-1261942.

[25] Antonia Blyth, "James Corden On How He Got Paul McCartney On 'Carpool Karaoke' & Tom Cruise's Comedy Doughnuts," *Deadline*, August 22, 2018, https://deadline.com/2018/08/james-corden-paul-mccartney-carpool-karaoke-tom-cruise-1202447271/.

pressings on high-quality vinyl with ultra-deluxe packaging. For baby boomers, the motivation may in part be the nostalgia of memories rekindled, but for audiophiles there is also a preference for the perceived "warmer" sound of vinyl over digital. Young collectors though, according to Vinyl Me, Please, a vinyl LP subscription service catering to twenty and thirty somethings, are more intrigued by the idea of "exchanging convenience for an experience." To customers who did not grow up with vinyl, they say, "the idea of owning is really interesting ... [Vinyl Me, Please] wanted to offer a service that puts the album as the central piece of ... listening experience ... this incredible thing that you sit down and participate in, ... the Napster generation" craving a "tangible, tactile relationship with music."[26]

Notable Beatles anniversaries have also spawned the release of deluxe attention-getting vinyl albums. For example, 2018 saw the release of a 50th anniversary repackaging of *The Beatles, aka The White Album*, the original a double vinyl gatefold album released in 1968. The new package offers a 164-page book with a collection of original and new mixes by George Martin's son Giles, demos and unreleased takes, all sequenced by recording date, 107 tracks in all. Platform options, in addition to CD and Blu-Ray disks, include for record buffs four LPs pressed on high quality 180-gram vinyl and gloriously packaged in a special box with replica gatefold sleeves and additional lithographed graphics not part of the original package.

We Hope You Have Enjoyed the Show

Well into the twenty-first century, the Beatles remain an indelible presence in the American entertainment landscape. What happens in Las Vegas, for example, does not necessarily stay in Las Vegas. Running there since 2006 at a specially built theater at the Mirage Hotel is *The Beatles LOVE* by Cirque du Soleil, a multimedia performance that delivers Beatles songs in grand spectacular fashion. The show features sixty costumed aerialists, dancers, and acrobats performing to surround-sound classic Beatles recordings remixed, reimagined, and revitalized by both George and son Giles Martin. Tourists from around the world come to see the show and leave Vegas with a fresh experience of the Beatles, the youngest hearing songs for the first time emerging as Beatles fans same as their parents and

---

[26] Laura Entis, "Millennials Are Blamed for a Lot of Things but They're Reviving the Vinyl Record Industry," *Fortune*, August 4, 2017, http://fortune.com/2017/08/04/millennials-vinyl-industry/.

grandparents before.[27] "The show," reports the *New York Times*, "has turned the Mirage into a bona fide pilgrimage site – the only place in the world you can see a Beatles-approved theatrical production with an enveloping surround soundtrack, direct from the master tapes. A spokeswoman for Apple said that the continuing demand for the production suggests that fans would come back for more ... And, in the end, *Love* is a measure of how the Beatles' music continues to speak to new listeners, and how the group's constituency has continued to expand: the show's audience of eight million is vastly larger than the number of people who saw the Beatles perform live. And its run is even longer than the group's recording career.[28]

Once There Was a Way to Get Back Homeward

Once when the Beatles were new, a spirit of rebellion was in the air, at the extreme, palpable rancor, or at least a schism between those of the World War II generation and their offspring, the children of the 1960s, inheritors of new age technologies, relative prosperity, freewheeling opportunity, and idealistic values. Pundits called it the "generation gap." Rock 'n' roll was fired in that rebellion, part of the border wall that demarcated division. The dissipation of that generational gap is another reason the Beatles live on.

There will always be friction between children and parents, but in the broadest sense, that dynamic no longer holds. Paul Taylor, formerly of the Pew Research Center, writes in *The Next America* that "today's young adults get along better with their parents than older adults did when they were young," and that part of the reason for the "low level of generational tension" is because "more than 50 million Americans, a record, are living under the same roof in multi-generational family households, their fortunes braided together by the bonds of love and the stress of economic insecurity."[29]

If anything, the music of the Beatles and of the 1960s in general has in large measure contributed to the narrowing of the distance between parents and children. Today's young people frequently describe growing up in homes where the Beatles were part of a shared and positive family

---

[27] "The Beatles Love," *Cirque du Soleil*, www.cirquedusoleil.com/beatles-love.
[28] Allan Kozinn, "In Las Vegas, All You Need Is 'Love' and Eight Million Beatles Fans," *New York Times*, August 1, 2016, www.nytimes.com/2016/08/02/arts/music/beatles-love-cirque-du-soleil.html.
[29] Paul Taylor, "Generational Equity and the 'Next America,'" *Pew Research Center*, April 18, 2014, www.pewresearch.org/fact-tank/2014/04/18/generational-equity-and-the-next-america/.

experience, particular songs emblematic of family harmony and love, the stuff of twenty-first-century childhood memories. As Taylor points out, what there is of present-day rebellion is not so much generational as societal and political. Points of view on environmental, social, economic, and world issues can no longer be compartmentalized by generational differences. The style and content of Beatles songs continue to have cachet across the demographic spread as the twenty-first century unfolds. Personally, as both musician and educator, I am often enough heartened and even somehow validated when twenty-somethings and younger tell me that their musical embrace includes 1960s music and especially the Beatles. Beatles songs continue to resonate. The songs are still in rotation. We are in an age, after all, when Sirius satellite radio finds it profitable to feature an entire 24/7 channel devoted exclusively to the Beatles.

If, however, the Beatles had left nothing worth remembering, they would not be remembered. They unlike the majority of their rock 'n' roll counterparts were not "one hit wonders." The Beatles literally top the record books as multi-hit wonders, according to the Record Industry Association of America, having sold over 178 million units and still counting.[30] The Beatles songbook via recordings is inextricably woven into our cultural fabric.

The Beatles are now iconic, seminal in pop music history. When they came on the scene, rock 'n' roll had essentially been stalled, in a stale doldrum. The Beatles broke out of the pack to become a force in a cultural shakeup that redefined what rock 'n' roll could be. By the mid-1960s, they had set a new standard by revolutionizing the sound and being of rock 'n' roll. The Beatles had taken an American pop music genre and given it a boost that exploded it worldwide. Even their physicality, their look, their demeanor was game changing. The outrageous (as it then seemed) long hair, and the comically snarky media interviews. The Beatles set a foundational template that, love their music or not, perseveres to this day as a reference point for aspiring and established musical artists no matter the genre.

Consider, for example, the track record of cross-genre tributes to the Beatles.

In jazz, Herbie Hancock with vocalist Corinne Bailey Rae performing "Blackbird" at the 2010 Gershwin Prize Ceremony at the White House; that same year Ramsey Lewis releasing *Ramsey Lewis Plays the Beatles Songbook*; or

[30] "Top-selling Rock Bands of All Time," *CNN*, January 2, 2017, www.cnn.com/2016/12/28/entertainment/gallery/successful-rock-bands-history-of-chicago/index.html.

the 2014 multi-artist compendium, *The Beatles: A Jazz Tribute – Celebrating 50 Years* with jazz covers of "Something," "Taxman," and "Here Comes the Sun" (High Note – HCD 7260).

In hip-hop, covers such as "Help!" by Lil Wayne on his 2007 album *The Drought Is Over Pt.2* (The Carter III Sessions MixTape) and in 2011 at the Hollywood Bowl Usher performing "With a Little Help from My Friends." Or sampling such as "Hold On John" by Los Angeles artist Blu, John Lennon's original "Hold On" looped and interwoven into Blu's reimagined rap track.[31]

In R&B, Bettye LaVette's 2010 Interpretations: *The British Rock Songbook* (-Anti) with covers of "The Word," McCartney's "Maybe I'm Amazed," Harrison's "Isn't it a Pity," and Starr's "It Don't Come Easy, "Can't Buy Me Love," "Help!," and "Revolution."[32]

In Americana, that folky minimal production homespun mostly acoustic genre, the album *Let Us In Americana* (Reviver Records, 2013) with "I Will" by Steve Earle, Lee Ann Womacks's "Let 'Em In," Matraca Berg's "Yesterday," mandolinist Sam Bush's "I've Just Seen a Face," singer/songwriter Bruce Cockburn's "The Fool on the Hill," and by the McCrary Sisters a gospelized version of "Let It Be."[33]

There are karaoke singalong Beatles albums, tributes to each Beatle individually, and multi-artist cross-genre collections such as the 2005 album, *This Bird Has Flown – A 40th Anniversary Tribute to the Beatles' Rubber Soul* (Razor and Tie) with covers of "Michelle," "Drive My Car," "Norwegian Wood," "Nowhere Man," "The Word," "Girl," and "Run for Your Life" by a diversity of artists including Dar Williams, Ben Harper, the Fiery Furnaces, the Donnas, the Cowboy Junkies, Ben Kweller, and Albert Hammond, Jr.

The implication that can be drawn from all this is that a significant number of contemporary artists think enough of the Beatles to want to tribute them in song. In the end and in the main, though, the continued popularity of the Beatles may not be so much about who has covered them and when, but rather about their inextricable presence in the very DNA of American and world pop music. Innumerable contemporary artists owe

---

[31] Christian Medina Beltz, "The Beatles On Beat: How the Fab Four Influenced Hip-Hop," *Medium*, May 7, 2017, https://medium.com/@C.Medina/the-beatles-on-beat-how-the-fab-four-influenced-hip-hop-2c3d0d466d3f.

[32] "Big Time Rush," *IMDb*, www.imdb.com/title/tt1131746/.

[33] "Various – Let Us In – Americana | The Music of Paul McCartney...For Linda," *Discogs*, www.discogs.com/Various-Let-Us-In-Americana-The-Music-Of-Paul-McCartneyFor-Linda/release/4821100.

something to the Beatles in one way or another. It could be identifiable in a style, in the instrumentation, in vocal harmonies, in songwriting, in the sonic character of a track, in a choice of chords or how chords are hung together, a melody line, an altered sound, an idea, or even the ambition to experiment. Bruce Springsteen, another 1970/80s icon, told the audience at an emotional 1980 concert in Philadelphia shortly after John Lennon's death, "The first record that I ever learned was a record called 'Twist and Shout.' It was a Beatles record. If it wasn't for John Lennon, we'd all be some place very different tonight." And some thirty years later on being invited by Paul McCartney to join the band at the 2012 Grammy Awards in a performance of the *Abbey Road* closing medley, Springsteen, referring now to McCartney, remarked, "There's a basic realization that you simply would not be here, the way you are here, without this specific person. Who actually is a person!"[34]

Dave Grohl of the Foo Fighters, partner with Kurt Cobain in Nirvana, was also influenced by the Beatles. Grohl and the surviving members of Nirvana performed with "Sir" Paul McCartney as "Sirvana" at a 2012 Concert for Hurricane Sandy Relief. "When I was young," said Grohl, "that's how I learned how to play music – I had a guitar and a Beatles songbook. I would listen to the records and play along. Of course, it didn't sound like the Beatles, but it got me to understand song structure and melody and harmony and arrangement. So, I never had a teacher – I just had these." And as to his Nirvana bandmate, "the Beatles [were] such a huge influence. Kurt loved the Beatles because it was just so simple. Well, it seemed simple ... they sound easy to play, but you know what? They're hard!"[35]

The entry on the Beatles in *Rolling Stone* magazine's *Encyclopedia of Rock & Roll* reads as follows:

> The impact of the Beatles – not only on rock & roll but on all of Western culture ... is simply incalculable ... [A]s personalities, they defined and incarnated '60s style: smart, idealistic, playful, irreverent, eclectic ... No group has so radically transformed the sound and significance of rock & roll ... [they] proved that rock & roll could embrace a limitless variety of harmonies, structures, and sounds; virtually every rock experiment has some precedent on a Beatles record.[36]

[34] Frank Mastropolo, "Top 11 Musicians Influenced By the Beatles," *Rock Cellar*, www.rockcellarma gazine.com/2014/02/04/top-11-musicians-influenced-by-the-beatles-50th-anniversary/2/.
[35] Mastropolo, "Top 11 Musicians Influenced By the Beatles."
[36] Holly Warren-George, Patricia Romanowski Bashe and Jon Pareles, *The Rolling Stone Encyclopedia of Rock & Roll* (New York: Fireside, 2001).

And in the end, records – recorded sound – are what matter in both coalescing and sustaining the legacy of the Beatles. They even told us that in titling one of their most significant albums. "We suddenly thought," said Paul, "Hey, what does a record do? It revolves. Great! You know – and so it was a Revolver."[37]

---

[37] "Revolver," *The Beatles*, www.thebeatles.com/album/revolver.

PART V

The Beatles as Sociocultural and Political Touchstones

CHAPTER 23

The Beatles, Fashion, and Cultural Iconography

Katie Kapurch

The history of the Beatles' fashion is summed up in the famous "Mocker" statement that Paul McCartney gave to the press in 1964. This response quickly found its way into the shooting script of *A Hard Day's Night*. In the film, when Ringo Starr is asked whether he identifies as a Mod or a Rocker – subcultures whose styles were integral to clashing identities that erupted in bloody conflict in the spring of that year[1] – the drummer answers, "I'm a Mocker." That dry rejoinder, which sidesteps the politics of pledging allegiance, is the story of the Beatles' changing fashion. Throughout their tenure as a group, the Beatles try on popular styles. Without seeming to take themselves too seriously, they mix elements that suit their needs, then discard them when they don't. "It wasn't like we were following a trend; we were in the trend," remembers Paul McCartney, recollecting the early days.[2] Just as they did with musical innovation, once the Beatles mastered a fashion, they were on to the next one. The ability to change, to be "in the trend" rather than in front of or behind it, is a key factor in the sustained popularity of the Beatles and their cultural iconography.

Whether they had matching suits or matching mustaches, the Beatles' fashion choices consistently threatened the status quo. Their now-iconic looks, which evolved as their music did, also invited imitation by fans. As such, the objects associated with their styles have graduated to the rank of iconography, sacred relics whose images stand in for songs, as well as the

---

[1] The seaside riots of spring 1964 are immortalized in *Quadrophenia* (1979), the fictional film based on the Who's 1973 concept album.

[2] Paul McCartney, "You Gave Me the Answer – Jake from Surrey Asks," *Paul McCartney*, May 31, 2018, www.paulmccartney.com/newsblogs/news/yougavemetheanswerjakefromsur reyasks. McCartney remembers: "By now we were starting to earn money, so you would buy those things and then you'd see guys in other groups who would be like, 'Where did you get your shirt man? Cecil Gee? Ah right, OK!!' You'd trade information. But the thing is, it wasn't so much that we were following fashion, so much as being part of it." McCartney's explanation of the Beatles' early process models the kind of behavior associated with the Mods, who aspired to transcend their working-class stations through style.

story of the band. The "mop-top" is the crowning glory of their most famous and most unifying style, whose history explains the radical impact of the hair, suits, and boots. The "Fab," as I term it, is a cohesive look born out of previous fashions, but the style is also a foundation for subsequent Beatles aesthetics. The "Pepper" is another unifying style, at once nostalgic and psychedelic, that reinvents the Beatles. The Pepper look includes one ingredient – Lennon's glasses – that begins to signal the band's end, which is also prefigured in the House of Nutter clothing (or lack thereof) that appears on the last album the band recorded.

Fab Style: "Man You've Been a Naughty Boy"

The transformation to Fab was finally complete early in 1962.[3] In January, at the encouragement of new manager Brian Epstein, the Beatles donned the tailored, fitted suits that replaced the leather gear and tight jeans of their "Gene Vincent" rocker look. Reminiscent of "what was progressively becoming British Mod fashion in London,"[4] which signified social and economic striving, those blue, single-breasted mohair suits were the final ingredient.[5] The trouser legs were cut narrow, tailoring that made the Beatles' legs appear long and youthful. The straight cut all the way down the leg to the hem accommodated their recently acquired footwear. The subsequently dubbed "Beatle boots" were "Spanish flamenco ankle boots, 'Chelsea'-style in black leather, with black elastic sides, a tag at the back, pointed toes and Cuban heels," purchased from a London shoe shop that served theater and ballet performers at the end of 1961.[6] These matching suits and boots completed a look that really began with their hair.

Before they were Fab, the pre-fame Beatles went through a series of "uniform" self-stylings that articulated and re-articulated their groupness.[7] The tough-looking leather during their wild Hamburg days was accompanied by the hairstyle of their Liverpool adolescence. That hair was influenced by the style of the Teddy Boy, who quiffed his hair into a ducktail and stuffed his legs into tight "drainpipe trousers" ("drainies") covered with a large Edwardian-style jacket known as a "brothel creeper."[8]

---

[3] Because there is so much legend surrounding the Beatles and their iconic style, I draw on Lewisohn due to his painstaking attention to detail and biographical accuracy. I condense the facts he presents to offer a useful resource that succinctly answers most common questions about the Beatles' early look. Any reader desiring more detail should consult *Tune In: The Beatles – All These Years, Extended Special Edition* (London: Little, Brown, 2013).

[4] Lewisohn, *Tune In*, 555. [5] Lewisohn, *Tune In*, 555. [6] Lewisohn, *Tune In*, 534.

[7] Lewisohn, *Tune In*, 332. [8] Lewisohn, *Tune In*, 66.

The look of a "Ted," which John Lennon especially tried to cultivate (much to the horror of parents and teachers), bespoke rebelliousness, as well as group membership as a rough boy. The Ted prohibited Lennon from wearing his glasses, rendering him visionless much of the time[9] – but that also coincided with his boyhood preference to be always surrounded by a gang of followers.[10] Ironically, as I consider in the conclusion, his future wire frames will be an early signal of his independence from his musical gang, the Beatles, eventually becoming the iconography of his own Lennon brand.

While Fab trousers favor the slim fit reminiscent of the "drainies," other remnants of these earlier looks are absent from the Fab, a gender-fluid style influenced by gay men, especially Brian, as well as exposure to the Continent and women. The Beatles' famous mop-top was modeled by their German art-school friends, specifically Astrid Kirchherr, the future wife of then-bandmate Stuart Sutcliffe. Along with another long-time Beatles player Klaus Voorman, Kirchherr copied fellow photographer and art-school friend Jürgen Vollmer, who "fashion[ed] his hair differently from everyone else, in the modish Paris student style, combed down and a little to the side."[11] In the fall of 1961, Paul and John visited Vollmer, who had moved to Paris, and their holiday marked the real beginning of Fab style. Paul and John admired Jürgen's heeled boots – and they took notice of the popular French cosmopolitan styles, especially the round-neck Pierre Cardin suits, which they purchased at the time.[12] Rejected by Parisian women largely due to their "Elvis hair and leather jackets," McCartney and Lennon had Vollmer cut their hair into the "clean, combed-down Paris" style to appeal better in a city that was not into the garishness and juvenilia of American rock.[13] That initial styling had a diagonal part, but after some wash and wear it settled into the straight-across fringe.[14] Soon after John and Paul returned to Liverpool from their transformative holiday, George right away adopted the look (sans diagonal), an expression of group solidarity with significant consequences.

Epstein would later commission his barber, Jim Cannon, for tidying trims of a haircut that gave the illusion of length because it sat down on the forehead,[15] but the Beatles' Fab hair was in place by the fall of 1961. In many ways, it was the hairstyle itself that initiated the process of ousting

---

[9] Lewisohn, *Tune In*, 88.   [10] Lewisohn, *Tune In*, 44.
[11] Lewisohn, *Tune In*, 372. Vollmer explains, "We called it the Caesar haircut. I always cut it myself because the barbers in Hamburg were totally square."
[12] Lewisohn, *Tune In*, 372   [13] Lewisohn, *Tune In*, 484.   [14] Lewisohn, *Tune In*, 487.
[15] Lewisohn, *Tune In*, 552.

drummer Pete Best, whose Tony Curtis curls either would not or could not accommodate the new group look. Neil Aspinall remembers, "this was a real tester for Pete. It was like a gauntlet had been thrown down. And Pete absolutely didn't want to put his hair down. A decision had to be made – and he decided no."[16] In another stroke of congruity, the mop-top style obscured the shocking streak of white at the center of Starr's forehead (which made him look much older and "nasty" according to George[17]). Fab mop-top hair rendered Ringo youthful and loveable, the persona he has cultivated ever since. In 1962, the Beatles finally got the drummer whose foot passed their glass-slipper test: Ringo had the skill – and hair – for the job. The Beatles' Fab style was finally complete in its uniformity, and the group was ready to take on the USA and the rest of the world.

Even though early 1960s comedians donned Beatle wigs for an easy laugh, the symbolic importance of the mop-top cannot be underplayed. The Parisian hairstyle was a post-war leftist political and philosophical response associated with the resurgence of existentialism. When adopted by the Beatles' German art-student friends, the hair was a specifically pro-European, anti-Nazi stance in a country still recovering from the horrors it had imposed on the rest of the continent. Astrid, Klaus, and Jürgen adopted a look that dissolved gender barriers – the very definitions the Nazis sought to foster in their obsession with the physically fit, robust bodies of German youth.[18] Along with the combed-down hair, the "Exi" favored skinny slenderness – in men and women – the kind of androgynous body favored by the early working-class Mods, whose look derived from the Exi, along with the Beatnik. That gender-fluid body is the one Twiggy would make famous as the icon of mid-1960s "swinging London," when Mod style gave way to the color blocks of Warholian pop art and psychedelia.[19] Thus, when the Beatles invaded in February 1964, American adults were threatened by a hairstyle that was indeed born out of resistance to the status quo, especially when it came to gender. Recognizing Fab hair as a menace to conventional middle-class values, American adults tried to mock the mop-top into impotence. But the Beatles and their "long" hair were not going anywhere.

---

[16] Lewisohn, *Tune In*, 490.   [17] Qtd. in Lewisohn, *Tune In*, 366.
[18] Steven D. Stark, *Meet the Beatles: A Cultural History of the Band That Shook Youth, Gender, and the World* (New York: Harper, 2006), 90–92.
[19] "Twiggy," *The Mod Generation*, 2009, www.themodgeneration.co.uk/2009/01/twiggy.html. Twiggy herself was a Mod before she began modeling and sums up the early 1960s Mod's gender-fluid style: "we all dressed alike."

One only needs turn so far as *A Hard Day's Night* to get the best view of Fab style in its peak. Director Richard Lester shoots "the boys" (as he and other "adults" called the Beatles[20]) from a variety of angles, often with a handheld camera and unconventional close-ups. As such, the viewer has a multi-dimensional view of the mop-top hair that was causing such a stir – along with their suited boyish bodies and what would soon be hawked as "Beatle boots" in the USA. The close quarters of the train scenes allow for non-traditional shots of the back of the head, showing how the mop-top descends in layers. Much shorter than the front, the back of Fab hair is not altogether neat given the unruliness of their very thick hair. (Looking in a train compartment mirror, Paul even runs a comb across his head, a gesture held over from the Teddy Boys, which demanded an ever-present comb for the Vaselined quiff.[21]) The black and white film stock eliminates the nuances of each Beatle's brunette hair, giving the sense of even more sameness. When the boys play in the abandoned field, a range of aerial views to low-angle shots capture the youthful, buoyant movement facilitated by the fitting of their trousers and those heeled boots made for dancing. In the final concert sequence of the film, Fab style is wholly visible all over again in full-body shots and mid-shots of hair-shaking woos (withheld until now), while close-ups feature the sweat-glistening faces and singing lips so many in the audience yearned to kiss. The Fab Beatles were something new, both girlish and boyish in their presentation of gender and sexuality.[22]

In addition to their first feature film, Fab style was on display on television, such as BBC1's *Top of the Pops* and the *Ed Sullivan Show* in the USA, as well as album covers and in other print media. The effect was instant imitation, especially when it came to hair. As film critic and *A Hard Day's Night* devotee Roger Ebert claims, "The film was so influential in its androgynous imagery that untold thousands of young men walked into the theater with short haircuts, and their hair started growing during the movie and didn't get cut again until the 1970s."[23] Both boys and girls, especially those in the USA, adopted Fab style, buying up Beatle-boot knock-offs and wigs or making their own clothing. But hair was really the thing.

---

[20] "You Can't Do That": The Making of "A Hard Day's Night," 1994, *A Hard Day's Night*, Criterion Collection, 2014.

[21] Lewisohn, *Tune In*, 66.

[22] See Katie Kapurch, "The Beatles, Gender, and Sexuality: I Am He as You are He as You are Me," in *The Beatles and Fandom*, ed. Kenneth Womack and Kit O'Toole (Oxford: Oxford University Press, forthcoming).

[23] Roger Ebert, Review of *A Hard Day's Night* (1964), October 27, 1996, www.rogerebert.com/reviews/great-movie-a-hard-days-night-1964.

Countless households in post-February 1964 America saw disputes between parents and children – mostly, though not only, boys – who grew their hair "long" like the Beatles. As one first-generation male fan remembers: "They burst into my consciousness and I thought they were the coolest thing when I saw them on *Ed Sullivan*. Dad was driven to distraction by the long hair. All the guys combed their hair down the next day."[24] Girls, who were likewise expected to have groomed and kempt hair, also adopted Beatle hairstyles, an expression of gender-fluidity that mirrored the Beatles' own. Then 14-year-old Donna Lynn's 1964 *Billboard*-charting Capitol single, "My Boyfriend Got a Beatle Haircut," bemoans the attention her guy is receiving – so she concludes, "to keep him true, I got a Beatle haircut, too."

Chrissie Hynde of the Pretenders was another girl inspired to imitate the Beatles. In 1964, the Beatles' and other UK bands' Britishness was an immediate point of appeal for 13-year-old Hynde; she saw their look as a departure from the stifling orthodoxy of her hometown, Akron, Ohio. Recalling her entrance into college five years later, Hynde compares herself to her groomed roommate: "She had big bouffant hair, which she set in those rollers that I'd stopped using way back when I went 'Beatle chick.' She looked like a singer out of a group like the Shangri-Las; she wasn't flying her freak flag in army fatigues like me."[25] For Hynde, Beatle style meant a natural, floppy fringe, hair she adopted while inaugurating her musical career through another form of Beatle imitation, guitar playing and songwriting. Hynde illustrates the radical consequences of the Beatles' Fab style for girls: the Beatles' gender-fluid look and music were like keys to open the world, an idea expressed so frequently by first-generation fans in feminist analyses of Beatlemania.[26] Hynde's recollection is also valuable because she references another aspect of 1960s fashion, constructing a continuum between early Fab style and the later countercultural military garb common among hippies and protesters. The latter is previewed by the Beatles' playful adoption of Edwardian uniforms on the cover of *Pepper*.

---

[24] Qtd. in Candy Leonard,.*Beatleness: How the Beatles and Their Fans Remade the World* (New York: Arcade, 2014), 49.

[25] Chrissie Hynde, *Reckless: My Life as a Pretender* (Norwell, MA: Anchor, 2015), 65.

[26] See Barbara Ehrenreich, Elizabeth Hess and Gloria Jacobs, "Beatlemania: Girls Just Want To Have Fun," in *The Adoring Audience: Fan Culture And Popular Music*, ed. Lisa Lewis (London: Routledge 1992); Susan Douglas, *Where the Girls Are: Growing Up Female with the Mass Media* (New York: Three Rivers Press, 1994).

The Pepper: "You Let Your Face Grow Long"

The mid-1960s Beatles let the mop-top and sideburns ("sidies") grow longer and more unruly. This transitional look is captured well in the 1966 promotional film for "Paperback Writer," which opens with four close-ups, one of each Beatle face (still clean shaven) looking rather somber. In that video, they wear similar but not completely matching black corduroy jackets and trousers that are complementary; Paul's turtle-neck appears to be the same taupe as the accent color of John's lapels. The videos for "Paperback Writer" and "Rain" shed the identical suits of their touring days, which ended in August of that year.

The Beatles' "street clothes," much more visible when they stopped touring, resembled the fashions of the day. The band members were heavily influenced by fellow musicians and friends in the London scene; Paul McCartney's girlfriend, actress Jane Asher, and George Harrison's wife, model Pattie Boyd, were particularly significant. Asher introduced McCartney to Leslie Cavendish, the hairstylist who began cutting the Beatles' hair in 1966.[27] And it was Boyd who first discovered Transcendental Meditation; its leader, the Maharishi Mahesh Yogi, along with Ravi Shankar, Harrison's guitar guru, influenced the Beatles' Indian aesthetic in music and clothing.[28]

The emerging psychedelic fashions found their way into subsequent promotional videos, particularly "Strawberry Fields Forever," as well as their self-made film, *Magical Mystery Tour* (1967). As McCartney remembers of that time:

> We just kind of wore what we liked and then as time went on we got into the psychedelic era and we met some people, a collective called "The Fool". They designed clothes and would custom make them for you. And those were very much the sort of psychedelic brightly coloured things that still, to me today, when you look at those clothes – they look like clothes from the future! They don't look like clothes from the past! Those pictures, if you look at "Magical Mystery Tour", something like "I Am the Walrus". Those are basically made by those people. They were Dutch kids – students – but they made clothes. Again, we were part of the trend rather than following it.[29]

[27] See Leslie Cavendish, *Cutting Edge: The Story of the Beatles' Hairdresser Who Defined an Era*, Kindle edn (London: Alma Books).
[28] See Pattie Boyd with Penny Junor, *Wonderful Tonight: George Harrison, Eric Clapton, and Me* (New York: Three Rivers Press, 2007), 96–97; see also Kathryn B. Cox, "The Road to Rishikesh: The Beatles, India, and Globalized Dialogue in 1967," *The Beatles, Sgt. Pepper, and the Summer of Love*, ed. Kenneth Womack and Kathryn B. Cox (Lanham, MD: Lexington, 2017) for the detailed history of the Beatles in India.
[29] McCartney, interview.

The Beatles absorbed and reflected what was popular around them – and part of that was LSD. Aspinall, noting the Beatles' naiveté, points out the inaccuracy of seeing the Beatles as style "leaders": "I saw them influenced by all sorts of nonsense a number of times. In general, they went along with everything that was happening in the sixties."[30] Still, their enormous cultural presence meant that, even if they did not inaugurate a trend, "for much of the youth in the sixties, the Beatles were the 'four wise men'. They were the heralds of an alternative culture."[31] To young people listening around the world and who would never get to visit the cool shops, clubs, and happenings associated with the London Underground scene,[32] the Beatles seemed to give away countercultural secrets, such as a visible style to imitate.

McCartney's recollection sees the future-signaling potential of clothes that evoke the past. This is the very rhetorical outcome achieved with *Sgt. Pepper's Lonely Hearts Club Band*. The Beatles' apparel on the cover of this album is a visual touchstone in the military styling popular in the latter part of the decade. McCartney remembers, "At the back of our minds, I think the plan was to have garish uniforms which would actually go against the idea of uniform."[33] Especially as the Vietnam War escalated, clothing evocative of military uniforms bespeaks a simultaneous protest of military action and co-opting of militarization. Like Hynde, who wore a grown-out Fab haircut with fatigues, Lennon also saw Beatles' looks in a continuum:

> *Pepper* was just an evolvement of the Beatle boots and all that. It was just another psychedelic image. Beatle haircuts and boots were just as big as flowered pants in their time. I never felt that when *Pepper* came out, Haight Ashbury was a direct result. It always seemed to me that they were all happening at once. Kids were already wearing army jackets on the King's Road, all we did was make them famous.[34]

For the Beatles, the uniforms directly communicated their new membership in Sgt. Pepper's band, an artifice McCartney imagined would free them from expectations about what constitutes "Beatles music."[35]

The Beatles' Pepper look is another radical metamorphosis akin to Fab style. While Fab signifies the origins of global fame, Pepper style overtly

[30] Qtd in Sheila Whiteley, *The Space Between the Notes: Rock and the Counter-Culture* (London: Routledge, 1992), 43.
[31] McCabe and Schonfield, qtd. in Whiteley, *Space Between*, 43.
[32] See Joe Boyd, "The London Underground," in *Sgt. Pepper's Lonely Hearts Club Band* (book accompanying album), 23–31, Capitol, 2017.
[33] The Beatles, *The Beatles Anthology* (San Francisco: Chronicle Books, 2000), 248.
[34] Beatles, *Anthology*, 248.   [35] Beatles, *Anthology*, 241.

tries to shed that skin and its baggage of mop-top cuteness, a theme that informed the album's concept. Fed up with the screaming chaos of touring, the Beatles wanted their musical innovation to be taken seriously. And yet Pepper style is still one that upends conventional masculinity. Once again, they don mostly matching styles that – like their earlier Beatle boots – were acquired from costume makers: "The Beatles wore colourful military tunics made by costumiers Berman's in the West End of London. While this type of clothing was primarily chosen to fit the retrospective image of Sgt. Pepper's band, it was also a current fashion style."[36] Their Edwardian military costume corresponds to late 1960s penchants for nine-teenth-century and early twentieth-century fashions,[37] an anti-Modern impulse that gave rise to the style and characteristic flamboyance of the British Pop Dandy.[38] That kind of Romantic nostalgia finds voice on the album itself with songs such as "When I'm Sixty-Four" and "Being for the Benefit of Mr. Kite!"[39]

But the Pepper style also references a more recent time, specifically the Beatles' 1950s adolescence. Paul's recollection again reveals the mix-and-match impulse: "We just chose oddball things and put them together. We all chose our own colours and materials . . . We went for bright psychedelic colours, a bit like the fluorescent socks you used to get in the Fifties (they came in very pink, very turquoise, and very yellow)." Like the colors, the choice of the Edwardian long-waisted jacket also evokes an earlier Edwardian reboot, again familiar to their 1950s youth: the "Ted" and his favored jacket, the "brothel creeper." The Pepper look thus involves a disguised disguise, one that recalls their original offensive style, which most of the public had never seen on the Beatles. After all, before American parents panicked about Beatle hair, the Beatles' own British parents and teachers were scolding them for sporting the Teddy Boy ducktail. Thus, in

---

[36] Kevin Howlett, "The Cover Story," in *Sgt. Pepper's Lonely Hearts Club Band* (book accompanying album), 107–14; see also Beatles, *Anthology*, 248.

[37] Benjamin Poore, *Heritage, Nostalgia and Modern British Theatre: Staging the Victorians* (New York: Palgrave Macmillan, 2012), 38. Poore notices the simultaneity of the "growing bourgeois fondness for the individualities of Victorian housing" and "the countercultural trend, in the late 1960s, for dressing in Victorian-style pea-coats, military jackets, top hats, ruffled shirts, boating blazers, capes and velvet suits." He goes on to discuss places frequented by the Beatles and their crowd, shops that directly influenced Pepper style: "Two of the most mythologized fashion boutiques in accounts of the 1960s are Granny Takes a Trip, on King's Road, and I Was Lord Kitchener's Valet, on the Portobello Road, both names drawing attention to the idea of young people dressing up in the clothes of their grandparents' generation, eclectically mixing styles to give them a 'psychedelic makeover.'"

[38] See Stan Hawkins, *The British Pop Dandy: Masculinity, Popular Music and Culture* (New York: Ashgate, 2009).

[39] See Beatles, *Anthology*, 248.

their Technicolor brilliance, the Pepper jackets are the cheerful gear needed for a psychedelic trip away from the straight Modern world. As Teddy Boy reboots, the jackets can be looked upon as a rebellious middle finger to the establishment that accused the Beatles of being finished prior to *Sgt. Pepper*'s long-awaited release.[40]

Along with their clothes, Pepper head-hairstyles are general variations on the mop-top, with the front of the hair still falling on the forehead. Like the Fab, the Pepper is still one of group cohesion – with the exception of Lennon's glasses and perhaps McCartney's shorter haircut, which he got earlier that year in order to go on vacation in "disguise."[41] Like the Edwardian uniforms, the mustaches were also motivated by the vintage impulse that signaled countercultural protest against modernity: "The longer hairstyles, sideburns, and moustaches that were to dominate male fashion until the early 1980s constituted the most hirsute look for men fashionable since the turn of the twentieth century."[42] The mustaches were the Beatles' *adult* statement of togetherness, claiming a grown-up masculinity with a thinly veiled mustache-mask that nevertheless allows the "real" Beatles' faces to shine through.[43] American audiences were not all wholly enthusiastic about the Beatles' new look, particularly the mustaches, with some kids reading the look as dour and too adult. This was the reaction Dick Clark witnessed when he played the promotional film of "Strawberry Fields Forever" for a group of young people, one of whom said, "They look like grandfathers or something."[44] Of course, this was the point of the Beatles' vintage look. That nostalgic persona-building would not, however, be the motivation for the following year's double album, *The Beatles*, whose album cover featured no Beatles at all.

The End: "Expert, Texpert"

Before they realized their corporate maneuvers would help speed along their disintegration, the Beatles had high hopes in 1968 for Apple Corps to become a countercultural trendsetter. In addition to sponsoring up-and-coming musicians (James Taylor, Mary Hopkin, Billy Preston) on their label, the Beatles opened Apple Tailoring on King's Road and Apple Boutique on Baker Street. The fashion venture is generally remembered

---

[40] Kevin Howlett, "The Path to Pepper," in *Sgt. Pepper's Lonely Hearts Club Band*, 11–21.
[41] Cavendish, *Cutting Edge*, loc. 1240. As with the *Sgt. Pepper* personas he dreamed up, disguise was a recurring theme for McCartney around this time.
[42] Poore, *Heritage*, 38.   [43] See Whiteley, *Space Between*, 39.
[44] Jeff Slate, "Sgt. Pepper in America," in *Sgt. Pepper's Lonely Hearts Club Band*, 129–35.

for the clothing shops intended to showcase the top styles of the day, made by the Fool and worn by the Beatles themselves. The King's Road location also included their hairdresser's salon, "Leslie Cavendish's Hairdressing Studio at Apple Tailoring."[45] These original Apple stores localized the kind of total-package trendsetting from which the earlier Beatles had been unable to profit given the loose licensing of their images that resulted in Beatle-image proliferation without proceeds. Apple Boutique, however, was a failure, largely due to a countercultural ethos of not paying and not reporting shoplifting – while also sourcing expensive materials that could not possibly turn a profit.[46] This venture might be another fashion metaphor: the Beatles' trendsetting always worked best when it was organic and unforced – when they were on the inside. The magic of Beatles' iconography is its open invitation, rather than a conscious demand.

In January 1969, when the Beatles ascended onto the rooftop for the concert that concluded the film *Let It Be* (1970), their disparate styles and hair lengths (on both face and head) are telling indications of what is to come. Likewise, for the photoshoot that would become the cover of *Abbey Road* (1969), George was not wearing the "Nutter" suits sported by the others in various colors: Paul in dark blue, Ringo in black, and John in the beautiful cream. The Nutter was the signature look of Savile Row tailor Tommy Nutter, yet another fashion-forward gay man significant in the Beatles' story.[47] Early influences on his look include none other than the precursors to Fab and Pepper, the Teddy Boy and "Neo-Edwardian dandyism." Nutter's suits became known for their extra-wide lapels, tapered waist, and flared trousers, which worked together to create a gender-fluid silhouette on the male body.[48] This silhouette is less discernable, however, on the cover of *Abbey Road* given their profile positions and in-motion strides as well as George's apparel abstention. As a result, the Beatles' *Abbey Road* look is seldom described as British dandyism, despite the House of Nutter's association with that trend. Moreover, Harrison ominously chose gravedigger denim, rather than the kind of matching or complementary style that historically signaled the Beatles' groupness. His choice, echoed in McCartney's famous shoelessness, is a dramatic indication of the looming dissolution. The break-up, however, was previewed

---

[45] Cavendish, *Cutting Edge*, loc. 2993.   [46] Cavendish, *Cutting Edge*, loc. 3073.
[47] Lance Richardson, *House of Nutter: The Rebel Tailor of Savile Row* (New York: Crown/Archetype, 2018), 107, 156. Nutter's "clobber" was also worn by Lennon at his Gibraltar wedding to Yoko Ono, as well as by Mick Jagger, whose preference for Nutters took off in 1971.
[48] Richardson, *House of Nutter*, 104.

even earlier by the wire-framed glasses that would come to stand for John's imagined future without the Beatles.

The Beatles' fashion and style iconography were – and still are – invitations to listeners to join the Fab Four, to find and express their own identities through imitation. The band's fashion-metamorphoses signaled new beginnings, communicating the early Beatles' cohesion as a band, later reinvention, and finally their disbanding.

CHAPTER 24

The Rise of Celebrity Culture and Fanship with the Beatles in the 1960s

Jeffrey Roessner

As the jet engine whine fades in and begins to fall in pitch, mimicking the descent of a landing plane, the band starts chugging away on a classic Chuck Berry-inspired rock riff. In many ways, the opening of the Beatles' "Back in the USSR," from the 1968 *White Album*, uncannily parodies the band's arrival in the USA some four and a half years earlier. In February 1964, they were flush from the musical conquest of their British homeland, and stepped off the plane in New York to the roar of over 4,000 shrieking, sobbing, *excited* fans – nearly all of whom had skipped school to be there to greet the invaders from across the Atlantic.[1] By that point, the band had its first No. 1 single in the USA, "I Want to Hold Your Hand" (a song that, like "Back in the USSR," begins with a strong rush to the dominant V chord for four measures before settling into a similarly propulsive riff). In many ways, the sound of the jet engine and the sound of those screams merged, laid over the driving beat of rock 'n' roll, re-energized and delivered back to its American birthplace with a twist of Scouse: this was the soundtrack of fame in the 1960s, and the Beatles' arrival in America – and subsequent artistic flourishing – defined the spectacle of rock celebrity for every band that followed.

Chuck Berry famously sang about planes, of course, with his ironic declaration, as a black man in 1950s America, of how glad, oh glad he was to be jet-propelled back home to the USA. But no matter how exciting high-speed travel sounded then, we do not typically associate early rock with jet-set culture. That phrase conveyed money and class and a Martini-swilling sophistication far beyond the biggest dreams of early rock stars. Even the king himself, Elvis Presley, mainly traveled by car. The 1960s changed all that. The jet engine signals money, power, speed, sex, and most important, movement – and the Beatles rarely stood still. It is significant that the band

---

[1] Mikal Gilmore, "How the Beatles Took America", *Rolling Stone*, January 16, 2014, 40–69.

arrived in America by jet and that many of the earliest scenes of hysteria occurred at airports. By the 1960s, commercial air travel was becoming a more common mode of transportation, and the Beatles spearheaded the economy class assault on the privileged, just as they transgressed so many other social and cultural barriers. In this regard, the jet stands metonymically for a broad set of technological advances that made the Beatles phenomenon possible.

The Beatles did not do anything radically different from their rock 'n' roll forbearers to promote their music or image – the difference was in scale, aided by advances in post-World Ward II technology. Presley's career in the 1950s, for example, stands as a clear template for the fab four: Elvis appeared on national television programs such as *The Ed Sullivan Show*, made movies (which featured set-pieces that can be viewed as early rock videos), toured the USA extensively, played large outdoor sports arenas, and evoked mass hysteria, much as Frank Sinatra had before him.[2] Presley even had a curtailed national touring career of just a few short years before joining the army – much as the Beatles themselves spent a mere two years playing large shows before retiring from the road. But all the Beatles' marketing efforts were accelerated by a host of post-World War II advances in technology. Millard offers an extensive analysis of the range of developments that made Beatlemania possible: the expanding shift to Top 40 radio format in the USA, the birth of pirate stations in the UK, the growth and competition of television programming, particularly variety shows, the extension of tabloid newspaper power and the rise of music journalism, the advances in recording and reproducing sound, along with the growing ease and affordability of commercial air travel and the advent of the mega-stadium concert – all fanned the "media saturation" underpinning the Beatles' celebrity in the 1960s.[3]

The technology would not have meant much if it had not been directed toward an audience, however. And with the baby-boom generation, the Beatles found their fans. In 1956, Presley had a potential American teen audience (aged 12–17) of over 15 million; in 1966, a decade later, that number had grown by more than a third, to over 22 million.[4] And teens in general had an increasing amount of cash to spend. The economic

---

[2] Jeffrey Roessner, "From 'Mach Shau' to Mock Show: The Beatles, Shea Stadium, and Rock Spectacle", in *The Arena Concert*, ed. Robert Edgar et al. (New York: Bloomsbury, 2015), 18.

[3] André Millard, *Beatlemania: Technology, Business, and Teen Culture in Cold War America* (Baltimore: Johns Hopkins University Press, 2012), 137–69.

[4] "Pop1 Child Population," Forum on Child and Family Statistics, *childstats*, www.childstats.gov/a mericaschildren/tables/pop1.asp.

engine after World War II not only spurred the purchase of consumer goods, houses, and cars by adults, but also allowed for colonization of a new, eager youth market. In his famous study of British teen culture in the late 1950s, Mark Abrams estimated that teenage spending power since World War II had increased as much as 100 percent, to roughly 830 million pounds.[5] And one thing teens spent the money on was vinyl aimed directly at them: by 1963, 45 rpm singles represented fully 80 percent of British record sales.[6] With their leisure money, record players, fan clubs, steadfast loyalty and above all their conviction that the world changed in some important way when the Beatles arrived, the fans re-shaped their culture and propelled the Beatles to an unprecedented level of celebrity.

"In the beginning was the scream," Steven Stark claims, the biblical echo appropriate for the foundational element of the Beatles' mythology.[7] Indeed, early coverage of the Beatles focused not on music or personality, but on the overwrought reaction of female fans. Airing in late November 1963, the earliest American television reports on the band showcased the "compulsive scream-ing" of frenzied girls, the enormous queues for tickets to their shows, and the volume of fan mail they generated.[8] These reports, and the Beatles themselves in a CBS news profile, dismiss their originality, with both Harrison and McCartney claiming that their music did not really differ from early rock 'n' roll.[9] Dripping with condescension about the band's music, performances, and appearance (the haircuts get almost as much attention as the songs), the newscasters wryly present theories about the band's "sociological" signifi-cance.[10] More prescient than they realized, the reports emphasize the fault line about to rupture into a cultural chasm. For their devoted fans, the Beatles came to represent a revolt against such priggish adult scorn; their humble origins, unpretentiousness, and direct wit all helped break tired barriers of class and taste and, ultimately, gender. They seemed astonishingly free. And in promising such liberation to millions of others like themselves – their fans –

---

[5] Cited in Bill Osgerby, "Youth Culture," in *A Companion to Contemporary Britain 1939–2000*, ed. Paul Addison and Harriet Jones (Malden, MA: Blackwell, 2005), 129.

[6] Osgerby, "Youth Culture," 129.

[7] Steven Stark, *Meet the Beatles* (New York: HarperCollins, 2005), 9.

[8] See Bill Crandall, "CBS News Reports on the Beatles in 1963," *CBS News*, last modified January 21, 2014, www.cbsnews.com/news/cbs-news-reports-on-the-beatles-in-1963/; "The Beatles on CBS News, 21 November 1963," *YouTube*, www.youtube.com/watch?v=UeolhjIWPYs; and "The Beatles' First Appearance on American TV – NBC News," *YouTube*, www.youtube.com/watch?v=wVjuKaJjsNA.

[9] "The Beatles on CBS News, 21 November 1963."

[10] Over a live audio performance of "From Me to You" saturated with screams, NBC reporter Edwin Newman notes, "One reason for the Beatles' popularity may be that it's almost impossible to hear them."

the band signaled a newly emerging "authenticity of democratic celebrity," as
P. David Marshall has argued.[11]

The power of that celebrity, quickly dubbed Beatlemania, proved to be
much larger than the press, the fans, or even the Beatles themselves could
have imagined. Mobs greeted them at every airport and hotel, and the
unceasing wave of screams saturated the music. The band's first feature
film, *A Hard Day's Night*, perfectly captures the intense reactions they
provoked in 1964. In the opening sequence, the title song's famous guitar
chord shatters the silence, a startled moment of attention seized, before the
fans realize who they are seeing and the screaming and running commence.
Yes, the film showcases the band's personalities, their wit, and their music –
but we should remember that its original title was *Beatlemania*, an apt
description of the quasi-documentary content: the exhilarating crush of
fans, the sense of primordial energy tensely coiled and sprung loose, the
media-fueled meta-frenzy (a film about a band making a TV appearance),
and for the band, the not-yet-draining sense of being inside the bubble
("a train and a room, and car and a room, and room and a room," as Paul's
fictive grandfather says in the movie).[12]

The film underscores a central truth about the Beatles: their celebrity
arose from a series of symbolic, perfectly communicated liberatory gestures, particularly in the thrilling escape from adult conformity and repres-
sion. If we wanted one image to perfectly capture the iconic import of the
Beatles for the 1960s, it occurs during the first "Can't Buy Me Love"
sequence in *A Hard Day's Night*, when they are being shepherded down
a narrow stairway and they burst out a side door into the light of an open
field quite literally to play. No handlers, no managers, no producers, no
adult authority of any kind. At one moment in the sequence, the film
shows them in slow motion jumps: they float across the screen, arms
splayed, seemingly unencumbered even by gravity. It feels like flying –
and it remains one of the most thrilling moments in cinema history.

Although the Beatles are generally seen as emblematic of the 1960s, and
of rock counterculture in particular, their meaning cannot be separated
from the wider context of post-World War II consumer culture. The
emphasis on their artistic integrity and their role in defining key trends
(in the 1960s it was hard not to feel that everyone was following them) have
obscured their marketing genius. From the outset, their celebrity status

[11]   P. David Marshall, "The Celebrity Legacy of the Beatles," in *The Beatles, Popular Music and Society*,
       ed. Ian Inglis (New York: St. Martin's, 2000), 173.
[12]   *A Hard Day's Night*, dir. Richard Lester (London: United Artists, 1964).

accelerated as they defined themselves against previous trends. Elvis had his Hollywood good looks and his distinctive side-burns, pompadour, and lip-curl. In contrast to the largely solo rock idols of the 1950s, however, the Beatles consciously presented themselves as a group, and their look, with their shared haircuts and custom suits, cemented them together as what Mick Jagger called the "four-headed monster."[13] The compelling look resulted from a mixture of Brian Epstein's thoughtful management and their own striking intuition: the cleaned-up stage act and tailored suits came from Epstein, for example, while the haircuts and the artful, half-shadowed cover of their second LP, *With the Beatles*, were their ideas. Lennon later praised Epstein as "an intuitive, theatrical guy who presented us well," but the Beatles' popularity was grounded in their own almost unerring aesthetic sensibility; they projected an aura of authenticity that made them "real" and powerfully sutured them to their devoted fans.[14]

Celebrity demands iconography, of course, and the Beatles repeatedly engraved their images in the consciousness of Western culture. Remarkably for the sphere of popular music culture at that time, those images were never static. With his trademark brand, Elvis always looked like Elvis, even when he donned his leather outfit for his 1968 "Comeback Special." But each phase of Beatles' career brought innovation and another fresh set of iconic representations: a new look, a new sound, a new quest for freedom or transcendence or drug-enabled escape. They understood that the audience continually wanted the next *now* thing, and the band supplied it through their restless re-invention, both as artists and as people. Producing such consumable imagery, the Beatles staged themselves in successive tableaux vivants: from the half-revealed photo on *With the Beatles* to the silhouettes of their spread-eagled leaps in *A Hard Day's Night*, to the outline of their early stage set and their stride across the Abbey Road crosswalk – has a celebrity ever been so instantly identifiable by so many distinctive shadows? As Marshall notes, innovative pop musicians function like modern artists in this respect, continually signal their authenticity by "the breaking of codes and the creation of new or transformed codes of style."[15] In *A Hard Day's Night*, George Harrison mocks

---

[13] Annie Nightingale, "Interview: Annie Nightingale Talks to Sir Paul McCartney," *Radio Times*, www.radiotimes.com/news/2011–06–03/interview-annie-nightingale-talks-to-sir-paul-mccartney/.

[14] "John Lennon at *The Tomorrow Show* 1975 (Entire Interview)," *YouTube*, www.youtube.com/watch?v=boT-4wbUbAU.

[15] P. David Marshall, "The Meanings of the Popular Music Celebrity: The Construction of Distinctive Authenticity," in *The Celebrity Culture Reader*, ed. P. David Marshall (New York: Routledge, 2006), 204.

the company trying to manipulate rapidly shifting trends to sell ugly shirts ("They're dead grotty"), but the Beatles nonetheless took part in and reaped the fruits of the accelerating consumer culture.

Indeed, in its participation in Beatlemania, *A Hard Day's Night* both documents and propagates the modern popular music spectacle. Concerts, tours, personal appearances, and even random sightings evoked the ritual performances of fandom: for the fans, it was crucial to be at the event and participate. Even if they could not hear and only barely see the band, they were there, lending their voices with the rest of the faithful, signifying a communal force and testifying to their own commitment to liberation. Beatles concerts became youth rallies for the revolution. The apex of such fan culture – and, ironically, a clear emblem of the band's increasing entrapment – was their first Shea Stadium concert on August 15, 1965. Occurring at precisely the mid-point of their two-year international touring career, this concert marked the culmination of their early fame and signaled things to come. Four small figures on a stage at second base surrounded by 55,600 barely controlled fans. By this point, Beatles concerts had become spectacles, mediatized events that were newsworthy not for musical performance, but because they confirmed the band's celebrity status. Within this cultural logic, the concert spectacle functions primarily as "the carrier of celebrity content," as it trades on "allure, glamour and charisma constructed around myths of transformation, belonging and affect" – hence, the importance fans placed on being there for the collective experience, though often unable to hear a single note.[16] In these early stages, success at that level still brought its own kind of intoxication for the band. Reflecting on the event many years later, Lennon simply said, "at Shea Stadium, I saw the top of the mountain."[17]

While the excitement at first proved a contagious thrill, the intensity finally became wearying: the band's predictable set list dwindled to just twelve songs for their entire final tour in 1966, and their irritation at not being able to hear themselves spiked. In George Harrison's famous summary, "They used us an excuse to go mad, the world did."[18] With the music increasingly eclipsed by the mania, the suffocating atmosphere became the dominant theme in their lives as "performing fleas."[19] Resentful of being

---

[16] Finola Kerrigan et al., "'Spinning' Warhol: Celebrity Brand Theoretics and the Logic of the Celebrity Brand," *Journal of Marketing Management*, 27, 13–14 (December 2011), 1505–06.
[17] Quoted in Michael O'Keefe, "The Beatles Punch Ticket to Ride for Shea Stadium Rock," *The New York Daily News*, September 20, 2008.
[18] *The Beatles Anthology*, dir. Bob Smeaton et al. (1995; Los Angeles: Capitol, 2003), DVD.
[19] John Lennon, *Skywriting by Word of Mouth* (New York: Harper & Row, 1986), 18.

imposed upon and trundled between cages, they were constantly planning their escape routes and worried about safety.[20] Such fears were not without cause, as they endured protests and assassination threats. When someone set off firecrackers at a show in Memphis, they looked at each other to see if one of them had been shot.[21] While the band symbolized freedom and movement for their ecstatic fans, they themselves stood inside a shrinking circle. Not surprisingly, after performing on a stage surrounded by a wire fence at San Francisco's Candlestick Park on August 29, 1966, they abandoned the road for good. On the jet back to England, Harrison declared simply, "That's it, then, I'm not a Beatle anymore."[22]

But of course, as they would all discover, they could stop touring but they could never stop being Beatles, as the torrent they unleashed swept through the rest of their lives. The level of celebrity they achieved traps as much or more than it liberates. In keeping with their resolute status as a foursome, the celebrity of the band became bigger than any individual member, and not one of them could out-pace it. As he forcefully tried to free himself from every illusion and idol, Lennon vehemently declared, in his 1970 song "God," that he did not believe in Beatles. But his personal declaration hardly mattered. While the lyrics reveal his desperate assertion of an independent artistic identity, the level of fame he and his band had achieved by that point was not under his control. He might have ceased to believe in Beatles, but the rest of the world had not. Everywhere he went for the next decade, he was dogged with the recurring question: when are the Beatles getting back together?

As we move further from those originary, mythic events, the fans' spirit remains vital. The Beatles' celebrity in the 1960s has cascaded through succeeding generations, promoted by both devoted corporate and fan cultures. Apple Records has very ably husbanded the band's legacy, overseeing a measured stream of releases, re-releases, and re-re-releases. When it seems as though there is nothing else to buy, another re-mix with bonus tracks emerges to mark another anniversary. Scholars too feed the mythology with biographies, cultural histories, and multiple yearly conferences and festivals. But perhaps most significantly the fans themselves have increasingly taken ownership of the band's fortune – particularly in the digital age. Generation after generation, creative, insightful devotees continue to make new meaning out the Beatles' catalog of sounds and images:

[20] For consideration of the band's "sheer terror" induced by unhinged fans, see Millard, *Beatlemania*, 27.

[21] The Beatles, *The Beatles Anthology* (New York: Chronicle Books, 2000), 227.

[22] Mark Lewisohn, *The Complete Beatles Chronicle* (New York: Harmony, 1992), 214.

they mash-up and re-mix the music, create vivid and insightful data visualizations of the band's history, and design clever web resources to keep the band current in the twenty-first century.[23] These contemporary fans want a relationship with the band, for the same unmistakable reason their predecessors flocked to shows in the 1960s: to be *there*, close to that space of exaltation, with these men who evoked such riotous joy. As the decades roll by, the community born of Beatlemania still exists and, remarkably, still takes its relationship with the band personally.

But of course, fan obsession produces an uncanny double. It should give us pause to consider that we almost lost two Beatles to murder. The December 8, 1980, attempt on Lennon succeeded. But the assault on George Harrison at his estate on December 30, 1999 – in which he received a near-fatal knife wound to his chest – has been overshadowed by his death from cancer some two years later. After Lennon's murder, Harrison reported being "absolutely terrified," particularly as he had received numerous death threats over the years.[24] Harrison had always been wary of the adulation generated by the band, and seemed more publicly concerned by the threat it represented than the others. With the attempt on his life, he barely escaped the cruel fallout of his mythic cultural status.

Lennon, of course, was not so lucky. Ironically, his murder was stoked by his very attempt to retreat from celebrity culture. After trying to use his fame to promote a political agenda in the late 1960s and early 1970s – with bed-ins for peace and anti-war billboards and songs – he spent an unhinged "lost weekend" of eighteen months separated from Yoko, before settling into quiet domesticity. From 1975 on, he proudly lived the life of house-husband, doting on his son Sean, focusing on baking bread, and not paying much attention to the music culture around him. His return to mass media coverage with the release of new material for the *Double Fantasy* album in 1980 simultaneously removed the space of fantasy for his killer, who could no longer sustain the illusion that he was John Lennon, and highlighted the supposed decadence of Lennon's retreat: he had abandoned the liberatory countercultural dream for a lavish cocoon, holed up in New York City's Dakota building, insulated by investments in expensive livestock. Tragically, even after a period of deliberately defusing the mythology,

[23] See Jeffrey Roessner, "Revolution 2.0: Beatles Fan Scholarship in the Digital Age," in *New Critical Perspectives on the Beatles*, ed. Ken Womack and Katie Kapurch (London: Palgrave, 2016), 221–40.
[24] Sarah Lyall, "George Harrison Stabbed in Chest by Intruder," *New York Times*, www.nytimes.com/1999/12/31/world/george-harrison-stabbed-in-chest-by-an-intruder.html.

Lennon did not survive his attempt to return to public life simply as a musician and songwriter.

More than any of his bandmates, McCartney maintained the career of a relatively normal, though immensely wealthy, touring and recording musician. But he too remains acutely aware of the perils of his fame and the overwhelming shadow cast by his legacy. A 2007 *New Yorker* profile depicts McCartney on a casual walk through London, stopping to take photos in an alley as research for promoting his new record.[25] First one fan and then another recognizes him and starts to intrude on his space, rudely taking selfies and trying to engage in conversation. Sensing that he is being cornered, McCartney moves off down the street at a pace, only to be caught again by one of the fans asking for an autograph.[26] After determining that the man has nothing for him to sign, McCartney thanks him and walks away even more hurriedly. Apologizing to the interviewer, McCartney explains, simply, 'That was my fault ... I stopped moving.'[27]

---

[25] John Colapinto, "When I'm Sixty-Four," *New Yorker*, www.newyorker.com/magazine/2007/06/0 4/when-im-sixty-four-2.

[26] A similar though less aggressive dynamic can be seen on film, during McCartney's 2018 appearance on *Carpool Karaoke* with James Corden. After visiting his childhood home in Liverpool, McCartney steps outside and is greeted by a large group of fans; we see how easily the situation could become overwhelming: "All right, folks, we'll keep it moving," he says, as people push forward to shake hands and Paul keeps walking toward his vehicle. "Paul McCartney Carpool Karaoke," *YouTube*, www.youtube.com/watch?v=QjvzCTqkBDQ.

[27] Colapinto, "When I'm Sixty-Four."

CHAPTER 25

"Swinging London," Psychedelia, and the Summer of Love

Kathryn B. Cox

"It was right and inevitable that one of Them should have been there in those times": thus proclaimed Derek Taylor, press officer for the Beatles, in his recollection of George Harrison's trip to the Haight-Ashbury district of San Francisco, California during the summer of 1967.[1] It was the Summer of Love, and Haight-Ashbury served as its epicenter as thousands of countercultural youth gathered there, ostensibly to live out a communal fantasy fueled by flower power, free love, hallucinogenic drugs, and rock music, thereby creating an experimental living village of a lifestyle alternative to the established post-war Western culture. These ideas resonated with the members of the Beatles, and Harrison was curious to experience the scene for himself. He flew in a Lear jet to San Francisco and soon found himself walking its streets at the height of the Summer of Love with his wife Pattie Boyd, her sister Jenny Boyd, Derek Taylor, the Beatles' friend and assistant Neil Aspinall, and Alexis Madras ("Magic Alex"), the electrical engineer with grand schemes for the Beatles that never quite came to fruition. In true countercultural fashion, this merry company consumed the hallucinogenic drug lysergic acid diethylamide (LSD) shortly before their outing.[2] The trip took a bad turn, however, as what seemed idyllic to Harrison in theory was a nightmare in reality: upon his arrival, the love-filled hippie paradise he had envisioned turned out to be a frightening mob of drug-addled youth that overwhelmed him.[3] After shaking some hands and demonstrating some chords on a guitar that materialized from the adoring crowd, Harrison left Haight-Ashbury to return to London. Yet he had been there in those times. Harrison's presence in San Francisco, and Taylor's retrospective assurance at the inevitability of at least one of the

---

[1] The Beatles, *The Beatles Anthology* (San Francisco: Chronicle Books, 2000), 259.
[2] Pattie Boyd, *Wonderful Tonight: George Harrison, Eric Clapton, and Me* (New York: Three Rivers Press, 2007), 104.
[3] George Harrison, *I Me Mine: The Extended Edition* (Guildford: Genesis Publications, 2017), 512.

Beatles – "one of Them" – being there at the time, speaks to the influential role of the Beatles during the Summer of Love. Indeed, one can hardly imagine that summer without the presence of the Beatles, whose 1967 album *Sgt. Pepper's Lonely Hearts Club Band* is now hailed as the sound-track to the Summer of Love. Through their music, their artistic collabora-tions, and their lifestyle choices, the Beatles were crucial to the development of psychedelic culture and to helping launch the Summer of Love.

The Beatles dominated the summer of 1967. Released May 27 in the UK and June 1 in the USA, *Sgt. Pepper's Lonely Hearts Club Band* held the top spot on the *Billboard* Top LPs chart for fifteen weeks, and sales of the record were over 2.5 million by August 1967.[4] The Beatles had seized the popular imagination once again, this time with a bold assertion that popular music could be consumed as high art. Their prevalence on the airwaves placed them in a leading role for countercultural trends, for music was a key component in constructing and cohering the Summer of Love. Musicologist Nadya Zimmerman argues in her study on the history of San Francisco in the late 1960s that while the counterculture in 1967 was "far from being an organized sociopolitical community," its cultural output, including the music and lifestyle tenets, were what came to define the era in collective memory.[5] For example, American singer Scott McKenzie's "San Francisco (Be Sure to Wear Flowers in Your Hair)" – and to a lesser extent its British counterpart "Let's Go to San Francisco" from a recording studio quartet called the Flower Pot Men – galvanized youth on both sides of the Atlantic during 1967 to join together in the Summer of Love's head-quarters, sonically cementing San Francisco's place in the cultural memory of the era. Psychedelic music from the Grateful Dead, Jefferson Airplane, Jimi Hendrix, the Doors, Pink Floyd, the Beach Boys, and many other artists shaped a collective – albeit somewhat nebulous – vision of the counterculture in 1967 that revolved around peace and love. The Beatles were part of this vision, holding their court during the Summer of Love in London rather than San Francisco.

The idealism of the Summer of Love was not solely relegated to Haight-Ashbury, and pockets of countercultural youth gathered elsewhere in the USA, Canada, Holland, France, India, and the UK. An ancillary geo-graphic locus for the Summer of Love was London, as the energy of

---

[4] Walter Everett, *The Beatles As Musicians: Revolver through the Anthology* (New York: Oxford University Press, 2001), 123.
[5] Nadya Zimmerman, *Counterculture Kaleidoscope: Musical and Cultural Perspectives on Late Sixties San Francisco* (Ann Arbor, MI: University of Michigan Press, 2008), 3.

Swinging London that started a few years prior transferred to the psychedelic London underground counterculture scene. The cosmopolitan capital became "Swinging London" during the mid-1960s as the UK finally experienced a brief economic upturn after a long post-war struggle to rebuild from the devastation of the Blitz and the collapse of the British Empire.[6] A new sense of pop optimism and modernization infiltrated the city, manifesting on the cultural front in fashion (led by model Twiggy's androgynous look and Mary Quant's mini skirt design), music (driven by British mod and rock bands, including the Beatles, who were attaining global popularity), and television (conveyed by the entertainment program *Ready Steady Go!*). It also permeated national politics. In 1963, Harold Wilson, then the leader of the Labour Party in the UK and who would later become prime minister, gave a rousing speech about a new Britain that would be forged in the "white heat" of a scientific and technological revolution.[7] As the decade progressed, these optimistic visions of a modern Britain found a degree of resonance with the utopic visions of the Summer of Love.

The American fascination with the Beatles, Beatlemania, and the ensuing British Invasion played no small role in bringing London onto the global fashion scene and amplifying the concept of London as Swinging.[8] The Beatles had already acted as trendsetters across Europe and North America since the early 1960s. In a 1966 *Time* article that took a quasi-anthropological approach to describing contemporary London, the Beatles were at the forefront of the Swinging London scene, so much so that the traditional symbols of the British monarchy were infiltrated by Beatles music and haircuts, and the word "beatle" itself pops up throughout the article as a common noun referring to any young man in London: "The city is alive with birds [girls] and beatles, buzzing with minicars are telly stars, pulsing with half a dozen separate veins of excitement. The guards now change at Buckingham Palace to a Lennon and McCartney tune, and Prince Charles is firmly in the longhair set."[9] The following year, *Time* ran

---

[6] See Simon Rycroft, *Swinging City: A Cultural Geography of London, 1950–1974* (Surrey: Ashgate, 2011).

[7] Harold Wilson, "Labour's Plan for Science: Reprint of Speech by the Rt. Hon. Harold Wilson, MP, Leader of the Labour Party, at the Annual Conference, Scarborough, Tuesday, October 1, 1963" (London: Victoria House Printing Company, 1963).

[8] One of the Beatles' many contributions to the culture of the Swinging City was to demonstrate that working- and middle-class citizens could bring Britain to the global stage. Historian Peter Clarke points to the power of British popular culture at the time as being of particular importance for its ability "to override, or at least mask, long-standing social distinctions . . . setting styles which marked off generations rather than classes." Peter Clarke, *Hope and Glory: Britain 1900–1990* (London: Penguin Books, 1996), 292.

[9] "Great Britain: You Can Walk Across It On the Grass," *Time*, April 15, 1966.

an article on the gathering of hippies in San Francisco, and while the youth movement was described as "leaderless and loose," the authors pointed to the Beatles as "the major tastemakers in hippiedom" due in large part to their being the "forerunners of psychedelic sound and once again at the forefront with their latest album, *Sgt. Pepper's Lonely Hearts Club Band.*"[10]

Just as the album cover of *Sgt. Pepper's* visually showcases the Beatles as part of a larger group of celebrity figures, by 1967 the Beatles were part of a larger network of boundary-pushing artists who constituted the "taste-makers in hippiedom." Paul McCartney likened his London apartment during 1967 to eighteenth-century European salon culture, where artists, musicians, and gallery owners gathered to share ideas: "My place was almost the centre of the social scene at one point, because I was on my own ... It was like a salon, almost."[11] These figures included artist Andy Warhol, gallery owner Robert Fraser (who aided McCartney in building his collection of works by surrealist painter René Magritte), musicians Marianne Faithfull, Mick Jagger, and Brian Jones, among others. The Beatles also began collaborating with the Dutch band and collective of designers called The Fool, famous for their psychedelic paintings and costume designs. Collaborations such as these opened the doors to new musical influences – McCartney was taking an interest in avant-garde composers Karlheinz Stockhausen, Luciano Berio, and John Cage – and the Beatles directed these artistic inspirations into the work of their psychedelic period, which began in late 1965 as they finished *Rubber Soul*, apexed in 1967 with *Sgt. Pepper's* and *Magical Mystery Tour*, and waned by the beginning of 1968 as they began work on *The Beatles (The White Album)*.

"Psychedelia" is a neologism from 1957 that combines the Greek words for "spirit" (*psyche*) and "reveal" (*delos*).[12] Proponents of psychedelia advocate expanding one's consciousness; in other words, to "turn on, tune in, and drop out," as expressed in the slogan popularized by leading counter-cultural figure, psychologist Timothy Leary. While music scholar William Echard notes that "psychedelia is not inherently about drug use" but rather mostly concerned with "the expansion and exploration of consciousness," he also recognizes that drug use can be an integral part of psychedelic

---

[10] "Youth: The Hippies," *Time*, July 7, 1967.
[11] Paul Du Noyer, *Conversations With McCartney* (New York: Overlook Press, 2015), 65.
[12] Russell Reising and Jim LeBlanc, "Magical Mystery Tours, and Other Trips: Yellow Submarines, Newspaper Taxis, and the Beatles' Psychedelic Years," in *The Cambridge Companion to the Beatles*, ed. Kenneth Womack (Cambridge: Cambridge University Press, 2009), 91.

culture as a means of expanding one's consciousness.[13] This was certainly true of the Beatles in the mid-1960s. By the time the Summer of Love commenced in 1967, the Beatles had already established a long history of drug use. Their early days of energetically performing in Hamburg (1960–62) were driven by the stimulant Preludin (phenmetrazine), which they referred to in their Liverpudlian slang as "prellies." The Beatles were familiar with marijuana from their Hamburg days, but after a meeting with Bob Dylan in August 1964 where the musicians smoked pot together, the Beatles heartily embraced the drug during the following years, which influenced their songwriting, as well as impacted the filming of *Help!*[14] LSD, first synthesized by Swiss chemist Albert Hofmann in 1938, gained popularity in the 1960s as the psychedelic drug of choice, and Leary championed the hallucinogen for its potential to facilitate altered modes of mental perception. Lennon and Harrison first experienced LSD unwittingly during a dinner with dentist John Riley in April 1965. The two Beatles and their wives at the time, Cynthia Lennon and Pattie Boyd, joined the dentist and his girlfriend for dinner before a planned outing to the Pickwick Club in London. Riley slipped the drug into their coffees after dinner, and the ensuing psychedelic journey went down in Beatles history as "The Dental Experience," becoming the inspiration for the *Revolver* track "Doctor Robert."[15] Lennon and Harrison began consuming LSD recreationally, and by the end of 1965, Starr and McCartney were also partaking of the hallucinogen. McCartney infamously and very publicly admitted to having taken LSD in an interview with *Life* magazine published June 17, 1967 and then again in a televised statement to Independent Television News (ITN) on June 19, 1967. By that point, the Beatles had been taking LSD for a couple of years, and were soon to abandon it in favor of practicing Transcendental Meditation. For those early months of the summer of 1967, however, the public attention to the Beatles' LSD consumption ballooned amidst a larger dialogue surrounding hippies and drug use.[16]

The Beatles' experiences with LSD informed their songwriting. In his autobiography, Harrison claimed, "That was also the result of the LSD really, writing songs to try and find out, to see who you are."[17] This

[13] William Echard, *Psychedelic Popular Music: A History Through Topic Theory* (Bloomington, IN: Indiana University Press, 2017), 11.
[14] As Starr remarks in the *Anthology*, "A hell of a lot of pot was being smoked while we were making the film." Beatles, *Anthology*, 167.
[15] Beatles, *Anthology*, 177.
[16] The *Time* feature on the counterculture stated: "If grass is the staple of hippiedom, then lysergic acid diethylamide (LSD) is its caviar." "Youth: The Hippies," *Time*, July 7, 1967.
[17] Harrison, *I Me Mine*, 36.

introspective turn is apparent in several Beatles tracks from this psychedelic period, including "Tomorrow Never Knows" ("You may see the meaning of within"), "Strawberry Fields Forever" ("Always, no, sometimes think it's me / but you know I know when it's a dream"), and "Within You Without You" ("Try to realize it's all within yourself"). While a psychedelic encounter can entail aspects of self-realization, it also encompasses other aspects of altered mental perceptions. Musicologist Sheila Whiteley's seminal work on psychedelic coding in rock music theorizes some of the ways in which artists translated the psychedelic experience into music.[18] Some of the sonic characteristics of psychedelic music include changing tempi to mirror the distortion of time that one might perceive during a psychedelic experience, lyrics that are often inscrutable and filled with sensory imagery to reflect heightened perceptions, and alterations of vocal and instrumental timbres, as well as performance and recording techniques such as echo effect, reverb, distortion, and tape delays to mimic altered states of mind.[19] Examples of each of these musical techniques are found throughout the Beatles' discography during their psychedelic years. The shifting tempi of "Magical Mystery Tour" make the listener question exactly what kind of trip the Beatles are singing about. Lennon professed to intentionally writing incomprehensible lyrics for "I Am the Walrus," and the confounding imagery of "Lucy in the Sky With Diamonds" provided a thrill for countercultural conspiracy theorists who saw the hidden initials of LSD within the song's title. The Beatles highlight and explore the sense of sight in the color-laden "Yellow Submarine" with its "sky of blue" and "sea of green" to the more cerebral sensory images in "Lucy in the Sky With Diamonds" with its "tangerine trees and marmalade skies." The recording process behind *Sgt. Pepper's* "Being for the Benefit of Mr. Kite!" is a sonic exercise in synesthesia, as Lennon asked producer George Martin to make the track sound like the "smell of the sawdust" and "wanted the music to 'swirl'."[20] Music theorist Walter Everett identifies "Tomorrow Never Knows" as the Beatles' first recording to "reflect the LSD experience," and it is the preeminent example of the Beatles using distorted sounds through the manipulation of tape loops to psychedelic effect.[21] Some of the

---

[18] See Sheila Whiteley, *The Space Between the Notes: Rock and the Counter-Culture* (London: Routledge, 1992).

[19] Reising and LeBlanc, "Magical Mystery Tours," 92.

[20] Reising and LeBlanc, "Magical Mystery Tours," 94.

[21] To create Lennon's desired sound of "thousands of monks chanting," Martin "put [Lennon's] voice through a loudspeaker and rotated it." Also among the many innovations on this song was Harrison's guitar solo, which was recorded backward, "treated with a Leslie speaker and run through a Leslie cabinet." Everett, *The Beatles As Musicians*, 34.

Beatles' most innovative studio work arose out of experimenting with producing psychedelic sounds.

For many British artists – including the Beatles, the Kinks, and Pink Floyd, among others – the psychedelic journey into the psychological landscape was also deeply connected to memory. Although the Summer of Love did not manifest in as obvious a way in the Beatles' hometown as it did in London, the Liverpool of the Beatles' imagination was integral to the development of psychedelic music, specifically in terms of distinguishing British psychedelia from American psychedelia.[22] British music critic Ian MacDonald wrote that the true subject of psychedelia in Britain was "neither love nor drugs, but nostalgia for the innocent vision of the child."[23] The Beatles began 1967 with an homage to their hometown through their February release of the double-A-sided single "Strawberry Fields Forever"/"Penny Lane." The Lennon-penned "Strawberry Fields Forever" draws listeners into a dreamlike reverie on a childhood haunt of his, while the McCartney-penned "Penny Lane" takes listeners on a delightful, but no less surreal, romp through the pedestrian scenes of Liverpool. This was the start of a nostalgic thread that wove throughout the year in the Beatles' music, as the brass bands and Victorian circuses of *Sgt. Pepper's Lonely Hearts Club Band* and the charabanc holiday tours of *Magical Mystery Tour* revealed a longing for the imagined innocence of the past. As the site for childhood memories, at least in the music of the Beatles, Liverpool came to represent an idyllic mental escape through time, and their musical explorations of their hometown emphasized the temporal facets of the psychedelic experience.

Another one of the sonic markers of psychedelic rock that the Beatles, especially Harrison, gave particular attention to is that of references to Indian classical music, most often through the use of a harmonic drone,

[22] London was a site for the Summer of Love, while Liverpool was decidedly not. Ringo Starr asserted, "A lot of Flower Power didn't translate in say, Oldham or Bradford, and not really in Liverpool." While in London flower power flourished, Liverpool continued to trudge along in its industrial Northernness relatively untouched by the Summer of Love. Stephen Daniels, "Suburban Pastoral: 'Strawberry Fields Forever' and Sixties Memory," *Cultural Geographies*, 13, 1 (January 2006): 36. Starr quoted in Paul Du Noyer, *Conversations With McCartney* (New York: Overlook Press, 2015), 90.
[23] Ian MacDonald, *Revolution in the Head: The Beatles' Records and the Sixties* (Chicago: Chicago Review Press, 2007), 216. British historian Dominic Sandbrook further explains: "This emphasis on nostalgia helped to distinguish the Beatles and the Kinks from their American counterparts while linking them with British creative artists in other genres, from fiction and poetry to the theatre and television, whose gaze was similarly fixed on the past. Nostalgia was one of the most powerful forces in post-war British culture, which was hardly surprising, given the collapse of the empire and all the talk about national political and economic decline." Dominic Sandbrook, *White Heat: A History of Britain in the Swinging Sixties 1964–1970* (London: Little, Brown, 2006), 420.

through the incorporation of Indian musical instruments such as the tabla and the sitar, or through formal construction.[24] This countercultural interest in Indian classical music stemmed from a desire to seek out alternatives to Western culture.[25] As the post-war, post-Independence Indian diaspora spread globally and grew in the UK and the USA, so too did Indian cultural products, including classical music, which British and American rock musicians then encountered and incorporated into their own compositions.[26] There is some contention as to which rock band in the mid-1960s was the first to be influenced by Indian classical music.[27] Ray Davies of the Kinks expressed his interest in Indian classical music as early as 1964 in an interview for *Melody Maker*, and the subsequent July 1965 single "See My Friends" features a drone-like guitar motive throughout most of the track.[28] The Beatles, however, were the first to prominently include an Indian classical instrument in one of their songs. "Norwegian Wood (This Bird Has Flown)" from *Rubber Soul* (1965) features Harrison on the sitar, repeating melodic material from the guitar lines. This timbral evocation would have been novel to the ears of most European and American pop listeners at the time, and in combination with ambiguous lyrics, the track exuded a mysteriousness that appealed to countercultural listeners. The Beatles continued to demonstrate their interest in Indian classical music on the following album *Revolver* (1966) through the use of Indian instruments and the Indian-inspired formal structure of "Love You To," through the tambura drone in "Tomorrow Never Knows," and through the ornamental figures in McCartney's modal guitar solo in "Taxman."[29] Between the

---

[24] See Echard, *Psychedelic*, 53–64.

[25] "Orientalist representations have always been, among other things, a matter of European Americans appropriating signs of the Asian other as a way to explore and expand their own self images." Echard, *Psychedelic*, 58.

[26] For example, the Yardbirds ("A Heart Full of Soul"), the Byrds ("Eight Miles High"), the Rolling Stones ("Paint It Black"), the Hollies ("Bus Stop"), the Doors ("The End"), and the Moody Blues ("Om"), among many others, incorporated elements of Indian classical music into their psychedelic songs.

[27] Jonathan Bellman, "Indian Resonances in the British Invasion, 1965–1968," *The Journal of Musicology*, 15, 1 (Winter 1997), 116–36.

[28] The Davies brothers revealed their fascination with Indian classical music in a *Melody Maker* interview: "'We're always looking, searching for new sounds,' said Dave. 'Ray likes Indian music for instance.' 'Yeah, I like going to Indian restaurants and listening to the records there. I like that drone they got on them,' Ray broke in. 'I liked that Rolf Harris record, "Sun arise" was it? We've got a bit of a drone on our record, about halfway through.'" Chris Roberts, "Kinks Ready for the New Wave," *Melody Maker*, August 22, 1964.

[29] Everett, *The Beatles As Musicians*, 34–49. See also Bellman, "Indian Resonances," and David Reck, "Beatles Orientalis: Influences From Asia in a Popular Song Tradition," *Asian Music*, 16, 2 (1985), 83–149.

releases of *Rubber Soul* and *Revolver*, Harrison began studying sitar with
the world-renowned sitarist Pandit Ravi Shankar, and this collaboration
grew into a lifelong friendship.[30] The influence of Indian music in the
Beatles' oeuvre reached its peak in "Within You Without You" on *Sgt.
Pepper's Lonely Hearts Club Band*.[31] Composer and sole Beatle on the
track, Harrison was joined by musicians from the Asian Music Circle –
an organization in London that promoted Indian classical music –
including Anna Joshi and Amrit Gajjar on dilruba, Buddhadev
Kansara on tambura, and Natwar Soni on tabla.[32] The lush Indian
orchestration accompanies lyrics that draw from Vedic philosophies
Harrison studied under the guidance of Shankar. These lyrics also
aligned with countercultural ideals, specifically the line, "With our
love we could save the world," which encapsulated what came to be a
driving concept behind the Summer of Love.

While *Sgt. Pepper's Lonely Hearts Club Band* was the representative LP
of the summer of 1967, the Beatles track that best embodied the ethos of
the Summer of Love was a single that they rush-released a few weeks later:
"All You Need is Love." The band performed the song during the first
international live satellite broadcast, *Our World*, on June 25, 1967.[33]
Somewhere between 400,000 and 700,000 viewers worldwide tuned in
to see performances from artists from different nations, and the highlight
of the England segment was the debut of the Beatles' "All You Need Is
Love." The Beatles had certainly sung about love before, but this track
presented listeners with an affectual transformation on the subject of
love. Where earlier Beatles lyrics emphasized personal romantic relationships, in "All You Need Is Love," the lyrical focus shifted to a love that
was an overarching, spiritually aimed concept. As Zimmerman explains
in her discussion of the counterculture, "the countercultural sensibility
was pluralistic, not oppositional; it embodied an anything-goes mind-set,
not an antiestablishment stance."[34] At the end of the day, the main

---

[30] See Ravi Shankar, *Raga Mala: The Autobiography of Ravi Shankar* (New York: Welcome Rain Publishers, 1999).
[31] Harrison would continue his exploration of Indian classical music throughout his solo career, but as the Beatles moved away from their psychedelic period, they also left behind overt references to Indian classical music.
[32] "Unrecognized Sgt. Pepper Indian Musicians to Perform After Being Tracked Down by Liverpool Academic," *University of Liverpool News*, June 6, 2017, https://news.liverpool.ac.uk/2017/06/06/u nrecognised-sgt-peppers-indian-musicians-perform-tracked-liverpool-academic/.
[33] Kit O'Toole, "'All You Need Is Love': The Beatles in the Global Village," in *The Beatles, Sgt. Pepper, and the Summer of Love*, ed. Kenneth Womack and Kathryn B. Cox (Lanham, MD: Lexington Books, 2017), 101.
[34] Zimmerman, *Countercultural Kaleidoscope*, 5.

requirement to be a part of the Summer of Love was to promote love, and the Beatles achieved that through singing their simple, repeated message, "All you need is love / love is all you need." The song fittingly closes with a psychedelic musical collage that performs the symbolic work of joining disparate musical ideas into one, reflecting the optimistic belief of the Summer of Love that disparate people could peacefully join together: all they needed was love. With this song, the Beatles decisively bound themselves with the Summer of Love and affirmed their roles on the forefront of psychedelic culture.

CHAPTER 26

Leaving the West Behind: The Beatles and India

Steve Hamelman

To address the question of the Beatles' relationship to India is to begin by
trying to understand what it was like for Western listeners to hear the
sound of India in the band's music for the first time. While it is easy to
verify items on the long list of their breakthroughs – for example, Artificial
Double Tracking or the double fade-out ending – open to debate is
whether or not George Harrison's sitar part on "Norwegian Wood (This
Bird Has Flown)" was the first appearance of an Indian sound in a rock
song. Not as debatable is that those sitar notes, strange as they may have
seemed to many English and American fans, were not the first aural sign of
Indian music in the Beatles canon. The Capitol Records soundtrack of
Help! (August 1965), which preceded "Norwegian Wood," the second track
on *Rubber Soul*, by four months, contained incidental music with Indian
instrumentation. But overarching this discographical detail is the fact that
the Indian influence, though not consciously explored by the band before
1965, had been with the four Beatles, coming of age as post-war subjects of
the British Empire, all along.[1]

How could it not? The historians S. M. Burke and Salim Al-Din
Quraishi write that in the year 1600, Queen Elizabeth I granted the
British East India Company permission "to trade everywhere to the east
of the Cape of Good Hope." The third voyage, in 1608, "brought a British
ship to the shores of India for the first time," thus launching an imperial
enterprise that led in 1833 to the Government of India Bill, which "asserted
the sovereignty of the Crown in India and declared that the territory was
held by the [East India] Company in trust for Her Majesty."[2] The British
would not leave their prize colony until 1947, when the Liverpudlian lads
John Lennon and Richard Starkey were seven years old, Paul McCartney

---

[1] All references to Beatles music are to *The Beatles Collection* vinyl box set (1978).
[2] S. M. Burke and Salim Al-Din Quraishi, *The British Raj in India: An Historical Review* (New York:
Oxford, 1995), 5, 44.

Figure 26.1 The Beatles and their wives and girlfriends at Rishikesh in India with the Maharishi Mahesh Yogi, March 1968. The group includes Maureen Starkey, Jane Asher, Patti Boyd, Cynthia Lennon, Beatles roadie Mal Evans, Prudence Farrow, Jenny Boyd, and Beach Boy Mike Love. Photo by Hulton Archive/Getty Images

five, and George Harrison four. In other words, by the time the individual Beatles were born, there had been dynamic political, social, and economic interaction between the two nations for centuries.

Though not a significant percentage of the population of Liverpool – or, for that matter, of Great Britain as a whole – in 1940, Indian immigrants were far from unknown. The population of Great Britain that year was an estimated 48 million; among these lived upwards of eight thousand Indians.[3] In his 2014 history of Liverpool, Ken Pye notes that "Indian sailors had first settled in the town in the 1860s," where they found work on the docks or as street pedlars. With the Partition of 1947, the influx accelerated, which allowed the four young Beatles to see, along with the rest of England, "the greatest numbers of people from the Indian subcontinent into Liverpool."[4]

[3] Rozina Visram, *Asians in Britain: 400 Years of History* (London: Pluto, 2002), 254.
[4] Ken Pye, *Liverpool: The Rise, Fall and Renaissance of a World-Class City* (The Hill, Stroud: Amberley, 2014), 121.

In London, meanwhile, notices of Indian music on radio and television[5] appeared in the *Daily Mail* as early as the mid-1940s, about the same time the toddler George Harrison heard, in his words, "comparable music ... from Algeria or elsewhere" on the family's shortwave radio.[6] Although far from mainstream – music historian Peggy Holroyde observes that "the sound [of raga] irritated [the English concert-goer], and the only people during the years of British rule who took a sympathetic view were a very few music scholars" – the renowned sitarist Ravi Shankar had been performing in Europe since the 1930s.[7] By the early 1960s, *The Times* was regularly reporting on recitals by Shankar and other masters, lavishing praise on their brilliant improvisations, as in this ecstatic review from 1963: "[Shankar] drew from his instrument a fantastically evocative range of tone and spun a melodic line of an intensely subtle complexity, making us rather uncomfortably aware of the power music can possess even when shorn of such western essentials as harmony and rhythm."[8]

In tune with the increasing English delight in Indian raga and drone were several English rock bands, the Beatles among them. In his study of what became known as "raga rock," Jonathan Bellman explains that with "See My Friends" (July 1965), the Kinks achieved a "jangling, drone-based, and unquestionably quasi-Indian" sound, and that in June 1965 the Yardbirds attempted a sitar part on "Heart Full of Soul," failing only because "the engineer was unable to satisfactorily record the sitar."[9] This left the Beatles first to record the sitar itself, in October 1965, on "Norwegian Wood."

As they revealed from first album to last, the Beatles absorbed and then re-constituted everything they heard in their inimitable way: American rockabilly, country and western, girl group, British music hall and comedy, skiffle, and so on. As such, it was only a matter of time before Indian classical music would leave its mark. The tipping-point was *Help!*, whose opening notes of a gong and sitar set the tone for its "Orientalist" plot: attempts by bumbling members of an Indian religious cult pursuing a sacrificial ring worn by Ringo Starr are stymied repeatedly by English pluck

[5] "Indian Music at 6 on the Third Program," (radio listing) *Daily Mail* (London, UK), August 12, 1947, 2, *Daily Mail Historical Archive*, May 15, 2018; "Indian Music on Television, Surya Sena and Nelun Devi 9.45–10.00," (television listing) *Daily Mail* (London, UK), January 25, 1947, 2, *Daily Mail Historical Archive*, May 15, 2018.
[6] Timothy White, "A Portrait of the Artist," *Billboard* (December 5, 1992), 23.
[7] Peggy Holroyde, *The Music of India* (New York: Praeger, 1972), 9.
[8] "Indian Music of Subtlety and Wit," *The Times*, October 14, 1963, 14. Web, June 30, 2018.
[9] Jonathan Bellman, "Indian Resonances in the British Invasion, 1965–1968," *The Journal of Musicology*, 15, 1 (1997), 122–24.

and luck. In London, the cultists prove their incompetence in an Indian restaurant where Bengali musicians provide entertainment.[10] As the musicians played, "George was looking at them," recalls Lennon in *Anthology*, confirming that the guitarist's transformation had begun.[11] Another key moment occurred while on location in the Bahamas, where the author Swami Vishnu Devananda, bearing four gift copies of his *The Illustrated Book of Yoga*, approached the boys between takes. Intrigued by these incidents, Harrison promptly acquired his first sitar.[12] In the ensuing months came two more major enticements for Harrison to explore this music further: first, hearing a recording by Ravi Shankar at a party in Los Angeles (August 1965); and second, meeting Shankar in London (June 1966), upon which he gave the curious Beatle his first sitar lesson. Intense instruction with Harrison's new mentor and friend took place during Harrison's six-week stay in Mumbai (September to October).

From its seeds in Orientalist slapstick, Harrison's initial interest in the "funny sound" of a sitar on a movie set evolved quickly into a lifetime immersion in Indian music, religion, and culture.[13] But until releasing, in late 1968, his pioneering solo album *Wonderwall Music* – a half-experimental, half-traditional soundtrack fusing Indian and Western styles – Harrison used the Beatles as his outlet for songs that incorporated sitar, tabla, sarod, and other instruments, as well as Vedic lyrics inspired by the mystical texts and Hindu scripture he began devouring in 1966: Paramahansa Yogananda's *Autobiography of a Yogi*, Swami Vivekananda's *Raja Yoga*, the *Yoga Sutras*, and the *Bhagavad-Gita*.

"Love You To," from *Revolver* (August 1966), reflects this sea change in Harrison's life, showing too the extraordinary speed at which the Beatles synthesized their influences. The group's acrimonious break-up in 1970, brought on partly by each member's different artistic temperament, came

---

[10] In the Beatles, writes David Reck, the "orientalist Indian influences were to peak and to reverberate through the pop music world" (95), the group's Orientalism ranging from the "campish" (99) features of *Help!* to authentic explorations of raga and Hindu philosophy. Regarding *Help!*, Peter Lavezzoli is blunt: "the film smacks of shameless Orientalism" (173). See Reck's "Beatles Orientalis: Influences from Asia in a Popular Song Tradition," *Asian Music*, 16, 1 (1985), 83–149 and Lavezzoli's *The Dawn of Indian Music in the West* (New York: Continuum, 2007).

[11] The Beatles, *The Beatles Anthology* (San Francisco: Chronicle, 2000), 171.

[12] Marc Shapiro, *Behind Sad Eyes: The Life of George Harrison* (New York: St. Martin's, 2002); White, "A Portrait of the Artist," 23.

[13] White, "A Portrait of the Artist," 23. In *Orientalism,* Edward Said defines the titular term "as a kind of Western projection onto and will to govern over the Orient" (95). The West constructs the Orient through a set of "timeless eternal" tropes that "are always symmetrical to, yet diametrically inferior to, a European equivalent" (72) resulting in an attitude that "vacillates between the West's contempt for what is familiar and its shivers of delight in – or fear of – novelty" (59). Edward Said, *Orientalism* (London: Penguin, 2003).

so suddenly that new or uninformed listeners may fail to appreciate Lennon's, McCartney's, and Starr's support of Harrison (Starr even guested on *Wonderwall*), even though they, lacking competence on Hindustani instruments, could not contribute much, if anything, to several of his tracks. For example, McCartney provides vocal backing, Starr tambourine, and Lennon nothing on "Love You To,"[14] a song about which David Reck, in a definitive study of Indian music's imprint on Western pop, enthuses, "One cannot emphasize enough how absolutely unprecedented this piece is in the history both of popular music and of European orientalism," praising the band's "sympathy and rare understanding"[15] of their Eastern source. By offering a somewhat glum view of humanity ("There's people standing 'round / Who'll screw you in the ground"), the tune's lyrics fall far short of the philosophical or mystical sentiments of Hinduism. Still, the breakthrough in form and instrumentation cannot be gainsaid, and credit is due to the Fabs for forgoing their guitars and drums in favor of guests playing sitar, tamboura, and tabla even though a 1960s rock treatment, played by themselves, with a "Satisfaction"-type four-beat groove driving the proceedings, can easily be imagined. (Despite his artistic explorations of India, Harrison had not renounced his rock bona fides: his Epiphone sears and jabs on the two crushing rockers he brought to *Revolver*, "Taxman" and "I Want to Tell You.")

No matter how unprecedented "Love You To" was in the annals of rock, *Revolver*'s tour de force is the Lennon composition "Tomorrow Never Knows," an electronic plunge into Buddhism in which Lennon's lines on the false binaries of Maya (the material world of illusion) are taken directly from *The Tibetan Book of the Dead*. This full-band effort brings *Revolver* to a staggering close in an amalgam of hypnotic raga drone, mystical text, lysergic vocals, backward tape effects, and hard rock (Ringo's gigantic, decidedly Western snare/tom/bass pattern).[16] Producer George Martin and the Abbey Road engineers also pitched in to fashion "a production which, in terms of textural innovation, is to pop what Berlioz's *Symphonie fantastique* was to nineteenth-century orchestral music."[17]

[14] Kenneth Womack, *The Beatles Encyclopedia: Everything Fab Four* (Santa Barbara: Greenwood, 2016), 583.
[15] Reck, "Beatles Orientalis," 102.
[16] Rob Sheffield describes Ringo's pattern as "galactic skull-crush kabooms" (68). See *Dreaming the Beatles: The Love Story of One Band and the Whole World* (New York: HarperCollins, 2017).
[17] Ian MacDonald, *Revolution in the Head: The Beatles' Records and the Sixties* (London: Fourth Estate, 1994), 152.

Not counting Harrison, the Beatles efface themselves completely on the next significant Indian-based track, "Within You Without You," which opens side two of *Sgt. Pepper's Lonely Hearts Club Band* (June 1967). Harrison's three bandmates are superseded altogether by Indian performers and a Western string ensemble, revealing how far Lennon, McCartney, and Starr were willing to go in order to give Harrison free reign to create an authentic Indian sound. Lyrics drawn from Harrison's studies in Hinduism mesh with the music: in a droning vocal, he reflects on emptiness and the salvation attainable in selfless, limitless love once the concept of duality is transcended. Kathryn B. Cox traces Harrison's lyrical debt to Vivekananda's *Raja Yoga*, while Michael Hannan unpacks the song's "complex timbres" deriving from "three tamburas ... combined to create a denser-than-usual, pulsating jivari [buzzing]," doubled dilrubas, sitar, and the closely mic'ed dayan (small tabla) and bayan (large tabla), all of these musical and vocal elements blending to generate a "deep meditative state."[18] On the LP cover, the band pays visual homage to Indian mysticism: nestled among the gallery are the three swamis Yukteswar Giri, Mahavatar Babaji, and Paramahansa Yogananda.

Spiritually and musically, Harrison had traveled far in a mere two years, blazing a trail into Indian music and culture that the whole band, with entourage (partners, wives, friends, a handful of rock stars) in tow, would follow into the northern Indian city of Rishikesh in February 1968. There, at the ashram of Maharishi Mahesh Yogi, the trend-setting avatar of Transcendental Meditation (TM) whom the boys first heard speak at a lecture in London in August 1967, the band would commune with nature, study sacred texts, meditate, shop in the village, and write rock masterpieces.

The Indian sage Maharishi Mahesh Yogi arrived in the West in the late 1950s as the pioneer/popularizer of this mind-calming discipline, which he had perfected after years of practice. This cheerful, captivating guru extolled the rewards of TM to ever bigger, ever receptive European and American audiences, who, he taught, would experience a decrease in the stress and anxiety that defined the chaos and fragmentation of modern life, with a corresponding increase in inner serenity. In the Maharishi's words, TM was "a technique for surrendering to the almighty power of nature and

---

[18] Kathryn B. Cox, "The Road to Rishikesh: The Beatles, India, and Globalized Dialogue in 1967," *The Beatles, Sgt. Pepper, and the Summer of Love*, ed. Kenneth Womack and Kathryn B. Cox (Lanham, MD: Lexington, 2017), 67–88; Michael Hannan, "The Sound Design of *Sgt. Pepper's Lonely Hearts Club Band*," *Sgt. Pepper and the Beatles: It Was Forty Years Ago Today*, ed. Olivier Julien (Aldershot: Ashgate, 2008), 54, 55.

arriving at the absolute, eternal field of divine intelligence."[19] The Beatles and other celebrities were the most visible of tens of thousands of votaries yearning for peace of mind achieved by centering their breath and meditating in 20-minute (or longer) sessions once or twice daily. Abetting this ritual was the practitioner's repetition of a mantra to ground his or her consciousness in transcendent oneness. In her book *Virtual Orientalism*, Jane Naomi Iwamura explains the movement's irresistible appeal to high-stressed Westerners such as the four Beatles: "The 'bliss consciousness' and 'illuminating expansion of the mind' the Maharishi promised made his spiritual alternative extremely compelling, if not magical."[20] That their 32-year-old manager Brian Epstein unexpectedly died while the band was attending the Maharishi's TM seminar in Wales in August 1967 strengthened their attachment to him, with his message of acceptance, during this difficult time.

Once ensconced in the Maharishi's bucolic fourteen-acre retreat on the banks of the Ganges at the edge of the Himalayas, Starr liked the meditation ("It was pretty exciting") but not the food, thus he left after two weeks. McCartney "loved it there," but with obligations in London departed after six weeks. Lennon gave it his best – despite missing Yoko Ono, recently met, and experiencing bouts of depression, he allowed that "It was a nice scene"; and Harrison, undeterred in his devotions, nonetheless threw in his lot with Lennon, both of them storming off a few weeks after McCartney upon hearing rumors of the Maharishi's impropriety (never substantiated) with Hollywood acolyte Mia Farrow.[21]

The first bunch of the dozens of pop/rock treasures penned by the Beatles during their winter stay in Rishikesh debuted on *The Beatles* (*The White Album*), released in November 1968. Using Kenneth Womack's *Encyclopedia* as a guide, one tallies nineteen of thirty tracks on *The Beatles* composed in Rishikesh. Other Indian-penned songs came out later, such as Lennon's "I'm Just a Child of Nature" (re-tooled as "Jealous Guy" on the 1971 *Imagine*), McCartney's "Teddy Boy" (the 1970 *McCartney*), and Harrison's "Sour Milk Sea" (a single for Apple Records artist Jackie Lomax). Oddly overlooked (many people find it superior to a number of cuts on *The Beatles*), "Sour Milk Sea" had lyrics based on a Tantric picture titled (in Sanscrit) *Kalladadi Samudra*, advocating

[19] Maharishi Mahesh Yogi, *The Science of Being and Art of Living* (Livingston Manor, NY: Maharishi International University Press, 1966), 104.
[20] Jane Naomi Iwamura, *Virtual Orientalism: Asian Religions and American Popular Culture* (New York: Oxford University Press, 2011), 64.
[21] Beatles, *Anthology*, 281, 285.

meditation for the discontented, thus making its rejection for *The Beatles* the more ironic, its Indian provenance being so clear.

The numbers that most baldly reflect events in Rishikesh are "Dear Prudence," "The Continuing Story of Bungalow Bill," and "Sexy Sadie," all by Lennon. Less well known than the story that it was written to tempt Prudence Farrow, who had been meditating so extensively that the others in the ashram feared for her health, is that "Dear Prudence" was recorded without Starr's input – the drummer having quit the band for about two weeks during the LP sessions. Lennon's gentle lyrics, reflecting the serene atmosphere of the retreat – "The sun is up, the sky is blue, / It's beautiful, and so are you" – do not prepare listeners for stand-in drummer McCartney's thunderous drum fills and cymbal crashes played over the last verse. "Bungalow Bill" is the first of the LP's several satires, this one skewering an American male who shot a tiger during a hunting junket. Perhaps more cutting than this profile of a callous, entitled young American is Lennon's attack – a "remarkably well restrained" one, according to Alan Pollack, "in spite of its confrontational, ridiculing, and questioning stance"[22] – on the Maharishi in "Sexy Sadie," so named, said Lennon, at Harrison's request, apparently to obscure the identity of the song's subject, who in actuality was perplexed by Lennon's and Harrison's abrupt departure, his transgression seemingly concocted by a Beatles insider. More spiritually focused products of the group's time in Rishikesh are Harrison's "Long, Long, Long" and McCartney's "Mother Nature's Son," the inspiration for each of them clearly conveyed in word and sound. Harrison's anguished yearning for godhead suffuses a soothing melody in 12/8 time interrupted by Starr's crashing drums, and McCartney's acoustic hymn to natural beauty lulls the listener into a momentary withdrawal from the human/nature duality.

These five tracks, as well as the many others on *The Beatles* written in Rishikesh, lack the overt references to sacred Hindu texts heard the previous year in "Within You Without You." They are instead anecdotal or spiritual in nature rather than didactic or scriptural. In other words, the songs written in India for *The Beatles* came about because the Beatles had a lot of time to write songs about the experience, not because they (Harrison excluded) had suddenly become lifelong converts to transcendental meditation or Hinduism.

---

[22] Alan W. Pollack, "Alan W. Pollack's Notes on 'Sexy Sadie,'" *Soundscapes.info*, August 9, 2018, www .icce.rug.nl/~soundscapes/DATABASES/AWP/ss.shtml.

The paradox at the core of *The Beatles* is that this most Indian of their releases – and a double-album, to boot – has no Indian instrumentation. Walter Everett's close reading of this music turns up no sitar, tabla, or tamboura, not to mention some of the more (to the Western ear) exotic instruments that had fleshed out "Within You Without You" and "Love You To." This absence is especially conspicuous on a recording renowned for its panorama of popular musical styles, from funk ("Savoy Truffle") to metal ("Helter Skelter"), calypso ("Ob-La-Di, Ob-La-Da") to vaudeville ("Honey Pie"). One suspects that the band's satisfaction with Harrison's "The Inner Light," taped January–February 1968 and released as the B-side of "Lady Madonna," made unnecessary another India-centric study for the upcoming album. As Everett explains, "The Inner Light," begun in Mumbai where Harrison was overseeing *Wonderwall*, features diverse Indian instruments, lyrics adapted from the *Tao Te Ching*, and a beautiful melody: "The peace and joy of nirvana are made palpable in this most sincere effort."[23] The Beatles had topped out the Indian sound, but not on the album they wrote in India.

What did that leave in the remaining eighteen months of the band's existence? A handful of tunes with mystical or philosophical ideas embedded in Western pop-rock form. Lennon's "Across the Universe" (begun in February 1969) blends two mantras, "Nothing's gonna change my world" and, showing that the composer had learned a great deal from the Maharishi about the serenity to be attained through meditation, "Jai Guru Deva Om" ("glory to the Indian teacher Dev"). Guru Dev (1868–1953) – that is, Swami Brahmananda Saraswati – had been the young Maharishi's master, and was largely responsible for laying out the fundamentals of his now famous disciple's TM program. Lennon prized "Across the Universe" highly among his compositions, for good reason: the archetypal play of light, wind, and rain animates a contemplative mind in harmony, at last, at least for the moment, with the universe. ("Cold Turkey" was on the horizon.) The April 1969 "Old Brown Shoe" is Harrison and his bandmates in full-blast rock mode, nearly eclipsing in its fury the metaphoric title's probable message: leave the material world behind; one's physical body is as useless as an old brown shoe. A bit more didactic and direct is the last song recorded by the Beatles (Lennon *in absentia*): "I Me Mine" (January 1970). In this short (the original take was 1:44) and tuneful sermon about the perils of the grasping ego, Harrison

---

[23] Walter Everett, *The Beatles as Musicians: "Revolver" Through the "Anthology"* (New York: Oxford University Press, 1999), 153.

gains powerful support from Starr's attack and McCartney's simpatico keyboards and bass guitar.

Post-Beatles, the predictable occurred. Neither Paul McCartney nor Ringo Starr turned to Indian music again, save for McCartney's "Riding to Jaipur" on *Driving Rain* (2001), and neither of them, in all their many tours (solo, Wings, All-Starr Band), played a show in India. John Lennon abjured all gods, all religions on Plastic Ono Band's "God" (1970). Meanwhile, George Harrison's Eastern-bred spirituality blossomed on the 1970 grand solo affair *All Things Must Pass*. With this achievement, raga rock had its *Sgt. Pepper*. Nothing else by the former Beatle would come close to surpassing it, not even albums such as *Living in the Material World* (1973) and *The Concert for Bangladesh* (1971) or productions such as *Chants of India* (1997). Nevertheless, these fine creations stand out among Harrison's numerous 1970s through 1990s releases, just as the Indian-tinged songs he made with Lennon, McCartney, and Starr are among the most memorable in the Beatles canon, the most sacred one in rock music.

PART VI

The Beatles' Critical Reception and Cultural Legacy

CHAPTER 27

Phantom Band: The Beatles after the Beatles

Jacqueline Edmondson

The word "phantom" conjures images of something elusory, abstract, or dream-like. A phantom may be a figment of one's imagination, something we think we see but are not quite sure. Phantoms can be fleeting yet haunting, apparitions that resemble real life and impact us in some way. Phantoms may influence how we see, feel, and engage or understand the world.

In what follows, I will explore the idea that the Beatles' in their post-Beatles lives were a phantom band, an illusory apparition of their lives while on stage or in the studio as the Fab Four. Although Lennon, McCartney, Harrison, and Starr struck out in different directions to establish their own individual identities and careers in their post-Beatles years, they still played in tandem, performing with and against one another as they learned to do from their early days in Liverpool and Hamburg. In other words, their collective performance continued, an embodiment of what French sociologist Pierre Bourdieu (1977) referred to as a "habitus," a force or set of established practices that always oriented them one toward the other, whether they were physically together or not.[1] This habitus was created and deeply ingrained through the intense time they spent together in their youth and early adulthood, and the habits and tendencies that formed during Beatlemania and the pressure to sustain their fame never really changed.

Creating Myths and Fantasies

As Beatles, the group thrived on myths and fantasies about their lives that surfaced during their early years. Most famously perhaps was the myth that Paul McCartney died in a tragic car accident November 1966 and was replaced by a look-alike named Williams Shears Campbell (or Billy

---

[1] Pierre Bourdieu, *Outline of a Theory of Practice* (London: Cambridge University Press, 1977).

Shears). Fanzines like *The Beatles Book* acknowledged the rumor, and fans believed there were secret messages encoded in songs like "Revolution 9," which allegedly had the phrase "Turn me on, dead man" when played backward. Paul eventually did an interview with reporters from *Life* magazine, published in November 1969, and this began to quell rumors about Paul's untimely death.

Other myths ranged from mundane claims about whether manager Brian Epstein talked the Beatles into wearing suits rather than leather clothing in their early days to rumors about the band's demise and the role Yoko Ono played in their break-up. Paul later commented on some of the rumors about John in particular. When dispelling a rumor that John participated in trepanning, which involves drilling a hole in the skull, he stated:

> John was a kooky cat. We'd all read about it – you know, this is the '60s . . . The "ancient art of trepanning," which lent a little bit of validity to it, because ancient must be good. I don't think he was really serious. He did say it, but he said all sorts of shit.[2]

Paul attributed John's propensity toward danger and lying to the fact that he did not have a father figure as a young man, and he contrasted this with his more stable home environment and the role his father played in his upbringing.

Myths and fantasies about the band certainly continued after they broke up, some of which were created through songs by the Beatles about the Beatles. One example is Ringo Starr's song "Early 1970." The lyrics describe Paul, John, and George's life post-Beatles. As Ringo questioned whether Paul would play with him, he acknowledged that John *would* play with him, and he described George as "playing for you with me." The piece captured the divide between Paul and the rest of the band when the Beatles broke up.

In the song "I'm the Greatest," Starr contributed to fantasies about his life while referencing his identity with the Beatles. In the song, written by John Lennon but performed by Ringo Starr (with Lennon and Harrison appearing on the track), Ringo reflected on aspects of his life, including growing up in Liverpool and falling in love. Each phase of his life was confirmed by someone who told him he was great. Starr then claimed he

[2] Antoinette Bueno, "Paul McCartney Addresses Most Scandalous John Lennon Rumors, Including Acid Use, Orgies, and His Jesus Complex," September 11, 2018, *etonline*, www.etonline.com/paul-mccartney-addresses-most-scandalous-john-lennon-rumors-including-acid-use-orgies-and-his-jesus.

was Billy Shears, a reference to his alter ego in "Sgt. Pepper's Lonely Hearts Club Band." Shears was listed as the singer when Starr performed the song "With a Little Help From My Friends" on the Sgt. Pepper's album.

George Harrison also had songs that referred to his time with the Beatles. "Sue Me, Sue You Blues" referred to the bitter break-up of the Beatles, while "I'm Not Guilty," which was recorded during *The White Album* period but not released until after the band broke up, described George's experiences in the aftermath of the Beatles visit to India with Maharishi Mahesh Yogi. In this song, Harrison conveyed the sense of responsibility he felt for the failed experiences in India, but with the line "I'll not upset the Apple cart," he also expressed his concern about the lavish campaign Apple Records prepared. Harrison's "When We Was Fab" (1987), co-written with Jeff Lynne, is a nostalgic reflection on Beatlemania, while the "Wah-Wah" song expressed frustration with the band and "Living in the Material World" described the trappings of wealth and Beatles.

McCartney's album *Ram* included the song "Too Many People," which contained oblique references to John and Yoko.[3] It took Paul years to publicly admit the extent to which the song was aimed at John. The piece begins with "Piss off, cake" and contains the lines "Too many people preaching practices," and "You took your lucky break and broke it in two." In a 2001 interview, Paul reflected on the piece:

> I felt John and Yoko were telling everyone what to do. And I felt we didn't need to be told what to do. The whole tenor of the Beatles thing had been, like, each to his own. Freedom. Suddenly it was "You should do this." It was just a bit the wagging finger, and I was pissed off with it. So that one got to be a thing about them.[4]

John thought there were other stabs at Yoko Ono and him throughout the album, including the songs "Dear Boy," "Three Legs" and "The Back Seat of My Car," but Paul denied this. While John and Ringo both publicly stated their dislike for the album, it hit No. 1 on the UK charts and No. 2 on the US charts.

John's "How Do You Sleep," from his 1971 album *Imagine*, is clearly directed toward Paul and written in response to Paul's attacks in *Ram*. The song begins with the line "So Sgt. Pepper took you by surprise" and goes on

---

[3] Philip Norman, *Paul McCartney: The Life* (Boston: Little, Brown: 2016), 437.
[4] Paul Du Noyer, *Conversations with McCartney* (London: Hodder and Stoughton, 2015), ch. 8.

to claim that the only thing Paul did was "yesterday" and that a "pretty face will last a year or two." John parodied Paul's album cover where Paul posed with a black-faced ram – John wrestled a pig. John openly admitted that the song was written in response to *Ram*, but he denied having any real or lasting resentment of Paul. John's *Rolling Stone* interview around the same time included comments about Paul's *McCartney* album where John "adopted the tone of a master sadly watching a former pupil go astray."[5]

After the Beatles broke up, each of the former Beatles took some effort to distance themselves from their Fab Four image as they established their solo careers. John's first solo album after the Beatles disbanded was the *John Lennon/Plastic Ono* Band, which included the track "God" where he sang "I don't believe in *Bea-tles*." In the final line of the song, he claimed "the dream is over." John mentioned the Beatles during his benefit concerts at Madison Square Garden on August 30, 1972. John introduced "Mother" as a song as coming from an album he made "when he left the Rolling Stones," and later he said he would "go back in the past just once" as he began to sing "Come Together."

Harrison once explained that "The whole Beatles thing is like a horror story, a nightmare. I don't even like to talk about it. I just hate it."[6] Much of his discontent was due to his songwriting status with the group. It is well known that Lennon and McCartney received songwriting credits, but Harrison did not. George's song "Only a Northern Song," expressed his discontent with the Beatles' publishing company Northern Songs and their practice of retaining copyrights for the songs he wrote.

As they established their solo careers, the former bandmates' songwriting consistently reflected stories of their personal lives and journeys, much as their songs did when they were in the band together. John's music post-Beatles was often autobiographical, similar to Paul who, with a different style, reverted to love songs and lyrics about his life. McCartney's work in the 1970s reflected his family life. The album *Ram* (1971) captured Paul's life with Linda on their farm in Scotland, including songs like "Eat At Home." Lennon's *Double Fantasy* (1980) reflected on his life with Ono and their young son Sean. Harrison wrote of his spirituality and reflections on life. Starr, likewise, engaged in songwriting about his own life experiences. In some way, they were still writing and performing together with their earlier tendencies in place.

---

[5] Norman, *Paul McCartney: The Life*, 428.
[6] Rob Sheffield, *Dreaming the Beatles: The Love Story of One Band and the Whole World* (New York: Dey Street, 2017), 51.

Competitions and Egos

All four of the former Beatles seemed to compete with one another in their Beatles years and in their post-Beatles lives. Their habitus involved having egos that were either hurt or built up, if only temporarily, through their exchanges.

Perhaps the biggest competition, albeit a mostly friendly one, was during the Beatles years as John and Paul wrote songs in a way that Shenk referred to as a "sort of call and response."[7] For example, John wrote "Strawberry Fields" about a place near his childhood home, and then Paul wrote "Penny Lane" about a street near his home. Paul thought this competition made them better. They wrote songs separately but together as creative partners and some of the most productive songwriters in the history of rock music.

Another source of competition and tension within the Beatles concerned who the de facto leader was. Ringo was perhaps the only Beatle who did not vie for leadership or influence. Lennon was clearly the first leader as he made decisions about whether to bring McCartney into his first band, and McCartney introduced Lennon to Harrison. In fact, Lennon once described his early relationship with Harrison in the following way:

> George is ten years younger than me, or some shit like that. I couldn't be bothered with him when he first came around. He used to follow me around like a bloody kid, hanging around all the time, I couldn't be bothered. He was a kid who played guitar, and he was a friend of Paul's which made it all easier. It took me years to come around to him, to start considering him as an equal or anything.[8]

In the band's first radio interview in 1962, an interviewer asked George if he was the band's leader since he played lead guitar. Paul corrected the interviewer by stating, "He's solo guitar, you see. John is in fact the leader of the group."[9] After manager Brian Epstein's death in August 1967, Paul exercised more influence on the band, convincing them to spend the summer filming the *Magical Mystery Tour*. By 1968, George

[7] Joshua Wolf Shenk, "The Power of Two," *The Atlantic*, July/August 2014, www.theatlantic.com/magazine/archive/2014/07/the-power-of-two/372289/.

[8] Jann Wenner, "Lennon Remembers, Part 2," *Rolling Stone Magazine*, February 4, 1971, www.rollingstone.com/music/music-news/lennon-remembers-part-two-187100/.

[9] Todd Van Luling, "11 Stories You Still Haven't Heard About the Beatles, Based on Their Earliest Interviews," *Huffington Post*, December 6, 2017, www.huffingtonpost.com/2015/06/18/beatles-trivia_n_7572788.html.

attempted to change the direction of the band by taking his bandmates to India to study with the Maharishi Mahesh Yogi. Tensions between George and John escalated further when George perceived that Yoko Ono was having some influence on the direction of the band.[10] The fatal struggle, however, was ultimately between Lennon and McCartney (with Ringo and George siding with Lennon) and the contract dispute with Allen Klein and Apple.

Perhaps the most public competition post-Beatles involved McCartney's continued effort to alter authorship of Beatles' songs, even decades after Lennon's death. As Womack notes, "the ramifications of authorship and the compensation and status that it derives, may be the most significant issues in the post-break-up lives of the Beatles – exception of course, John Lennon's murder in December 1980 and George Harrison's death in November 2001."[11] McCartney's insecurity with authorship also was manifest in imitation. He included "Let Me Roll It" on the 1973 album *Band on the Run*. Some critics, including Jon Landau of *Rolling Stone*, thought the song imitated John and Yoko's sound.[12] Paul denied this was intentional, but he admitted that it did sound like John. John was complimentary of the album.

Starr was the first to release a solo album, just as the Beatles broke up. *Sentimental Journey* (1970) was a compilation of Ringo's mother Elsie's favorite songs. Produced by George Martin, the album had moderate reviews and some wondered why he covered standards.[13] The album was a Top 10 hit in the UK. Five months later, Ringo released *Beaucoup of Blues* (1970), which reflected his interest in country and western music. The album did not fare well in the UK or USA, and fans wondered about yet another change in genre.

Ringo benefited from the fact that he got along well with the other Beatles. His former bandmates contributed to Ringo's solo work, and Ringo contributed to their efforts. John and George contributed to Ringo's third album. Paul had to send his track from London because he could not re-enter the USA due to a drug conviction in Scotland.

[10] Mikal Gilmore, "Why the Beatles Broke Up: The Inside Story of the Forces that Broke Up the World's Greatest Band," *Rolling Stones Magazine*, September 3, 2009, www.rollingstone.com/mus ic/music-news/why-the-beatles-broke-up-113403/.

[11] Kenneth Womack, "Authorship and the Beatles," *College Literature*, 34, 3 (Summer 2007), 161.

[12] Jon Landau, "Paul McCartney: Band on the Run," *Rolling Stone,* January 21, 1997, www.rolling stone.com/music/albumreviews/band-on-the-run-19970121.

[13] Robert Rodriguez, *Fab Four FAQ 2.0: The Beatles' Solo Years, 1970–1980* (New York: Backbeat Books, 2010).

After the Beatles broke up, George had the first No. 1 single with "My Sweet Lord." His triple album *All Things Must Pass* (1971) was met with critical acclaim as people responded to the range and creative abilities George demonstrated in these albums. While some of the songs were written when George was a Beatle, none had been released. Biographer Simon Leng, noted the paradoxical nature of the album. He wrote:

> While it was obviously Harrison's attempt to break free from his Beatles identity, the whole venture was framed by the mythologized history of the group ... The entire album is concerned with the group and Harrison's experiences in it. The themes – the nature of friendship, failed relationships, the search for spiritual peace, and escape to a safe haven – all result from the distortion of his life through his years within the Beatles.[14]

Harrison reissued a remastered edition of the album in 2001, which was both a critical and a commercial success, and EMI reissued a limited edition of the original album in 2010. In 2014, the album was again remastered and included in a box set of Harrison's work *The Apple Years 1968–75.*

Paul's first No. 1 single, "Uncle Albert/Admiral Halsey," was co-written with Linda and appeared on the album *Ram.* The song had a number of story fragments Paul wove together in a narrative. Uncle Albert was his uncle, and Admiral Halsey is based on the American admiral William "Bull" Halsey (1882–1959), someone Paul thought should be ignored.[15]

John was the final Beatle to have a No. 1 hit with the 1974 single "Whatever Gets You Through the Night." It was his only No. 1 single on an American chart. The song was inspired by a late night television evangelist who used the phrase on his show. British artist Elton John featured on piano and back-up vocals. Lennon performed the song on stage with Elton John on November 24, 1974, at Elton's concert in Madison Square Garden, Lennon's last appearance at a major concert.

After John's death, tensions related to the Beatles and their post-Beatles life still surfaced. Biographer Philip Norman wrote of Paul's apparent hurt when Norman published an article in the *Sunday Times* recounting a conversation with Yoko Ono shortly after John's death. Ono spoke of John's insecurities and bitterness toward his former bandmates, particularly Paul. Ono shared "John always used to say ... that no one ever hurt

---

[14] Simon Leng, *While My Guitar Gently Weeps: The Music of George Harrison* (Milwaukee, WI: Hal Leonard Corporation, 2006), 76.

[15] Vincent P. Benítez, *The Words and Music of Paul McCartney: The Solo Years* (New York: Praeger, 2010).

him the way Paul hurt him." Paul contacted Norman's office after the article was published, and Norman's interpretation was that Paul "seemed upset rather than angry."[16]

After Lennon's death, McCartney joked "that in the contest they'd always waged, John's death had been the final act of one-upmanship."[17] By 1972, Paul and John seemed to put aside their differences and began speaking again. Paul visited John in the West Village in New York where he lived with Yoko. Paul called John regularly when Paul was in New York, but he was not always able to anticipate how John would receive him.[18]

The World Stage

The Beatles enjoyed the world stage when they performed together, and they became accustomed to the international attention and recognition they received. They realized how their statements impacted their fans and people around the world. One example was in 1966 when John Lennon stated that the Beatles were "more popular than Jesus" during a news conference. He observed:

> Christianity will go . . . It will vanish and shrink. I needn't argue about that; I know I'm right and I will be proved right. We're more popular than Jesus now. I don't know which will go first – rock & roll or Christianity. Jesus was all right, but his disciples were thick and ordinary. It's them twisting it that ruins it for me.[19]

When Lennon's comments were printed in an American teen magazine, protests ensued. American radio stations, particularly in the Bible belt, banned the Beatles' music. Churches threatened to excommunicate members who attended a Beatles concert, and the Pope denounced Lennon's words. Lennon eventually apologized when he realized the severity of the situation and how his words set off a firestorm that threatened the band and their tour.

In their post-Beatles years, the former Beatles all pursued creative outlets beyond music, and all found a voice on their world stage to promote social causes that interested them. In fact, they were among the first rock stars to

---

[16] Norman, *Paul McCartney: The Life*, 8–9.   [17] Norman, *Paul McCartney: The Life*, 570.
[18] Norman, *Paul McCartney: The Life*, 479.
[19] Jordon Runtagh, "When John Lennon's 'More Popular Than Jesus' Controversy Turned Ugly," *Rolling Stone Magazine*, July 29, 2016, www.rollingstone.com/music/music-features/when-john-le nnons-more-popular-than-jesus-controversy-turned-ugly-106430/.

engage in diplomacy and advocacy, and they set a standard for others who followed.

John and Yoko were at the forefront as they promoted world peace and other social causes. On their honeymoon, John and Yoko famously advocated for world peace through their bed-ins. They invited the press to their room in the Amsterdam Hilton Hotel presidential suite between 9 am and 9 pm each day between March 25 and 31, 1969. On March 31 in Vienna, they introduced Bagism, which was intended to satirize prejudice and stereotyping. In April, John and Yoko sent acorns to heads of state around the world with the hope they would plant them as a symbol for world peace. In May 1969, they repeated the bed-in in Montreal at the Queen Elizabeth Hotel. They invited celebrities, including beat poet Allen Ginsberg, psychologist Timothy Leary, and comedian Tommy Smothers. To end the year, the couple paid for billboards in eleven major cities that stated "War is Over! If you want it – Happy Christmas from John and Yoko." John's songs "Imagine," "Gimme Some Truth," and "Power to the People," further conveyed his political views about world peace and his concerns about politicians.

In the years that followed, John and Yoko were vocal in their support of feminism. In some ways, this seemed an unlikely cause for Lennon to support. He admitted to having a history of mistreating women, and offered this explanation:

> That was me. I used to be cruel to my woman, and physically – any woman. I was a hitter. I couldn't express myself and I hit. I fought men and I hit women. That is why I am always on about peace, you see. It is the most violent people who go for love and peace. Everything's the opposite. But I sincerely believe in love and peace. I am a violent man who has learned not to be violent and regrets his violence. I will have to be a lot older before I can face in public how I treated women as a youngster.[20]

But his experiences with Yoko and his engagement with social causes influenced how he thought about and treated women. By 1972, Lennon co-wrote with Ono the controversial pro-feminist anthem "Woman Is the Nigger of the World." In 1980, Lennon wrote "Woman" as a personal apology for pain he caused Yoko and a declaration of his love for her.

John and Yoko supported other causes together. In 1970, John and Yoko cut their hair, which was then auctioned off to benefit Britain's Black

[20] Joe Raiola, "John Lennon's Journey to Feminism and Why It Matters in the Age of Trump," *Huffington Post*, October 10, 2016, www.huffingtonpost.com/entry/john-lennons-journey-to-feminism-and-why-it-matters_us_57f9601ee4b090dec0e71412.

Power organization. In August 1972, they played benefit concerts in New York City to raise funds for handicapped children. They also walked in protest marches.

George led the first major benefit concert as he, along with other artists, sought to provide relief for Bangladesh. The Concert for Bangladesh involved two concerts held on August 1, 1971, in Madison Square Garden (one concert at 2:30 pm, and the other at 8:00 pm). George and Ringo performed together with a star-studded lineup that included Eric Clapton, Leon Russell, Billy Preston, Bob Dylan, and the band Badfinger. Approximately 40,000 people attended, raising $250,000 in humanitarian aid for people displaced during the Bangladesh Liberation War. This concert set the standard for other major humanitarian concerts that followed, including Live Aid.

Paul brought attention to concerns in Cambodia. In 1979, he led the Concerts of the People of Kampuchea, which involved musicians and dignitaries. The concert was a response to the Khmer Rouge reign which brought 3 million deaths in Cambodia. Wings, members of Procol Harum, and the Who were among those who performed, along with Elvis Costello, the Pretenders, Queen, the Clash, and members of Led Zeppelin.

With Linda, Paul advocated for vegetarianism and animal rights, causes he continued to support after her death. In 2018, Paul proclaimed that "meat-free is the new rock and roll," a comment that brought criticism from dairy farmers.[21] Linda's cookbooks and food line continued to sell.

Paul's activism continued after Linda's death. With his second wife, Heather Mills, McCartney advocated for the elimination of landmines. Together they launched a campaign and engaged in raising awareness and funds for charity to support the cause. Paul also participated in efforts to eliminate gun violence, and on March 24, 2018 he joined a March for our Lives rally in New York to honor John Lennon. McCartney stated: "One of my best friends was killed in gun violence right around here, so it's important to me."[22]

As a Beatle, Ringo Starr took political stances. He advocated against segregation, stating:

[21] Maria Chiorando, "Sir Paul McCartney Blasted for Saying 'Meat Free Is the New Rock n Roll,'" *Plant Based News*, May 21, 2018, www.plantbasednews.org/post/sir-paul-mccartney-meat-free-new-rock-n-roll.
[22] Jennifer Calfas, "'One of My Best Friends Was Killed in Gun Violence.' Paul McCartney Honors John Lennon at March For Our Lives," *Time Magazine*, March 24, 2018, http://time.com/5213991/paul-mccartney-john-lennon-march-for-our-lives/.

Segregation is a lot of rubbish … As far as we're concerned, people are people, no different from each other. We'd never play South Africa if it means a segregated audience. What a lot of rubbish.[23]

Ringo also engaged in political causes during his post-Beatles years. He joined the anti-apartheid movement, appearing with his son Zak in Artists United Against Apartheid in 1985. He participated in the protest song "Sun City" with an array of other artists with the hope of bringing change. Sun City was a resort in South Africa that hosted entertainment banned elsewhere in the country, and anti-apartheid protests included boycotting the resort.

In 2014 with fashion designer John Varvatos, Ringo launched "PeaceRocks" an anti-violence campaign. Varvatos included Ringo in advertisements with #PEACEROCKS, and each time the hashtag was used on a photo, Varvatos donated $1 to the campaign. This continued a trend of Ringo advocating for peace and love. Starting in 2008, Ringo shared that all he wanted for his birthday was some peace and love, and he asked people to join him in thinking about peace and love on his birthday. This tradition continued over the next decade as people honored his request in cities around the world each year on his birthday. In 2014, Ringo's efforts were recognized. His efforts with the David Lynch Foundation (DLF) which supported using transcendental meditation in education won him the DLF Peace and Love Award. Ringo was also awarded the GQ UK's Men of the Year Humanitarian Award in 2014.

Conclusion

While the Beatles may have ended when they officially split up on April 10, 1970, they did not stop their collective performance. Although the form of their performance did not materialize in an onstage reunion with all four Beatles, the Beatles continued in a phantom form as they created music, competed with one another, and promoted their various causes. The Beatles were still a band, still part of the habitus of the Beatles as they influenced one another and continued the practices they engaged as young men through the remainder of their lives.

Some believe the most significant contribution of the Beatles post-Beatles was the influence they had on creative musical forms that followed, including 1970s Anglo-American art rock and punk.[24] I would add that

---

[23] Runtagh, "'More Popular Than Jesus'."
[24] Dean Biron, "Towards a Popular Music Criticism of Replenishment," *Popular Music and Society*, 34, 5 (2011), 661–82.

this influence came from the creative work they did together yet separately in their post-Beatles years, and perhaps the biggest influence may be the example they set related to promoting peace and justice. Others have followed their lead, particularly as various artists engage the world stage to promote social causes and protest inequities.

CHAPTER 28

The Beatles, Apple, and the Business of Music Publishing

Stuart Rosenberg

Following the unexpected death of their manager, Brian Epstein, in August 1967, the Beatles accelerated their plan to gain control of their own financial affairs. Epstein's team at NEMS, the management company that managed the Beatles' business affairs, had actually hatched this plan at least two years earlier as a way for John Lennon, Paul McCartney, George Harrison, and Ringo Starr to invest their income into a business venture, since the British government's corporate tax rate was significantly lower than the individual rate. Consequently, the Beatles severed all ties with NEMS to focus their attention on their own company, named Apple Corps, which was founded in London in January 1968, with headquarters at 94 Baker Street. With regard to the company's income (excluding songwriting royalties that were paid to the composer of a particular song), each of the Beatles would own 5 percent, while the new corporation – which would be owned collectively by all four Beatles – would own the remaining 80 percent.

The Beatles wanted to employ friends and people that they trusted to form Apple's inner circle; a prime example was Neil Aspinall, the band's road manager, who became the entertainment conglomerate's managing director.

Apple's subsidiaries included Apple Films, Apple Retail, Apple Electronics, Apple Publishing, and Apple Records. Both Apple Films and Apple Retail began operations in late 1967. The film *Magical Mystery Tour*, which was broadcast by the BBC over the Christmas holiday, was panned by the British press. Apple Films went on to produce only seven more films. The Apple Boutique, which sold records, psychedelic fashions, and jewelry, lost money from the start and closed its doors by July 1968. Apple Electronics also quickly failed, due to the inability to develop any meaningful products. Clearly, the primary focus of the Beatles was on music publishing and the development of their independent record label.

Apple Publishing

Music publishers are vital to songwriters for the promotion of their catalog and to protect their copyright. Music publishing emerged as the original commercial music business in the early nineteenth century when the printing of the sheet music containing the notation and lyrics of popular songs made it possible for the songs to be performed in saloons and restaurants. Following the growth of radio and films in the first half of the twentieth century, US and UK music publishers relied on song pluggers to visit popular night spots and to help promote their songs to be performed by the biggest singers of the day in order to earn their royalty checks. Later, the advent of pop music led to an increase in record sales, and royalties on recorded versions of a song became an important source of income in addition to the royalties on public performances and broadcasts of a song. By signing with a publisher, a songwriter effectively sells a proportion of the copyright (i.e., ownership) of the song to the publisher who in turn markets the song and then splits income from the song with the songwriter on an agreed percentage. Under UK law, copyrights for original literary, dramatic, musical, and artistic works generally last for seventy years after the death of the creator; in the case of writing partnerships, the copyright exists until seventy years after the death of the last surviving member. Consequently, this would prove to be significant to the songs of Lennon and McCartney.

Back when the Beatles were first signed by EMI Records in 1962,[1] Brian Epstein had been unhappy with the promotion that the group's first single, "Love Me Do," received from its music publisher, Ardmore & Beechwood. Perhaps more importantly, he recognized that the Beatles represented a new breed of pop artist who wrote and recorded their own songs,[2] and together with music publisher Dick James he formed Northern Songs Ltd in 1963 to publish the songs of just two songwriters – Lennon and McCartney. Over time the two songwriters grew to resent the arrangement, where Dick James Music would have ownership of 50 percent of the publishing and the other 50 percent was split between NEMS and the two songwriting Beatles. Although they were receiving royalties as songwriters

---

[1] The record contract, which was offered by EMI in-house producer George Martin, had a low royalty rate because it required that all records be made at EMI's own Abbey Road studios at the company's rather than at the artists' expense.

[2] This was a huge departure from New York City's Tin Pan Alley in the 1920s and Brill Building in the 1960s, where publishers, songwriters, and pluggers worked together in small offices equipped with a piano to get major singers to record their songs, spawning a significant share of the hit records of the day.

and now as music publishers, Lennon and McCartney felt they were taken advantage of by Epstein and James. The Beatles had little or no understanding of how music publishing worked. Because a song was not a physical object, they did not know that it was possible to "own" it. Both Epstein and James, however, would become very wealthy within a short amount of time. Royalties from sheet music sales of Beatles songs reached unheard of levels. It was claimed that a Beatles record was played on the radio somewhere around the world almost every minute of every day and sales of singles and albums were exceeding capacity at factories in the UK and USA. Income also started to come in from an added piece to the Beatles portfolio, as Epstein agreed to a film deal with United Artists featuring the group and its music.[3] In 1965, NEMS accountants and advisers decided to issue shares in Northern Songs on the London Stock Exchange as a means to relieve Lennon and McCartney of their tax burden, thereby enabling the public to share in the success of the Beatles' compositions. With the release of their fifth album, *Help!*, the same year, George Harrison's songs were also assigned to Northern Songs.[4]

By the time they formed Apple, all four members of the Beatles had become more aware of their monetary worth, which sparked their interest in their financial security. They saw their songs such as "Yesterday" and "Michelle" become favorites for other artists to record.[5] They saw how Dick James was able to make use of the financial strength of Northern Songs to purchase the copyrights of other catalogs and build it to become one of popular music's most valuable music publishers. They spoke with other artists and various business people to compare record and publishing deals. With Apple, the group followed the business model established for the Beatles through Northern Songs. They looked to sign songwriters and give them 50 percent of the ownership for their compositions. Apple Publishing took the other 50 percent.

Apple Records

The Beatles had not been happy with their deal with EMI Records. They were under contract to the company's Parlophone label in the UK and to Capitol Records in the USA. With the formation of Apple, EMI and

[3] Epstein also agreed to a large merchandising deal for Beatles memorabilia that proved to be ill conceived. The deal was poorly structured, losing the Beatles millions of dollars.
[4] Beginning with his four compositions on *The Beatles* (*The White Album*) in 1968, Harrison's songs would be copyrighted to Harrisongs.
[5] Over 3,000 versions of "Yesterday" would be recorded over the next four decades.

Capitol agreed to distribute Apple Records until 1975. EMI retained ownership of the Beatles' recordings, while the rights to recordings of other artists signed to the new label would be owned by Apple.

The Beatles saw Apple Records as revolutionizing the recording industry. It was aimed at placing power in the hands of the artists instead of the artists having to kowtow to business people who might not understand the creative process involved in making records in the first place. The Beatles altruistically wanted to use their good fortune for this artist-friendly company to give a chance to aspiring artists who would not have a chance with large established companies like EMI. McCartney declared that the Beatles had all the money they needed, and by establishing a business in an environment where everyone would prosper "it would be a sort of Western communism."

While the Beatles traveled to meet Maharishi Mahesh Yogi in India in early 1968, an advertising campaign had commenced calling for artists to send demo recordings to Apple's offices. In May, Lennon and McCartney went to New York to promote the new company. Upon their return to London, Lennon met Yoko Ono, so McCartney and Harrison quickly took charge looking for new artists to sign. Harrison began working with Jackie Lomax, who had had modest success in the Merseybeat band the Undertakers. The celebrated model Twiggy recommended a teenage Welsh folk singer to McCartney, Mary Hopkin, who became his first project. Peter Asher, the brother of McCartney's girlfriend, Jane (and also one half of the recently disbanded recording act Peter and Gordon, who had topped the charts with the Lennon and McCartney composition "A World Without Love"), was hired by Apple as head of its A&R (artists and repertoire) division in order to bring in new artists. Asher soon acted on a recommendation from the New York City guitarist Danny Kortchmar, and signed an American singer-songwriter, James Taylor. Meanwhile, Mal Evans, a former bouncer at Liverpool's Cavern Club and an assistant roadie for the Beatles, recommended another Welsh act, the Iveys, a four-man group from Swansea who had relocated to London, where they lived in the loft of the house of their manager in Golders Green. Along with these signings, the Beatles received an endless stream of demo tapes that ensured that Apple would fulfill its goal of building a broad catalog of eclectic musical genres.

On August 30, 1968, Apple released its first four singles, each featuring the iconic apple logo on their labels: "Thingumybob" by the Black Dyke Mills Band; "Sour Milk Sea" by Jackie Lomax; "Hey Jude" by the Beatles; and "Those Were the Days" by Mary Hopkin. "Thingumybob" was a brass band instrumental written by Lennon and McCartney that was not commercially successful. More surprisingly, "Sour Milk Sea," a Harrison composition, did not chart. The sales of Lomax's single and subsequent album were disappointing despite Harrison getting McCartney, Starr, and Eric Clapton to perform on the records. Lomax knew that the Beatles did not need to go out on concert tours to sell their records; he believed, however, that this neglected promotional strategy would have benefited him to generate attention for his records. More than 7 minutes in length, "Hey Jude" became the longest single ever to top the British charts. "Those Were the Days" was also a huge hit, selling 8 million copies worldwide, and it was not very long before the company had grown so much that it needed to move to a larger location, at 3 Savile Row.

The Iveys' first single, "Maybe Tomorrow," and James Taylor's self-titled debut album were both released in late 1968. "Maybe Tomorrow," produced by Tony Visconti, failed to chart in the UK due in part to comparisons between the Iveys' sound to that of the Beatles. Similarly, *James Taylor*, produced by Peter Asher, showed strong promise but received little fanfare. Although these releases did not meet expectations, the atmosphere at Apple in its first year was a very encouraging one. It all seemed quite utopian and the company continued signing new bands from across the musical spectrum.

Apple did have an impractical signing policy, though, since one of the Beatles had to be around to give his stamp of approval. The Beatles were often busy with their own projects and Apple simply could not finalize the deals on a number of artists who went on to achieve commercial success over the next decade. One example was when Mick Fleetwood, who was Harrison's brother-in-law, tried and failed to get his band Fleetwood Mac signed to Apple. A second example was when Harrison decided not to sign Crosby, Stills and Nash after they came to Apple for an audition.

By early 1969, the press was reporting about underlying tensions among the Beatles and within Apple. In an interview with the British weekly *Disc and Music Echo*, Lennon voiced the concern that "We're losing money hand over fist." It was rumored that Apple was spending more money on the Beatles' personal expenses, like airfare – as well as on business expenses for company employees such as expensive lunches, alcohol, and drugs – than on developing the other artists on the label. Allen Klein, the aggressive American business manager of the Rolling Stones, seized upon Lennon's comment that the Beatles would be broke in six months if Apple were to continue operating the way it had been. Klein got ahold of Lennon and Yoko Ono through Derek Taylor, Apple's press officer, and assured them that he could shore up the company's finances. As sessions were beginning for the band's final album, *Abbey Road*, Lennon convinced Harrison and Starr that Klein should be brought on as financial adviser, outnumbering McCartney's vote for entertainment lawyer Lee Eastman, the father of his soon-to-be wife, Linda. Once on board, Klein wasted little time in beginning a full assessment of Apple, firing twenty staff members to bring the company's headcount down to about thirty people. He indicated that he was putting a number of new record releases on hold until he could sort things out. As a result, in a very short amount of time the atmosphere inside Apple turned, as people were afraid they might be fired.

During this period at Northern Songs, Dick James had become increasingly worried about Klein. Moreover, he was aware of the disharmony within the Beatles. He was also concerned about John Lennon's drug bust in October 1968 and the cover of his *Two Virgins* released on Apple Records in November 1968 on which he and Yoko Ono appeared fully nude. Speculation of James selling his share of the publishing company became a reality in March 1969, with the sale to the British company, Associated Television Corporation (ATV), which was run by Lew Grade. As a result of the sale, ATV owned 35 percent of Northern Songs and Grade was knighted a few months later. Lennon and McCartney, who claimed they had no prior knowledge of the deal, felt betrayed, and they proceeded to sever their ties with Northern Songs by selling their shares to ATV and losing the rights to the first fifty-six songs that they wrote together. The two songwriters would not be able to control the copyrights to their solo compositions for another three years, when their formal agreement with Northern Songs and ATV expired.

Work had already begun on James Taylor's second album, but Peter Asher resigned and wanted to take his discovery with him to Warner Brothers. Taylor was bound to a five-year contract with Apple, but Harrison told Klein that he did not want any negative publicity for the Beatles' artist-friendly label and they agreed to let him go. Taylor's album, *Sweet Baby James*, made him a star.

Another artist that was signed to Apple who eventually departed for greater commercial success was Billy Preston. The Beatles had known the Houston-born keyboardist from their early days in Hamburg, when he played in Little Richard's band. He was signed by Harrison in spite of the cost-cutting that Klein had recently initiated. Preston, who had an infectious personality, helped to ease the tension among the Beatles in the recording studio; this was rewarded when the single "Get Back" was credited on the label to the Beatles with Billy Preston (the only time a non-Beatle was named on one of their records). His single "That's the Way God Planned It," produced by Harrison, peaked at No. 11 on the UK charts in June 1969. He remained with Apple for another two years, but Apple did not quite know how to promote R&B records and, like James Taylor before him, he achieved greater mainstream success once he moved on, at A&M records.

Mary Hopkin's second single, "Goodbye," written by Paul McCartney, was kept out of the top spot on the UK charts by "Get Back," another McCartney composition. Hopkin would become increasingly disenchanted with the saccharine pop songs that McCartney, and later Mickey Most, produced for her. She finally would migrate to the folk vein in which she was more comfortable a couple of years later under the guidance of Tony Visconti, who at the time was producing the band T. Rex, but there was no inclination by Apple to promote her album *Earth Song/Ocean Song*. Soon afterwards, she left Apple, married Visconti, and withdrew from the spotlight.

After Paul McCartney read an interview with bassist Ron Griffiths of the Iveys in *Disc and Music Echo* that complained about the lack of support for the artists at Apple, he offered the band a song that he had written for an upcoming film based on a novel by Terry Southern and starring Peter Sellers and Ringo Starr called *The Magic Christian*. The song, "Come and Get It," released in December 1969, was a hit, reaching No. 7 in the USA and No. 4 in the UK, but by that time Griffiths was replaced in the band by Joey Molland and the band's name was changed to Badfinger. Badfinger would go on to become the biggest act in the history of Apple outside the Beatles, and behind the songwriting of the band's Pete Ham and Tom Evans, they would help define the Power Pop genre with big hits like "No Matter What" from the album *No Dice* and "Day after Day" from the album *Straight Up*. One of the commercial highlights in Apple Publishing's history was the Ham–Evans song "Without You," from *No Dice*, which the singer Harry Nilsson had heard while at a party and decided to record; Nilsson's version was released in 1971 and hit No. 1 in the USA, UK, and several other countries. During the recording sessions for *Straight Up*, producer George Harrison abandoned the project when he was approached by his friend the Indian sitarist Ravi Shankar to help raise awareness and funds for the victims of the Bangladesh genocide. Harrison enlisted several of his friends, as well as surprise headliner Bob Dylan, to perform two benefit concerts at Madison Square Garden, while Todd Rundgren finished the production chores for Badfinger's album, which was released to both critical and commercial acclaim.

The ongoing comparisons between Badfinger and the Beatles, however, plagued the band. *Rolling Stone* magazine said that *No Dice* was the album that the Beatles would have made if they were still together. Criticism of these "Beatle clones" was harshest in the UK, where glam rock was all the rage and made Badfinger's music sound passé. With Apple experiencing deteriorating financial conditions, Badfinger's business manager, Stan Polley, who had recently been identified in a US Senate investigation for his ties to organized crime, convinced the band to leave Apple to sign a contract with Warner Brothers. The Warner Brothers contract ended up being a worse deal than Badfinger had at Apple.[6]

Apple Records' financial woes coincided with the disintegration of the band that had founded the company. The Beatles' naiveté concerning their utopian mission as well as concerning their ability to operate a business would lead to the company's ultimate demise. Less than two years after the founding of the company, Lennon informed the Beatles that he wanted to quit the band so that he could focus on his Plastic Ono Band. McCartney, who was devastated that the Beatles were coming to an end and that Klein was still the band's manager, wanted no further part in Apple Records and moved to Scotland. He served court papers in 1971 against his three former bandmates and Apple Records to extricate himself from the relationship.

Lennon soon moved to Greenwich Village in New York City, where he immersed himself in the activities of the radical left. His involvement with countercultural figures such as Abbie Hoffman and Jerry Rubin led him to street musician David Peel, whom he signed to Apple, but Lennon's name could not influence sales of Peel's album *The Pope Smokes Dope*. It was apparent that while McCartney and Harrison had signed acts with commercial potential, Lennon now tended to sign acts that he simply liked. He also signed the band Elephant's Memory, which had contributed two songs to the soundtrack of the film *Midnight Cowboy*. The band backed Lennon on his album *Some Time in New York City*, released in 1972. The album was the first flop that Lennon had ever experienced, which greatly disappointed him, causing him to terminate his association with the New York City underground and with Apple Records altogether.

Over the years, Apple kept signing artists. This list included Brute Force (whose single "King of Fuh" received no radio airplay); the Hot Chocolate Band (who had a string of hit singles post-Apple as Hot Chocolate); the

---

[6] In April 1975, a disillusioned Pete Ham hanged himself in his studio. In his suicide note, he blamed Polley, who seemed to have vanished when the band had stopped receiving its paychecks. In the ensuing years, Badfinger tried to carry on, but Tom Evans, who had never overcome the grief of losing his songwriting partner, hanged himself in the garden at his home in November 1983.

Modern Jazz Quartet; Radha Krishna Temple; Ronnie Spector; John Tavener (a classical artist who was one of the few signings by Ringo Starr); Doris Troy, Lon and Derrek Van Eaton, and Yoko Ono. With the exception of Ono, Apple did not have the resources or direction to promote its artists. Ono, on the other hand, who was intent on having a musical career despite tremendous criticism of the cacophonous sound of her experimental style, had a number of records released by Apple, especially in the company's final years. These releases were expensive, as she got more promotion than Apple's other artists even though there was no commercial return. Allegedly, it was just a matter of Allen Klein not being able to tell Lennon how much money his wife was costing the company.

Allen Klein's contract as manager of the Beatles and Apple mercifully expired in March 1973. It was far too late, of course, to right the ship. Two years later, the Beatles' partnership was finally dissolved, legally freeing each of their interests from Apple while allowing them to be co-owners of the company. In May 1975, Apple Records ceased operations. The revolutionary label and the foundation of the Apple enterprise never really was able to live up to its promise.

* * *

By the mid-1970s, Paul McCartney had gained a very clear understanding of how music publishing worked, and he began to accumulate an impressive catalog for his newly formed publishing company, MPL (McCartney Productions Limited). In 1976, MPL became one of the world's largest independent music publishers after buying the prestigious Edwin W. Morris Music catalog, which included songs from the musicals *Grease* and *A Chorus Line* as well as the entire Buddy Holly catalog. When McCartney's American contract with Capitol Records expired in 1979, CBS incentivized him to sign by offering the music catalog of the great American songwriter Frank Loesser (including "Standing on the Corner," "Once in Love with Amy," "Luck be a Lady Tonight," and hundreds of others).

While ATV Music, which had been formed to manage all of ATV's publishing interests, was cautioned that the use of Beatles songs in commercials was restricted, the company did grant approval to use the group's music and lyrics for the 1977 Broadway musical *Beatlemania*. This was granted without ever consulting any of the Beatles or Apple Corps. They also were not consulted when ATV Music allowed the use of the Beatles' songs in the 1978 film *Sgt. Pepper's Lonely Hearts Club Band*. The royalty

income from such ventures added to ATV Music's success, but Lew
Grade's interest was in the film business. Following the critical and
commercial success of *The Pink Panther*, *The Muppet Movie*, *Sophie's
Choice*, and *On Golden Pond*, *Raise the Titanic* went disastrously over
budget. In 1982, Robert Holmes à Court was named to the board of
Associated Communications Corporation (the parent company of ATV),
and promptly removed Grade from the board, fueling speculation that
ATV Music would soon be sold.

Paul McCartney was interested in buying Northern Songs, but he did
not want to pay what he felt was too much for it. Yoko Ono, who was now
John Lennon's widow, made the prospect of such a deal more complicated.
McCartney also did not want to buy the whole company. Around this
time, he collaborated with Michael Jackson on his 1983 song "Say Say Say",
which was published by MPL, and the two became very close. McCartney
introduced Jackson to the idea of owning songs and copyrights; on the
heels of 50 million in world record sales for his landmark album *Thriller*,
Jackson had cash to spare. He ultimately bought the ATV Music catalog in
August 1985 for $47.5 million. The irony is that Jackson learned about
music publishing from McCartney, and their friendship was never the
same again.

Jackson was free to exploit the songs from the Lennon–McCartney
catalog however he pleased, and they soon began to appear in a
number of commercials. Jackson also continued to invest aggressively
in the ATV Music catalog. His record label, Sony, decided to merge
with ATV Music so that Sony could handle the worldwide adminis-
tration of the combined company Sony ATV. Jackson would eventually become embroiled in a bitter dispute with Sony for not fulfilling
his commitment for the delivery of new recordings and for owing the
company millions in advances and loans. His personal finances were in
a perilous state, as he was spending around $1.5 million per month to
maintain his Neverland ranch and extravagant lifestyle. In 2006, a year
after Jackson was brought to court in Santa Monica, California on
child molestation charges, Sony gained operational control of Sony/
ATV and obtained an option to buy half of Jackson's stake in the
company. With song royalties now also coming from music downloads
and mobile phone ringtones, as well as from their use in commercials,
films, television, computer games, videos, and DVDs, the value of the
ATV Music catalog and its cornerstone Northern Songs songbook that
Jackson bought for $47 million was valued somewhere between $400
and $500 million.

In 2016, Sony acquired the Michael Jackson estate's share in Sony/ATV in a deal valued at around $750 million. A lawsuit filed by Paul McCartney in district court in New York sought to reclaim ownership of his share of the Lennon–McCartney song catalog in 2018 based on US copyright law. McCartney agreed to a confidential settlement with Sony, finally allowing him to recapture the ownership of his songs. Together with Ringo Starr and the estates of John Lennon and George Harrison, he also still had his ownership share in Apple Corps, which in recent years had remastered and re-issued the entire Beatles catalog.

CHAPTER 29

Rebooting Beatlemania in the Digital Age

Joe Rapolla

At 2:30 pm Thursday, April 7, 1966, the Beatles, producer George Martin and engineer Geoff Emerick (all of 20 years old) began work on a session at Studio Three of EMI Recording Studios, 3 Abbey Road, London NW8, honing the first song for the album *Revolver*.[1] Why such a granular level of detail? Because: the next four-plus hours forever changed the history of recorded music.

Recording studios until that point had always been used to document musical performances, and eventually performances with modest over-dubbing. But this afternoon and early evening saw the four Beatles, at least as many studio personnel, and five tape machines enlisted in a here-tofore unattempted feat: feeding five homemade cassette tape loops supplied by Paul McCartney into Studio Three's REDD.51 mixing console.[2] Emerick played the mix board faders like keys on a synthesizer to control the loops (which included a laughing male voice played at double speed to simulate a seagull, and an orchestra playing a B♭ chord – likely "sampled" from a classical record before sampling as a concept existed.)

In an era before computers, this mix could never be reproduced, as George Martin would emphatically contend years later. And for a time, this session put the Beatles ahead of anything digital technology could do.

Eager to pursue such new horizons, they finished their last-ever concert that year at Candlestick Park in San Francisco.

It was 10:00 pm August 29.

Perhaps fifty hours later, on September 1, 1966, American inventor James T. Russell filed for US patent 3,501,586 – his ten-page document describing an "analog to digital to optical recording and playback system."

---

[1] Mark Lewishon, *The Beatles Recording Sessions* (New York: Harmony Books, 1988) 72.
[2] Brian Kehew and Kevin Ryan, *Recording The Beatles* (Houston, TX: Curvebender Publishing, 2006), 412, 431.

Figure 29.1 The Beatles on iTunes (2009). Photograph by Anthony Olszewski

Russell's invention laid the foundation for the compact disc, though his patent would not be awarded until March 17, 1970; oddly enough, less than one month before Paul McCartney announced his split from the Beatles on April 10.

Call those coincidences if you like. But it proves no accident that the Beatles' career would interweave so closely with the development of modern recording technology, and eventually the ascent of digital music technology. In fact, it is no stretch to contend that in the 1960s, they started the ball rolling. On the "Tomorrow Never Knows" sessions alone, they hit three more historic landmarks: the first use of dense fabric (in this case a fan-made sweater) to muffle the kick drum – now standard practice in recording studios across the world; the first-ever backwards guitar solo (played by McCartney); and the first use of a technology called artificial double tracking (ADT), invented for them by EMI studio engineer Ken Townsend. That effect is now also standard in every major studio you can name.

In fact the Beatles were "the first" popular music group in many, many other regards: as stadium headliners, music video stars, record label owners, and holding down all of the Top 5 slots on the *Billboard* Hot 100 – along with numbers 31, 41, and 46 – on April 4, 1964.

Yet the Beatles (and their estates) lagged behind in most regards when it came to releasing their music and content in the digital era. That is right. Late, but certainly not least – and perhaps in a way that in hindsight reveals some clever calculation.

Not that the band was intimidated by technology, as proven by their feats on "Tomorrow Never Knows" (a title concocted by Ringo). Consider their self-styled "proto-synth" mix approach; though the synthesizer had been introduced in the 1960s by Dr. Robert Moog and Don Buchla, it was not commercially used until the 1970s.[3] There as well, the Beatles were steps ahead, using a real synthesizer on a commercial pop song in 1969 – long before their contemporaries – with "Here Comes the Sun."

Still, they took their time entering the digital ecosphere. For a band that was always on the leading edge of sound innovation, the Beatles did not run to digital. To understand the "why," whether intentional on their part or not, requires a closer look at how popular music entered the realm of ones and zeroes.

When CDs Were Fab

After Russell landed his patent, he completed his first operating prototype of an optical disc recorder and playback system in 1973. Independent of each other, Philips and Sony developed more advanced prototypes during the decade, and in 1979 joined forces through a task force of engineers dedicated to honing the technology for consumer use. The very first commercial release came on August 17, 1982, a 1979 recording of Claudio Arrau performing Chopin waltzes.[4] (CDs were standardized to their maximum length of 74 minutes because that was just enough to hold Beethoven's Ninth Symphony on a single disc.)

Philips released the first CD in the pop music realm, ABBA's *The Visitors*, in November 1982.[5]

It would take more than four years for the Beatles' music to arrive on CD in February 1987. That placed them behind countless pop music artists. Why the delay?

[3] George Martin, ed., *Making Music: The Guide to Writing, Performing, & Recording* (London: Frederick Muller, 1983).

[4] "Debut of the Compact Disc," *chonday*, www.chonday.com/16551/decbucdkl3/.

[5] "Sony History: A Great Invention 100 Years On," *Sony*. Archived from the original on August 2, 2008. Retrieved February 28, 2012.

Those present will testify that those first Beatles releases were an event. Like everything associated with the Beatles, the world waited. And the Beatles certainly made it wait – which amplified demand to a fever pitch, a Digital Beatlemania 1.0.

For the Beatles in the early digital age, late had no penalty. Nor has it hurt the group's catalog and subsequent releases in the years since. Simply put, "late" acts naturally as a strategy. In the mid-1980s, "late" sent hordes of Beatles fans back to music stores to rebuy their favorite albums on CD. And the Beatles were just late enough: in a conceptual/verbal twist John Lennon would have no doubt loved, late was in fact perfect timing. With the compact disc format still early in its product cycle – just barely crossing into its growth stage – a ripe and growing mass of CD buyers stood register-ready. With Digital Beatlemania 1.0, fans were ready to bust down record store doors for their band's "debut," some seventeen years after their last official release of new studio material.

Bust them down they did. Highly anticipated like anything Beatles, the discs flew off the shelves when released across seven batches in 1987 and 1988.

For a band whose co-founder died in 1980, this marked a barely comprehensible achievement. And as with so many things the group touched, it reflected a mixture of planning and happenstance, calculation and kismet. At the very least, it mirrored the experiments-turned-happy accidents that marked every stage of their creative output. A radio broad-cast weaved on-the-spot into the mix of "I Am The Walrus" just happens to be a gripping death scene from *King Lear*;[6] the chicken cluck sound effect that finishes "Good Morning, Good Morning" rams via hard edit into a frighteningly identical guitar note; a stray tape fragment of "Her Majesty," accidentally left on the master reel of *Abbey Road*'s side two by tape op engineer John Kurlander, crashes 20 seconds after when the album was supposed to conclude and creates a surprise ending that complements the cut-off of John Lennon's "I Want You (She's So Heavy)," the closer of side one.[7]

And when the Beatles bang out a single chord on acoustic, twelve-string electric and bass guitars – joined by George Martin on a Steinway piano and Ringo Starr hitting a snare drum and cymbal – it creates the unmistak-able opening chord of "A Hard Day's Night." This is arguably the very

---

[6] Kehew and Ryan, *Recording The Beatles*, 466.
[7] Geoff Emerick, *Here, There, and Everywhere: My Life Recording the Music of The Beatles* (New York: Gotham Books, 2006), 291.

condensed essence of Beatlemania, and yet no one quite knows what it is. Academics and music experts have tried to dissect it for years, offering at least fourteen guesses. George Harrison seemed to confirm it was F^{add9} (an F chord with a G note on top) in a 2001 online chat but even he confessed: "You'll have to ask Paul about the bass note to get the proper story."[8]

Now with Digital Beatlemania 1.0, fans got to hear those nuances in sharper sonic detail than ever before.

More Is All You Need

Whether late to the party by design, complexity, or politics, the Beatles could not use any creative sleight of hand to sidestep some of the hurdles that held them up until 1987. The sheer effort to administrate, manage, and exploit a catalog as vast and revered as theirs cannot be exaggerated. Think of a Fab Four times ten: multiple catalog owners, estate managers, record labels, publishing companies and attorneys working together (or not) to forge a path to compromise and agreement.

But in the case of the Beatles – more so than any popular music group or act in history – what looks like delays to those on the inside comes across as a tantalizing holdout to those on the consumer side.

Fast forward to 2019, and what was true thirty-two years ago still applies today: holding out only increases the high level of anticipation by their large-scale, loyal fan base and keeps demand at a frenzied level. So what would kill any consumer electronics company, for example, actually breathes life into the Beatles enterprise: a slow-to-market pace creates more of a business benefit than a drawback.

Not that those CD-hungry fans were universally happy – far from it. The rudimentarily digitized and packaged compact disc sets were met with some level of disenchantment by avid Beatles fans, collectors, and certainly audiophiles. Complaints railed that these reboots amounted to nothing more than the UK albums reformatted onto CD. The blandly packaged releases had not have lived up to the wait, the hype, or a group with a status like the Beatles.

Any other band might have suffered a black eye. Not these guys.

When the Beatles finally released their catalog on CD across 1987 and into 1988 (including *Past Masters Volume 1* and *Volume 2*), they once again owned popular music. Most of the albums re-entered the charts in the Top

[8] "The 'Hard Day's Night' Opening Chord," *Beatles Bible*, www.beatlesbible.com/features/hard-days-night-chord/.

40, and *Sgt. Pepper's Lonely Heart Club* climbed all the way to No. 3. This, some forty years after its original 1967 release and without a single bonus track, outtake or fan-friendly freebie.[9]

Mastering the Art of Remastering

In 1995 and 1996, the Beatles released three double-CD sets as part of their *Anthology* series. For a band that had long sworn that the studio material it released as a working unit was all that would ever see the light of day, the *Anthology* sets marked a 180-degree turn. Remarkably, the surviving band members dubbed on top of two Lennon demos to produce the first new Beatles songs in a quarter-century: "Free As A Bird" and "Real Love." Even the heavy-handed production of Jeff Lynne on these tracks (which some mocked as "BLO," a pun on Lynne's ELO, or Electric Light Orchestra) could not hold back the tears and elation from fans deprived of an in-the-flesh reunion.

Meanwhile, the Beatles tape vault transmogrified into a mother lode for outtake-hungry fans and the band's bottom line. (Even Pete Best, the drummer the Beatles fired on the eve of conquering the world, may have earned as much £4 million ($10 million in today's money) for his appearances on the *Anthology 1* tracks recorded at a Decca Records audition on New Year's Day 1962.)[10]

The public's appetite had already been whetted the year before with the release of the double-CD *Live at the BBC*. Though it peaked only at No. 3 on the *Billboard* charts – great for any other artist but perhaps a disappointment in the eyes of Beatlemaniacs – it also went quadruple platinum, selling more than 2 million units.

Anthology and the ABC-TV documentaries that accompanied it were hailed as well-conceived, well-produced retrospectives of the iconic band's journey. Whatever gaffes may have accompanied those 1987–88 releases were now beyond forgiven. And instead of fading with each passing generation, the fame and acclaim only grew. So too, remarkably, would the statistics as the band doubled and tripled down on its new-found strategy of releasing cuts that perhaps only the band's intimates and obsessed bootleg collectors had ever heard – or in some cases, never heard.

---

[9] Kenneth Womack, *The Beatles Encyclopedia: Everything Fab Four, Volume 1* (Santa Barbara, CA: Greenwood, 2014).

[10] "Pete Best," *Beatles Bible*, www.beatlesbible.com/people/pete-best/3/.

This was followed by the remarkably successful *1*. This compilation of No. 1 hit singles from the USA and UK, released in 2000, lived up to its cocky moniker: it soared to the top of the charts and became the best-selling album from 2000 to 2010, topping charts in thirty-five countries and going on to sell more than 31 million copies worldwide.[11]

And in September 2009 – cleverly on 09/09/09 – the Beatles whipped up a perfect storm of simultaneous digital releases, including a remastered box set available in mono and stereo. This catalog re-release included remastered audio, new liner notes, rare photos and embedded digital content on an included Enhanced CD. Knowing how much the first set of discs disappointed, the ad for this set directly gave a nod (and a Liverpudlian wink) to those 1987 releases.

Game Over, before It Started

But there was more. That same day, the *Beatles Rock Band* was released – painstakingly curated and crafted by Giles Martin, son of Beatles' producer George Martin. It allowed gamers of every age to play faux instruments along with forty-five Beatles tracks, interlinked with behind-the-scenes studio banter. This highly interactive, multimedia platform release introduced a whole new and different audience to their music. It was also precisely prescient. Many big bands of that time had just begun to realize that kids were discovering much of the music they loved via gaming as opposed to radio or video.

And after a protracted legal dispute and settlement, the Beatles released their music on iTunes on November 16, 2010. With Apple using a late-era, black-and-white Beatles photo against a stark white background – in sync with the company's minimalist aesthetic – the promotional synergy of two titanic brands proved nothing less than "yeah, yeah, yeah" to the 100th power.

According to Apple, more than 450,000 albums and 2 million individual songs were sold on iTunes worldwide during the first week of the Beatles' catalog release.[12]

Enter Digital Beatlemania 2.0.

[11] "The Beatles 1", Amazon.com editorial review, September 13, 2011, www.amazon.com/Beatles-1/dp/B0058HDHAK.
[12] Billboard Staff, "Beatles Sell 2 Million Songs in First Week on iTunes," November 23, 2010, www.billboard.com/articles/news/950355/beatles-sell-2-million-songs-in-first-week-on-itunes.

The Beatles and the Vinyl Revival

Still, younger generations must have tired of hearing their elders repeat it: nothing could match holding and owning a Beatles album on vinyl. Even the printed labels had an aura of magic to them; first the black Capitol Records label with its silver logo and rainbow circle. It had so enthralled a young Doug Fieger that when his band released the 1979 *Get The Knack* (known for the classic hit "My Sharona"), he requested that Capitol use that long-mothballed design.

Later, the Beatles treated the vinyl label as nothing less than another canvas for their creativity. When Apple Records bowed in 1968, the green Granny Smith apple – whole on side one, split in half on side two – was like nothing that came before it. As the Beatles went their separate ways, they would take turns being cheeky, making the apple orange (George), white (John), blue (Ringo) or sometimes non-existent (Paul).

Vinyl also represented a much more deliberate way to consume music. When you heard a song you liked on the radio, you likely needed repeated listens before you committed to buy. Then you could play it anytime you wanted, on demand! It was a deliberative decision marked by physical rituals.

In the 1990s, "ripping" meant the digital assembly of tracks onto a CD compilation of your own making. Up until a decade before, it could only mean tearing off the shrink wrap once you got your new long-player home. You reached inside the cardboard cover and carefully allowed the vinyl disc to slide from its inner sleeve and into your outstretched hand, carefully straddling the disc edge and record label between your thumb and middle finger. You lowered it onto the turn-table, dropped the needle and listened as a few warm crackles teased the aural bliss of that first track.

For all the time this took (an eternity by Gen Z standards), it dwarfed the commitment to earn the needed discretionary funds: close to five hours of pay for the average teenager.[13]

It was wonderful. Interactive. And, often communal, experienced via living room stereos and in the company of family and friends. Downloading or streaming a track is an isolated event; breaking open the latest Beatles single was for many high school students in the 1960s a rite of

---

[13] "History of Federal Minimum Wage Rates Under the Fair Labor Standards Act, 1938–2009," *US Department of Labor*, www.dol.gov/whd/minwage/chart.htm.

passage – never done alone if you wanted to experience an extra jolt of shared joy.

After decades of decline, vinyl is now enjoying a healthy resurgence. Vinyl album sales in the USA hit their thirteenth consecutive year of growth, and the Beatles are contributing to that growth, according to *Billboard*. Vinyl LP sales accounted for 11.9 percent of all album sales in 2018, almost double the percentage of just one year prior. And in 2018, the Beatles were the top-selling act on vinyl at 321,000 copies spanning their catalog. Their biggest seller, *Abbey Road*, finished 2018 as the fourth largest-seller with 76,000 copies. The Fab Four also have two more titles among the year's Top 15: their self-titled *The White Album* is No. 11 (56,000 units) and *Sgt. Pepper's Lonely Hearts Club Band* is No. 13 (50,000 units).[14]

I'm Only Streaming

Vinyl of course demands a quite different effort and process than what many listeners use to find and consume music today. In 2018 and for the most part the decade previous, music fans have the vast and essentially complete, universal catalog of music at their fingertips: the proverbial "celestial jukebox."

Streaming has forever changed how we discover and listen to music. Curated playlists and computer-driven algorithms (which emerged in nascent form through Pandora in the mid-2000s)[15] assist in aligning the listeners' tastes with songs and artists they will have a high propensity to like. Calling up songs takes no more than a few clicks on a keyboard or smartphone screen. Instantly, any song in most any version is served up on demand via a handful of competing digital platforms.

This technology has also enabled the Beatles find and win new fans. As "digital natives" who have never known life without computers, the Internet and mobile, the current generation discovers and experiences the Beatles in an entirely different way: song by song, sorted by their streamed popularity. Search for Beatles songs on Spotify and you will see "Here Comes The Sun" on top. The opening track of side two on their second-to-last album, *Abbey Road*, "Sun" was not the first song most Beatles listeners came across before the digital age.

New fans are discovering the Beatles – in their own way.

---

[14] Keith Caulfield, "U.S. Vinyl Album Sales Grew 15% in 2018, Led by the Beatles, Pink Floyd, David Bowie & Panic! at the Disco," *Billboard*, January 12, 2019, www.billboard.com/articles/columns/chart-beat/8493256/vinyl-album-sales-growth-2018-beatles-david-bowie-pink-floyd.

[15] Lou Carlozo, "Opening Pandora's Box," *Chicago Tribune*, April 23, 2006.

Would-Be Beatles

Larry Mattera, general manager at Warner Brothers Records, took the digital playlist concept to the next level of Beatles imagination. He created what he thinks would have been the next Beatles record post-1970, collecting some of the better Beatles solo songs released soon after the break-up of the band. These include "Photograph" and "It Don't Come Easy" (Ringo); "My Love," "Jet," and "Band On The Run" (Paul); and of course many more from George and John.

As Mattera puts it:

> [When the band was together] you had the music coming in from three guys. Think about why those albums were so great. Part of it was because you had three incredibly strong songwriters. When you get to the Beatles' solo careers, those albums don't stand up as much as The Beatles work, for a lot of reasons. But some of it is that there's definitely more filler on the solo albums, because you don't have the unit that's only bringing the A-list songs.
>
> The way the idea manifested itself for me was when they went onto Spotify. I'd been thinking about this for years and I finally had a chance to do it. Think about the songs that came out in 1971, 1972, 1973 and 1974, post-break-up. The album they created would have been songs from those years, written by the three of them. [As noted above, Mattera also includes some of Starr's compositions.][16]

For being a band that stopped making music as a group five years before the first personal computer was available, the Beatles have mastered the digital age and continue to leverage the spectrum of technology to support and sell their art.

The Beatles have more than 2.6 million YouTube subscribers on the band's official channel. There are of course many other Beatles channels on YouTube, which is the most popular streaming platform with about 2 billion active monthly users and more than 1 billion hours watched daily. One-third of YouTube users are between 18 and 34 and in an average month, eight out of ten 18-to-49 year olds watch YouTube.[17]

Paul McCartney may be closing in on 80, but that has not stopped him from embracing all of the opportunities that exist in the digital ecosystem today, especially to connect with his fans. Leading up to the release of

---

[16] Larry Mattera, general manager, Warner Brothers Records, Burbank, CA, in discussion with the author, February 2019.

[17] Celie O'Neil-Hart and Howard Blumenstein, "The Latest Video Trends: Where Your Audience is Watching," Video, Consumer Insights, *Think with Google*, April 2016, www.thinkwithgoogle.com/consumer-insights/video-trends-where-audience-watching.

Paul's most recent album, *Egypt*, in 2018, the McCartney team made sure the record was everywhere – not just on Egypt or Planet Earth but in the cyberverse as well. Paul takes full advantage of the digital sphere to connect with today's fans while his team makes sure there is a constant stream of fun, interesting content and updates to keep friends, followers, and registrants engaged.

The viral shot across the bow came when McCartney appeared with James Corden on *Carpool Karaoke*. Sir Paul, like many artists and celebrities before him, jumped in a car with Corden for some cheeky conversation before launching into a lively karaoke 2.0 version of Beatles' songs. In Paul's case, they reminisced while driving through the streets of Liverpool – including a visit to his childhood home – and capped the event with Paul playing at a local pub, acting as a "human jukebox" whenever a customer thought they were requesting a prerecorded Beatles song.

The 24-minute episode took on a life of its own. It has 39.3 million views to date. McCartney, ever the showman, gets how YouTube boasts the ability to go beyond original broadcast TV. Its thousands of channels and constant live feeds wait to be called up, on-demand, by millions of viewers, readers, and listeners. Paul's fun, reminiscent *Carpool Karaoke* piece reached half as many eyeballs as the Beatles debut appearance on the Ed Sullivan show way back in 1964. In 1964 there were three broadcast networks. So reaching a concentrated audience was not quite the challenge it is today.

Yet it did not just "happen," even for a Beatle. Paul has 3.9 million Twitter followers and 6.9 million on Facebook. You can even receive an occasional email from Sir Paul himself. It may be about an upcoming event, tour or release, or a seemingly personal greeting. Of course, it is nothing like the Christmas cards the boys sent out between 1963 and 1969 to a few thousand fans. But here is a nice stocking stuffer: December 2017 saw the release of a limited box set that contained their Christmas holiday messages, first sent exclusively to fan club members.

Turn Off Your Mind, Relax and Float on Stream

Another holiday gift came on December 24, 2015, when the Beatles finally made their music available on major streaming music services such as Spotify, Apple Music, and TIDAL. To differentiate itself from the other digital streaming platforms offering the Beatles music, TIDAL – the lossless audio streaming service – assembled a true multimedia, interactive experience that included timelines, interactive graphics, and interview clips with band members telling backstories and insider tales.[18] This original offering saw the Beatles once again accomplish another first, seven years after the launch of the most popular music service, Spotify, and fourteen after the first music streaming service Rhapsody, currently known as Napster.

Once again, being late had major benefits. Among them: this open avenue to Digital Beatlemania 3.0.

"In seven short years, the Beatles created a body of work that changed the world", said Spotify's Daniel Ek. He wrote in his blog on December 28, 2015:

> In the first three days since THE BEATLES landed on Spotify, fans have streamed more than 70 million songs. What's even cooler is that over 65% of their listeners on Spotify are under the age of 34, so we're helping introduce a new generation of fans to the most important band in history.
>
> Think about it. The Beatles have remained the most listened-to and influential artists for almost 60 years, and almost half a century after their last release as a group.

Given their embrace of the digital ecosystem and steadfast commitment to leverage the utilization of digital activities, the Beatles have maintained the attention of their original and long-term fans, and continue to accumulate new ones.

And with streaming firmly planted as the primary mechanism for music consumption, the Beatles stand well positioned to demonstrate their ongoing dominance.

In 2018, Spotify hit 96 million paying subscribers and reported its first-ever profitable quarter. Spotify has 180 million active monthly listeners in sixty-five countries, with all age groups fairly represented and 55 percent between the ages of 18 and 34.

There, the Beatles average 17,060,300 monthly listens. To date, they have surpassed 4 billion streams on digital channels. These numbers do not lie. As legacy recording artists, the Beatles are unparalleled in the digital ecosphere: still selling records (or "album equivalents" as they are calculated today) at charting speed. They outsell most current artists and top the list of any legacy artist. On average the Beatles sell approximately 32,000 album equivalents *per week* across digital platforms, according to Nielsen Music Connect.

---

[18] Chris O'Brien, "For Real Beatles Fans, Tidal Offers the Best Multimedia Experience and Sound," *Venture Beat*, December 24, 2015, https://venturebeat.com/2015/12/24/for-real-beatles-tidal-offers-the-best-multimedia-experience-and-richest-sound/.

Think of any other legendary act who has not released an album in decades – Elvis Presley, Frank Sinatra, Led Zeppelin – or even those who have, such as the Rolling Stones. Who is even close from a numbers perspective?

The Rolling Stones sell about 14,000 album equivalents per week. The Eagles, Fleetwood Mac, and the Beach Boys combined can barely match the sales penetration. Ariana Grande, an artist who just this week rivaled the Beatles with simultaneous No. 1, 2, and 3 positions on the *Billboard* Hot 100, averages 80,000 album equivalencies per week.

Though Beatles' catalog did not make it onto Spotify until 2015, their numbers already put them neck and neck with pop's current top artists who were on the platform since its launch.

As Ben Kline, head of digital strategy and streaming at Warner Music Nashville puts it:

> There's the Beatles and there's everyone else. The Rolling Stones have to work at it. The Beatles are The Beatles – they are so important. Every generation's artists cite them as influences and they're really good at preserving their brand. They probably have to utilize social media and the like less than any other artist. The numbers tell us that they are being consumed like the iconic important musicians that they are.[19]

The digital era created opportunities that the Beatles and Apple Corps masterfully capitalized on. Sales? Listens? Likes? Absolutely. By the millions. Billions. But the digital era also helped lock their status in popular music history beyond any chance of their fading from view.

Apple Corps CEO Jeff Jones had this to say at a panel discussion on the release of "Eight Days A Week" at the University of New Haven on September 23, 2016:

> I think it's hard in today's fragmented media society that we live in, for one group to have that kind of impact. If you just take the [Ed] Sullivan example, 73, 74 million people watched them at the same time. I don't think that's possible in today's media world. I don't think it's possible for one group to dominate the attention span of that many people because there's so many choices.[20]

[19] Ben Kline, SVP, Global Revenue & Touring, Warner Music, Nashville, TN, in discussion with the author, February 2019.
[20] Jeff Jones, CEO, Apple Corps, Ltd, "Jeff Jones, CEO of Apple Corps Ltd, Talks about Whether There Ever Will Be another 'Beatles' at @UNH," *YouTube*, www.youtube.com/watch?v=AwbZ2ggMmf8.

Hot 100 Years from Now

The Beatles have been getting it done for almost six decades. The Beatles still earn in a digital era. They are still rank No. 1 on the *Billboard* Hot 100's Top Artists of All Time. The Greatest of All-Time 60th Anniversary *Billboard* Hot 100 Songs and Artists rankings are based on weekly performance on the Hot 100 from its inception on August 4, 1958, through July 21, 2018.[21]

The Beatles have remained the most consumed and studied band since they released their first single in 1962. But just as John, Paul, George, and Ringo did from that time forward, the band's team continues to search for ways to exploit new channels for promotion and distribution: digital channels unimaginable when the foursome were together.

Even academia has been touched in the era of Digital Beatlemania 3.0.

John Covach, professor of music and director at the Institute for Popular Music, University of Rochester, said more than 20,000 people have registered for his next course on the Beatles:

> It's incredible how people can't get enough of them. The first time I taught my Music of the Beatles class online for Coursera in early 2014, the enrollment topped 40,000 students worldwide. In the time since the MOOC boom, the course has attracted tens of thousands of additional students, probably topping 100,000 over the last five years. My total enrollment for all of my online rock courses is about 350,000.
>
> Coursera went to an on-demand format some time back, but we still get more than 1000 new students in the Beatles class a year. None of this would have happened without the dramatic advances in digital technology we've seen over the years.[22]

We'll end our exploration by returning to EMI Studios (now known as Abbey Road Studios) one last time. It is easy to forget that in the 1960s, EMI's engineers wore lab coats. Microphones and outboard gear were watched with military fervor for any signs of misuse. Everyone knew the rules. Except for – well, you know by now.

It is said that on one day of sessions, the band inquired as to why they could not get more high-end EQ onto one of their tracks. They were told, politely, that the board's channel had reached its limit. To which they

---

[21] Billboard Staff, "HOT 100 TURNS 60: The Hot 100's Top Artists of All Time," *Billboard*, August 2, 2018, www.billboard.com/articles/news/hot-100-turns-60/8468147/hot-100-top-artists-all-time-list.

[22] Mark Koba, "Beatles Business: Still Making Money, 50 Years On," *CNBC*, February 7, 2014, www.cnbc.com/2014/01/24/beatles-business-still-making-money-50-years-on.html.

replied something to the effect of, "Why can't you just take the signal from that fader and move it onto the next fader? We want more."

By 1968, they got their wish. To make his guitar distort on "Revolution" like no one had attempted before, Lennon's signal was fed directly into one channel of a REDD.47 mixing console, its gain turned up to distort. Emerick then took that signal, fed it into another channel, and turned that one way up: as he recalled, "the maximum amount of overload the board could take without bursting into flames."[23]

Emerick feared it that if caught, he would be fired. To make matters worse, a pissed-off Lennon was tearing into him as he desperately tried to dial in the sound John wanted. The resulting tone was so dark and angry, many record buyers returned their discs, assuming they were defective.

For fifty-plus years guitar players have chased that sound – a grail full of flaming sludge – in hopes of matching it, to no avail.

Emerick: "This ended up being precisely the guitar sound every grunge band in the world aspired to."[24]

Another Beatles engineer, Ken Scott, would go on to produce David Bowie and Supertramp but never reproduce the third-degree burn of "Revolution's" guitar: "I've tried since to recreate the sound and you just don't get even close."[25] "Revolution," which peaked at No. 12 in the USA, was just the B-side of the band's first single on their own Apple Records in 1968. The A-side? "Hey Jude": at the time, the longest song ever to hit No. 1 and the longest stay in that slot for any Beatles song (nine weeks). As for longer still: who knows how much the Beatles will out-sing, out-sell, out-stream, and outhustle the competition for the next fifty years, during which time all four members will have passed away? Surely, in musical formats known and still unknown, they will continue to live and cannot be out loved.

---

[23] Emerick, *Here, There and Everywhere*, 253.   [24] Emerick, *Here, There and Everywhere*, 253.
[25] Kehew and Ryan, *Recording The Beatles*, 485.

CHAPTER 30

The Beatles in the New Millennium

Michael R. Frontani

In the twenty-first century, the Beatles are the focus of thousands of books and analyses and, fittingly, the subject of an every-growing body of college and university curricula. Liverpool Hope University has offered an MA degree in "The Beatles, Popular Music & Society," which graduated its first student in 2011.[1] Even a cursory search of the web presents scores of courses and syllabi from across the globe. The wealth of courses and interest in such courses has prompted countless academic presentations and publications concerned specifically with the Beatles and pedagogy.[2] This is not surprising. The Beatles have long been the subject of serious music scholars, and the band's interaction with nearly every aspect of 1960s culture makes them an ideal entry point into that decade. Their imprint is easily read into nearly every field and discipline of the arts, humanities, and social sciences, and the technical aspects of their recordings and cinematic presentation make them suitable for scientific and technical investigation.

Still, the Beatles are more than a historical or academic artifact and, despite the temporal distance between now and the 1960s, they have remained a commercial force, releasing a daunting amount of material to generally good, even ecstatic, response from fans and critics, alike. The Beatles continue to sell music, and they continue to be attached to well-regarded films, and – most radically – they continue to *be*. That is, their "image" thrives and evolves, as always linking the band's present to its past. With the *Anthology* project, the surviving Beatles' assembled behind a united effort to construct an image they intended to support the future commercial and creative viability of the Beatles entity. To that end, the image has since been mobilized in at least two significant ways, one

---

[1] Valerie Strauss, "A Master's Degree on the Beatles – Really," *Washington Post*, February 6, 2014, www.washingtonpost.com/news/answer-sheet/wp/2014/02/06/a-masters-degree-on-the-beatles-re ally/?utm_term=.a1847ib66170.

[2] For a recent collection of various approaches from across the Arts & Sciences, see Paul O. Jenkins and Hugh Jenkins, eds., *Teaching the Beatles* (New York: Routledge, 2018).

predicated on the Beatles' singular artistic achievement and critical reception during the *Pepper* period and afterwards, and the other based on the rapturous affirmation of life embodied in the "Fab Four" image of 1964–66, and carried forward in the communal spirit of the counterculture and youth culture. This chapter explores the considerable presence that the Beatles' past continues to enjoy in twenty-first-century culture and music, as the band gathers new generations of fans through the landmark release of the band's *1* album, Cirque du Soleil's *Love*, and the *Rock Band* video game, among other media inroads.

The Beatles' Image, 1995, 1963, and 1967

The *Beatles Anthology* project (1995) brought together the Beatles' inner circle, including Lennon (via archival audio and video materials), Harrison, McCartney, Starr, Brian Epstein (archival materials), George Martin, Derek Taylor, and Neil Aspinall, to present their perspective on the band's history and accomplishments, and, for the first time since the 1960s, the Beatles (with Yoko Ono, in Lennon's stead) actively and jointly participated in the construction of their image. At the end of the *Anthology* documentary, McCartney commented on the band's legacy in remarks undoubtedly found suitable by all. "I'm really glad that most of the songs dealt with love, peace, understanding," he said, and added, "It's all very 'All You Need is Love' or John's 'Give Peace a Chance'. There was a good spirit behind it all, which I'm very proud of."[3] Largely absent from the *Anthology* project are the strife within the band that led to its break-up, the tales of infighting, drug excess, and neuroses, or the tensions arising from Yoko Ono's arrival, all of which were publicized in numerous books, magazine articles, and television interviews, particularly since Lennon's death, in 1980.

The literature on star image is voluminous and nuanced, but, for our purpose, suffice it to say that an image coalesces out of all that is publicly known of a star, and that this mass-mediated construction of the star, to quote Dyer, "encourages us to think in terms of 'really.' What is [the star] really like?"[4] The image, then, is a contested ground encompassing what is promoted by a star and their handlers, on one hand, and, on the other, information published as a part of journalistic and critical assessment, in

[3] The Beatles, *The Beatles Anthology* (San Francisco: Chronicle Books, 2000), 357; see also, The Beatles, *The Beatles Anthology*, eight episodes, 1995 (Apple Corps, 2003), DVD.
[4] Richard Dyer, *Heavenly Bodies: Film Stars and Society*, 2nd edn (New York: Routledge, 2004), 2.

newspapers, broadcasts, and so on. Space precludes an exhaustive discussion of the Beatles' image in the 1960s but it is useful for our purposes to briefly consider some key elements and their context. Of particular interest are the constellations of ideas threading through the image at two critical points in the Beatles' progress: the first is the teen idol-inflected image introduced to Americans in early 1964 and dominant throughout the years of touring and Beatlemania (1964–66); the second is the countercultural, "flower power" image revealed in 1967.

The teen idol-inflected image came together in the UK in promotion of the Beatles in the fall of 1963, and was honed to commercial perfection in Capitol Records' promotion of the band in early 1964, in the lead-up to the Beatles' first visit to the USA and their historic performance on the *Ed Sullivan Show*, on February 9, 1964. Capitol's promotion of the Beatles shed much of the uniquely British aspects of the image[5] in favor of a more broadly appealing construct. It focused upon the Beatles' commercial success; their talent, particularly that of the songwriters, Lennon and McCartney; their youth and cheekiness; their unique sound and appearance, particularly their hairstyle; the individuality of each Beatle; their broad appeal; and, above all else, the frenzied ardor of young, primarily female fans, that is, "Beatlemania." These elements dominated the image throughout the touring years, which ended with the last show of the American tour in late August 1966.

With the release of *Sgt. Pepper's Lonely Hearts Club Band* (June 1967), the Beatles' image incorporated notions of the band's unrivaled commercial success with notions of their artistic importance and centrality to contemporary popular music and the youth culture, particularly the counterculture. At the height of "flower power," in 1967 and 1968, the Beatles were held up as countercultural ideals, hippies pointing the way to a better way of being as humans, whether as part of the LSD-laced culture of "flower children" or, later, as ambassadors for Transcendental Meditation, specifically, and self-improvement, generally. Additionally, the mass-mediated critical response to *Pepper* accorded them unequaled artistic and cultural status that they continued to the end of the decade and beyond. In the twenty-first century, the Beatles' image has evolved to encapsulate both the ebullient youth and joy of the days of Beatlemania and their unequaled artistic achievement and centrality within the youth culture.

---

[5] For instance, the Beatles' Northern English working-class identity and Liverpool roots, including the rave culture from which the Beatles emerged, held implications for the image in Britain that were not present or of interest in the US promotion of the band.

Reissues, Remasters, and Archival Releases

In retrospect, one can push the start of the Beatles' grand re-imagining of
the image back a full year before the *Anthology* broadcast to the release of
the compilation double-CD collection, *Live at the Beeb* (Apple, 1994). The
set, which contained performances on numerous BBC Light Programme
shows between 1963 and 1965, rose to the top of the charts on both sides of
the Atlantic. *Rolling Stone*'s Anthony DeCurtis opined, "[I]nnocence floats
by again – unmistakably, ephemerally, too late and not a moment too
soon"[6] and Jon Savage, in a review appearing in *MOJO*, wrote that the
early records of the Beatles, "who epitomized the youth principle in
Western society," retained "an innocent and first-time energy which still
makes them fresh. It will lift your spirits . . . *Live At The BBC* returns The
Beatles to the beginning, from where their scarcely believable story can be
retold yet one more time."[7] And so it has been ever since.

Archival materials and remasters continue to be released with some
regularity in the twenty-first century, serving to keep older recordings in
circulation and, just as importantly, allowing the works to be redefined on
terms set by the Beatles. In November 2000, thirty years after their break-
up, the Beatles released *1* (Apple/Parlophone, Capitol), a collection of
remastered No. 1 hits put out between 1962 and 1970 in the UK and
USA. "'The Beatles are still saving the industry's ass',"[8] quipped one
retailer as the album quickly sold 18,000,000 units before, ultimately,
becoming the best-selling album of the decade (2000–09), according to
Nielsen SoundScan,[9] and one of the top-selling albums of the new
millennium.

Emblematic of the Beatles' incorporation of the digital realm into their
enterprise, the initial promotion of the album included video, games, and
activities on the Beatles' web portal, Beatles.com. A remixed version of the
album, *1+*, was released in 2015 and benefited from the services of George
Martin's son, Giles Martin, who effectively took over his father's role as
producer and keeper of the music following their collaboration on the *Love*
project. *Let It Be . . . Naked* (2003), reimagined the "Get Back" project

---

[6] Anthony DeCurtis, "Live at the BBC", album review, *Rolling Stone*, January 26, 1995, www.roll
ingstone.com/music/music-album-reviews/live-at-the-bbc-252205/.

[7] Jon Savage, "The Beatles: *Live At The BBC*", *MOJO*, January 1995, www.rocksbackpages.com/Libr
ary/Article/the-beatles-ilive-at-the-bbci.

[8] Peter Doggett, *You Never Give Me Your Money: The Beatles After the Breakup* (New York: Harper,
2009), 344.

[9] People Staff, "Top Ten", *People*, December 28, 2009, https://people.com/archive/top-ten-vol-72-no-
26/.

without Phil Spector's production and, so, is an alternative and preferred mix of the 1970 album. It was followed by *The Capitol Albums, Volumes 1 & 2* (2004 and 2006, respectively), which gathered together all of Capitol Record's pre-*Sgt. Pepper* albums, which carried different track listings from the British albums.

In 2009, the Beatles released a remastered British catalog, available as single albums and in monophonic and stereo box sets augmented by video essays. This was followed by the release of vinyl versions, also available in a box set, in 2012. *On Air – Live at the BBC Volume 2* was released in 2013, as was *Beatles Bootleg Recordings 1963*, a collection of fifty-nine unreleased recordings initially available exclusively on iTunes that allowed for the extension of the copyright of those recordings under European Union law. *The Beatles at the Hollywood Bowl* (remaster of the 1977 album) was released in September 2016 to coincide with release of the documentary *Eight Days a Week* (Apple Corps/Imagine, 2016), and was another hit in the UK and USA. *Sgt. Pepper's Lonely Hearts Club Band* fiftieth anniversary release was the top-selling vinyl album of the year in 2017[10] and a critical triumph, as was *The Beatles (The White Album)* fiftieth anniversary reissue, released in 2018.

These last two albums were released in deluxe packaging that provided remasters and remixes of the monophonic and stereophonic original albums, outtakes, and other archival material, as well as books detailing the reminiscences of the band, the production of the album, and original critical reception for the works. Releases of such vast amounts of material indicate the degree to which the surviving Beatles and Beatle families intended that the projects be given their historical due, and critics accepted them on those terms. The *Financial Times* blurb contained in the promotion of *Pepper* notes, "The Super Deluxe version of the new edition takes pop archaeology to new levels."[11] *Rolling Stone, MOJO, The Guardian*, and others gave the package five stars. *Entertainment Weekly* called it an "unprecedented look at the making of a masterpiece," and, the quote from *Forbes* judges the album "arguably the greatest rock album of all time. Fifty years later it is still inspiring me."[12] The advertising for the *The Beatles* (i.e., *The White Album*) indicates a similar concern with establishing

[10] Nielsen SoundScan, "2017 U.S. Music Year-End-Report," *Nielsen*, January 3, 2018, www.nielsen.com/us/en/insights/reports/2018/2017-music-us-year-end-report.html.
[11] "It's here – Sgt. Pepper's Lonely Hearts Club Band Anniversary Edition is out now", *The Beatles*, www.thebeatles.com/news/it%E2%80%99s-here-sgt-pepper%E2%80%99s-lonely-hearts-club-band-anniversary-edition-out-now.
[12] "It's here," *The Beatles*.

the preeminence of the band and the album.[13] Critical acclaim is splashed across one advertisement. Five star reviews from *Mojo*, *Q magazine*, *The Mirror*, *The Times*, *Rolling Stone*, among others, are joined by other rave reviews: "The Beatles' sprawling masterpiece" (*Newsweek*); "sprawling oddness, vulnerability, wit and daring" (*Record Collector*); and, "astonishing" (*People*). Significantly, the *New York Times* declares, "hours of previously unreleased tapes reveal a band patiently and often jovially working together," and *Q magazine* writes, "Thrillingly raw ... The Beatles were clearly having a ball here." The focus upon the band's togetherness reflects how the Beatles and their legacy are being repositioned for new audiences – *The White Album* has long been described as one rife with tension, with group dynamics breaking down and each Beatle pursuing his own interests and leading his own sessions. Starr famously left the band, briefly. Yet, with the release of the fiftieth anniversary album, the alienation and tension that marked the popular narrative of the album are jettisoned in favor of one promoting an opposite characterization of the album's recording, one in which the Beatles' story is allowed to proceed in happiness rather than rancor. In the cases of *Pepper* and *The Beatles*, then, the Beatles have taken effort to re-establish the band's 1960s bona fides but also to reframe an important period in their history.

New Fields, New Audiences

In the last year of his life, though gravely ill, George Harrison began discussions with his friend, and a founder of Cirque de Soleil, Guy Laliberté, about a possible Beatle-inspired production. After three years of further negotiations between the surviving Beatles, the Beatle widows, Apple Corps Ltd, Cirque du Soleil, and the MGM Mirage, and two years of production, *The Beatles Love* premiered to great popular and critical acclaim in June 2006, in the theater constructed especially for it, and continues its run to this day. The *Love* album, a soundtrack to the Cirque du Soleil production, was also released to critical plaudits. As the *Love* project suggests, the Beatles were exploring success in areas that would extend their appeal and provide another avenue for Beatle projects. In 2009, in the midst of the reissue of the Beatles' catalog, a Beatles edition of the video game *Rock Band* was

---

[13] "Out Now: The Beatles White Album," *The Beatles*, www.thebeatles.com/news/out-now-beatles-white-album-50th-anniversary-editions.

released to brisk sales[14] and generally positive reviews. An ever-cautious Apple Corps allowed the project to proceed after urging from George Harrison's son, Dhani, who rightly argued that the game provided a platform to court younger fans and position the band with a new generation of listeners that was not even born when Lennon was murdered, in 1980.[15] The trailer[16] for the game debuted at the Electronic Entertainment Expo (E3), 2009, and featured gameplay and a chronological journey through the Beatles' past, in song and place: from the Cavern Club in Liverpool, circa 1963, where the Beatles play "I Saw Her Standing There," to the *Sullivan Show* and "I Want to Hold Your Hand," then Shea Stadium and "I Feel Fine," and so forth through the Beatles' history. The 2:37 minute spot ends with "Get Back" on the Apple rooftop, and Lennon jokingly pleading, "I'd like to say thank you on behalf ... ". Another trailer for the game featured "Come Together." The chorus chimes in as virtual Beatles cross Abbey Road and are photographed for the famous album cover. The Beatles' presence sparks a sudden street party as people of all stripes gather on the zebra crossing and join John, Paul, George, and Ringo in a spontaneous celebration of community. A voice with a British accent rings in, and script urges, "Meet the Beatles, rock the world," then, "09/09/09" (i.e., release date).[17]

As with any modern entertainment entity, the Beatles' have a broad footprint in contemporary social media, including official pages on Facebook, Instagram, Twitter, and these have been utilized to promote interest in the band's past and, above all else, current Beatles projects and releases. The Beatles are also heavily involved in music streaming and other modes of finding listeners on their preferred platforms. Beatles' music streams over various services, including Spotify, Pandora, and iTunes, and Sirius XM radio debuted a Beatles station in 2017. As to iTunes, finally, in 2010, after years of negotiations between Apple Corps and Apple, the Beatles' catalog was finally

---

[14] See Chris Remo, "MTV Games: We Outsold [Guitar Hero] Two to One", *Gamasutra*, October 19, 2009, www.gamasutra.com/php-bin/news_index.php?story=25708; and Brendan Sinclair, "Beatles: Rock Band Outsold Guitar Hero 5 – Analysts", *Gamespot*, October 8, 2009, www.gamespot.com/news/6232261.html.

[15] Peter Doggett, *You Never Give Me Your Money: The Beatles After the Breakup* (New York:It Books, 2011), 349.

[16] "The Beatles: Rock Band Trailer—E3 2009," *YouTube*, www.youtube.com/watch?v=NFgEmu9ARVA.

[17] "The Beatles: Rock Band Commercial Spot", *YouTube*, August 28, 2009, www.youtube.com/watch?v=c-qt5szlQ_U.

made available on the streaming service. Indicative of the import placed on this relationship are the promotional materials released by each side. For example, one Apple iTunes commercial focused on the record, "Let It Be,"[18] and featured black and white photos of the band, then, white letters on a black field, "The band that changed everything" followed by "Now on iTunes." For Apple, this is a marriage of giants.

The Beatles put its relationship with iTunes to work in service of ongoing efforts to position the Beatles for new generations. The Beatles' commercial, "The Beatles on iTunes,"[19] offers a smart audio and visual collage that manages to incorporate a great deal of Beatle music and Beatles-authorized video and audio releases in a cascade through the Beatles' history and catalog. It starts with a short sound collage of the orchestra tuning and poised to open *Sgt. Pepper's Lonely Hearts Club Band*. This dissolves into the sound of screaming fans and chants of "We want the Beatles – We want the Beatles," and a snippet of Ed Sullivan's introduction of the band at Shea Stadium. Suddenly, Ringo's drumming leads the band into "She Loves You" over a montage that intercuts segments of the opening sequence of *A Hard Day's Night*, in which the band is chased down the street (toward the camera) and into "Liverpool Lime Street Station" (actually, Marylebone Station), with footage of frenzied fans and shots of the band. This segues into footage of Ed Sullivan's introduction of the Beatles for their historic first appearance on the *Ed Sullivan Show*, "Ladies and gentlemen, the Beatles!," and a quick shot of his erupting studio audience brings in the opening vocals of "I Want to Hold Your Hand," which play over quick cuts of footage of the band and their frenzied fans during the historic first visit to America, in February 1964 (from the Maysles' documentary, *The Beatles: First American Visit* [MPI Home Video, 1991; Apple Films, 2004]). And so it continues, through the touring years to *Help!* Then, on through *Revolver*, and *Sgt. Pepper*, etc., ultimately arriving at "The End" of *Abbey Road*. "And, in the end . . ." the Beatles sing, as a rapid montage takes us back to a still of the band at the Cavern Club in 1963. Then, images sweep us forward into a vast array of framed film cells documenting the Beatles' story. The lyric is completed, and the commercial ends. The

---

[18] Apple, iTunes "Let It Be" commercial, *YouTube*, November 10, 2010, www.youtube.com/watch?v=4XBt_opD8RU.
[19] The Beatles, "The Beatles on iTunes", *YouTube*, January 8, 2013, www.youtube.com/watch?v=4Pf3s1KNYvI.

Beatles' presentation of the material is within a narrative of unparalleled success and fame, evolution, and artistic accomplishment.

Conclusion

In their time, the Beatles enjoyed unprecedented success and their image encapsulated an idealized notion of youth that encompassed joyful, guileless, freedom, and the Beatles' singular artistic and cultural standing. Even after the break-up, in 1970, the Beatles continued to enjoy success.

George Harrison once commented, "It's some little magic chemistry that happened between us that seems to appeal to each generation as it comes up."[20] In the twenty-first century, the Beatles' image incorporates what it can of that magic and, despite the intervening years and ravages of time, it continues to resonate with new generations of fans and critics. But, what is this magic? Back in late 1963, before the Beatles went to the USA, the *Evening Standard*'s Maureen Cleave, always a perceptive observer of the band, offered one explanation for their success, "There they are, about the stage, pumping the happiness over the footlights."[21] Shortly afterward, in February 1964, the famed conductor Leopold Stokowski attributed the Beatles' appeal to their ability to give youth a "vision" of "something in life that can't always be found, a joie de vivre."[22] And, in 1997, Kurt Vonnegut wrote, "I say in speeches that a plausible mission of artists is to make people appreciate being alive at least a little bit. I am then asked if I know of any artists who pulled that off. I reply, 'The Beatles did'."[23] Surely, few words better explain why the Beatles mattered, or why they always will.

---

[20] The Beatles, *Eight Days a Week – the Touring Years official Trailer 1*, *YouTube*, www.youtube.com/watch?v=NzYyVj6N9y8.

[21] Maureen Cleave, "How the Frenzied, Furry Beatles Took Over England", *San Francisco Examiner*, February 2, 1964, www.rocksbackpages.com/Library/Article/how-the-frenzied-furry-beatles-took-over-england.

[22] Richard F. Shepard, "Stokowski Talks Something Called Beatles", *New York Times*, February 15, 1964, late edn, 13.

[23] Kurt Vonnegut, *Timequake* (New York: Berkley Books, 1997), 1.

Further Reading

Abbey Road Studios. www.abbeyroad.com.

Babiuk, Andy. 2001. *Beatles Gear: All the Fab Four's Instruments, from Stage to Studio*. San Francisco: Backbeat.

Badman, Keith. 1999. *The Beatles After the Breakup, 1970–2000: A Day-by-Day Diary*. London: Omnibus.

    2001. *The Beatles Off the Record: Outrageous Opinions and Unrehearsed Interviews*. London: Omnibus.

The Beatles. http://beatles.com.

The Beatles. 2000. *The Beatles Anthology*. San Francisco: Chronicle.

The Beatles Bible. 2008. www.beatlesbible.com.

Carlin, Peter Ames. 2009. *Paul McCartney: A Life*. New York: Touchstone.

Carr, Roy, and Tony Tyler. 1975. *The Beatles: An Illustrated Record*. New York: Harmony.

Cott, Jonathan, and Christine Doudna, eds. 1982. *The Ballad of John and Yoko*. San Francisco: Rolling Stone.

Cross, Craig. 2005. *The Beatles: Day-by-Day, Song-by-Song, Record-by-Record*. New York: iUniverse.

Davies, Hunter. 1968. *The Beatles: The Authorized Biography*. New York: McGraw-Hill.

Doggett, Peter. 1998. *Abbey Road/Let It Be: The Beatles*. New York: Schirmer.

Dowlding, William J. 1989. *Beatlesongs*. New York: Simon & Schuster.

Emerick, Geoff, and Howard Massey. 2006. *Here, There, and Everywhere: My Life Recording the Music of the Beatles*. New York: Gotham.

Epstein, Brian. 1998. *A Cellarful of Noise: The Autobiography of the Man Who Made the Beatles*. New York: Pocket.

Everett, Walter. 1999. *The Beatles as Musicians: Revolver through the Anthology*. Oxford: Oxford University Press.

    2001. *The Beatles as Musicians: The Quarry Men through Rubber Soul*. Oxford: Oxford University Press.

Everett, Walter, and Tim Riley. 2019. *What Goes On: The Beatles, Their Music, and Their Time*. Oxford: Oxford University Press.

Frontani, Michael R. 2009. *The Beatles: Image and the Media*. Jackson: University Press of Mississippi.

Harrison, George. 1980. *I Me Mine*. San Francisco: Chronicle.

Harry, Bill. 1992. *The Ultimate Beatles Encyclopedia*. New York: Hyperion.

Hertsgaard, Mark. 1995. *A Day in the Life: The Music and Artistry of the Beatles*. New York: Delacorte.

Inglis, Ian, ed. 2000. *The Beatles, Popular Music, and Society: A Thousand Voices*. New York: St. Martin's.

The Internet Beatles Album. 1995. www.beatlesagain.com.

Jackson, Andrew Grant. 2012. *Still the Greatest: The Essential Songs of the Beatles' Solo Careers*. Lanham, MD: Scarecrow.

Kozinn, Allan. 1995. *The Beatles*. London: Phaidon.

Lennon, John. 1970. *Lennon Remembers*, interview by Jann Wenner. New York: Verso.

Lennon, John, and Yoko Ono. 2000. *All We Are Saying: The Last Major Interview with John Lennon and Yoko Ono*, interview by David Sheff and edited by G. Barry Golson. New York: Griffin.

Lewisohn, Mark. 1986. *The Beatles Live!* London: Pavilion.

1988. *The Recording Sessions: The Official Abbey Road Studio Session Notes, 1962–1970*. New York: Harmony.

1995. *The Complete Beatles Chronicle*. London: Pyramid.

2013. *Tune In: The Beatles – All These Years*. New York: Crown.

MacDonald, Ian. 1994. *Revolution in the Head: The Beatles' Records and the Sixties*. New York: Holt.

Martin, George. 2002. *Playback: An Illustrated Memoir*. Guildford: Genesis Publications.

Martin, George, with Jeremy Hornsby. 1979. *All You Need Is Ears*. New York: St. Martin's.

Martin, George, with William Pearson. 1994. *With a Little Help from My Friends: The Making of Sgt. Pepper*. Boston: Little, Brown.

McCabe, Peter, and Robert D. Schonfeld. 1972. *Apple to the Core: The Unmaking of the Beatles*. London: Martin Brian and O'Keeffe

McKinney, Devin. 2003. *Magic Circles: The Beatles in Dream and History*. Cambridge, MA: Harvard University Press.

Mellers, Wilfred. 1973. *Twilight of the Gods: The Music of the Beatles*. New York: Schirmer.

Miles, Barry. 1997. *Paul McCartney: Many Years from Now*. New York: Holt.

Moore, Allan F. 1997. *The Beatles: Sgt. Pepper's Lonely Hearts Club Band*. Cambridge: Cambridge University Press.

Neaverson, Bob. 1997. *The Beatles Movies*. London: Cassell.

Norman, Philip. 1981. *Shout!: The Beatles in Their Generation*. New York: Simon & Schuster.

O'Donnell, Jim. 1995. *The Day John Met Paul: An Hour-by-Hour of How the Beatles Began*. New York: Penguin.

Peel, Ian. 2002. *The Unknown Paul McCartney: McCartney and the Avant-Garde*. London: Reynolds & Hearn.

Pollack, Alan W. 2000. "Alan W. Pollack's 'Notes On' Series." www.recmusicbea tles.com/public/files/awp/awp.html.

Reising, Russell, ed. 2002. *"Every Sound There Is": The Beatles' Revolver and the Transformation of Rock and Roll*. Aldershot, UK: Ashgate.

Riley, Tim. 1988. *Tell Me Why: A Beatles Commentary*. New York: Knopf.

2011. *Lennon: The Man, the Myth, the Music – The Definitive Life*. New York: Hyperion.

Russell, Jeff. 2006. *The Beatles Complete Discography*. New York: Universe.

Ryan, Kevin, and Brian Kehew. 2006. *Recording the Beatles: The Studio Equipment and Techniques Used to Create Their Classic Albums*. Houston: Curvebender.

Schaffner, Nicholas. 1977. *The Beatles Forever*. Harrisburg, PA: Cameron House.

Shotton, Pete, and Nicholas Schaffner. 1983. *John Lennon: In My Life*. New York: Stein and Day.

Southall, Brian. 2008. *Northern Songs: The True Story of the Beatles Song Publishing Empire*. London: Omnibus.

Spitz, Bob. 2005. *The Beatles: The Biography*. Boston: Little, Brown.

Spizer, Bruce. 1998. *Songs, Pictures, and Stories of the Fabulous Beatles Records on Vee-Jay*. New Orleans: 498 Productions.

2000a. *The Beatles on Capitol Records, Volume One: Beatlemania and the Singles*. New Orleans: 498 Productions.

2000b. *The Beatles on Capitol Records, Volume Two: The Albums*. New Orleans: 498 Productions.

2003. *The Beatles on Apple Records*. New Orleans: 498 Productions.

2005. *The Beatles Solo on Apple Records*. New Orleans: 498 Productions.

2007. *The Beatles Swan Song: "She Loves You" and Other Records*. New Orleans: 498 Productions.

2011. *Beatles for Sale on Parlophone Records*. New Orleans: 498 Productions.

Sulpy, Doug, and Ray Schweighardt. 1997. *Get Back: The Unauthorized Chronicle of the Beatles' Let It Be Disaster*. New York: Griffin.

Turner, Steve. 2015. *The Complete Beatles Songs: The Stories behind Every Track Written by the Fab Four*. London: Carlton.

2016. *Beatles '66: The Revolutionary Year*. New York: HarperCollins.

Unterberger, Richie. 2006. *The Unreleased Beatles: Music and Film*. San Francisco: Backbeat.

Williams, Allan. 1975. *The Man Who Gave the Beatles Away*. London: Macmillan.

Winn, John C. 2003a. *Way Beyond Compare: The Beatles' Recorded Legacy, Volume One: 1957–1965*. Sharon, VT: Multiplus.

2003b. *That Magic Feeling: The Beatles' Recorded Legacy, Volume Two: 1966–1970*. Sharon, VT: Multiplus.

Womack, Kenneth. 2007. *Long and Winding Roads: The Evolving Artistry of the Beatles*. New York: Continuum.

ed. 2009. *The Cambridge Companion to the Beatles*. Cambridge: Cambridge University Press.

2017. *Maximum Volume: The Life of Beatles Producer George Martin (The Early Years, 1926–1966)*. Chicago: Chicago Review Press.

2018. *Sound Pictures: The Life of Beatles Producer George Martin (The Later Years, 1966–2016)*. Chicago: Chicago Review Press.

2019. *Solid State: The Story of Abbey Road and the End of the Beatles*. Cornell: Cornell University Press.

Index

Index

Lightning Source UK Ltd.
Milton Keynes UK
UKHW022149111221
395517UK00009B/85